Planning in Ireland and Beyond: Multidisciplinary Essays in Honour of John V. Greer

John V. Greer

Planning in Ireland and Beyond: Multidisciplinary Essays in Honour of John V. Greer

Edited by Malachy McEldowney, Michael Murray,
Brendan Murtagh and Ken Sterrett

School of Environmental Planning
Queen's University, Belfast

Published in 2005
by the School of Environmental Planning
Queen's University, Belfast

British Library Cataloguing in Publication Data
A Catalogue record for this book
is available from the British Library

ISBN
0-9551347-0-6
978-0-9551347-0-8

Cover design "Participatory Village Planning" by Jonathan McHugh, 2001
Layout by Page Setup, Belfast
Printed by W&G Baird, Belfast

Contents

List of illustrations   *viii*

List of tables   *ix*

List of photographs   *x*

Notes on contributors   *xi*

Foreword   *xiii*
Niall Fitzduff

John V. Greer   *xv*
Malachy McEldowney, Michael Murray, Brendan Murtagh and Ken Sterrett

SECTION 1: PERSPECTIVES ON THE CULTURAL DOMAINS OF PLANNING

1. **Estyn Evans's geography of Ireland**   3
    Brian Graham

2. **Craigavon: locality, economy and the state in a failed 'new city'**   23
    Liam O'Dowd

3. **Identity, place and conflict in rural Northern Ireland**   49
    Brendan Murtagh

4. ***Berlin Babylon*: the spatiality of memory and identity in recent
    planning for the German capital**   63
    William J V Neill

SECTION 2: PERSPECTIVES ON REGIONAL PLANNING

5. **From undeveloped areas to spatial strategies: reflections
    on Irish regional policy**   91
    Thomas A. Boylan

6. **The Irish BMW Region – towards convergence or divergence?**   107
    Michael J. Bannon

7. **Spatial planning frameworks for Ireland: critical reflections
    on the Dublin – Belfast corridor**   125
    James A. Walsh

SECTION 3: PERSPECTIVES ON RURAL PLANNING AND DEVELOPMENT

8. The social shaping of rural vernacular housing 139
    Ken Sterrett and Jayne Bassett

9. Preserving character in the towns and villages of
    Northern Ireland 157
    Karen Latimer

10. Consultation and rural planning in Northern Ireland 169
    Michael Murray

11. Connecting rural dwellings with rural sustainable development 187
    Mark Scott

12. The rural economy: value added creation, market
    sustainability and the limits of policy measures 205
    Michael P. Cuddy

SECTION 4: PERSPECTIVES ON THE PLANNING SYSTEM

13. Planning methodology and the rational
    comprehensive paradigm 225
    Patrick L. Braniff

14. Prizes and pitfalls in planning enforcement 235
    Stephen McKay

15. Retailing theories: attempts to explain an
    ever-changing industry 249
    Anthony Quinn

16. The city of the black stuff: Belfast and the autism of planning 261
    Geraint Ellis

SECTION 5: PERSPECTIVES ON PLANNING GOVERNANCE

17. **Towards a theory of state – community partnerships:
    interpreting the Irish Muintir Na Tire movement's experience**   271
    Tony Varley and Diarmuid O'Cearbhaill

18. **Community planning in Northern Ireland: participative
    democracy in practice?**   289
    Colin Knox

19. **Cross border tourism cooperation on the island of Ireland**   301
    Jonathan Greer

20. **The rural urban interface: outskirts of European cities**   319
    Malachy McEldowney

21. **Campus and community: changing times for the
    urban university**   333
    Frank Gaffikin

Publications of John V. Greer   345

Index   353

List of Illustrations

Figure 2.1   Aerial view of the linear core of Craigavon as it might appear in the year 2000

Figure 2.2   Brownlow planned land use structure

Figure 4.1   (i) Central Berlin around 1940,
(ii) Central Berlin around 1989,
(iii) Central Berlin proposed in Planwerk Innenstadt around 2010

Figure 6.1   The Border, Midland and Western Region and its constituent local authorities

Figure 8.1   Traditional rural dwelling, County Cork

Figure 8.2   (i) Direct-entry dwelling, County Donegal, (ii) Hearth-lobby dwelling, County Tyrone

Figure 8.3   Formal facade of hearth-lobby farmhouse, County Fermanagh

Figure 8.4   Clachan grouping, Murphystown, County Down

Figure 8.5   Contemporary vernacular expression, County Down

Figure 8.6   The contemplative northern Irish landscape

Figure 11.1   Map of County Mayo and County Donegal case study areas

Figure 12.1   Factors influencing the market sustainability of rural communities

Figure 18.1   Proposed community planning model

Figure 18.2   Joined-up government

Figure 20.1   BAB context map

List of Tables

Table 2.1   Unemployment rates by religion, gender and locality in 1989 (percentages)

Table 3.1   Attitudes to community relations between Whitecross and Glenanne between 1996 and 2003

Table 3.2   Activity analysis for Whitecross

Table 3.3   Activity analysis for Glenanne

Table 3.4   The Regional Development Strategy and community relations

Table 6.1   Administrative authorities within the BMW Region

Table 6.2   Population change in the BMW Region, 1991-2002

Table 6.3   Population change in the larger centres, 1996-2002

Table 6.4   Estimated persons at work by sector, BMW Region, 1992-2002

Table 6.5   Gross value added per person at basic prices, 1995-2002 in €

Table 6.6   EU agricultural payments to the BMW Region, € million

Table 6.7   Cohesiuon Fund commitment distribution, 1993-2002 (€ million)

Table 6.8   ESF expenditure through FAS, 2000-2001 (€ million)

Table 6.9   Direct payments to companies (all principal agencies) 1992-2002 (€ 000s)

Table 6.10   National Development Plan, 2000-2006 expenditure levels by Operational Programme and NUTS II Region (€ million)

Table 12.1   Leontief input / output framework

Table 17.1   Two models of state / community partnerships

Table 18.1   Common elements of an effective integrated local strategy

List of Photographs

Photograph 4.1   A trademark identity for the nation's capital

Photograph 4.2   A Berlin Wall fragment close to Potsdamer Platz, 2004

Photograph 4.3   Doubt sits on the Palast der Republik, 2005

Photograph 4.4   Past and present: Memorial to the Murdered Jews of Europe as overlooked by Potsdamer Platz, 2005

Photograph 9.1   Almshouses at Seaforde

Photograph 9.2   Drumbeg Lockhouse

Photograph 9.3   Curry's Cottage with new annex, Derrylin

Photograph 9.4   Turnly's Tower, Cushendall

Photograph 20.1   Good quality high rise residential development in the Limmatal Valley

Photograph 20.2   Shopping centre development in the Limmatal Valley

Photograph 20.3   Derelict streetscape in the buffer-zone, Nicosia

Photograph 20.4   Urban sprawl in Nicosia

Notes on Contributors

Michael J. Bannon is Professor Emeritus in the Department of Planning and Environmental Policy at University College Dublin

Jayne Bassett is Lecturer in the School of Environmental Planning at Queen's University, Belfast

Thomas A. Boylan is Professor of Economics in the Department of Economics at National University of Ireland, Galway

Patrick L. Braniff is Director of Braniff Associates, Belfast

Michael P. Cuddy is Professor of Economics in the Department of Economics at National University of Ireland, Galway

Geraint Ellis is Senior Lecturer in the School of Environmental Planning at Queen's University, Belfast

Niall Fitzduff is Director of Rural Community Network (Northern Ireland)

Frank Gaffikin is Reader in the School of Environmental Planning at Queen's University, Belfast

Brian Graham is Professor of Human Geography in the School of Environmental Sciences at University of Ulster

Jonathan Greer is Consultant in Public Policy with PriceWaterhouseCoopers, Belfast

Karen Latimer is Agriculture and Food Sciences Librarian at Queen's University, Belfast

Colin Knox is Professor of Comparative Public Policy in the School of Policy Studies at University of Ulster

Malachy McEldowney is Professor of Town and Country Planning in the School of Environmental Planning at Queen's University, Belfast

Stephen McKay is Lecturer in the School of Environmental Planning at Queen's University, Belfast

Michael Murray is Reader in the School of Environmental Planning at Queen's University, Belfast

Brendan Murtagh is Reader in the School of Environmental Planning at Queen's University, Belfast

William J.V. Neill is Reader in the School of Environmental Planning at Queen's University, Belfast

Diarmuid O'Cearbhaill has retired as Lecturer in the Department of Economics at National University of Ireland, Galway

Liam O'Dowd is Professor of Sociology in the School of Sociology and Social Policy at Queen's University, Belfast

Anthony Quinn is an Associate Planner with Braniff Associates, Belfast

Mark Scott is Lecturer in the Department of Planning and Environmental Policy at University College Dublin

Ken Sterrett is Senior Lecturer and Head of School of Environmental Planning at Queen's University, Belfast

Tony Varley is Lecturer in the Department of Political Science and Sociology at National University of Ireland, Galway

James A. Walsh is Professor of Geography and Head of School of Geography at National University of Ireland, Maynooth

Foreword

Niall Fitzduff

This book is a fitting testimony to the work of John Greer. In preparing for a talk on leadership recently, I asked a wide range of people what makes a difference. Almost without exception the reply was 'someone who cares', put together with a sharp intellect, ability to listen and rooted perception. You have in the man and the pages that follow, a story of planning and development which reaches deep into our imaginations and cultures, far beyond the narrow concepts of land use planning.

My association with John stretches back to 1970 when as a young development officer with Voluntary Service Belfast I accompanied Maurice Hayes, who had been recently appointed Chairman of the Community Relations Commission, to meet with planning students at Queen's University and to make the connection between planning and some of the tenants' associations and other community organisations in different parts of Belfast. The Troubles had bitten deeply, causing large displacements of people. But so too had redevelopment and the proposed route of the Belfast Inner Ring Road. My contact with MSc students at that time and with Professor Cliff Moughton was not only interesting because it made the connection between community development and planning, but in the background I became aware of John Greer's work in taking students out to rural areas on field trips, challenging the predominant interest in urban planning. The many hundreds of students who have left Queen's in the intervening years, moving into many different professions, have taken with them an appreciation of rural community life, and the importance of people and place.

Much later I had the good fortune to meet with John during his explorations for development strategies in Tydavnet and for my own place of Ardboe / Ballinderry / Moortown. This work came on the back of John's involvement with the Rural Action Project and the pilot community planning initiative in County Fermanagh. Indeed John's work with the Rural Action Project, in the context of the emerging document *The Future of Rural Society* in 1988, began to lay the foundations for a new Rural Development Programme for Northern Ireland.

Like the poet, John is always looking for the authentic currents which lie outside the mainstream. Thus his interest in the formation of Rural Community Network (RCN) in 1990 was no surprise. At that time community groups, then numbering just 60, established Rural Community Network to articulate the voice of rural people on issues of poverty and disadvantage and to support community development as an important approach in meeting the needs of rural communities. From those early days rural housing and planning were major issues for consultation. RCN has benefited tremendously from his students past and present, both on the staff and as volunteers, whether it is planning in a divided society, reviews of area plans, or how RCN has measured up to its advocacy role in relation to the policy arena.

For John Greer planning is not about lines on maps. It is certainly not about the predominance of an urban landscape casting a shadow on a rural remainder. Rather it is about people, community and place and the wisdom and commitment which can be harnessed to throw shape on the contributions that rural communities can make to society as a whole. It is to this vision that John Greer will remain identified with for many years to come, both within the island of Ireland and beyond. In the last fifteen years of the Rural Development Programme whether as mentor, critic or analyst to the Department of Agriculture and Rural Development, the Rural Development Council or Rural Community Network, his influence will live on long beyond his well deserved retirement.

On many occasions John came to visit RCN for the long chat. I was honoured to think that our mutual interest was in exploring the degree to which Rural Community Network had fulfilled its obligations to rural communities in Northern Ireland. As we struggled to gain equity for rural communities in, for example, the Regional Development Strategy, it remains a shared hope that this policy prescription will translate into a comprehensive rural policy for Northern Ireland.

It is indeed an honour to commend this book to the reader and to have in one volume so many connections and tributes to the career and contribution of a very special sage.

John V Greer

The emergence and development of the planning profession in Ireland is inextricably linked to the name of John Greer. His enormous contribution to teaching, research and practice has helped fashion a critical appreciation for planning intervention at different spatial scales. His firm belief in the integrity of the discipline, combined with a deep affection for Irish places and cultures, have guided an impressive portfolio of work that encompasses national, regional, urban and rural settings. John's capacity to interpret very complex planning challenges through a combination of careful reflection, engaging conversation and tireless fieldwork are the hallmarks of his personal 'take' on the Geddesian model of survey, analysis and plan. In this regard John has always been quick to eschew the veneers of technocracy and the well-meaning expert. His contributions to planning consistently emphasise method in order to unpack and discover the facts and values of the situations to hand. The mark of a great planner is informed judgement and it is this quality that defines how John Greer consistently voices 'truth to power'. In short, people listen when John Greer speaks!

John Greer graduated from Queen's University in 1963 with an Honours degree in Geography and, following a period as a Research Assistant with the Department of Geography at Queen's, he joined the Craigavon Development Commission. His appointment as a planner over the period 1964 to 1968 brought him into the world of master plan preparation, population forecasting, commercial development and strategic planning for small communities. In 1968 he accepted a Lectureship post on the newly established postgraduate course on Town and Country Planning in his *alma mater* and was promoted to Senior Lecturer in 1976. While his teaching interests have long embraced history of settlement, planning theory and planning methodology, John Greer is specifically recognised for his contribution to the field of rural planning and development in Ireland. There can be little doubt that he has drawn a substantial intellectual stimulus from the work of Estyn Evans under whose tutelage John had read for his primary degree. Indeed the advocacy of Professor Evans for a 'trilogy of regional studies, of habitat, heritage and history' profoundly informed his teaching preferences. John Greer has laboured hard to create a comprehensive programme in the theoretical and practical aspects of rural planning and development as a core element of the planning curriculum at Queen's. It is interesting that course documentation from 1978 describes his input to Rural Resource Planning in the following way:

> The object of this course is to provide students with an insight into the interaction of man and his habitat, and to examine the forces at work in the evolution of the cultural and physical landscape of rural areas. The course begins with a discussion of the relationship of man and the natural environment, and continues with an analysis of rural planning in Britain and the contrasting circumstances in Ireland. Concentration is then focused upon the land uses and activities in rural areas particularly agriculture, forestry, industry and tourism. Case studies of approaches to rural resource planning problems in Britain and Ireland are then discussed, followed by an analysis of techniques in landscape survey and evaluation. The emphasis throughout is not purely on the physical landscape, but on the interrelationship of social, economic, cultural and physical factors, with particular reference to the development of a planning approach suitable for application in the Irish context.

Over twenty-five years later John Greer is still intensely loyal to the sentiments embedded in this statement of teaching endeavour. His many publications across both planning practice and academic inquiry have consistently argued for an integrated approach to rural planning and development and, significantly, long before this appeared as a mainstream policy objective of the European Union and national governments. He was, for example, the principal author of the 1980 Erne Catchment Area Study that assessed the potential of arterial drainage and tourism for rural development in the borderlands of Ireland. This study, undertaken on behalf of the European Commission and the Governments of Ireland and the United Kingdom, received the international award of *Distinctions Europeennes en Amenagement du Territoire* from the European Council of Town Planners in 1990. When in Northern Ireland an Interdepartmental Committee on Rural Development was established by the Secretary of State in 1989 to advise on how best to tackle social and economic problems in the most deprived rural areas of Northern Ireland, it is appropriate that John Greer should have played a central consultative role in shaping its action agenda.

A second and related dimension to John's view of the rural world, which emerges from the teaching statement above, is the need to appreciate the Irish context and to avoid the slavish application of British planning orthodoxy on rural concerns in both Northern Ireland and the Republic of Ireland. Again this is well evidenced by his submission (now held by the Public Record Office of Northern Ireland) to the Government appointed Rural Planning Policy Review Committee in September 1977 where, in his concluding paragraph, he states:

In general it may be said that the major shortcomings of the present policy are (1) that it is a blanket policy which does not recognise differences between areas and (2) that it is derived, without further analysis, from the rural settlement policies which have been devised for the densely populated and highly urbanised areas of lowland Britain. What is required is a policy that reflects the condition and problems of rural life in Northern Ireland, and this can only be achieved by closer study and research.

John Greer's analysis received an overwhelming endorsement in the follow-on Cockcroft Report published by the Department of the Environment in 1978. The issue of housing in the countryside continues to provoke contestation in 2005, but for John the central issue has never been about housing *per se*. Nor indeed has John been an advocate for a laissez-faire approach to countryside planning. His constant theme is that the connectedness of rural housing into the local social, cultural and economic dynamics of dispersed rural communities should define the planning policy challenge.

The contemporary formulation of public policy champions the insights provided by evidence and it is to John Greer's credit that during his academic career he has immersed himself in extensive empirical investigations to add solid weight to his opinions. Two Social Science Research Council Awards were, for example, received by John in 1981 and 1983 to progress his interest in the rural. The first, shared with his longstanding departmental colleague and friend, John Caldwell, concerned itself with *Planning for peripheral rural areas and the effects of policy change in Northern Ireland*. The second involved a collaborative project with Jimmy Armstrong (then with the Department of Geography at Queen's) on *The relevance of Integrated Rural Development to the Northern Ireland context*. In 1986 John Greer was awarded the Degree of Master of Science by Research from Queen's University for work based on these projects.

The eventual acceptance by Government in Northern Ireland of the need for a rural development policy commitment led to the opening up of a suite of exciting research opportunities during the 1990s. It is not surprising that John Greer should be to the forefront of this applied research agenda. At the beginning of that decade Ministers agreed to create an agency outside Government – the Rural Development Council, and to support the establishment of a voice for rural communities through Rural Community Network. Both organisations have from the outset been committed to community-led rural development and have embraced strategic planning processes as a mechanism to strengthen group capacity and delivery potential. John's theoretical grounding in participatory governance has equipped him well for a succession of research projects on single and multi-community strategic planning in both Northern Ireland and the Republic of Ireland. Critical reflection around these experiences has translated well into significant contributions to Irish planning practice and the wider international academic literature.

John Greer's research interests in the rural have substantially enriched his teaching to the multiple cohorts of students that have passed through Queen's. But John's willingness to travel to other universities and wide-ranging conference venues has also made him a much sought after authority. He has been an Accredited Lecturer on the Master of Rural Development course at NUI Galway from its inception in 1986, and he assisted with the devising of degree programmes in Rural Development within Northern Ireland at Queen's and the Rural College at Draperstown. He has served as a Board member of the Rural Innovation and Research Partnership (a partnership between Queen's University and the Rural Development Council which was funded by LEADER 2 with a grant from the Department of Agriculture and Rural Development), and as a Board member of the Gibson Institute for Land, Food and the Environment at Queen's. His respect among the academic community has made him a popular external examiner for teaching programmes and doctoral candidates in Ireland and Great Britain, a respect which is recognised in equal measure by the planning practice fraternity. John served as a Member of the Executive Committee of the Royal Town Planning Institute (Irish Branch – Northern Section) between 1969 and 1976. He was elected to membership of the Council of the Irish Planning Institute in 1986 and in 1991-1992 he held its Presidency. He has gone on to represent the Institute at the European Council of Town Planners between 1993 and 1997 and served as Vice-President of the European Council of Town Planners between 1995 and 1997. In 1996 he acted as a planning expert adviser to the House of Commons Northern Ireland Affairs Committee.

During his recent tenure of the post of Vice Chancellor at Queen's University, Professor Sir George Bain placed emphasis on 'balanced excellence' across contributions to teaching, research and administration. John Greer provides powerful witness to this set of interlinked activities, whether it is the reassuring eyes over the shoulder of an anxious doctoral student or first year undergraduate, the capacity to articulate complex issues with stunning simplicity, or the ever-ready willingness to take charge of an administrative task. Planning at Queen's is much the richer for John's presence. In this regard it is a happy task for us as editors, and on behalf of all the contributors, to present this *festschrift* on "Planning in Ireland and beyond" to John Greer as a mark of the great esteem with which he is held by his many friends and colleagues.

The Editorial Team

Section One:

PERSPECTIVES ON
THE CULTURAL DOMAINS
OF PLANNING

Chapter 1

Estyn Evans's Geography of Ireland

Brian Graham

Introduction

'Where to find the loyalties a people needs to live'[1]

Few geographers have found themselves acknowledged in verse, but the tribute paid by John Hewitt in his poem, 'Roll call' (1942) to Emyr Estyn Evans (1905-1989) is one notable acknowledgement of the work of a man who was 'a genuine Irish heretic'.[2] Born in Shropshire and educated at Aberystwyth under the tutelage of H.J. Fleure, Evans spent his career at Queen's University, Belfast, first as Head of the Department of Geography and, latterly, as Director of the Institute of Irish Studies.[3] Evans was an academic of international stature, whose methodology and personality strongly influenced several generations of Irish geographers, particularly those working in the north of the island. Many of his students, including John Greer, went on to become professional planners. Although his geographical world was very much defined by the nine counties of the historic province of Ulster, Evans's interests extended well beyond this adopted domain to embrace not only Ireland as a whole, but also, for example, the Irish in North America, peasant life and the geography of France.[4]

This chapter has two particular aims in its critical assessment of Evans's ideas and their continued relevance to the unresolved issues of identity that characterise the island of Ireland. First, it seeks to relate something of Evans and his relationship to geographical knowledge in general and that of Ireland in particular. Evans's geography is seen as a cultural product, derived from the interaction of a particular geographical philosophy with the specific social and political circumstances of Ireland. It was a resource for himself and his own agenda as he worked in one part of a newly partitioned island, both elements of which were struggling to establish their own identities, primarily through the adoption of mutually exclusive cultural and political discourses. Throughout his work, however, Evans was disinclined to be explicit about class, power, religion or politics; indeed, in *Irish Heritage*, he consciously eschews such 'controversial realms'.[5] Nevertheless, it is argued here that

Evans did have a political agenda, signified particularly by a refusal to accept the assumptions of traditional Irish nationalism. The difficulty remains that this dimension was never made explicit in his published work, creating an unresolved dissonance between its exploration of Irish identity and the political expressions thereof. Secondly, Evans's geography is interrogated in terms of the insights which it might offer into the political, economic and cultural conflict engendered by the existence within Ireland of various contested bases for social understanding. His work remains a resource to be used in contemporary analyses of the nature and meaning of Irishness and its inevitable sub-text of partition. While issues of regional identity are much to the fore in these debates on Ulster's meaning and location within Ireland, there is little overt cognisance of Tuan's observations that regions may have no existence outside the consciousness of the geographers who may persuade other people to accept these entities.[6]

Evans is often linked with John Hewitt in attempts to establish an Ulster identity which may owe something to both Britain and Ireland, but, primarily, is particular to the province itself. Politically, however, the concept of a native Ulster tradition, which is broader than either unionism or republicanism, can find expression, either as Ulster separatism or, less radically, as a form of regional identity within a greater United Kingdom, itself regionally disparate. Consequently, Evans's views on regional distinctiveness can be – and have been – depicted as no more than a convenient prop to unionist ideology, which, intellectually, minimises their importance to wider Irish and international contexts in which a chauvinistic Irish nationalism is entirely acceptable while, conversely, an Ulster identity can be rejected dismissively as being merely sectarian.[7] I argue here, however, that Evans's *oeuvre* addresses the intellectually more challenging concept of a regionally diverse Ireland in which Ulster is but *one* variant of a heterogeneous vision of Irishness.

Evans in his Geographical Context
Before exploring the themes diagnostic of Evans's interpretation of Ireland, something needs to be said of their underlying geographical philosophy. His work demonstrates a very high degree of internal consistency and coherence, the product of a sustained loyalty to a set of particular geographical principles. The most immediate influence was the holistic philosophy of H.J. Fleure who was concerned with the elaboration of a moral geography which 'intertwined his anthropometric localisation, pastoral preferences, cultural survivals and behavioural traits'[8] into a conviction that the Celtic fringes of Wales formed the 'ultimate refuge' of old thoughts and visions otherwise lost to the world.[9] Fleure's direct influences upon Evans were heavily modified, however, by their mediation, first through an engagement with the work of the French geographer, Paul Vidal de la Blache and, subsequently, by a long-standing

admiration for the *Annales* school of *géohistoire*. Vidal emphasised the significance of ordinary people and their environment: to him, the region was not simply a convenient framework, but rather a social reality.[10] Evans shared in this idea that the landscape was a democratic text, recording the history of the undocumented.[11] Later, it became a tenet of *géohistoire* that any social reality must be referred to the space, place or region within which it existed.[12] These Vidalian-derived ideas were fundamental to Evans's geographical philosophy and, late in his career, he continued to profess admiration for Marc Bloch, Lucien Febvre and, perhaps above all, Fernand Braudel, applauding – like his American contemporary, Carl Sauer – the French genius for regional synthesis.[13] From Vidal, Evans also took the idea of the *pays* as the geographical mediation of synthesis and continuity, the product of human 'interaction with his physical environment over centuries'.[14] Larger generalisations could emerge only gradually from a series of detailed and exact case studies of various *pays*. Finally, like Vidal's own work, Evans's geography is framed within a possibilist epistemology, best summed up in Febvre's famous dictum that 'there are nowhere necessities, but everywhere possibilities; and man as master of the possibilities, is the judge of their use.'[15] Evans also maintained a strong relationship with Sauer and other North American geographers who had rejected determinism and shared a similar conception of 'geography as cultural history in its regional articulation'.[16] These influences meshed with Fleure's theory of regions as places of lived experience, and his concept of contact zones was to inform Evans's geography of Ireland: regions were 'not just the product of a symbiotic union of people and places' but also the 'consequence of the shifting relationships between people and people'.[17] Geography was 'the common ground between the natural world and cultural history'.[18]

Evans's work retains an internal coherence because he held to this geographical philosophy throughout his career. It was accompanied by a methodological orientation that was almost entirely fieldwork-based and included not merely those attributes of material and spiritual culture which might be observed in the countryside through detailed field study, but also archaeological survey and excavation.[19] As Whelan somewhat inelegantly remarks, Evans was a 'six-inch geographer', the reference being to the First Edition Ordnance Survey Six Inch Maps of the 1830s and 1840s.[20] Unsurprisingly, this splendid cartographic legacy has influenced the methodology and scale of numerous geographical studies of Ireland, although Evans and many other geographers have tended to accept the maps at face value rather than as social documents. However, Evans also explored the human interaction with environment, expressed through minute regional variations, by gathering evidence from meticulous field observation of all aspects of the cultural environment. He was more concerned with material artefacts and their meanings – partly due perhaps to the linguistic inaccessibility of documentary and oral evidence in the Irish language – than with folklore and beliefs. All this was to be 'absorbed through... the senses, including the soles of the feet'.[21] He distrusted history – and historians – as over-dependent on documentation, which, inevitably, could serve only to demonstrate the values of an élite: to depend on written sources alone was to see Ireland through the eyes of successive conquerors – 'whether saints or swordsmen'.[22] It is this geographical heritage which interweaves with, and underscores, Evans's understanding of Ulster and, in turn, his portrayal of its relationship with the remainder of Ireland and the broader archipelago.

The Themes of Evans's Geography of Ireland
Although there are other dimensions to his work, I concentrate here on three themes that define Evan's contribution to defining Ireland's conceptual space.[23] It is argued here that these are directly derivative of the epistemological influences outlined above, mediated through a consistent attempt to define Ulster's cultural space within Ireland. This is an explicit rather than hidden agenda, but while it may have been stimulated by Evans's political aspirations as well as his geographical philosophy, the themes are worked through in cultural terms alone. They are: regionalism, human society and environment; the common ground – peasants, rurality and continuity; Ulsterness and Irishness.

Regionalism, human society and environment
First, and basic to every other aspect of Evans's methodology, was a belief that the relationship between people and their environment is expressed within a regional dimension, itself a constraint upon human behaviour. Consequently, at the very core of Evans's geographical cosmos was the holistic belief that people, with their shared past, cultural artefacts, values, beliefs and emotions, and land, 'go together and have shaped each other, and you cannot understand one apart from the other.'[24] He visualised the most genuine bonds as occurring in the *pays*, areas which were much smaller spatially than the four provinces of Ireland. The examples he most often quoted were the Kingdom of Mourne and West Cork, areas sufficiently small that 'interpretation might be checked against observation and local knowledge'.[25] More generally, Evans inclined to the belief that innovations were diffused from Scotland through the east and south of Ireland towards its north and west. Consequently, relicts, such as openfield agriculture in Gweedore, Co. Donegal, became part of a 'complex of cultural survivals, persisting in this far corner of the island.'[26] The west became the real Ireland for Evans, the *pays* where the peasant folk-culture of the common person remained – if not untouched – at least identifiable.

Ironically, this was exactly the same Ireland portrayed in Gaelic nationalism as the heartland of the island's cultural consciousness, the region of unspoilt beauty where the influences of Anglicising modernity were at their weakest.[27] Nonetheless much of Evans's geography of Ireland evolved within the overriding constraint of his explicit antagonism to the sectarian nationalism of Irish-Ireland.[28] He was determined to reject the notion of a racially pure genetic Irishness in favour of a mongrel identity: 'in the long run', he wrote, it was a geography created both by the variable physical landscape of the island and the patterning of its human occupation that counted 'for more than genes.'[29]

Inconsistently, perhaps, Evans saw Ulster as being 'in many ways the strongest, and most fully Celtic', of all the Irish regions,[30] archaeologically, at least, the island's 'most representative region'.[31] It is a land and people, 'in some ways more British than the British, yet in other ways more Irish than the Irish.'[32] Crucially, however, he did not accept the exclusivist premises of Irish-Ireland in which identity is conferred by the Gaelic past; to Evans, Irishness was plural. The argument contained in the pamphlet, *The Common Ground*, is perhaps the clearest account of Evans's culturally heterogeneous and regionalist view of Ulster and Ireland, albeit one characterised by distinct tinges of ethnic stereotyping.[33] He saw the hidden closed-in drumlin lands of south Ulster as a Protestant landscape, occupied by a people of limited vision and imagination, marooned in their 'psychic stockade'.[34] In contrast stands the other tradition of Ulster, the open, naked bogs and hills, the lands of the poetic and visionary in the Ulster soul, 'the spiritual hinterland of ancient memories of freedom and passion.'[35] Evans believed that this diversity could be reconciled as a single theme with many variations, the *personnalité* of Ulster deriving from the fusion of many small *pays*. He recognised that the landscape and material heritages were also a potent source of dissension, but argued that we must live with and exploit these as 'a total inheritance irrespective of formal creeds'.[36] The physical manifestation of this conviction is the Ulster Folk and Transport Museum at Cultra Manor, Co. Down, which opened in 1961. Evans was one instigator of this institution which embodies a belief in the integrative role of culture, and does reflect his conviction that it is the duty of geographers to explore its spatial patterning and meaning.[37] To Evans, these regional variations constituted a diagnostic indicator of Ulster's and, by implication, Ireland's personality, his riposte to the orthodox nationalist belief in the 'God-given inviolate island'.[38] Thus while Evans regarded Ulster as a single theme with many variations, he was not arguing for its separateness from a homogeneous south for his philosophy denied the existence of the latter. Despite the shared fascination with the 'West', it is that perspective that distances Evans decisively from Irish-Ireland.

The common ground – peasants, rurality and continuity

Evans regarded peasant culture as both the product of the mediation of the human-environment relationship and also as a repository of the vitality and continuity of lasting social values which urbanism tends to destroy. His geographical theme was very much 'the common people and the land itself, the land that they've helped to make: because the land is far older than us all, far older than all human cultures.'[39]

Perforce, this was largely – indeed almost entirely – a rural world, full of resonances – transposed to Ireland – of Fleure's ideas about the furthest fringes of Wales being the 'ultimate refuge' of the true values and visions of Welshness. As Fleure himself wrote in a tribute to Evans: 'Ireland has been looked upon as an ultimate corner of western Europe, a treasury of the past, the last place to which a culture would spread and the last place in which an out-of-date culture would linger.'[40] To some extent, it was seen in this way by Evans too, for – as has been argued here – the epicentre of his vision of Ireland was the west in general, and the far north-west in particular. It is a powerful imagery but, in a telling point, Whelan observes that by the nineteenth century, the west of Ireland was scarcely a far-flung periphery but, through emigration and trade, looked to and had intimate connections with North America.[41] Nevertheless, for Evans one of the common bonds that linked all the peoples of Ireland was this loyalty to local traditions and regions expressed through the symbiosis of human society and its physical environment.

The concept of continuity, dependent on 'habitat and heritage' is intrinsic to this second theme in Evans's *oeuvre*. Further, it is perhaps the one most crucial to an understanding of his perspectives on Ulster and Ireland, a reason why it has become one of the more controversial aspects of his work. 'I have tried', Evans wrote, 'to read the rural landscape and have come to see it as the key to the continuity of Irish history.'[42] He believed that the 'foreshortening of time', so characteristic of Irish nationalism,[43] was no more than a necessary legitimation of the twentieth-century state by linking it backwards to some mythical origin-legend. The claimed linear continuity of this narrative was 'derived from an annexation and misuse' of that Gaelic past.[44] So Evans's search for a common ground, and his arguments concerning continuity owed much to his objection to the nationalist notion that the 26-county state, as constituted in 1922, was the embodiment of Irish aspirations. His conceptualisation of continuity invokes far more than the mere long-term survival of artefacts and customs through time, representing instead a belief that the very particularities of cultures are forged through 'a renewal of the old in contact with the new'.[45] Thus the centrality of continuity to Evans's representation of Ireland originated in Fleure's moral geography and ideas on regional conceptualisation, mediated through the notion of the *pays* as an embodiment of – and control on - peasant values.

Despite urbanisation and industrialisation, Evans saw in Ireland the preservation 'to a remarkable degree [of] the customs and social habits of the pre-industrial phase of western civilisation'.[46] Although this could be held to imply cultural stasis, Evans did not see the island as a mere repository of archaic cultural artefacts. First, his disputes with other Irish archaeologists revolved around movement, including contrasting views on 'cultural evolution, of independent origin as opposed to diffusion, of links with Britain or direct with continental Europe.'[47] Secondly, peasant life was not an archaic social form in Evans's geographical cosmos. What we can detect, however, is an uneasy tension between a concept of continuity which invoked ceaseless movement, and, simultaneously, an almost mystical belief that to the Irish peasant, 'all time is present here and now... a view almost certainly megalithic'.[48]

Evans's insistence upon the importance of the pre-Celtic civilisation of Ireland was predicated upon an objection to the presumptions of orthodox nationalism. He held that the sequestering of the Celts' past as the foundation stone of Irish nationalism ignored the historical verity that they too had once to adapt to and be changed by settlement in Ireland. His thesis – derived from studies on megalithic tombs – was that Ireland imported little of developed Celtic culture and tended to transmute what it did receive in the light of native forms; more simply put, the Celts were planters too.[49] To Evans, Irish culture stretched back to the megalithic world 'in which so many of the Elder Faiths are rooted.'[50] 'There were many strains in those traditions', he wrote, 'not only of Celtic but of pre-Celtic antiquity',[51] quoting with approval an aphorism attributed to the archaeologist, Seán 'O Ríordáin: 'the Irish are megalith-builders who somehow learned to speak Gaelic.'[52] There was no 'Celtic Golden Age', a centrepiece of the orthodox nationalist myth, even if it was a product of the Anglo-Irish 'Gaelic Revival'. But the tension in his reasoning is again apparent. Evans opposed the concept of Celtic hegemony – proposing different variations of cultural movement – but at root within his work, there remains the same foreshortening of time that also characterises the rhetoric of Gaelic nationalism, albeit on a different scale.

While Evans may have been involved in what, ostensibly, were academic disputes over the origins of early Irish society, his arguments do possess a clear political import in terms of the contested bases for social understanding in Ireland. First, they were fundamental to the case against the usurpation of Irishness by the Gaelic myth in favour of a more pluralistic view of Irish culture. Secondly, as I have observed, they can be used to depict him as a unionist or even Ulster nationalist. However, despite the unresolved problems created by the tension between the dual emphasis on ceaseless movement and the predominance of the old stream, the key element in Evans's perception of continuity remains the pluralistic idea of successive immigrant groups adapting to pre-existing societies which their arrival must also have changed, a concept illuminated by Fleure's concern for cultural contact zones. By continuity, therefore, Evans meant not simply the survival of townlands and place-names or customs through time, but the constant renewal of the old through its contact with new ideas and cultures.[53] He saw Irish culture as diverse, the archaeological record demonstrating the enrichment of that cultural continuity, but also its enduring characteristics. The Norse were absorbed and the Normans failed, their several colonisations leading, however, to an enduring Anglo-Irish tradition.[54] Evans did not use the term, 'assimilation', referring instead to a process of absorption. It was precisely the clash of native and newcomer which struck the sparks in Irish culture and, consequently, Evans's interpretation is the very antithesis to the nationalist image which depicts Gaelic Ireland assimilating almost seamlessly the encroachments of various invaders.[55] To him, the island's particularity of place resulted from the specific cultural matrix which emanated from this concept of a continuity defined as 're-birth'.[56] In many ways, this is a very present-centred interpretation with its explicit relevance to the notion of a pluralistic Irishness. But it is one compromised by Evan's insistence upon the predominance of the old streams, a perspective which ultimately derives from his geographical philosophy, albeit mediated through his objections to the sequestration of Irishness by the Gaelic metanarrative.

Ulsterness and Irishness

All these various elements – regionalism, habitat, peasants, rurality and continuity – are necessary precursors to an understanding of Evans's particular representations of Ulster and of Ireland. Evans was an Ulsterman by adoption and the nine-county province became the laboratory for his geographical ideas. He objected to the usurpation of the place-name, 'Ulster', by 'extreme Protestant spokesmen' to define the six counties,[57] the boundary of Evans's Ulster not being that of partition, but, characteristically, the difficult drumlin belt, stretching east-west from County Down to Donegal Bay, through Cavan, Monaghan and Fermanagh. His central concern was to define the meaning of Ulster, to isolate its *personnalité* which he saw as one manifestation of Irishness, separate from but part of a larger entity which, in itself, was less than homogeneous.

Evans held – as we have seen – that Ulster was the most intensely Irish of all the island's regions, a *de facto* recognition that Ireland constituted one socio-cultural unit - albeit far from homogeneous – rather than the two distinct entities of the Ulster nationalist. One of his favourite indicators was the incidence of Gaelic place-names in the province, an unspoken contrast to the anglicised Pale around Dublin.[58] It is tempting to read into this something of the complex identity dilemma of northern Protestants, opposed to the sequestration of Irishness by Irish-Ireland and emphasising the legitimacy of their own long-lived claim to Ireland's land. As a riposte to the exclusivity of orthodox Irish nationalism, Evans was concerned to establish the essential Irishness of an ethnically complex Ulster in which the Planters have 'inherited a land full of Irishness, full of things Gaelic and pre-Gaelic'.[59] To Evans, these constituted a shared heritage while denying the nationalist appropriation of the artefacts of Irishness.

A logical extension of the conception of a geographical world, defined by the small scale of the *pays*, is the notion that, although it may constitute a single theme, Ireland's character is defined by its numerous regional variations. Indeed, most European nations have evolved through such a 'fusion of regional loyalties'.[60] This relatively small island of 70,000 sq. km. is characterised by regions which 'have long developed their own orientations and experiences', even if the 'compacting insular qualities' of the place have meant that these experiences have had to 'be contained and shared within a narrow, often introverted, ground.'[61] It is within such a context that much of Evans's work can be read as a rejection of the homogenising and sectarian certainties of orthodox Irish nationalism in favour of plurality or heterogeneity. However, and it is a significant qualification to the success of his endeavour, he never did systematically explore the distinctiveness of other regions. For example, although both *Irish Heritage* (1942) and *Irish Folk Ways* (1957) do invoke a surprisingly catholic selection of places, they also confirm that the extent of Evans's world was largely defined by the more rural parts of Ulster, together with a significant representation from the west of Ireland generally. It would be unsurprising if this was not so, because rural areas of the north and west – hypothetically beyond the contamination of an expanding metropolitan world – were precisely the *pays* which Evans's geographical beliefs would have isolated as the repositories of the true attributes of Irishness.

Both traditional nationalist and unionist myths depend upon an assumption that Ulster is *the* particular region in Ireland. To Evans, however, it was one variant amongst a number, Irish heritage being a single theme with many variations.[62] He saw Irishness as a complex of regional and national qualities, the uniformity of Catholicism as its distinguishing mark a product largely of the nineteenth century.[63] But he did not explore this island-wide heterogeneity systematically. The essence of Evans's definition of Irishness depended upon a combined rejection of spurious assumptions of homogeneity, together with the nationalist sequestration of customs and habits popularly supposed 'to be the peculiar possession of the Gaeltacht'.[64] Thus again we find the dilemma of continuity to the fore. 'A large part of the Irishness of the Irish, is, I believe, a pre-Celtic heritage.'[65] Evans's rejection of Gaelic nationalism required its own origin-myth, thereby introducing the tension between movement and stasis which is apparent in all his work. The essence of his interpretation of Irishness derived from the process of renewal under the stimulus of cultural contact and interconnection, a continual re-birth through exposure to the outside world and fresh cultural forces. The very vitality and originality of Irish culture were created through this constant renewal. But, simultaneously, a paradoxical stagnation emanates from the retention of his belief in the timelessness of peasant life. Despite this difficulty, I believe that it can be argued that Evans's geographical philosophy and his enduring loyalty to its values of habitat, regionalism and diversity, led him to a vision of Ireland which, although requiring many and important qualifications, remains a potent resource for present society.

A Critique of Evans's Ideas

It is readily apparent that there are real internal contradictions and lacunae in Evans's geographical philosophy, in particular its failure to engage explicitly with the realms of political discourse and action. His work can be questioned in both epistemological and methodological terms but it also constitutes a discourse which, in seeking to define an identity for Ulster, would allow that province to be part of a politically changed Ireland. Inevitably, therefore, Evans's *oeuvre* is involved in the issue of the contested representations of Irishness because the social construct of knowledge remains a resource for successive generations, even though meanings will change as contexts alter. Although much earlier, Evans's work remains relevant insofar as it can be read as an attempt to define an Ireland acceptable to all its inhabitants. Nevertheless, there are at least three specific grounds on which issue can be taken with his view of Ireland.

First, it has been criticised for its artefactual rather than ideational or humanistic basis. As John Hewitt observed, Evans's emphasis upon folklife was largely affirmed through the study of material culture, particularly house-types and implements such as the spade, as opposed to things of the spirit - expressed in ballads, poetry and speech[66] As observed earlier, this is not to say that Evans was unappreciative of the oneness of culture, or of the socio-cultural contexts of artefacts, for he regarded the rich heritage of Irish folklore as being a measure of the intimate association between people and their immediate surroundings.[67] This artefactual emphasis, however, partly accounts for Evans's failure to engage with power, class, religion or politics. His methodology, particularly in its bias against documentary sources, was ill-equipped to consider such issues. Only on the rarest of occasions did he allude to the political repercussions of his ideas for the island of Ireland: inevitably, their outcome would be 'a federal solution of some kind'.[68] Secondly, serious questions must attach to Evans's views on continuity. While these are consistent with his epistemological orientation towards the timelessness of peasant cultures, they also evolve from the attempt to refute the sequestration of Irishness by the Gaelic myth. Thus Evans was forced to try and demonstrate the pre-Celtic antiquity of the critical artefactual elements of peasant life, including settlement forms and field systems. But as Whelan argues, peripheral western areas such as County Donegal were not refuges of some long-established folklife, but actually experienced close and permanent settlement by farming peoples only in the eighteenth century in the wake of the Ulster Plantations and population increase. It was Evans's argument that a particularly Irish variant of openfield - rundale - and its associated nucleated settlement form – the clachan – which he held to be characteristic of such western regions, dated back to the Iron Age.[69] Thus, the examples recorded by the First Edition Ordnance Survey Six Inch Maps of *c.* 1840 were cultural survivals in an inaccessible region, demonstrative of long-term continuity. In contrast, Whelan argues cogently, both for the recency and polygenetic origins of the complex of rural settlement recorded by these maps. Indeed, Evans did point to the lateness of much settlement in the Gweedore area of Donegal, one of his postulated refuge areas, but failed to address the implications for his earlier argument.[70] Whelan's case does not actually invalidate Evan's claim for long-term continuity of material artefacts, permanent settlement along Donegal's wild and inaccessible Atlantic fringe dating back as early as the Early Bronze Age. It does serve, however, to demonstrate that Evans was incorrect both in positing a single characteristic Irish field and settlement system, and in assuming a uniform origin for the elements of that complex. As I have suggested, Evans's ideas on continuity were constructed from his wider geographical philosophy; mediated through an aversion to traditional Irish nationalism; only the latter point makes them specific to Ireland as his generalist work on peasant societies amply demonstrates. Further, Evans believed in far more than the mere preservation of folk-culture through time. To reiterate, although internally inconsistent, his view of continuity emphasised the rebirth or renewal of the old in contact with the new, which distinguishes it from the perpetual survival of a set of fixed ethnic certainties, one of the guiding tenets of traditional Irish nationalism.

Further, this issue of continuity does point to a final area of criticism. Evans considered cultural renewal in a highly selective fashion, a perspective which, through its exclusion of influences which did not fit into the peasant complex, or were amenable to his methodology, led to a most particular view of Ulster in Ireland. The rebirth took place within the framework of the *pays*, but many elements of the Irish past were given short shrift. Those included the influence of the Anglo-Normans, admittedly muted in Ulster but nonetheless significant, and the landlord-inspired improvements which transformed rural and urban landscapes in the eighteenth and early nineteenth centuries.[71] But perhaps most significant, there was almost no place in Evans's world for the transformations of Irish social space occasioned by the nineteenth-century penetration of industrial capitalism and urbanisation, particularly into the north-east of the island. Ironically, even the remote 'rundale' areas of west Donegal were affected by this process, Evans's Gweedore 'peasantry' evolving into a rural proletariat heavily dependent on migrant labouring in the Scottish Lowlands. Evans, it might be concluded, created a representative Ulster and Ireland to which the working classes could not relate except insofar as their ancestors came from the West, and the Irish state under de Valera was prepared to endorse that particular image in its cultural representations. His selective vision of continuity, derived from the belief in the primacy of peasant culture, curtailed the development of a fully convincing *personnalité* of Ulster.

Conclusions: Evans's Geography as a Resource for Ireland Today

Consequently, Evans's geographical philosophy produced a less than absorbing interest in certain elements of the diversity of his own landscape. Although his later work in particular does have something to say about the post-Plantation heterogeneity of the Irish landscape, this topic is neither central to his arguments nor is it treated in a particularly convincing fashion. Despite this serious reservation, Evans's work retains a significant relevance to contemporary Ireland through particular aspects of the vision of identity which it proffers. In the context of the contested bases of social understanding in the island, it is a text which addresses the variety and diversity of Ireland – the traits submerged in the monolith of the Gaelic myth – while acknowledging it as a source of dissension; Evans believed that it was those characteristics of our island which we had to learn to live with and exploit.[72] Any essential unity emerges from this diversity, and not through assumptions of a false homogeneity: to Evans, Sinn Féinism was the antithesis of Irishness.[73]

Therefore, Evans's ideas must be distinguished carefully from the agendas of those who seek to demonstrate Ulster's separateness from the remainder of Ireland. Such representations embrace both the concept of Ulster as a nationality conflict and its depiction as a separate regional entity within the United Kingdom which is largely defined by the interpenetration of Britain and Ireland within its territory. Their common function is to deny Irish nationalist assumptions about Ulster (Northern Ireland in this context). John Hewitt is more easily suborned to such concepts than is Evans. He shared Evans's interests in regionalism, producing what is perhaps a more significant – and indeed modern – interpretation of the region as 'some grouping smaller than the nation, larger than the family, with which we could effectively identify... the region, an area of a size and significance that we could hold in our hearts.'[74] Both Evans and Hewitt had a shared belief in the concept of the *pays,* the latter having something of the same relationship with the Glens of

Antrim – again a rural refuge – as Evans had with the Mourne country. But Hewitt made a more significant effort to come to terms with Belfast, the ethnically divided, urban-industrial capitalist landscape largely inimical to Evans's visions of Ulster and Ireland. Hewitt stressed the values of Ulster as a region, not as a symbol of creed, but as an area which could transcend sectarian division and command the loyalty of every one of its inhabitants.[75] Unable to fall back on religion, Hewitt's own nativeness was incomplete, birth and residence being insufficient qualifications so, like Seamus Heaney after him, he turned 'to the landscape that seems on occasions to join the sects.'[76]

All this could be construed as Ulster nationalism. However, it is clear from his hierarchy of values that Hewitt did not intend this. He visualised Ulster as a European region, set within a British archipelago, neither British nor Irish but simultaneously both.[77] We are dealing with fine distinctions here but his first loyalties were to the 'cross-sectarian ideal of regionalism',[78] an idea which momentarily regained some currency through the vision of 'a Europe of the regions'.[79] Hewitt's primary purpose, motivated by his own desire for inclusion, was precisely the creation of an identity based on the region rather than the nation. Both his work and that of Evans can be seen as denials of the notion that Ireland's landscape is a sectarian one. But there is a difference of degree in those denials.

While Evans did not demur from the integrative nature of regional individuality, as his pamphlet, *Ulster: The Common Ground* confirms graphically, he saw Ulster's landscape as more than a cultural code of provincial stability, however linked to the external world. For both Hewitt and Evans, part of Ulster's common ground was Ireland, as part of Ireland's was Ulster. Crucially, however, Evans's Ulster remained within Ireland. The key point – and perhaps the critical deficiency in Evans's work – is that such an understanding presupposes a regionally diverse Ireland. Evans regarded Ulster as one element of an Ireland characterised by regions defined by the interrelationship of people and their and his environment. But the philosophical necessity of refuting Celtic/Gaelic synonymity, and the nationalist abrogation of the Irish past, led to the particular perspective of continuity which substantially undermined his capacity for addressing heterogeneity. This, I believe, is the critical dissonance in Evans's work. But it should not conceal his concern for a unity in diversity, through which he sought a communality in Ireland's past to which all its inhabitants might subscribe. The importance of his interpretation lies less in the now inevitably dated empirical details of his work, as in the recognition that Irishness has to be defined as a 'many-ness'.

Therefore, Evans's work cannot be marginalised or dismissed as that of an Ulster nationalist. Conceivably, however, his *oeuvre* could be used to support those who support the concept of a self-contained Ulster regional identity or nationalism, largely because Evans never went beyond the constraints of his geographical philosophy to explore the island's heterogeneity systematically, either geographically, or in terms of class, religion and politics. Some of the criticisms of Evans's work are ideologically-driven, stimulated by re-revisionist disinclinations to admit a culturally pluralistic Ireland and undertones of that ambivalence which seeks to bolster the imagined communality of the Irish nation-state through an exploitation of a lost Ulster. More widely, Evans's *oeuvre* is a social construct, and its weaknesses are those of a geography situated in a particular epistemological and temporal context. Fleure's moral geography, the Vidalian concept of *pays*, the possibilist concerns for the interrelationship between human society and environment all now belong largely to the tradition of geography.

Again, it is now recognised that a society's material heritage is constituted not of actual artefacts, but rather of the interpretations which are attached to those. Just as knowledge changes its meaning through time, artefacts are created anew by successive generations; heritage is defined in and derives its authenticity from the present.[80] Clearly a major difficulty to conflict resolution in Ireland concerns the loss of a sense of Irishness amongst Protestants, who believe that Irish history, culture and language 'have been expropriated by nationalists as political weapons.'[81] Despite all the qualifications voiced here, Evans's life's work addressed this very dilemma, and that is why his geography still matters. Geographers can 'create place by their eloquence', and few have written as poetically, or with such emotional attachment to place, as Evans did about Ulster and its *pays*.[82] In so doing, he denied the exclusivity of Irish-Ireland. Thus his geography can be appropriated to support the very contemporary idea that the explanation of the complexities of Irish cultural identity are to be found in 'a plurality of continuities, interlocking, full of complexity'.[83] The heritage defined by it – in the sense of meanings attached to inanimate objects - urges all Ulster people to accept their Irishness. Evans's Ireland encompasses Planter and Gael, his work arguing for the centrality of immigration and colonisation in the sense that both Irish and Ulster identity have been forged through the continual renewal of the old in contact with the new.

It helps, too, that despite the essentially late-nineteenth and early twentieth-century derivation of his geographical philosophy, there does remain a curious modernity about Evans's ideas, particularly the concern with the eclectic and ordinary, with local particularity in a context of universal process. It has been argued here that the weaknesses of his geography reflect the social construction of knowledge, nor are they particular to him. Again, socially, although Evans's geography is devoted almost entirely to the undocumented in Irish society, it is the limited extent of his version of Irishness which seems most negative, in particular the little which it has to say on urban society in general, and the working classes in particular. Nevertheless, Evans's geography remains important politically for its ideals. His work can be seen as one sustained attempt – however flawed – to include all the peoples of Ireland within the ambit of Irishness. We should resist his marginalisation by those unable to come to terms with the poverty of their own vision, with 'the fingers of... evil', that dread ambiguity which undermines the morality of contemporary Ireland. [84]

Endnotes

1   J. Hewitt (1991) Roll call, in F. Ormsby (ed.) *The collected poems of John Hewitt*, Belfast, Blackstaff Press, p.486.

2   P. Durcan (1992) Foreword, in E.E. Evans, *The personality of Ireland: habitat, heritage and history*, Dublin, Lilliput Press, 3rd ed., pp. viii-ix.

3   J. Campbell (1996) Ecology and culture in Ireland, in E.E. Evans (1996) *Ireland and the Atlantic heritage: selected writings*, Dublin, Lilliput Press, pp. 225-44; G. Evans, Estyn: a biographical memoir, in E.E. Evans (1996) *Ireland and the Atlantic heritage: selected writings*, Dublin, Lilliput Press, pp.1-19; B. Graham (2004) Evans, Emyr Estyn, *Oxford Dictionary of National Biography*, Oxford, Oxford University Press.

4   For a complete bibliography of Evans's work, see: M.L. Henry (1971) A bibliography of the writings of E. Estyn Evans, in R.H. Buchanan, E. Jones and D.McCourt (eds.) *Man and his habitat: essays presented to Emyr Estyn Evans*, London, Routledge and Kegan Paul, pp.264-76; E.E. Evans (1996) *Ireland and the Atlantic heritage: selected writings*, Dublin, Lilliput Press, pp. 261-8.

5.   E.E. Evans (1942) *Irish heritage: the landscape, the people and their work*, Dundalk, Dundalgan Press.

6   Y-F. Tuan (1991) Language and the making of place: a narrative-descriptive approach, *Annals of the Association of American Geographers*, 81, pp.684-96.

7   Evans has attracted much virulent criticism, particularly from J.H. Andrews – see the discussion in: B. Graham (1994) The search for the common ground: Estyn Evans's Ireland, *Transactions Institute of British Geographers*, NS19, pp.183-201. For what can be described only as a very unpleasant attack, see: M. Stout (1996) Emyr Estyn Evans and Northern Ireland: the archaeology and geography of a new state, in J.A. Atkinson, I. Banks and J. O'Sullivan (eds.) *Nationalism in archaeology*, Glasgow, Cruithne Press, pp.111-27. For a robust rebuttal, see: G. Evans (1999) Emyr Estyn Evans, *Ulster Journal of Archaeology*, 58, pp.134-42.

8   D.N. Livingstone (1991) The moral discourse of climate: historical considerations on race, place and virtue, *Journal of Historical Geography*, 17, pp.413-34; see pp. 425-6.

9   R.P. Gruffudd (1988) Anthropology and agriculture: rural planning in Wales between the wars, in M. Heffernan and P. Gruffudd (eds.) *"A land fit for heroes": essays in the Human Geography of inter-war Britain*, Loughborough University, Department of Geography, Occasional Paper 14, pp.78-91; see p.87.

10   P. Claval (1984) The historical dimension of French geography, *Journal of Historical Geography*, 10, pp.229-45.

11   K. Whelan (1993) The bases of regionalism, in P. Ó Drisceoil (ed.) *Culture in Ireland – regions, identity and power*, Belfast, Institute of Irish Studies, pp.5-63.

12   A.R.H. Baker (1984) Reflections on the relations of historical geography and the *Annales* school of history, in A.R.H. Baker and D. Gregory (eds.) *Explorations in Historical Geography*, Cambridge, Cambridge University Press, pp.1-27. See also: A.R.H. Baker (2004) *Geography and History: bridging the divide*, Cambridge, Cambridge University Press.

13   E.E. Evans (1981) *The personality of Ireland: habitat, heritage and history*, Belfast, Blackstaff Press, 2nd ed.

14   Baker, 'Reflections', p.12.

15   L. Febvre (1925) *A geographical introduction to History*, London, Kegan Paul, p.236.

16   D.N. Livingstone (1992) *The geographical tradition*, Oxford, Blackwell, p.297.

17   Livingstone, *Geographical tradition*, p.285.

18   R.E. Glasscock (1991) Obituary: E. Estyn Evans, 1905-1989, *Journal of Historical Geography*, 17, pp.87-91; see p.87.

19   R.H. Buchanan (1984) Historical geography of Ireland pre-1700, in G.L. Herries Davies (ed.) *Irish Geography: The Geographical Society of Ireland, Golden Jubilee, 1934-1984*, Dublin, Geographical Society of Ireland, pp.129-48.

20   K. Whelan (1992) Beyond a paper landscape: J.H. Andrews and Irish historical geography, in F.H.A. Aalen and K.Whelan (eds.) *Dublin: city and county: from prehistory to present*, Dublin, Geography Publications, pp. 379-424; see p.386.

21   E.E. Evans (1951) *Mourne Country: landscape and life in South Down*, Dundalk, Dundalgan Press.

22   E.E. Evans (1968) *The Irishness of the Irish*, Belfast, The Irish Association for Cultural, Economic and Social Relations.

23   B. Graham (1993) Search for the common ground, in B. Graham, and L.J. Proudfoot (eds.) *An Historical Geography of Ireland*, London, Academic Press.

24   Evans, *Irishness of Irish*, p.2.

25   Evans, Personality, p. 88.

26   E.E. Evans (1971) Introduction, in Lord George Hill, *Facts From Gweedore*, Belfast, Institute of Irish Studies, reprint of 1887 5th ed., p.xviii.

27   See, for example: T. Brown (1981) British Ireland, in E. Longley (ed.) *Culture in Ireland: division or diversity*, Belfast, Institute of Irish Studies, pp.54-71; B. Graham (ed.) (1997) *In search of Ireland: a Cultural Geography*, London, Routledge, 1997;

       N.C. Johnson (1993) Building a nation: an examination of the Irish Gaeltacht Commission Report of 1926, *Journal of Historical Geography*,19, pp.157-68; C. Nash (1993)"Embodying the nation" - the West of Ireland landscape and Irish identity, in B. O'Connor and M. Cronin (eds.) *Tourism in Ireland: A critical analysis*, Cork, Cork University Press, pp.147-62.

28   B. Graham (1994) No place of the mind: contested Protestant representations of Ulster, *Ecumene*, 1, pp.257-81.

29   E.E. Evans, *Irishness of Irish*, p.1.

30   E.E. Evans (1951) *About Britain, No.15: Northern Ireland*, London, Collins, p.52.

31   E.E. Evans (1996) *Irish heritage*, p.2; E.E. Evans (1966) *Prehistoric and Early Christian Ireland: a guide*, London, Batsford, p.6.

32   E.E. Evans, *About Britain*, p.7.

33   E.E. Evans (1984) *Ulster: the common ground*, Mullingar, Lilliput Press.

34   J.W. Foster (1991) *Colonial consequences: essays in Irish literature and culture*, Dublin, Lilliput Press, p.159.

35   Foster, *Colonial consequences*, p.159.

36   Evans, *Common Ground*, p.8.

37   B. Graham (1996) The contested interpretation of heritage landscapes in Northern Ireland, *International Journal of Heritage Studies*, 2, pp.10-22.

38   E.E. Evans (1971) Foreword, in M.W. Heslinga, *The Irish Border as a cultural divide: a contribution to the study of regionalism in the British Isles*, Assen, Van Gorcum and Co., 2nd ed., no page numbers given.

39   Evans, *Common Ground*, p.10.

40   H. Fleure (1971) Emyr Estyn Evans: a personal note, in R.H. Buchanan, E. Jones and D.McCourt (eds.) *Man and his habitat: essays presented to Emyr Estyn Evans*, London, Routledge and Kegan Paul, pp.1-7.

41   Whelan, *Beyond paper landscape*.

42   Evans, *Personality*, p.10.

43   O. MacDonagh (1983) *States of mind: a study of Anglo-Irish conflict, 1780-1980*, London, Pimlico.

44   Evans, *Personality*, p. xiv.

45   Evans, *Irishness of Irish*, p. 6.

46   Evans, *Irish heritage*, p.6.

47   Buchanan, *Historical geography of Ireland*, p.134.

48   E.E. Evans (1941) An interpretation of Irish culture, *Ulster Journal of Archaeology*, 4, pp.12-18.

49   E.E. Evans (1939) The Celts in archaeology, *Ulster Journal of Archaeology*, 2, pp.137-47; Evans, *Interpretation of Irish culture*; E.E. Evans (1966) *Prehistoric and Early Christian Ireland: a guide*, London, Batsford.

50   Evans, *Mourne Country*, p. 203.

51   Evans, *Irish heritage*, p. 12.

52   Evans, *Irishness of Irish*, p. 5.

53   Evans, *Irishness of Irish*.

54   Evans, *Irishness of Irish*, p. 2.

55   Evans, *Common ground*.

56   Evans, *Prehistoric and Early Christian Ireland*.

57   Evans, *Common ground*, p.8.

58   Evans, *Irish heritage*; *Mourne Country*.

59   Evans, *Common ground*, p.12.

60   Evans, *Personality*, p.80.

61   W.J. Smyth (1993) The making of Ireland: agendas and perspectives in cultural geography, in B. Graham and L. Proudfoot (eds.) *An Historical Geography of Ireland*, pp.99-438; see p.400.

62   Evans, *Irish heritage*.

63   Evans, *Personality*; *Common ground*.

64   Evans, *Irish heritage*, p.2.

65   Evans, *Irishness of Irish*, p.4.

66   See: J. Hewitt, No rootless colonist. Originally printed in *Aquarius* (1972), reprinted in in P. Craig (ed.) (1992) *The rattle of the North: an anthology of Ulster prose*, Belfast, Blackstaff Press, pp.121-31; R.H. Buchanan (1991) The achievement of Estyn Evans, in G. Dawe and J.W. Foster (eds.) *The poet's place: Ulster literature and society*, Belfast, Institute of Irish Studies, pp.149-56.

67   E.E. Evans (1957) *Irish folk ways*, London, Routledge and Kegan Paul.

68   E.E. Evans (1971) The personality of Ulster, *Transactions of the Institute of British Geographers*, 51, pp.1-19.

69   E.E. Evans (1939) Some survivals of the Irish openfield system, *Geography*, 24, pp. 24-36.

70   Whelan, *Beyond paper landscape*.

71   J.P. Mallory, and T.E. McNeill (1991) *The archaeology of Ulster: from colonization to plantation*, Belfast, Institute of Irish Studies; B. Graham and L. Proudfoot (eds.) (1993) *An Historical Geography of Ireland*.

72   Evans, *Common ground*.

73   Evans, *Irishness of the Irish*.

74   Evans, *Personality*, p.127.

75   F. Ormsby (1991) Introduction, in F. Ormsby (ed.) *The collected poems of John Hewitt*, Belfast, Blackstaff Press, pp.xli-lxxiv.

76   Foster, *Colonial consequences*, p.159.

77   P. Arthur (1991) John Hewitt's hierarchy of values, in G. Dawe and J.W. Foster (eds.) *The poet's place: Ulster literature and society*, Belfast, Institute of Irish Studies, pp.273-84.

78   Ormsby, Introduction, p.lxv.

79   N. Ascherson (1991) Europe of the regions, in M. Crozier (ed.) *Cultural traditions in Northern Ireland*, Belfast, Institute of Irish Studies, pp.24-30; R. Kearney (ed.) (1988) *Across the frontiers: Ireland in the 1980s*, Dublin, Wolfhound Press.

80   B. Graham, G.J. Ashworth and J.E. Tunbridge (2000) *A Geography of heritage: power, culture and economy*, London, Arnold.

81   A. Pollak (ed.) (1993) *A citizens' enquiry: the Opsahl Report on Northern Ireland*, Dublin, Lilliput Press, p.122.

82   Tuan, Language and the making of place, p. 693.

83   G. Ó Tuathaigh (1991) The Irish-Ireland idea: rationale and relevance, in E. Longley (ed.) *Culture in Ireland: division or diversity*, Belfast, Institute of Irish Studies, pp.54-71; see p. 67.

84   Durcan, 'Foreword', p. ix.

Chapter 2

Craigavon: Locality, Economy and the State in a Failed 'New City'

Liam O'Dowd

Introduction

The research project[1] on which this chapter is based seeks to challenge a pervasive compartmentalisation in the study of socio-economic change in Northern Ireland. This compartmentalisation has taken a number of forms. First, the analyses of the dramatic transformation of Northern Ireland's economic structure since the 1960s have remained unconnected with the study of its impact on specific localities. More particularly, apart from some crude estimations, there has been little in-depth examination of the links between ethnic-national conflict and economic change at either local or regional level.[2] Second, the ethnic-national conflict has been linked to space and locality, especially in the work of Jones (1960) and Boal (e.g., Boal and Douglas, 1982). While carefully underlining the centrality of sectarian geography, this approach sees the latter as merely the outcome of inter-communal conflict. It pays relatively little attention to how the state and wider processes of economic restructuring interact with locality and ethnic conflict. Third, a variety of local community studies do exist but they too are largely compartmentalised from the study of structural changes at the political and economic level. Moreover, they have tended to concentrate less on urban industrial than on rural settings. They have shared the perspective of much of the anthropology of modern Ireland which has focused on the degeneration and decline of traditional rural society (important exceptions to this pattern are Eipper, 1986; Jenkins, 1983; Dilley, 1989; and Howe, 1990). The research reported here, however, concerns an urban environment with a long history of industrialization – marked at the time of the research between 1989 and 1991 by a combination of industrial change and decline as well as by an intensification of ethnic-national conflict.

Cast in broader terms, our research addressed an age-old issue in the social sciences - the links between structural change and the experiences and responses of local actors in specific communities. The initial problem was whether to begin the study with an account of structural change or alternatively with an examination of a delimited territorial area. The former posed serious data problems. While much socio-economic information exists for Northern Ireland as a whole, information was extremely patchy at lower levels of disaggregation. Two decades of changing local and administrative boundaries made historical comparisons difficult and, moreover, ensured that many of these local entities failed to correspond with popular territorial identifications.[3]

Starting from delimited territorial areas also posed problems. Existing studies of such areas often failed to address wider structural and political change adequately. There was little systematic comparative study of local communities (see Donnan and McFarlane, 1986, p.396), in part because of the practical difficulties of studying more than one community at a time. Existing ethnographies also seemed to concentrate on areas of limited size, i.e., small rural communities or urban housing estates. In the face of these kinds of problems it seemed to many observers that the 'community studies' tradition generally had run out of steam (Day and Murdoch, 1993).

On the other hand, in the 1980s, a tradition of 'locality studies' had emerged which seemed to link wider processes of economic change to particular localities (see, for example, Hausner, 1987; Cooke, 1989; Bagguley *et al.*, 1990). Many social scientists argued that, far from homogenising social space, modern capitalist development was a differentiating force – heightening the economic, social and political significance of localities (Urry, 1981, p.464). This perspective appeared promising in a Northern Ireland context, where the ethnic-national conflict also seemed to be enhancing the significance of localities. Regional analyses in Northern Ireland had underlined the central role of the state in mediating economic change (O'Dowd, 1986; Rowthorn and Wayne, 1988). It was also clear that the state was a key element in the relationship between the Catholic and Protestant communities. Thus, it appeared that the state provided a bridge between general processes of economic restructuring and local community consciousness heightened by the continuing conflict.

The Craigavon new city project neatly brought together all these issues. Craigavon was both a product of the radical economic change of the 1960s and a key means employed by the state to direct and influence that change. It underlined the territorial dimensions of state policy and brought the latter face to face with the problem of restructuring sectarian geography. By the early 1970s, sectarian geography was being exacerbated by the eruption of the Northern Ireland conflict which in turn was to have a decisive impact on the prospects of the new city. The overall result was the exposure of the territorial and ethnic strategies of the Northern Ireland state to critical scrutiny, an exposure which was to lead to the reshaping of the state itself.

The 'new city' plan was an attempt to merge two long established towns,

Lurgan and Portadown, into an enlarged urban area, Craigavon. In terms of local perceptions, at least, the plan failed. Not only have the two towns preserved their distinctiveness, a third entity has emerged – Brownlow – a legacy of new city housing policy. Although Craigavon is the official name for all three areas, significantly, locals identify only Brownlow as Craigavon, seeing its severe socio-economic problems as conclusive testimony of the ill-advised nature of the new city plan. Whatever the final outcome, however, the experience of the 'new city' allows us to examine the interface between economic change, state management and established local identities.

The first part of this chapter outlines the historical and 'structural' context of the new city project, drawing on official documents, newspapers and interviews. This project, which generated political controversy from the outset, was severely hampered by the international economic downturn after 1973, by political upheaval in Northern Ireland, by the vagaries of government economic and planning policy, and, not least, by popular resistance to the new city idea. The second part of the chapter probes the basis for this resistance among local residents who are coping with, and reflecting on, the 'failure' of the new city twenty-five years after its inception. The concluding section suggests that the 'failure' of Craigavon has arisen from the interaction of state policy, economic change, and local identity and local action. In particular, it highlights the importance of the interaction of state and local territorial strategies in a society marked by deep ethnic-national divisions.

Background, Origins and Development
The Craigavon project was conceived and partially implemented against a background of radical socio-economic and political change. Not only was the project perhaps the most ambitious example of urban planning in twentieth century Ireland, it was initiated at a time when there was a major shift in how Northern Ireland was being incorporated into the international economy. Indeed, the new city was intended as a means of influencing and shaping this incorporation. The global economy was undergoing radical alteration itself as multinationals were beginning to develop effective global strategies, including the decentralization and dispersal of production processes, which were undermining more locally-based industry in the towns and cities of the province.

The British government in the post-1945 period and, more belatedly, the Northern Ireland government (Stormont), had become committed to an interventionist role in influencing the geography of global economic change. This meant *inter alia* developing growth-centres, new cities, and industrial estates to act as poles of attraction for industry. In peripheral regions of the United Kingdom (UK) and the Irish Republic, this policy meant state sponsorship of branches of multinational corporations. The subsequent move away from interventionist policies in the 1970s and 1980s to more "market-led" strategies of development was to have far-reaching effects for Craigavon.

However, by the early 1960s, pressure was building on Stormont to take a more active role in promoting regional economic development. Persistent high unemployment in the province contrasted with near full employment in Britain. Large scale redundancies among Protestant workers in the Belfast engineering and shipbuilding industries had led to defections from the Unionist Party to the Northern Ireland Labour Party. The British Conservative government had begun to revitalise regional policy by attempting to re-direct employment to peripheral regions of the UK – a policy taken further by the new Labour government between 1964 and 1970. Moreover, multinational corporations were generating more mobile international investment and the Irish Republic had already embarked on its programme of state-sponsored multinational investment. Within the Northern Ireland civil service, there was mounting concern over the rapid and unplanned growth of the Belfast urban area (see e.g., Oliver, 1978). A small group of civil servants, in conjunction with some younger modernising government ministers (including the new Prime Minister Terence O'Neill, Brian Faulkner and William Craig), embarked on a regional development strategy which was to have far-reaching ramifications. By the 1960s, Stormont was ready to embrace a policy of new towns, growth centre planning, and the provision of industrial estates, roads and other infrastructural developments.

Two key reports were commissioned: one on physical planning (Matthew Report, 1963) and one on economic development (Wilson Report, 1965). These reports introduced the fashionable British planning rhetoric of the time without acknowledging the highly charged nature of Northern Ireland's sectarian geography. Matthew proposed a stop-line to Belfast's development. He urged that labour and industry be redirected to two major growth centres, Antrim / Ballymena and Lurgan / Portadown, and to a number of secondary centres in the east of the province. Among Matthew's more dramatic recommendations was a proposal for a new "regional city", incorporating the market and linen towns of Lurgan and Portadown, with a population of 20,000 each. This new city was to cater for a large overspill of population from Belfast and for unemployed migrants from the west of the province. The target population set for it was 120,000 by 1980 and 180,000 by the year 2,000.[4] Matthew (1963) declared the new city to be the "first priority" of the Plan and claimed that it would be "a major symbol of regeneration within Northern Ireland".

Matthew justified his choice of location on the grounds of proximity to Belfast, existing transportation routes with potential for expansion, land availability, and the existence of two established urban centres, Lurgan and Portadown. Significantly, unemployment rates were not a criterion. Both

Lurgan and Portadown rates were generally at or below the Northern Ireland average and much lower than in other potential locations such as Armagh, Derry and Newry. Nonetheless, the subsequent Wilson report on the economy, published two years later, endorsed Matthew's plans claiming that the new city could "weld the area together and provide a growth point capable of adding significantly to Northern Ireland's capacity to attract industry" (Wilson, 1965, pp.29-30). Even prior to the Wilson document, the O'Neill administration had moved with great alacrity to implement Matthew's new city recommendations despite considerable hostility from opposition members at Stormont. The latter accused the government of favouring a predominantly Protestant area over Catholic areas with higher levels of unemployment.[5]

Hostility provoked by the choice of location was further intensified by the Cabinet's decision to name the new city after the first Prime Minister of Northern Ireland (James Craig) and by the failure to appoint any nationalists to the new Development Commission. The debate over Craigavon continued in the midst of controversy over a series of other locational decisions, the alleged neglect of the west of the province, the closure of railway lines to the predominantly nationalist towns of Derry and Newry, and, subsequently, the preference of "unionist" Coleraine to Derry as the site of the province's new university.

Despite these objections and many others by both nationalists and unionists (see Blackman, 1988), the plan for Craigavon was prepared and a New Towns Act (NI) was passed in June 1965. In July 1965, the Ministry of Development designated a development area of approximately 100 square miles (67,553 acres), incorporating the boroughs of Lurgan and Portadown and the rural districts of Lurgan and Moira in County Armagh. The designated area had a population of 61,700. In June 1966, a Vesting Order was made and 68,000 acres of land were acquired for the project; a considerably larger area than acquired for similar new town developments in Britain (Carolan, 1987).

The first major conflict was between the government and local farmers concerning the value of vested land. The farmers' campaign, which temporarily brought together Protestants and Catholics, was unsuccessful. In October 1965, the Craigavon Development Commission was appointed to manage the development of Craigavon in accordance with the Plan. There was little representation of local interests, possibly to minimise competition between Lurgan and Portadown, while anti-unionists were excluded altogether. Neither was there any mechanism for public participation or consultation. The whole project had been the brainchild of a small elite of politicians, planners and civil servants. In conception and design, it paid little attention to the attachment of Northern Irish people to their localities, nor did it contemplate how difficult it would be to construct a new over-arching urban entity to which both locals and migrants could give their allegiance. The

Craigavon Master Plan provided for a sharp segregation of residential, industrial and retail zones reflecting the planning wisdom of the time and the belief that the new city dwellers would be car-owners (Figure 2.1).[6]

Figure 2.1: Aerial view of the linear core of Craigavon as it might appear in the year 2000

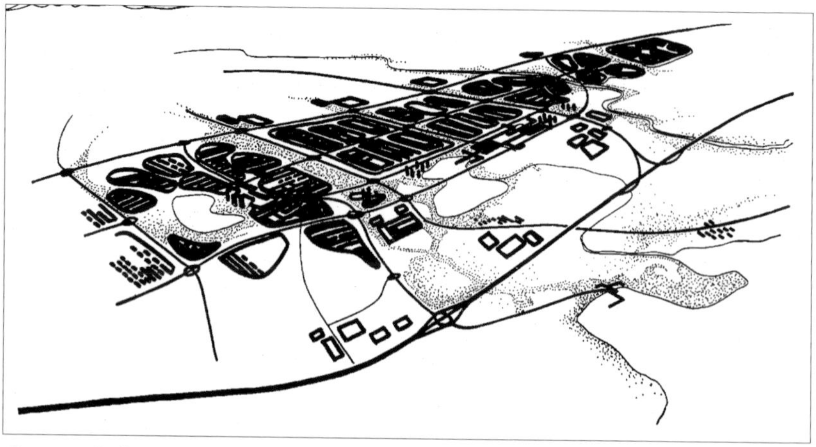

Source: Craigavon Development Commission (1967) *Craigavon New City: Second Report on the Plan*, p.29.

Although the Brownlow sector was the first to be initiated, it was already behind target by 1969. Its population in June of that year was only 1,600 against a target of 5,000. By 1969, the managing director of Goodyear was claiming major labour recruitment problems. Labour turnover was also becoming a problem. The company lost 254 employees in the first four months of 1969 and 'screened' the unemployed in Belfast, Strabane, Newry and Enniskillen with little success. The manager also claimed that new city housing was "too rich for the pocketbook" of potential workers (Belfast Telegraph, 17-19 June 1969). It seems likely that labour shortages and turnover were partly due to work-related factors and partly to a reluctance to move to, or remain in, an unfamiliar new city environment.

Problems in attracting migrants persisted. In 1971, a mobility office was established in Belfast to provide advice, publicity and financial assistance in the form of cash grants to encourage movement out of Belfast. The resettlement grant scheme met with little success and was often abused by 'moonlighters' who moved to Craigavon until they received the cash grant and then returned, mainly to Belfast (Lurgan Mail, 11 March 1982). The Craigavon Development Commission went on to build a total of 3739 houses in 22 estates. The Commission succeeded in making major investments – amounting to £500 million – in roads, advance factory units, housing, a government training centre and a 492-bed hospital with a projected employment of 750. Five new industrial estates were established at Annesborough, Silverwood, Seagoe, Carn and Mahon.

By the late 1960s, however, the development of Craigavon was becoming caught up in the general escalation of the 'troubles'. The reluctance of families of both communities to move away from their home territories or to live in mixed communities was now exacerbated. Belfast Catholics began to retreat back into West Belfast, while Protestants tended to move to the new estates on the fringes of the Belfast urban area. Neither were attracted to Craigavon in large numbers, although some 'problem families' were assigned housing there. Conversely, sectarian conflict in Lurgan and Portadown encouraged locals to move to Brownlow, to escape the violence. From the outset, Brownlow gained a reputation as being relatively free from sectarian conflict. However, it did not escape a considerable degree of physical segregation of Protestants and Catholics.

The planners intended to create an integrated community in Brownlow. They sought to avoid the physical separation of denominational facilities by grouping schools, churches, and shops near the centre of neighbourhoods (Figure 2.2). The sector was to be a model of integration located between two towns which had a long history of sectarian segregation. As early as 1973, however, there was considerable Protestant-Catholic segregation in Brownlow (Reid, 1973). The eastern area contiguous to the Catholic estates in Lurgan was predominantly Catholic, while those in the west nearest Portadown were largely Protestant. This tendency was confirmed by the later building of the Parkmore estate. Closer to Portadown, it became almost exclusively Protestant. While a mixed buffer area exists in the middle of Brownlow (Reid, 1973), Brownlow has remained a predominantly Catholic area. Demands for jobs and housing were greater among Catholics and from the outset the Goodyear factory near Lurgan employed large numbers of unskilled Catholic workers. Brownlow's subsequent image problem, however, derived less from sectarian considerations than from problems of marginalization, deprivation and unemployment.

By the early 1970s, other obstacles were mounting for the new city. As part of the reorganisation of local government in 1973, the Craigavon Commission was abolished. It had proved to be one of the shortest lived of any of the UK new town commissions, and its abolition removed the major agency with overall responsibility for coordinating development in Craigavon. The new Borough Council remit did cover the new city, but it had very limited powers. Moreover, it was dominated by rival Portadown and Lurgan interests with minimal representation from Brownlow. The dominant political interests were highly sceptical of the new city in any case, and argued that Brownlow had been developed at the expense of Portadown and Lurgan.

Figure 2.2: Brownlow planned land use structure

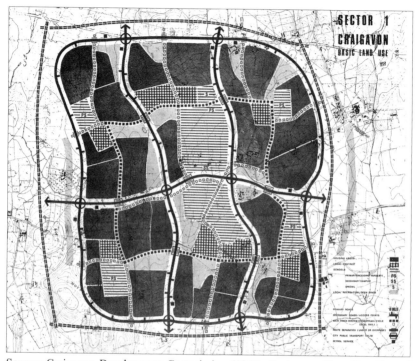

Source: Craigavon Development Commission (1967) *Craigavon New City: Second Report on the Plan*, p.35.

In fact, quite apart from local government re-organisation, regional and growth-centre policy was going out of fashion nationally. In 1975, a new Regional Development Strategy reversed the Matthew / Wilson plans and favoured the dispersing of development among 26 District towns. This further down-graded Craigavon, as did a subsequent shift in priorities to regenerating housing and infrastructure in Belfast and in the older towns. These changes in conjunction with the 'troubles' and international recession made industrial promotion more difficult. Unemployment began to rise rapidly in Craigavon in line with the overall Northern Ireland level. As happened in Britain, the juxtaposition of areas of low and high unemployment became apparent. While industrial employment in Portadown proved resilient, it declined considerably in Lurgan and disastrously in Brownlow with the demise of Goodyear. Brownlow was developing, not as a housing sector of an integrated new city, but, in the words of one state official, as a "collection of problem housing estates, located somewhere between Portadown and Lurgan". In fact, the fragmented nature of Brownlow was expressed physically in the layout of its housing estates. Built for a skilled, fully employed, car owning population, it proved unsuitable to a population characterised by low skill levels, low incomes, mass unemployment and limited mobility.

Overall, the story of Brownlow in the 1980s was one of continuous crisis involving housing surpluses, high tenancy turnover rates, declining job opportunities, and high debt levels. Over 800 houses were demolished (circa 20% of the total housing stock) and others privatised. While this reduced the housing surplus, it did not prevent the high tenancy turnover or the drift of people back to refurbished or new dwellings in Lurgan, Portadown and Belfast.

The politics of Brownlow in the 1970s and 1980s were not those of unionism and nationalism but of community groups, housing and social welfare issues. The Brownlow Community Council (1979) strongly criticised the ward boundaries which led to under-representation of Brownlow compared to Lurgan and Portadown. It suggested that the only hope for the area was a strong voice to offset the rivalries of the towns. This demand was to recur regularly from umbrella groups of community activists.

In spite of its internal divisions, a separate identity began to develop in Brownlow, rooted in part in its neglect and stigmatisation by Lurgan and Portadown interests and in part due to its dependency on state agencies. By the time our research got underway the Brownlow Initiative (and subsequently Brownlow Ltd.) had been set up as a "partnership" between state agencies, community groups and business to develop an economic strategy for Brownlow *per se*. Soon after, the government designated the area as the sole Northern Ireland recipient of funds under the EC's third anti-poverty programme. The Brownlow Community Trust was established as a partnership between statutory, voluntary and community organisations to administer the programme and tackle the social problems of the area. It seemed that the government was acquiescing to demands to have Brownlow treated as a separate local entity – yet another sign that the vision of an integrated new city had been laid to rest.

A deteriorating economic environment, lack of consistency in state policy, and a loss of political enthusiasm all combined to undermine the new city. Yet, such a general and 'top-down' assessment misses an important dimension to the story, i.e., the interaction of local identity and local action with state policy. At the outset, the Craigavon project seemed to meet two key requirements: for planners and administrators, it represented the opportunity to translate 'best' British economic and 'new town' strategy to Northern Ireland; for Stormont ministers, it was consistent with maintaining unionist economic and political dominance. Neither group reckoned with the strength of local resistance, however, and the difficulty of transcending deeply rooted communal and territorial identifications in Lurgan and Portadown. Our research in Craigavon, almost three decades after its designation as a new city, highlights not just local residents' reaction to failed state policies, but how local responses and perceptions helped ensure such failure in the first place. Perhaps the most striking failure of all was the failure of the new city advocates to grasp the problematical nature of state locality interaction in a society torn by territorially based ethnic national divisions.

Local Responses and Perceptions in a 'Failed' New City Context
By 1989, when this research began, residents of Craigavon were agreed that Lurgan and Portadown had retained their separate identities. Typically, Brownlow was also seen as distinct - a failed remnant of a failed new city. One life-long resident of Portadown remembered the rivalry between Lurgan and Portadown from her schooldays, adding:

> There's always rivalry between Lurgan and Portadown. . . . But the two towns are very similar, even in the shape of the towns. You would never get a Lurgan person saying that Portadown's a better town or vice versa. I've often thought that was the reason why the city didn't join up. Although we're supposed to be from Craigavon, if anybody asked me where I came from, I'd never think of saying I came from Craigavon. I come from Portadown. There are two main towns in themselves and a piece in between that's an outsider.

The long-standing rivalry between both towns was a recurrent theme among our informants. It was clear also that overarching local identities transcended the Protestant-Catholic divide. However, this did not mean that the internal communal divide was unimportant. Indeed, there were considerable differences in the population balance in each locality. The percentage of Catholics ranged from approximately 30 per cent in Portadown, to about 50 per cent in Lurgan and 70 per cent in Brownlow.[7] Moreover, religious affiliation fused in different ways with social class and local identity in each area. A senior manager in the Southern Health and Social Services Board made the issue of intra-locality division explicit:

> Portadown people are Portadown . . . you could say there's two separate communities in Portadown and two separate communities in Lurgan; they wouldn't even talk to themselves, let alone acknowledge this big lump in the middle. I think they are reasonably insular and it's a disaster in social planning for everyone to come together into one big brave new town with new industry and big jobs.

A male community worker in Brownlow noted the perception of the place as a dumping ground for 'problem-families':

> Every Tom, Dick and Harry has been shoved in here, and the place has a name
> for all sorts of perverts and weirdoes. This has been said to me by people I
> knew from Portadown . . . morale is low, self-esteem is low.

Brownlow's identity was portrayed generally in negative terms. An official in the Craigavon Training Centre located in Portadown observed that there was very little difference in trainees from Lurgan and Portadown but that those from Brownlow:

> would tend to have a very erratic attitude, and would tend to drop out, they'd
> have discipline problems, time-keeping and attendance problems. . . I feel that
> people who were encouraged to come into it (Brownlow) were possibly
> troublesome cases from elsewhere.

Brownlow Ltd. and Brownlow Community Trust aimed to reverse this negative image by generating improved job opportunities, welfare provision, and identification with Brownlow as an entity distinct from either Portadown or Lurgan. The development of separate strategies for Brownlow even included a proposal by the Brownlow Initiative to build a traditional town centre to give the area a focus. Such attempts to establish a separate identity for Brownlow were met with a mixture of scepticism and enthusiasm by state officials and voluntary sector workers dealing with the area.[8] Community activists, on the other hand, saw little alternative, given the stigmatisation and isolation of the area by Portadown and Lurgan, though they felt ambivalent about the possibility of success.

A leading voluntary sector worker involved in the regeneration plans acknowledged that "historically Brownlow was a white elephant" and "an administrative embarrassment" and that "a lot of senior civil servants would hope that it would go away". The consultants appointed to develop the Brownlow Initiative noted that there were only a few scattered shops in the area and one manufacturing business employing six people (four of them on training schemes) in an area of 10,000 people (Mackey, 1989). This was a sharp reminder of the difficulties of creating a settled urban identity comparable to that in Lurgan and Portadown.

Lurgan and Portadown: Contrasting Business Cultures

In terms of origins, size, location, and common industrial base in the linen industry, Lurgan and Portadown seem to have much more in common with each other than they do with Brownlow. Yet our respondents' images of Lurgan and Portadown not only stressed their differences from Brownlow, but the contrasts between one another. Portadown was uniformly represented as the most successful local economy, while Lurgan was portrayed as less well off – a point supported by our survey research. Both towns were perceived as very different in terms of business and trade union culture, and highly competitive historically *vis-a-vis* employment, trade and other resources. These responses illuminate the difficulties of merging the two towns into a wider urban entity. For example, one Catholic industrialist claimed that there was more "entrepreneurial flair in Portadown than in Lurgan", adding:

> I think there are more people owning their houses [9] and there's more of a sense of commitment in the community and to the community. It may have something to do with the Catholic/Protestant links. . . you have a higher percentage of Catholics in Lurgan than in Portadown. And for some reason there has never been as much capital available in the Catholic community.

A retired businessman active in bringing new industry to Portadown in the post-war period saw the ascendancy of Portadown in terms of a more proactive civic culture:

> You can get Portadown people to respond more quickly to a public need (for example, set up a committee). The Portadown Chamber of Commerce is an example – it has been going for 50 years, whereas Lurgan Chamber of Commerce, you never hear about them.

Our historical research into local economic initiatives in Portadown and Lurgan confirmed the pro-activity of a small business elite in the former and the relative inactivity in the latter. As early as 1946, an elite group of businessmen formed the Portadown New Industries Council (PNIC) to attract industrial investment to the town as the local linen industry began to decline. The PNIC was largely informal in nature with five permanent members: a store-owner, a solicitor, a builder and two linen industrialists. It linked the local Chamber of Commerce with the Junior Chamber, the Rotary Club and the Borough Council. Its first chairman was a highly influential linen industrialist at both local and regional level. For example, he used his position on the Electricity Board for Northern Ireland to persuade Unidare to locate in the town and he was able to persuade existing local employers to adapt to a more diversified industrial base. In the late 1950s, the PNIC was the first local body to produce an industrial promotion brochure to "sell the town" to potential investors. [10]

Not only was the Portadown business elite more active than its Lurgan counterpart, it pre-figured the systematic sponsorship of multinational investment by the Stormont government in the 1960s. Craigavon Development Commission took over the functions of the PNIC on its creation in 1966. Nevertheless, when the Commission disbanded in 1973 the newly formed Craigavon Borough Council expressed an interest in the old PNIC and in 1980 the Craigavon New Industries Council (CNIC) was established and re-named the Craigavon Industrial Development Organisation (ClDO) in 1985.

The old gulf between Lurgan and Portadown re-appeared, however. Although the CNIC was to act for Craigavon as a whole, representatives from Lurgan withdrew their participation within 18 months, claiming that the new body was primarily Portadown-oriented. ClDO took advantage of the Thatcher's government commitment to 'enterprise culture' to establish small business units in Portadown, while, belatedly, an Enterprise Trust was established in Lurgan in 1989. The slowness of Lurgan to respond to the new enterprise policies was explained by the manager of the Lurgan Job Market in terms of the absence of locals at management level in industry:

> If we had industrialists who were local, maybe they would band together and get things going. There are some, but not as many as other towns would have. They say that the Rotary here is more commercially-orientated than manufacturing-orientated.

Certainly, evidence of employment change suggested that Portadown had succeeded better than Lurgan in diversifying its economy and combating global economic changes. Between 1950 and 1970 both towns had similar unemployment rates - at or below the Northern Ireland average. Initially, both were heavily dependent on linen manufacture, but as this industry declined Portadown's economic diversification helped it to combat recession. Between 1971 and 1978 Portadown lost only 10 per cent of its manufacturing jobs, as compared to Lurgan's 21 per cent. In the same period, unemployment increased by 85 per cent in Portadown and by 139 per cent in Lurgan.[11] Thus, the Craigavon project coincided with a widening gulf between the economies of Portadown and Lurgan – a gulf that may be partly rooted in the history of their business communities. Both towns have seen the replacement of indigenous industry by national and multinational interests. Portadown, however, has retained a larger core of locally owned manufacturing which seems to provide the impetus for a more positive response to economic change and shifts in government economic policy.

Trades Union Culture
Business, of course, constitutes only one element in a complex local identity. Different trades union histories also distinguished the two towns. For example, unlike Portadown, Lurgan had a long history of trade union activity associated with the linen trade – a difference which lived on in the perceptions of local activists. One retired trade union official in Lurgan claimed that Portadown would not join the trade union in the 1950s while "Lurgan was 100 per cent trade union". Whereas Portadown had its leading business activists, Lurgan

had a prominent and influential union organiser called Mick Casey. While there was a trade union in Portadown, "there were never trade union principles. . . they accepted everything that was offered to them, whether they liked it or not". He felt that Portadown employees were always very respectful to their bosses.

Another trade union activist supported the point about worker deference in Portadown claiming that, in one factory, fully organised by the ATGWU, workers called their bosses 'Master' and were called by their surname in turn. He also noted the historical resistance in Portadown to trade union organisation claiming that it was 'a religious thing'. As in the case of business culture, religion is seen as interwoven with the history of trade unionism in both towns. According to the retired trade union official: "it was always considered a Catholic thing to be a member of a trade union. . . all the shop-stewards in the linen trade were Catholic. . . people were looked down on because they were associated with a 'Communist/Catholic' organisation" (i.e., the trade union).

Trade unionists acknowledged, however, that Portadown's better employment record and improved trade union organisation had led to a strengthening of trade union membership, whereas economic decline had undermined Lurgan's trade union tradition. Nevertheless, as another ATGWU official pointed out, Lurgan remained the traditional centre for trade union protests and parades.[12] These were unlikely to occur in Portadown. Although trades union membership was seen to have increased in the latter due to active local officials, membership was not to be confused with militancy. This view was supported by several female trade unionists concerned with opposing the privatisation of services in Craigavon Hospital (located near Portadown). They complained about the difficulty of mobilising opposition to privatisation of services in Craigavon Area Hospital (near Portadown) blaming it on conservatism, status snobbery and "culture". Although religion was not explicitly mentioned as a factor, unfavourable comparisons were made between the lack of militancy in Protestant Craigavon and the more militant response in Catholic Newry to the same privatisation plans.

The different business and trade union cultures in Lurgan and Portadown were compounded by local political rivalry between the two towns. While this rivalry found expression on Craigavon Council in terms of intra-unionist politics, it was also evident in wider lobbying for facilities and resources.

Ethno-sectarian Geography and Local Identity
The origins of both Lurgan and Portadown can be traced directly to the plantation of Ulster in the early seventeenth century. In Lurgan, for example, a planter family, the Brownlows, built the town and maintained an unbroken connection with it until recently. Memories of plantation and revolt are

preserved in local culture. Perhaps one of the more striking examples of this was the ceremony on the bridge in Portadown in 1991, presided over by the head of the Orange Order to commemorate the Protestants massacred there 350 years earlier in the Catholic rising of 1641. Both towns were strong centres of Orangeism from the inception of the Orange Order in the late eighteenth century.

Against this background, geographers and historians have noted how communal segregation became an integral part of the rapid development of both towns in the second half of the nineteenth century. The pattern of segregation established in Lurgan by 1911, after forty years of industrial growth, has changed little in the twentieth century – in 1971, it was the most segregated middle-sized town in Northern Ireland (Poole, 1982, pp.298-305).

Our interviews revealed a sharp awareness of religious segregation. Respondents spoke of an "invisible line" which divided Catholic from Protestant Lurgan. There was a sharp sectarian polarisation in working class estates in both Lurgan and Portadown and signs that these divisions were being replicated in Brownlow. Some of our respondents referred to cases of intimidation and assassination which led to the enforced movement of population in the early 1970s and a reversal of the degree of mixing that was beginning to occur in some of the newer estates.

Early signs of the failure of the planners' attempt to create religiously integrated areas in Brownlow were confirmed in the 1980s. The estates nearest Lurgan were overwhelmingly Catholic and became, in a sense, an extension of the Catholic part of Lurgan. Protestants in Brownlow, on the other hand, gravitated towards Portadown. Central Brownlow was more mixed but the demolition of some of the central estates was reducing its size. In the words of a Brownlow community worker, this demolition is:

> creating a lot of problems for the central area. The nationalist side is gravitating towards Lurgan, the loyalist side to the Portadown end, and the middle being totally devastated. I think that's going to create difficulties in the future – it could exacerbate sectarian difficulties of which there has not been much so far.

The housing schemes and industrial estates of the new city, far from providing new "integrated environments", soon began to demonstrate the power of popular as opposed to planners' definitions of locality. In our interviews with householders,[13] there was a tendency to distinguish between workplace and where it was located. Generally, there was a feeling that both religions can and do work together but that the location of the workplace and/or the areas through which one had to travel to get to it, could be problematic. A female Protestant factory worker in Lurgan commented:

> There isn't anything, you know, between Protestants and Catholics in work really. You know, everybody seems to be sort of friends like. It's a funny thing, that like. You can have a mixture of people and the troubles would never be mentioned at work.

This woman said her factory was in a Catholic area of Lurgan and that she had no fears at all about going to work. Her husband, however, remembered difficulties in persuading Catholics to travel through Protestant areas to work at his previous place of employment.

An unemployed Protestant in Portadown mentioned a food processing plant located in a Catholic area pointing out that: "there's no Protestants that would apply for that because of where it is". His wife added: "it's not in a really bad area but to get to it you have to go through a really bad area". The husband then referred to a Protestant factory where Catholics had similar problems.

A part-time Catholic shop assistant in central Craigavon was in no doubt that shops in Lurgan and Portadown employed workers on the basis of religion and that people would refuse to work in certain factories because of their religion. She then added: "I wouldn't go to Portadown - I'd go to Lurgan. There's girls I work with who've never been to Lurgan - they stay in Portadown." This comment is revealing in that it illustrates the self-contained nature of Portadown and Lurgan and the orientation of the Catholic part of Brownlow to Lurgan.

The manager of Lurgan job market stressed the separateness of Lurgan and Portadown and noted the difficulty of working with "three separate communities" within the Craigavon area. He mentioned the reluctance of Lurgan people to travel to work in Portadown, four or five miles away, although they would travel to industrial estates on the outskirts of Portadown or to work in Lisburn and Belfast. The reluctance to travel was particularly marked among Catholics who saw Portadown as a Protestant town. The Lurgan job market manager mentioned, in particular, the efforts being made to get people to attend the Job Club in Portadown, observing: "you can't tell whether it's a genuine fear or just an excuse or a perceived notion. There was always confrontation between Lurgan and Portadown anyway".

The difficulties posed by sectarian geography were underlined by an unemployed 35 year old Catholic man in Portadown:

> You don't go to certain factories because they are in bad areas. . . I've seen Manpower or the job market as it's called now, asking me to go to a job and I wouldn't go to it because of the area it was in. Because I can't drive and I've no form of transport and I'd have to walk or go on a bike, or whatever. But I thought it was highly dangerous going through the areas y'know.

The impact of sectarian geography on young people's opportunities was stressed by some of our key informants. A Portadown community workshop (training) manager noted:

> Ninety per cent of the trainees would come from the Tunnel (Catholic working class area of Portadown). Those trainees have a ghetto mentality – they won't go outside of this area. . . We had some trainees going for a job here this morning [mentions another Catholic area of Portadown], which is a quarter of a mile from here, and they wanted to know how they would get there. They have this ghetto mentality reinforced at home.

His opposite number in Lurgan also noted the reluctance of young Catholic trainees: "(they) will go to Protestant employers, but they won't go to a predominantly Protestant area to work". Employment that serviced the whole Craigavon area posed particular problems in negotiating sectarian geography. A Brownlow woman whose husband was a taxi-driver worried about him being "an easy target":

> If you are going around you're just stopped and asked who you are and what you are. . . There would be certain areas they would be afraid to go into. People would ring a certain company because they know what they are.

The difficulties of constructing an integrated local labour market in Craigavon are clear from our interviews, which show that there is more mixing at work than in housing, education and leisure pursuits. Nevertheless, workplaces are lodged within a sharply defined sectarian geography which they also help to shape. Mobility and willingness to travel to work are constrained not just by religious affiliation but also by age, gender and class. While none of our middle class, and few of our female, respondents indicated that their own access to work was limited by sectarian considerations, clearly they were a major consideration for our working class interviewees, especially for males in the younger age groups.

Territorial and ethnic-sectarian divisions, far from being undermined by economic change and state planning, were in many respects consolidated by them. One key indicator is unemployment rates. Our survey research reveals major territorial and religious variations in unemployment rates, ranging from 26.4 per cent in Brownlow to 17.3 per cent in Lurgan to 11.5 per cent in Portadown (the unemployment rates for the Craigavon Travel to Work Area and Northern Ireland as a whole were 13.7 per cent and 15.4 per cent respectively). These figures obscured very large variation within localities. In Brownlow, for example, a survey undertaken in 1989 (prior to our survey) reveals rates of zero and 9 per cent in two owner-occupied estates and a range from 30 to 38 per cent in the publicly owned estates (Mackey, 1989).

Differential unemployment rates by religion in each of the three areas further confirm the durable economic underpinnings of sectarian geography in Craigavon (see Table 2.1).

Table 2.1: Unemployment rates by religion, gender and locality in 1989 (percentages)

	Lurgan	**Brownlow**	**Portadown**
Catholic males	29.4 (51)	29.6 (27)	27.6 (29)
Other denominations males	12.8 (47)	36.4 (11)	10.0 (70)
Catholic females	13.3 (30)	17.4 (23)	15.4 (26)
Other denominations females	5.9 (34)	14.3 (7)	3.7 (54)
Total Catholics	23.5 (81)	24.0 (50)	21.9 (55)
Total other denominations	9.9 (81)	27.8 (18)	7.3(124)
Total	**17.3(162)**	**26.4 (68)**	**11.5(179)**

Table 2.1 lends support to information from our other sources that Portadown is the most successful local economy followed by Lurgan and Brownlow. However, "equality of misery" between Catholic and Protestant, as measured by unemployment rates, holds only in Brownlow. Although care must be taken in interpretation because of small numbers, the figures indicate that all denominations share the common economic marginalization of Brownlow. The position is very different in the two established towns where it is much closer to the Northern Ireland picture as a whole. Catholics are three times more likely to be unemployed than others in Portadown and 2.4 times more likely in Lurgan. Interestingly, the gap is widest in the most successful economy, suggesting that success in creating new jobs does not necessarily mean greater inter-communal equality. It is clear also that inter-communal inequality is generally greater for males than for females with the striking exception of Portadown, where Catholic women are over four times as likely to be unemployed as women from other denominations.

Territorial and communal identity, therefore, is not merely a matter of perception but is rooted also in material inequality. Differential experiences of work and unemployment, for example, combines with residential segregation to help define Catholic and Protestant communities. Inter-communal inequality seems to have been consolidated rather than undermined by the experience of the new city. Portadown has maintained a strong economy, benefiting from new industrial investments and government policy. Lurgan, and especially Brownlow, have suffered in comparison.

Conclusion

It now seems that the vision of an integrated new city at Craigavon has been finally abandoned, yet the project has had a major effect on the area, notably in the creation of Brownlow and in the investment of substantial government expenditure in a skeletal framework which links industrial estates, roads, housing estates, and an incomplete city centre. The elaborate, and now inappropriate, urban layout still visible in Craigavon is a reminder of the optimistic assumptions which informed the project in the early 1960s. These included beliefs in the efficacy of 'top-down' planning as an instrument of socio-economic change, in the continuation of economic expansion, and in a future of political stability in Northern Ireland, where communal divisions could be managed, if not avoided altogether. In the event, international economic downturn coincided with political upheaval, ensuring that multinational investment would no longer serve as the engine of new city development in the 1970s and 1980s.

Such broad explanations of failure, while necessary, are insufficient in themselves, however, and ignore the salience of local identities and local action. Craigavon is testimony to the durability and adaptability of territorial and communal identities despite the challenge which the new city project seemed to pose to the local *status quo*. In Northern Ireland, any attempt to implement a new spatial or territorial strategy inevitably means modifying the ethno-sectarian geography which comprises the province as a territorial unit. Territorial decision-making has always been a matter of contention since the creation of Northern Ireland, notably with respect to the location of housing and jobs, as well as the delineation of local electoral boundaries. Territorial strategies, however, are not just a matter for policy makers, they are of central significance in everyday life in the construction of local and communal identity. Our research suggests some of the ways in which communal affiliation, business, trade unions, the experience of work and unemployment are interwoven to forge local identities. The formation and negotiation of sectarian geography in Craigavon is not just a matter for policy makers, it is a matter for local residents also. They are influenced by historical and cultural memory, by fear and intimidation, and by the class, gender, religion and age group to which they belong.

The fate of the new city reveals the capacity of local groups to fit the altered urban environment to the contours of established sectarian geography. The polarised sectarian geography of Lurgan and Portadown has survived and has extended into the new Brownlow district. Superficially, both towns seemed to have common origins and a shared history of industrial development making them appropriate candidates for merger into the new city. Closer study, however, reveals significant differences in local culture which are expressed in intense rivalry – a rivalry which has survived a shared suspicion of the new city. Different local histories of inter-communal relations, of access to work and political power, and antagonisms over the state and over territory all contributed to resistance to the new city project. Far from the latter ameliorating such differences, it seems to have exposed and underlined them.

In societies where ethnic or national divisions are central, territorial strategies are routinely employed to link the economic, political and cultural dimensions of everyday life. Of course, such links are made in all societies, but in stable states they appear consensual, opaque or only partially contested. Where ethnic-national divisions persist, however, and where the state is largely identified with one ethnic group, state and local boundaries are routinely problematical and even violently contested because they delineate different ways of linking economy, polity and culture. Moreover, the various specialised functions of the state are regularly co-ordinated to protect ethnic dominance, which in turn is identified with the state itself.

The Craigavon project linked economic and spatial strategies while initially obscuring their political and cultural dimensions. It seems likely that, for some of the planners and economists involved, building a new city as a means of economic modernisation constituted an end in itself or held out prospects for greater political and cultural integration of both ethno-religious communities in Northern Ireland. From the outset, the nature of local response to the project, the emergent and enveloping Northern Ireland conflict, and changing international economic conditions, demonstrated the limitations of the Craigavon strategy. It failed, but it is an instructive failure for students of locality formation and locality-state relationships.

Locality formation is a complex dynamic process shaped by the interplay between local action, the state and the international economy. Confronted with the complexity of this process, a social science of compartmentalised disciplines is tempted by spatial, economic, political and cultural reductionism. Here the social scientist falls back on abstraction, either by choosing to privilege economic, political or cultural variables, or else by arbitrarily defining a locality as a fixed territorial and physical entity. While abstraction is necessary, the form it should take is debatable. This research suggests that abstraction should not obscure process.

Economists and sociologists who study local economies and labour markets must realise that these are not synonymous with 'locality'. This research supports Howe's (1990, p.72) observation in his Belfast study that local economies and labour markets are simultaneously cultural constructions which sustain the sectarian divide. As he points out, each ethnic group feels a 'proprietary right to jobs in its own area'. However, as Craigavon shows, what is 'its own area' is contestable. Many jobs in Craigavon service the whole area and demand territorial strategies to deal with a mosaic of segregated communities. Of course, joblessness also has territorial dimensions, which are particularly constraining on young males in the Craigavon area. Students of global economic development have underlined how modern business and technological innovation have allowed capitalist firms a growing freedom from territorial constraints. The history of Goodyear in Craigavon is a good example. Yet, ironically, such a capacity to transcend spatial boundaries has made territoriality and locality more, not less, important. Firms can choose where to locate; and localities and state agencies must compete for the jobs they provide. As a result, localities are often reshaped by processes to which they can only react, rather than control.

Recognising the impact of international economic change in ethnically divided societies should limit the temptation to reduce locality formation to accounts of ethnic struggle. Ethnic groups are typically heterogeneous with respect to their business and workplace cultures and their class composition. Such groups, and their internal divisions, relate to the economy and the state in different ways. Indeed, the state and the economy play a key role in constituting inter- (as well as intra-) ethnic relations and in building up the patterns of conflict and accommodation which mark these relations in particular localities. Access to power (state or otherwise) or degrees of powerlessness can in themselves constitute crucial elements of local and communal identity.

There is, therefore, no simple correspondence of ethnicity and territory. Lurgan, Brownlow and Portadown, are internally divided on ethnic lines (and in different ways). Each area is characterised by different patterns of inter-ethnic conflict and accommodation, and by different relationships to the state and the economy. Yet, in Lurgan and Portadown, and to a growing extent in Brownlow, there are types of overarching popular identifications strong enough to prevent the three areas from being merged into an integrated new city. Day and Murdoch's (1993) critique of locality studies includes a plea to restore 'community' to its place in the study of social space. They argue that the tendency to replace 'community studies' with 'locality studies' discounts the capacity of local actors to shape their environment. They criticise the way in which locality studies have accorded primacy to economic factors, thereby conceptualising localities as simply the contingent outcomes of wider processes. When greater weight is accorded to local action by these studies, Day and Murdoch (1993, p.85) argue, the term 'locality' takes on many of the connotations of 'community'.

While they are correct in warning against ascribing to localities the capacity to act, Day and Murdoch (1993) seem to leave open the possibility of using both terms, 'community' and 'locality'. Certainly, Craigavon suggests the utility of this approach. Each ethnic group may be seen as an 'imagined community' pursuing territorial strategies which help shape localities. As argued above, local identification can be different from communal identification. The construction, defence and management of local boundaries allows us to grasp the processes of interaction between economic actors, the state, and local groups.

Territorial strategies remain critical in all societies where states and communities seek to domesticate the dynamics of socio-economic change. However, they are particularly transparent in societies characterised by ethnic-national conflict. More stable, homogeneous societies are characterised by a popular amnesia about the degrees of historic conflict, coercion, and even duplicity involved in constructing national boundaries and in incorporating localities within states. Some of the thinking behind the Craigavon project seems to have assumed that the prospect of the new city would induce such amnesia, locally at least. In this, it failed to recognise the importance of local actors and of the historical and cultural memories they brought to the 'new city'. The significance of these memories, however, resides not in some pathological fixation with the past, but in the way in which they are provoked and re-activated by the territorial strategies of states and capitalist firms, by the politics of locational decisions, and by the continued material inequalities within and between communities. By giving a voice to local actors, social scientists and policy makers can begin to grasp the importance of historical and cultural memory and the local and communal identities to which it contributes.

Acknowledgement

This chapter was initially published under the same title in Curtin, C., Donnan, H. and Wilson, T.M. (1993) *Irish Urban Cultures*, Institute of Irish Studies, The Queen's University of Belfast. The editors of this volume are grateful that it has been possible to include this contribution as an important critique of the history of planning in Northern Ireland.

Endnotes

1. This research project, "Local Responses to Industrial Change in Northern Ireland: A Comparison of Newry and Craigavon", was funded by ESRC Research Grant: ROOO 23 1161. I would like to acknowledge the contribution of two research officers on the project: Michael Maguire, 1988-89, and Colm Ryan, 1989-91. The research, carried out between 1989 and 1991, employed a variety of methods including semi-structured (taped) interviews with local businessmen, officials, community activists, politicians and householders, as well as a questionnaire survey of 250 households randomly selected from the Craigavon area.

2. Economists have tended to incorporate 'the troubles' as a rather crude and undifferentiated variable into their analyses, estimating their effect on employment, unemployment, job promotion, external investment and public expenditure. Rowthorn and Wayne (1988) have provided the most detailed study of the links between economic change and the conflict but have focused on the regional, rather than the locality level. Studies of employment inequality and discrimination (e.g., Smith and Chambers, 1991; Cormack and Osborne, 1991) also concentrate on the regional rather than on the local levels. Eversley (1989) makes strenuous attempts at sub-regional analysis of labour market inequality between Catholics and Protestants but his analysis is greatly hindered by imperfect census data, by shifting administrative boundaries and by the lack of correspondence between popular and administrative definitions of locality.

3. While Northern Ireland is relatively well provided with statistical information at regional level, this is not the case at local level. Major data sets such as the Continuous Household Survey, the Labour Force Survey, and the Family Expenditure Survey cannot be disaggregated to local level because of sample size. Analysis of the census is also hampered by problems of non-response and non-completion in specific areas and by the shifting ward boundaries between censuses.

4. In fact, by 1991, the population of Craigavon Borough Council area had only reached 74,986, an increase of only 1,726 since 1981. Far from attracting new migrants, Craigavon showed a net out-migration of 7.8 per cent between 1981 and 1991 (Northern Ireland, 1992).

5. Portadown and Lurgan were significant centres of local Unionist power, even if they had relatively large nationalist populations. Early Catholic civil rights activists had criticised Lurgan's 15 person local council for operating "large religious ghettos". Although the 1961 census indicated that Catholics accounted for over 45 per cent of Lurgan's population, a system of block voting (i.e., every elector voting for every councillor with no ward divisions) ensured that there was no anti-unionist representation on the local council. In central and local government in the town, it was claimed that there was only one Catholic in a salaried position. Lurgan council's 156 employees included only 25 Catholics, 23 of whom were labourers (McCluskey, 1989). An early account of the Northern

Ireland 'problem' indicated similar difficulties with the block voting system in Portadown. In 1962, there was no direct Catholic representation on Portadown Council, although Catholics comprised over a quarter of the population (Barritt and Carter, 1962, p.125).

6. In 1966, the whole project got a major boost when the Minister of Commerce, Brian Faulkner, announced that Goodyear was to locate a £6.5 million factory between Lurgan and Brownlow, with a promise of 2,000 jobs. Goodyear, it appeared, would be at once the industrial anchor and launching pad for Craigavon as a whole. In fact, after a chequered local history, it reached a peak of nearly 1,800 workers in 1977. Thereafter, its workforce was run down to its eventual closure in 1983 with a loss of 770 jobs.

7. In our random survey of 250 households, 33 per cent were Catholic in Portadown, 52 per cent in Lurgan, and 70 per cent in Brownlow.

8. Some officials pointed out the need to plan for Craigavon as a whole. Others, such as the outgoing Director of Social Services in the region, placed more emphasis on the need to develop a separate strategy for Brownlow. The Department of the Environment, as owners of the land in the area, was a major force behind the economic regeneration plan. However, community activists and some voluntary sector workers believed that the plan was aimed more at reducing state expenditure in Brownlow than a genuine attempt to develop it as an urban locality in its own right.

9. Interestingly, this point was not confirmed by our survey of households.

10. This information is from an interview with a former secretary of PNIC.

11. Employment and unemployment data are derived from Northern Ireland (n.d.), Ministry of Health and Social Services, Abstract 8, page 8 for 1953-67 figures. Subsequent figures come from unpublished Department of Economic Development sources.

12. David Calvert, a former Democratic Unionist Party councillor in Craigavon, remembered Lurgan in the 1960s not as a trade union centre, but as a great location for (Protestant) religious meetings (BBC, "Places Apart, Lurgan" 2 July 1990).

13. In-depth interviews were undertaken with fourteen households in the Craigavon area. Interviewees were selected from respondents to our random survey of households, to reflect the balance of religion, household location and employment profile in the random sample.

References

Bagguley, P., Mark-Lawson, J., Shapiro, D., Urry, J., Walby, S. and Warde, A. (1990) *Restructuring: place, class and gender*, London, Sage.

Barritt, D.P. and Carter, C.F. (1962) The *Northern Ireland problem: a study in community relations,* London, Oxford University Press.

Blackman, T. (1988) *Housing policy and community action in County Durham and County Armagh*, Unpublished PhD thesis, University of Durham.

Boal, F.W. and Douglas, J.N.H. (eds.) (1982) *Integration and division,* London, Academic Press.

Brownlow Community Council (1979) *The future of Brownlow,* Craigavon, Brownlow Community Council.

Carolan, B. (1987) The *management of the Craigavon housing crisis: an assessment of the Northern Ireland Housing Executive's strategy, 1983-86*, Unpublished MSc thesis, University of Ulster.

Cooke, P. (1989) *Localities, the changing face of urban Britain*, London, Unwin Hyman.

Cormack, R 1. and Osborne, RD. (eds.) (1991) *Discrimination and public policy in Northern Ireland,* Oxford, Clarendon Press.

Day, G. and Murdoch, J. (1993) Locality and community: coming to terms with places, *Sociological Review*, 41, pp.82-111.

Dilley, R. (1989) Boat owners, patrons and state policy in Northern Ireland, in H.Donnan and G. McFarlane (eds.) *Social anthropology and public policy in Northern Ireland*, Aldershot, Avebury.

Donnan, H. and McFarlane, G. (1986) "You get on better with your own": social continuity and change in rural Northern Ireland, in P. Clancy, S. Drudy, K. Lynch and L. O'Dowd (eds.) *Ireland: a sociological profile*, Dublin, Institute of Public Administration.

Eipper, C. (1986) *The ruling trinity: a community study of church, state and business in Ireland,* Aldershot, Gower.

Eversley, D. (1989) *Religion and employment in Northern Ireland*, London, Sage.

Hausner, V. (ed) (1987) *Economic change in British cities*, Oxford, Clarendon Press.

Howe, L. (1990) *Being unemployed in Belfast: an ethnographic study,* Cambridge, Cambridge University Press.

Jenkins, R. (1983) *Lads, citizens and ordinary kids,* London, Routledge and Kegan Paul.

Jones, E. (1960) *The social geography of Belfast*, London, Oxford University Press.

McCluskey, C. (1989) *Off their knees: a commentary on the civil rights movement in Northern Ireland*, Galway, Conn McCluskey & Associates.

Mackey, D. (1989) *Brownlow skills survey*, Brownlow, Mackey Consultants.

Matthew Report (1963) *The Belfast regional survey and plan*, Cmd. 451, Belfast, HMSO.

Northern Ireland (1992) *Census of population 1991: Preliminary Report*, Belfast, HMSO. n.d. Ministry of Health and Social Services, Abstract 8.

O'Dowd, L. (1986) Beyond industrial society, in P. Clancy, S. Drudy, K. Lynch and L. O'Dowd (eds.) *Ireland: a sociological profile,* Dublin, Institute of Public Administration.

Oliver, J. (1978) *Working at Stormont,* Dublin, Institute of Public Administration.

Poole, M. (1982) Religious residential segregation in urban Northern Ireland, in F.W. Boal and J.N.H. Douglas (eds.) *Integration and division*, London, Academic Press.

Reid, J. (1973) Craigavon: what went wrong? *Lurgan and Portadown Examiner*, 27 December.

Rowthorn, B. and Wayne, N. (1988) *Northern Ireland: the political economy of conflict*, Cambridge, Polity Press.

Smith, D.J. and Chambers, G. (1991) *Inequality in Northern Ireland*, Oxford, Clarendon Press.

Urry, J. (1981) Localities, regions and social class, *International Journal of Urban and Regional Research*, 4, pp.455-474.

Wilson Report (1965) *Economic development in Northern Ireland*, CMD.479, Belfast, HMSO.

Chapter 3

Identity, Place and Conflict in Rural Northern Ireland

Brendan Murtagh

Introduction

One of the significant contributions that John Greer makes to our understanding of rurality is the way in which identity, attachment to place and culture impact on both opportunities and constraints for local development. The 'rural' is not conceived narrowly in terms of dispersed settlement patterns, agricultural productivity or the physicality of the environment. Rather, rural space is understood as a complex web of natural, economic and social variables that combine to create distinctive places that cannot be easily categorised using a conventional geographic taxonomy. This is especially the case in Northern Ireland. Well before equality legislation was introduced or planners turned their attention to the relevance of segregation, Murray and Greer argued for the "promotion of territorial identity to assist the processes of collaboration among diverse interest groups" (Murray and Greer, 1993, p.261).

In pursuit of this agenda John Greer's work is based on a strong commitment to empiricism and policy making based on evidence. Understanding the way in which people use and relate to their area has underpinned his powerful critique of rural planning policy and the limitations of a regulatory regime based on centralised urban settlement patterns. This chapter draws on these traditions in John's research. It looks at the way in which segregation and territoriality impact on rural life and development in Northern Ireland. In particular, it revisits research conducted in 1996 in two villages, Whitecross and Glenanne, in mid-County Armagh. The two villages are one mile apart and Whitecross has a mainly Catholic population whilst Glenanne has a predominantly Protestant one. The data in the 1996 survey act as a baseline of community relations attitudes and behaviour at a particular point of time, since when, political progress and European Union resources have impacted on the region, especially via the Peace and Reconciliation Programme. The chapter emphasises the strong imprint that the ethno-religious divide has made on rural change and the formidable obstacles to local development and community led regeneration. It also reminds us of the importance of place and the need to fuse a particular tradition of geographical enquiry with a normative policy agenda in land use planning.

Identity and Rural Segregation

In February 2005, the Rural Community Network launched a report on the experiences of Catholic communities in Counties Antrim and Down titled, *We Don't Feel As Isolated As You Might Think* (Rural Community Network, 2005). It makes the fundamental point that ethno-religious identity can determine access to services, quality of life and feelings of fear among the minority community. The study follows a similar research project on the attitudes of Protestants living in border areas which showed that many experienced a greater sense of isolation and abandonment than their Catholic neighbours (Rural Community Network, 2003). Murray and Murtagh (2004) highlight the importance of an integrated programme based on the *Equity, Diversity and Interdependence (EDI)* model to tackle, not just religious segregation, but the way in which a number of groups such as disabled people, women and older people experience exclusion in rural society. Segregation clearly matters and the powerful attraction of spatial segregation to communities experiencing high levels of conflict and fear should not be overstated. Avoidance, cultural preservation and attack functions underpin the desire of communities for separate living in strongly demarcated territory. But, the potential for cultural assimilation is also retarded by segregation and for Boal this sets out a central dilemma:

> Persistent segregation is likely to contribute to the perpetuation of long-standing prejudices, while at the very same time contributing to the maintenance of valued group attributes and providing a geographical basis for political action. Act to destroy the prejudice and you may undermine a rich social plurality; preserve the social plurality and you provide a fertile environment for prejudice to thrive in (Boal, 1987, p.112).

Whilst the literature on rural segregation and conflict is not as well developed as the material for urban environments, there are some important studies on the experiences of micro-communities. The seminal work in this area was carried out by Rosemary Harris in the early 1950s in an area she called 'Ballybeg'. Written in a period of relative peace it not surprisingly highlighted the frequent and positive nature of contact between neighbours. However, she also mapped out the character of separate socio-spatial worlds where religion and social institutions dictated mutually exclusive patterns of behaviour and interaction. Describing shopping patterns in the village, she pointed out that "the advantage offered by one shop over its rivals had to be very considerable before a Protestant owner could attract Catholic customers and vice-versa" (Harris, 1972, p.6). Leisure activities were also highly segregated in Ballybeg partly because they were organised by the respective churches and she pointed out that mixing was often the preserve of middle class social contexts in tennis and golf clubs.

Leyton's (1975) study of the small Protestant rural community of 'Perrin' observed that its inhabitants "see their village as a bastion of Protestant morality and Protestant virtue" (Leyton, 1975, p.11-12) but highlighted that, in areas experiencing high levels of violence, Protestants emphasised their political rather than their religious identity. Similarly, in their analysis of a small border village which they called 'Daviestown', Hamilton *et al.* (1990) described the damaging consequences for community relations of a prolonged paramilitary campaign in the area. In an extensive review of the anthropological literature on locality conflict, Donnan and McFarlane (1986) identified the significance of diverse social, kinship and ethnic cleavages in rural life. In her work, Harris (1972) linked these variables to a common identity, which is maintained by attachment to place and the sense of ownership and pride in being local. Thus, Donnan and McFarlane conclude that it is difficult to say whether kinship, social class or religion is the determining variable in explaining social relations generally and inter-group contact in particular:

> If people are continually switching from one identity to another from situation to situation, it becomes problematic to assign primacy to any single identity. Nevertheless, at particular times, in particular places, with particular people, some identities may be consistently more weighted than others (Donnan and McFarlane, 1986, pp.895-6).

Writing from a geographical perspective, Kirk (1993) offers one approach to prioritising types of social contact by distinguishing between individual interests (for example, by sharing labour and machinery between farmers) and the group interests of preservation of the sub-culture in a territorial space. In his analysis of land transfers between Protestant and Catholics in north Antrim between 1958 and 1987, he points out how Protestant and Catholic farmers accepted lower values for land by selling it within the ethnic group. Thus, he concludes "group interests are best served by the existence of social closure with an absence of land transfer across the religious divide" (Kirk, 1993, p.334). In their review of *Reconciliation and Social Inclusion in Rural Areas,* Morrow *et al.* (2003) highlighted the interrelated nature of these problems and the need for a comprehensive agenda to underpin local development and socio-cultural change:

Investment, peace-building and social inclusion should all be recognised as linked yet separate areas of policy concern in Northern Ireland. If development is to be sustainable, rural areas need all three areas to be given due weight. Both the differences and the interconnections are important and policy makers need to aim for ever-greater clarity about the nature of each and their dependence on one another (Morrow *et al.*, 2003, p.18).

Case Study in mid County Armagh

As noted earlier, the case study villages were initially selected as part of a wider programme of research into conflict and community in the area which itself was identified as a region that had experienced a process of population change close to the border over the last three decades (Murtagh, 2002). They are approximately 7 kilometres north west of Newry and 9 kilometres south east of Armagh city. *Glenanne* is predominantly Protestant and has a population of 140 persons whilst *Whitecross* is predominately Catholic, and has a population of 170 persons. The research used a household survey of residents in both villages as a context for more semi-structured in-depth interviews with community leaders. The 'head-of household', defined as the eldest adult in the family unit, was selected as the respondent and the qualitative interviews were held with local church-persons, community leaders and elected representatives. The fieldwork for the initial survey was carried out in 1996 and then repeated in 2003 using the same sample design and questionnaire.

According to the original survey data, Whitecross was 96 per cent Catholic while Glenanne was 92 per cent Protestant and by 2003 little had changed as the corresponding figures were 93 per cent and 88 per cent respectively. Moreover, respondents in Whitecross were most likely to describe the village as Catholic (96 per cent) while respondents in Glenanne strongly perceived their village to be Protestant (86 per cent). The survey highlighted the long established attachment to place in both villages. Nearly two-thirds (64 per cent) of respondents in Whitecross and half (50 per cent) of those in Glenanne had lived there all their lives. In 2003 the corresponding figures were 53 per cent and 67 per cent respectively and despite this, there were comparatively few close friendship or kinship ties across the religious divide. In 1996, more than three quarters (77 per cent) of people in Whitecross had most or all of their friends and relatives of the same religion compared to 86 per cent of people in Glenanne but by 2003 this had risen to 93 per cent in Whitecross but declined to 73 per cent in Glenanne. In Glenanne, 27 per cent of respondents said that half their friends and relatives came from the other religion which was an increase on the 1996 figure of 7 per cent.

There was a sharp contrast in the perceptions of respondents when attitudes to community relations within, and between, the villages were examined. Table 3.1 shows that community relations between the two villages have changed little in Whitecross although respondents in Glenanne were more likely to detect deterioration in relations between the two. For instance, in 1996 29 per cent of respondents in Glenanne described community relations between the two villages as very good, but by 2003, that figure had fallen to 7 per cent. When prompted for specific explanations of this pattern many rooted the cause in the lack of contact with neighbours (32 per cent of those who said relations were poor or very poor) and that the feelings of bitterness between the two villages were too deep to be addressed easily in the short term (32 per cent). It is clear that there is a disconnection between macro-political progress and strong economic performance at a regional level and attitudes and behaviour at a local level. The argument here is that despite the ceasefires, stumbling political development and EU investment, stubborn segregation permeates localities deeply scarred by the memory of violence and fear. It would be wrong to assume too much in terms of attitudinal or behavioural change, in the short term at least.

Table 3.1: Attitudes to community relations between Whitecross and Glenanne between 1996 and 2003

Attitude	Glenanne		Whitecross	
	1996	2003	1996	2003
Very good	0	3	29	7
Good	29	30	64	40
Neither	21	3	1	7
Poor	15	33	6	27
Very poor	21	20	0	7
Refused D/K	14	11	0	12
Total	**100**	**100**	**100**	**100**

The research carried out in 1996 showed that the residents of Glenanne mainly look north to largely Protestant towns such as Armagh, Markethill and Portadown for comparison goods, convenience goods and services. It was interesting that more people went to Markethill for these goods, rather than Newry, despite the latter's more dominant settlement status offering a wider number, range and quality of services than Markethill. When the activity profile for Whitecross was examined an almost mirror image emerges. Here, the population is drawn south to the mainly Catholic towns of Newry, Keady and even across the border to Dundalk. The demographic analysis and in particular the 'greening' of border areas explains part of the process but close inspection of local history reveals more immediate *push* factors on the

Protestant population. Tables 3.2 and 3.3 show that there has been comparatively little change in the structure of movement of the Catholic populated village. There is a slightly stronger draw from Belfast and higher order settlements for entertainment and doctors' services but the basic focus on Newry, especially for shopping, remains largely unaltered. Similarly, residents in Glennane maintained their affinity to Markethill although again, there is more activity towards Belfast, especially for entertainment. In order to summarise the degree of difference between the two villages the movement pattern data for both years was subjected to a correlation analysis. Given their physical proximity, we would predict a correlation close to 1.0 indicating a strong directional path to the services and facilities measured in the survey, yet the data show a very weak correlation of 0.16 over the two years of the survey. In short, there is very little in common between the way in which the two villages interact with their hinterland and wider urban and rural relations.

Table 3.2: Activity analysis for Whitecross

Destination	Convenience Goods		Comparison Goods		Entertainment		Doctors	
	1996	2003	1996	2003	1996	2003	1996	2003
Markethill	3	10	0	0	0	0	16	3
Belfast	0	0	3	7	0	0	0	0
Dundalk	0	0	0	6	17	17	0	0
Warrenpoint	0	0	0	0	0	3	0	0
Newry	97	87	91	87	32	40	26	33
Keady	0	0	0	0	4	0	52	0
Armagh	0	0	0	0	0	5	0	3
Portadown	0	0	0	0	0	0	0	0
Banbridge	0	0	0	0	0	0	0	0
Newtownhamilton	0	0	0	0	0	0	0	50
Whitecross	0	3	6	0	47	33	6	0
Castleblaney	0	0	0	0	0	3	0	0
Loughbrickland	0	0	0	0	0	0	0	3
Bessbrook	0	0	0	0	0	0	0	7
Total	**100**	**100**	**100**	**100**	**100**	**100**	**100**	**100**

Table 3.3: Activity analysis for Glenanne

Destination	Convenience Goods		Comparison Goods		Entertainment		Doctors	
	1996	2003	1996	2003	1996	2003	1996	2003
Markethill	63	83	27	53	67	23	80	77
Belfast	0	0	0	20	0	0	0	0
Dundalk	0	0	0	0	0	0	0	0
Warrenpoint	0	0	0	0	0	3	0	0
Newry	12	10	27	13	0	38	0	13
Keady	0	0	0	3	6	0	14	0
Armagh	19	3	40	7	23	3	0	3
Portadown	6	3	0	3	0	0	0	0
Banbridge	0	0	6	0	4	20	0	0
Newtownhamilton	0	0	0	0	0	0	0	0
Whitecross	0	0	0	0	0	13	6	0
Castleblaney	0	0	0	0	0	0	0	0
Loughbrickland	0	0	0	0	0	0	0	3
Bessbrook	0	0	0	0	0	0	0	3
Total	**100**	**100**	**100**	**100**	**100**	**100**	**100**	**100**

The 1980s and 1990s were particularly uncertain times for the community in Glenanne. A number of incidents, highlighted consistently in discussions with local people, reveal the extent to which the basic economic, commercial, cultural and security 'institutions', have been progressively eroded in a short period of time.

• The first major incident happened in 1976 during a period of sectarian murders, high paramilitary activity and a strengthening of the security force presence with the development of an Army base in the village. The main employment in Glenanne was a small textile factory whose labour force was drawn mainly from surrounding towns and villages. After a period of tit-for-tat sectarian murders in the area, ten employees (all male and Protestant) were taken from the factory bus and shot dead three miles outside the village.

- Another violent attack came in 1983 when the largest bomb set off in the Troubles destroyed the Army base and killed three soldiers. The base was not reopened.

- As the population declined this had a cumulative negative impact on local commerce and in the early 1990s the post office and local grocery shop both closed and what passed for the commercial core of the village fell into physical neglect.

- The decline in the Protestant population of the village also had an impact on the local Primary school which closed in 1995 and the remaining pupils were bussed to a school five miles away.

- Finally, the local Orange hall was destroyed by fire in the same year. Indeed 4 out of 5 Orange halls in the area had been attacked in 1994 and 1995.

When these events are placed in the context of wider demographic shifts, the northward orientation of the community is hardly surprising.

However, the 2003 survey also showed that 67 per cent of people in Whitecross and 93 per cent of people in Glenanne were aware of regeneration initiatives in the area. Since the first study was completed there have been a number of projects to develop the villages and engender a spirit of cross-community and inter-village dependency in local development. The most significant was the establishment of the Glenanne, Loughgilly and Mountnorris Community Association (GLM) in 1998, which initially concentrated on developing infrastructure and services within the triangle of mainly Protestant villages. A successful regeneration and environmental improvement scheme was launched in the small housing estate in Glenanne and a Millennium Hall was constructed in nearby Mountnorris. The idea behind these initiatives was to develop the capacity of the local community in small steps, as the chairman of GLM explained: "I am a great believer in sorting out our own area first, before expanding into the broader area of development". Moreover, it was also felt that this type of patient, single identity work was an essential prerequisite to cross-community contact and that this had led to a more sustainable agenda for the local group. A Committee Member explained that "Glenanne has taken off and this shows the value of building community infrastructure". The Hall is shared by both traditions and there is mutual respect and space given to culturally specific events including sports, music and dance. Moreover, the presence of the facility and growing confidence in the capacity of the local group has created a rationale for more purposive cross-community contact between the mainly Protestant GLM and a Catholic community group from Lislea in south Armagh. Here, common pursuits and interests in stage drama have created negotiable and non-threatening opportunities for mutual cooperation and trust, which has been extended to more recent cross-community contact between Senior Citizens Groups representing both Protestants and Catholics in the wider area. It would be wrong to overstate the impact of these initiatives, as the survey data has already shown that many attitudes and behaviours remained unaltered in the intervening period. However, collaborative working has created important channels for communication that did not exist before and on which longer term developments may be centred.

Space, Conflict and the Equality Agenda

For this to happen they should be identified, nurtured and sustained in the context of mainstream development and planning initiatives in the area and whilst there have been important policy changes, this section highlights the need for more concerted action in the rural arena. A critical response to continuing segregation, political violence and concentrated poverty in the 1970s was to centralise contentious, expensive and strategic functions including planning, roads and agricultural and rural development policy. Popular participation and democratic control was marginalised in favor of corporatised approaches to policy making and development. Here, the thrust of the research agenda set in place by John Greer was directed at governance, participatory planning and equality in the rural arena. Much of this drew on an emerging policy landscape more clearly shaped in response to urban based crises, especially in Belfast. By the late 1980s Targeting Social Need had emerged as a spending priority (rather than a specific programme) and Policy Appraisal for Fair Treatment (PAFT) was simultaneously introduced to check and proof policies for their impact on the two main religions. Area based regeneration programmes, principally Making Belfast Work, made specific commitments to tackle deprivation in the inner-city and in the suburban housing estates of North and West Belfast (Murtagh, 2002).

However, it was the paramilitary ceasefires in 1994 and the subsequent Belfast Agreement in 1998 that redefined equality and social need as constitutional rather than purely policy issues. The nature of the Agreement as a consensual product inevitably led to a degree of eclecticism and it lacked any real detail about how these political aspirations could be woven together as coherent programmes. The Northern Ireland Act (1998), which provided the legal interpretation of the Agreement, did set down formidable equality duties on all public bodies in the region. The Act established a Northern Ireland Human Rights Commission and introduced a statutory duty on public bodies to have:

Due regard to the need to promote equality of opportunity –

(a) between persons of different religious belief, political opinion, racial group, age, marital status or sexual orientation;

(b) between men and women generally;
(c) between persons with a disability and persons without;
(d) between persons with dependents and persons without (Section 75(1).

In carrying out their functions, public authorities must also "have regard to the desirability of promoting good relations between persons of different religious belief, political opinion or racial group" (Section 75(2)). Government Departments have to prepare Equality Schemes that show how these objectives will be met through current policies, and Equality Impact Assessments have been introduced to proof all new programmes against the needs of the nine groups identified in Section 75(1).

Whilst it was not given the same legislative weight, *New* Targeting Social Need (NTSN) aimed to revive a policy that had been criticised as ineffective and tokenistic. Ellis (2001) made the point that TSN was bolted on to existing commitments and that there few additional resources allocated to specific social objectives. The remodelled initiative had three elements including tackling unemployment, addressing social need (in health, education and housing) and coordinating the actions of Government Departments through a new commitment to Promoting Social Inclusion (PSI) (NTSN Unit, 1999). Departmental Action Plans again translated these themes into three-year programmes and in particular identified poverty reduction targets for specific policies and initiatives. These have been strengthened in the latest *Anti-Poverty Strategy* published by the Office of the First and Deputy First Minister in 2005. This focuses attention on economic, financial and social exclusion and is especially concerned with the potential of area-based programmes such as Neighbourhood Renewal and Rural Development to deliver change.

For land use planning the combined requirements of equality and social inclusion represent formidable challenges, especially given its historical 'contentless' and 'contextless' character. A key test was the preparation of the Regional Development Strategy, which is the first physical development plan for Northern Ireland in more than 30 years (Department for Regional Development, 2001). This is based on an extensive programme of consultation and during the production process both equality and NTSN were identified as policy informants (McEldowney and Sterrett, 2001). The strategy makes bold attempts to engage the issue of residential segregation and integration and strikes a balance between the two in the framing of Strategic Planning Guidance related to *Community Cohesion* (SPG3). Table 3.4 shows how notions of community cohesion and respecting choice and diversity can be mediated through the built environment as specific proposals are set out for more detailed interrogation at the local scale.

Table 3.4: The Regional Development Strategy and community cohesion

Strategic Planning Guidance (SPG SRC 3) objective
• To foster development which contributes to community relations, recognises cultural diversity and reduces socio economic differentials within Northern Ireland
SCR 3.1 Foster patterns of development supporting community cohesion
• Facilitate the development of integrated communities where people wish to live together and to promote respect, encouragement and celebration of different traditions • Promote respect, encouragement and celebration of different traditions, and encourage communication and social intercourse in areas where communities are living apart
SRC 3.2 Underpin the dual approach by fostering community interaction which could also contribute, over time and on the basis of choice, to greater community integration
• Develop partnerships between public, private, voluntary and community sectors to facilitate community co-operation and involvement in securing social, economic and environmental objectives • Facilitate the removal of existing physical barriers between communities, subject to local community agreement • Support the development of 'shared places' accessible to all members of the community • Revitalise the role of town centres and other common locations well served by public transport as focal points for shopping, services, employment, cultural and leisure activities for the whole community • Promote the development of major employment/enterprise areas in locations which are accessible to all sections of the community • Improve and develop public transport to assist in providing safe and equitable access to services, facilities and employment opportunities essential to the vitality of local communities • Strengthen the network of local museums and heritage centres and arts centres with a special focus on understanding cultural diversity • Promote cultural diversity through the creation of opportunities in the creative industries associated with the arts

Source: Based on DRD, 2001, pp.34-35.

However, there are inconsistencies in the way in which these strategic objectives have been interpreted in specific development plans, especially in rural areas where the pattern of ethno-religious segregation is less clear but, as we have seen, quite significant in shaping people's quality of life. A number of *Area Plan Issues Papers* have been published, to include rural districts, within the context of the Regional Development Strategy, but few make any real mention of specific proposals for neutral spaces, deal with contested territory or address the effects of 'interfaces' described earlier. Clearly, the commitments made at a strategic level might be more difficult to confront at the local scale, but institutional inertia, weak skills and inappropriate training, and the limited development of methodologies in equality and social need also account for the lack of progress. It is not just at different levels of the planning system, but it is also in different functional areas that policy thinking and practice are weakly developed.

In urban Belfast there are hopeful signs that the aspirations set out in the Regional Development Strategy are likely to be treated more seriously. The draft Belfast Metropolitan Area Plan has been published for consultation in which the need to tackle the legacy of segregation and provide opportunities for integration in 'neutral spaces' is at least identified in the background to the strategy. Moreover, the preceding *Issues Paper* did make an important connection between social need and equality in the city and the potential for local planning to act as some form of integrating mechanism where these problems are most acute.

The Government is committed to tackling social exclusion by targeting efforts and resources towards people, groups and areas objectively defined as being in social need. Land use planning alone cannot alleviate such problems of social deprivation and exclusion or problems associated with community division. It can, however, create a locational framework, which will provide the context for other initiatives (Department of the Environment, 2001, p.44).

In contrast, the *Issues Papers* for the Banbridge and Newry and Mourne Area Plan as well as the Armagh Area Plan, which cover the case study area presented earlier in this chapter, failed to address SPG 3 or the segregation that mediates movement patterns to shops, health facilities and entertainment services. This disconnection undermines the progress that has been made in the Regional Development Strategy, the real meaning of equality, and the potential to connect equity and social justice in a planning context. The commitment to empiricism, finding out how things actually work in rural settings, involving people properly in decisions that affect their future are at the core of John Greer's work and still provide the principles upon which real equality and debates about difference can find their way into the planning arena.

Conclusions

This chapter has highlighted the legacy of the Northern Ireland conflict for rural communities. The peace process and economic progress have brought significant benefits for some people and especially for some places. The renewal of Belfast's waterfront, new flagship urban projects and the recent development of high value suburban housing are all evidence of the differential spatial effects of the growth economy. However, many of these benefits have not trickled down to some rural communities facing the multiple effects of agricultural restructuring, the reform of EU farm support and increasingly stringent environmental and water quality directives. Suspicion, mistrust and fear still characterise social life and act as an obstacle to a unified agenda capable of connecting people across the religious divide. Important progress has been made and there is little alternative to the continuous management of contact and mutual working around socio-economic issues in local development. John Greer's farsighted analysis highlights the need to see rural life and place as an integrated system in which the emotional attachment to place needs to be both understood and respected. In Northern Ireland, this has a distinctive edge brought about by territorial behaviour and enduring segregation in many rural communities. Building these concerns and priorities into local development plans is essential in the creation of any genuinely integrated and credible regeneration agenda for rural areas in Northern Ireland.

References

Boal, F. (1987) Segregation, in M. Pacione (ed.) *Social geography: progress and prospects*, pp.90-128, London, Croom Helm.

Department of the Environment (2001) *Belfast Metropolitan Area Plan (BMAP) Issues Paper*, Belfast, Planning Service for Northern Ireland.

Department for Regional Development (2001) *Shaping Our Future: Regional Development Strategy for Northern* Ireland, Belfast, Department for Regional Development.

Ellis, G. (2001) Social exclusion, equality and the Good Friday Agreement: the implications for land use planning, *Policy and Politics*, 29(4), pp.393-411.

Harris, R. (1972) *Prejudice and tolerance in Ulster: a study of neighbours and strangers in a border community*, Manchester, Manchester University Press.

Leyton, E. (1975) *The one blood: kinship and class in an Irish village,* Social and Economic Studies, Newfoundland, Memorial University.

Donnan, H. and McFarlane, G. (1986) You get on better with your own: social continuity and change in rural Northern Ireland, in P. Clancey, S. Drudy, K. Lynch and L. O' Dowd (eds.) *Ireland: a sociological profile,* pp.21-37, Dublin, Institute of Public Administration in association with the Sociological Association of Ireland, Dublin.

Hamilton, A., McCartney, C., Anderson, T. and Finn, A. (1990) *Violence and communities,* Coleraine, Centre for the Study of Conflict, University of Ulster.

Kirk, T. (1993) *The polarisation of Protestants and Roman Catholics in rural Northern Ireland: a case study of the Glenravel Ward, Co. Antrim, 1956-1988,* Unpublished Ph.D. Thesis, Belfast, School of Geosciences, Queens University Belfast.

McEldowney, M. & Sterrett, K. (2001) Shaping a regional vision: the case of Northern Ireland, *Local Economy,* 16(1), pp.38-49.

Morrow, D., Wilson, D. and Eyben, K. (2003) *Reconciliation and social inclusion in rural areas,* Cookstown, Rural Community Network.

Murray, M and Greer, J. (1993) Rural development and paradigm change, in M. Murray and J. Greer (eds.) *Rural development in Ireland,* pp.255-268, Aldershot, Avebury.

Murray, M. and Murtagh, B. (2004) *Equity, Diversity and Interdependence: reconnecting governance and people through authentic dialogue,* Aldershot, Ashgate.

Murtagh, B. (2002) *The politics of territory,* London, Palgrave.

New TSN Unit (1999) *Vision into practice: The first New TSN annual report,* Belfast, Corporate Document Service.

Rural Community Network (2003) *The experiences of Protestant communities in border areas,* Cookstown, Rural Community Network.

Rural Community Network (2005) *We don't feel as isolated as you might think: the experiences of Catholic minority communities in Counties Antrim and Down,* Cookstown, Rural Community Network.

Chapter 4

Berlin Babylon: The Spatiality of Memory and Identity in Recent Planning for the German Capital

William J. V. Neill

Introduction.

The 2001 film *Berlin Babylon*, by the German director Hubertus Siegert, explores place-making tensions in reunited Berlin concerned with the spatiality of memory. Siegert's film, which documents in powerful images the physical rebuilding of central Berlin since the fall of the Wall, provides a portal to the city of the imagination where not just a city is being rebuilt but German identity itself. As one reviewer has pointed out, the film raises important issues concerning "the 'city' of memory and identity in an age of globalisation" (Stern, 2002, p.118). This chapter, reflecting on scenes in the film and informed by interviews with 'memory workers', traces the special tension in Berlin between, on the one hand, an impulse to forget the past, and on the other, the stranglehold which this past place of infamous events exerts over cultural self understanding in Germany.

Berlin provides a powerful reminder that the uniqueness of place in the formation of identity still matters. Focussing in particular on the rebuilt Potsdamer Platz, the Planwerk Innenstadt (the design plan for the inner city which sets the planning context in central Berlin) and the recently completed Memorial to the Murdered Jews of Europe, all featuring prominently in Siegert's film, links are made to current German identity ruminations. German identity angst, still intense, can be read in its capital city. Reverberating as capital cities do with symbolic power the physical planning of central Berlin, it is argued, makes its special but contested contribution to the exorcising of national ghosts – a process documented by Ladd but far from complete (Ladd, 1997).

The chapter proceeds by way of considering the special problems surrounding national identity narrative construction in Germany and the role of a spatial imagination necessarily invoked by this. This involves forgetting, remembering and imagining politically contested processes whose outcomes are constituted in concrete form in the actual city of bricks, mortar and, of course, glass. Foregrounding the role of capital city planning in etching or erasing memory traces in identity construction, the chapter argues that Berlin fortunately remains an uneasy place where a national narrative of continuity exists in tension with an identity narrative which seeks to incorporate rupture.

German National Narrative Construction

The historian Norman Davies describes how nationalism came from the late 18th century and 19th century onwards in two opposing variants: civic nationalism and ethnic nationalism (Davies, 1996). Ethnic nationalism, in its concept of nationhood, emphasises mythical notions of ethnic identity, language, culture, poetry, history and romantic feelings about the land. Civic nationalism is based on place bounded political institutions. Recognising that the civic / ethnic dichotomy is an ideal type distinction, and that the nationalism of every nation has romantic as well as constitutional and political elements, the question is well posed as to where most weight is placed (Buruma, 1998). In constructing a sense of shared belonging and identification out of cultural and civic elements a "national narrative" is essential to any nation state. Here collective memory, open to contestation, selects from history what is emphasised, remembered and forgotten.

While Maurice Halbwachs, the French sociologist, pointed out in the 1920's that it is present concerns that determine what of the past we include in collective memory (Novick, 1999), Easthope reminds us (not without significance for identity preoccupations in Germany) that, since the function of a national narrative is to confer a sense of identity on members of a nation, this is only possible if the national narrative retains a considerable degree of stability. The national narrative bestows a sense of "being a people", a "large scale solidarity" with a "perceived integration of past and present in an envisioned future" (Easthope, 1997).

However, while most major Western nation states now define their nationhood more in terms of common citizenship than by common ethnicity, one prominent exception, until recently, has been Germany (Ignatieff, 1995). It has been towards Berlin as a locale for the reassessment of the meaning of German nationhood and identity that debate has been channelled, since the 1991 decision of the German parliament by a narrow vote to restore the city as the nation's capital. While Berlin is historically associated with a cosmopolitan openness extending back from Weimar decadence to Prussian qualities of liberalism, toleration and enlightenment (Craig, 1991), and while almost three out of four Berliners voted against Hitler in 1932 (Read and Fisher, 1994), Berlin is irrevocably associated with the failure of a nation state under the Nazis that was based on a most extreme and grotesque form of ethno-nationalism. In the words of Daniel Libeskind, designer of the new

Jewish museum in Berlin and architect of other prominent memory projects:

> The Holocaust is not just another event in the time line of Berlin. It's an axial
> redefinition of Berlin. (Libeskind, quoted Range, 1996, p.116)

In Hitler and the Holocaust, the German national narrative was shattered in a way not permitting of easy suture. While it is possible to omit, for example, the behaviour of Oliver Cromwell at Drogheda in Ireland from the British national narrative, the "break in civilization", as Habermas calls it, during the Nazi period cannot easily be dismissed from the German theatre of memory (Habermas, 1998). Habermas has gone as far as to argue that in the construction of a new definition of Germanness only 8th May 1945 – "Null Stunde" (Zero Hour) – can be an appropriate starting point. It is 1945 that is seen as a crucial turning-point in German history when West Germans began a process of rediscovering "the muted legacy of humanism and the Enlightenment in their own tradition". It is the concept of a nation of citizens that Habermas embraces as opposed to the notion of a "community of fate shaped by common descent, language and history" (Habermas, 1998). Rather, democratic citizenship establishing "an abstract, legally mediated solidarity between strangers" is sought, which would ideally nest within an enhanced, European level, civic identity building project, involving a European constitution based on the recognition of diversity (Habermas, 1998). In Germany itself, the overhauling of hitherto ethnically restrictive citizenship laws goes down the path favoured by Habermas. In what has been called a "milestone" event, since 1999 naturalisation has been made easier for long term foreign residents and their children (Fessenden, 2002), although a pessimist might point out that holding a German passport signifies belonging only to the German state, not the German nation (Ignatieff, 1995).

In understanding German national narrative (re)construction and identity politics, it is useful to contrast the views of Habermas with those of former Chancellor Helmut Kohl influential as he was during the post Wende rebuilding of the German capital. In the opinion of Kohl it is the year 1989, not 1945, which is to be emphasised in the broad sweep of German history as it represents a return to normality and normal history. The year 1989, moreover, marks the return of a common past to East and West Germans, with a shared and rich cultural legacy in literature, philosophy, music and poetry. This difference in emphasis can perhaps be overstated. Kohl has candidly admitted that Germany needs to be anchored in Europe as a protection against the romantic temptations of its worst self (Selbourne, 2001). It is a position, however, which has been strongly criticised as seeing the Nazi past as "only" a "bad tributary" in Germany's past compared to the "mighty current" of German history where the Nazi past was something that happened to "victim

Germany" (Kramer, 1995). While any crude reading of the meaning of place in the new Berlin is to be avoided, it is argued in what follows that narratives emphasising both Kohl's continuity and Habermas's rupture are both present in Germany's capital city landscape of identity signification.

Spatiality of German Identity

Brian Ladd in his 1997 book *The Ghosts of Berlin* describes how much of the physical rebuilding of central Berlin in the 1990s has involved the problem of confronting German history, especially the Nationalist Socialist past, in the urban landscape. As expressed by Alexandra Richie (1999) in her highly acclaimed history of Berlin:

> The legacy of the years 1933 to 1945 presents enormous problems for Berlin
> as a whole, and it is not an exaggeration to say that the way in which its citizens
> face the past will help to shape both the future of the capital and the very
> identity of the new Germany. (p. xivii)

Albert Speer, installed by Adolf Hitler as Inspector-General of Building in 1937, began a process of inscribing a diabolically exclusivist national narrative in stone in the form of grand plans for a new Germania (Reichhardt and Schaeche, 1998). With the return in 1991 of capital city rank to Berlin, presiding again over a reunited Germany, the question of the spatial expression of identity has necessarily involved reaction to this perverse but animating city of the imagination sketched in prison by Hitler and remaining with him in his bunker to the end (Balfour, 1990). The German Democratic Republic had avoided difficult engagement with memory and identity questions with the international communist movement supplying heroes and memory figures and links that stressed the peasant and worker traditions of the German nation (Ardagh, 1995). In a *tabula rasa* approach, East Berlin planners and architects directly under political direction correspondingly inscribed through the Soviet version of modernism a new and stark beginning for identity formation on their half of the city (Cowan, 1989).

On the other hand the approach to the spatial expression of identity in Bonn, the capital of West Germany, has been described as one of self-effacement (Wise, 1998). In Bonn glass surfaces and floating white walls as opposed to the stone classicism of National Socialist buildings, became the architectural form in which the young democracy came to recognise itself (Bartetzko, 1995; Wilhelm, 2001). Bonn represented a reassuring sign of discontinuity for Germans with their troubled history or, as put by one commentator, in Bonn, Germany "stepped out of history and stepped into business" with the West German state uncomfortable in projecting a political image of itself (Duerrenmatt, quoted in Der Spiegel, 1998, p.57).

However, if Bonn was a new beginning, a "Null Stunde", in a provincial small town on the Rhine, the image of the new Berlin is more ambivalent in this respect. While the wrapped Reichstag of Christo in 1995 symbolically signalled a new beginning and a break with the past by reworking the identity of the building (Der Spiegel, 1998) and, while the new federal government quarter in general (the Band des Bundes or Ribbon of the Federation) is deliberately set at right angles to the North-South axis of Speer, other aspects of capital city planning can be best interpreted as part of a narrative of continuity and normalisation. The Bonn tradition is recognisable in the Band des Bundes with transparent functionalism as the architectural symbol of democracy represented in iconic form in the new Reichstag dome (Photograph 4.1). At the same time the central spine of government buildings is presented in "a severe Prussian Functionalist block-geometry" (Jencks, 1995, p.19), with the steadfastness of massive stone-faced walls expressing new German confidence and setting the tone for new construction in Berlin "as the architectural symbol for a recovery in self-esteem" (Bartetzko, 1995, p.15). One prominent critic has gone so far as to suggest that the promotional hype of the Band des Bundes as a "clasp" linking the West and Eastern parts of Berlin has the function, in conjuring up a return to normality, of permitting "the Germans to appear to be the victims, not the perpetrators, of 20th century history" (Guerra, 1998).

Photograph 4.1: A trademark identity for the nation's capital

Debate over how German identity should be reflected in Berlin has not, however, just been confined to the federal government quarter. Central Berlin, more generally, has been "in recent years a battleground for conflicting architectural visions reflecting political agendas" (Paulick, 2004). It is this wider canvas that is the focus of the film *Berlin Babylon*. The remainder of this chapter combines perspectives from the film on set piece plans and projects in Berlin with a broader consideration of how they relate to identity narratives of continuity and rupture.

Forgetting the Past on Potsdamer Platz: The *Angel of History* Takes Flight
In *Berlin Babylon* the director Siegert gives voice to Walter Benjamin's *Angel of History*. This is sandwiched between two 'chapters' of the film. The first depicts scenes of grandiose vision and implied hubris, involved in the corporate reinvention of Berlin's Potsdamer Platz. The subsequent 'chapter' of the film, looking to a difficult past, depicts scenes from Berlin's new Jewish Museum alongside the site for the Memorial to the Murdered Jews of Europe. Contemplating the wreckage of a second European war in his lifetime, Benjamin, a native of Berlin, imagined in the following words, quoted in the film, the animation of his *Angel of History*:

> The Angel of History
> His countenance faces the past
> Where we can see a chain of events he sees a single catastrophe.
> Rubble piles up relentlessly.
> Layers of it are hurled at his feet.
> He longs to linger,
> To wake the dead and reconstruct the rubble.
> But a storm has brewed in paradise.
> The tempest has unfurled its wings
> It is so strong he cannot lower them again.
> The storm drives him pell-mell into the future.
> He turns his back on what's to come.
> Meanwhile the pile of rubble grows sky high before his eyes.
> The phenomenon that we call progress is this mighty storm.
> (Benjamin, 1940)

The frenetic activity portrayed in much of *Berlin Babylon* in the rebuilding of Berlin in the 1990s conjures up the imagery of a city swept backwards into the future uneasily aware of the rubble of the past but wanting to escape at speed. The rush, with little public discussion, by Bonn and Berlin politicians post-unification to a major corporate and commercial centre as the future of Potsdamer Platz (Caygill, 1992) can be read as the embrace of a narrative of continuity with a direct line of succession from the novel and distracting 1920's Berlin arcades and department stores written about with fascination by Benjamin, to the modern shrines of commodification at the reborn Potsdamer Platz in whose worship the post-war German collective unconscious has found some comfort. As Brian Ladd (2004) says of Potsdamer Platz:

> Whereas the past is visible and palpable in so many sites across the city, however, the layers of history are not on display here…The new masters of Potsdamer Platz invoke the past but …this history is much closer to the Disney version. (p.132)

One is tempted in walking around the new corporate Berlin heart of Potsdamer Platz to recall Walter Benjamin's explorations of place character and identity in his hometown of 80 years ago where he discerned "the dream sleep" of capitalism (quoted by Gillock, 1996, p.104). Here, in an all-consuming present, continuity with the past is eased through the haze provided by historical amnesia. In the many shops, restaurants, bars and cafes of the new Daimler Chrysler and Sony developments and in the associated apartments and international penthouses on the reinvented public square, visitors and residents are orientated towards the future. As a spanking new mini-Manhattan nodal point in the network society, Potsdamer Platz is but a short distance from the new Lehrter Bahnhof, Berlin's "Station of the Future". (Deutsche Bahn AG, 1998). This is a mid-continental transportation crossroads of chilling airport-like sterility.

Standing in the audio-booth in the landmark red Info-Box overlooking Potsdamer Platz, which until 2000 showcased the flagship construction projects of the Berlin of the future, a city promotional process that commodified the building process itself (Lehrer, 2004), the listener was transported to the imaginary sounds of the city in the year 2020. From this vantage point even the present seemed like a dim memory or a place outside the booth to be escaped from. Here major architectural and urban design impulses in Berlin have also placed a premium on forgetting. The architecture of Potsdamer Platz, despite paying some respects to the traditional city block structure of Berlin development and despite the virtuoso modernist and post modernist design performances of those from the illustrious ranks of Helmut Jahn, Giorgio Grassi, Renzo Piano, Richard Rogers and others, ultimately speaks of and identifies with other prestige nodal network places preoccupied with an omni future present where identity is defined by consumption.

In his 1987 film, *The Sky Over Berlin* - an undoubted inspiration to *Berlin Babylon*, with both films invoking the concept of the angel as witness to history and events – the director Wim Wenders in a context where Potsdamer Platz has literally disappeared, has one of his characters roaming close to the

Berlin Wall exclaim: "I won't give up searching until I have found Potsdamer Platz". If Curt Bois, the character in Wenders's film was to be placed on the same ground today he would likely make the same poignant exclamation. Consumption and spectacular architecture, however, are not solely at work in etching an identity narrative of continuity. In Berlin the presumed normal future to be embraced with enthusiasm is connected to a "normal" past reconstructed with the aid of urban design. This involves largely forgetting the GDR years.

Planwerk Innenstadt and Return to "Normal" German Identity

A resolution passed by the Berlin Senat and House of Representatives in May 1999 makes an inner city planning and design concept known as Planwerk Innenstadt a standard to which inner city Berlin boroughs are obliged to abide in partnership with the Berlin Senat itself. This plan forms a major reference point for future planning explicitly concerned with changing the identity and character of central Berlin. That deliberations over the ideas in Planwerk Innenstadt should feature strongly in Siegert's film, especially as propounded by Berlin's former building director Hans Stimman, is hardly surprising. In the plan the urban designer's pen is used on the grand scale to consciously erase and etch physical traces of memory into the built fabric of the city. Berliners are to be reconnected with a shared history before 1933 when Berlin was a "normal" and more classically beautiful city in the European tradition (Figure 4.1).

The city will be sutured by privileging the urban ground plan and architectural principles of Berlin in the 19th and early 20th century (Neill, 2004). In a densification strategy, presented partly under the guise of sustainable development, wealthy western consumers are to be attracted to the new centre of Potsdamer Platz and Friedrichstrasse to underpin commercial development already there and to add cosmopolitan flair not always provided by less affluent Easterners. While the full actualisation of the Planwerk strategy awaits a general upturn in the development market in Berlin, the whole approach has been labelled by Simone Hain (2001), a former East Berlin planner and member of East Germany's prestigious Bauakademie, as "a declaration of war" (p.74) against the identity and experience of East Germans (Photograph 4.2). An exhibition in Leipzig in the autumn of 2004 organised by Hain and others and titled *Two German Architectures* continued to question the denigration for political reasons of an East German building tradition (Paulick, 2004a). However, it remains probable that less evidence of more discordant spatial testimony to 20th century ruptures in the built fabric will be less jarring to the dreaming consuming collectivity, the mass from which Benjamin laterally came to see Fascism as formed (Gillock, 1996). At the 15th anniversary of the fall of the Berlin Wall in November 2004 a spokesperson for the Berlin city planning department even went so far as to suggest that Berlin was in danger of becoming a Cold War theme park with the Checkpoint Charlie Museum for marketing reasons erecting a temporary memorial in the form of multiple crosses to the "victims of the Berlin Wall" helping in the process to turn the city into a "Disneyland" version of its former self (Damianakis, quoted in Paulick, 2004b). A narrative of continuity will be assisted by the balm of historical commercialisation.

Figure 4.1: (i) Central Berlin around 1940, (ii) Central Berlin around 1989, (iii) Central Berlin proposed in Planwerk Innenstadt around 2010

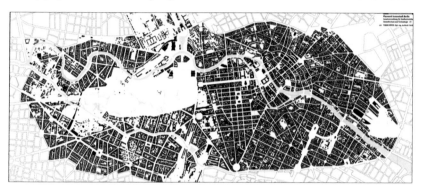

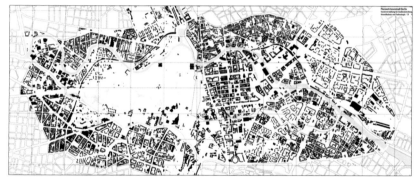

Photograph 4.2: A Berlin Wall fragment close to Potsdamer Platz, 2004

Within the framework of the Planwerk Innenstadt a decision made at the highest level by the German Bundestag in July 2002 will further contribute to the encrypting of a reassuring storyline of continuity into the Berlin cityscape. Following the advice of an "international commission" (Swoboda, 2002), the city is to see the reconstruction of the baroque facades of the famous Berlin castle, home of the Hohenzollern dynasty, which was dynamited for ideological reasons by the GDR in the 1950s. The modernist monolith, the Palast der Republik, built by the communists on the site and home to the rubber stamp People's Chamber of the GDR, was a popular meeting place for East Berliners, and took some delight as an edifice in completely "cocking a snoop" at the old aesthetic geometry of Berlin's centre as redesigned by its most famous 19th century architect, Karl Friedrich Schinkel (Neill, 1997). As one recent commentator has pointed out, until now "urban planning and the Planwerk Innenstadt have been circling the central area of the GDR state buildings between the television tower and the Palast der Republik as if it were a mined area" (Hartung, 2001). There are good reasons for this. Above all this is hallowed ground, a place of German historical self-understanding representing a spiritual void that places like Potsdamer Platz cannot fill. That the Palast der Republik on such a major meaning–impregnated representational space, to use Lefebvre's terminology (Lefebvre, 1991), should face the wrecker's ball is understandable even if an artistic display (Photograph 4.3) above the Palast in early 2005 cried out the simple word "Zweifel" (Doubt).

Photograph 4.3: Doubt sits on the Palast der Republik, 2005

A victorious global turbo capitalism celebrating itself at Potsdamer Platz threatens to erase all memory of Socialism, the other "wayward child of Enlightenment", to borrow a term from Günter Grass (Grass, 2002, p.65). The denial by neo-liberalism, now without the historical counterweight of communism, that there is any alternative to the free market (Grass, 2002, p.66) can be seen in the urban planning tendency in Berlin to repress the notion that there was once the possibility of a different system despite the irony that the world's most prominent socialist thinker was German. Benjamin's "dream sleep" will be compounded at the redeveloped site by the intention to rebrand Schloßplatz in the name of culture and science. The reconstructed castle will house history of science collections presently owned by the Humboldt University and collections of art and cultural artefacts now in the possession of the Foundation for Prussian Cultural Heritage. The centre of Germany will be associated with art, science and learning of the highest order. The old National Gallery (Alte Nationalgalerie), just across the road from Schloßplatz, after all had been marshalled in similar fashion to legitimise in high culture the unification of the German nation under Bismarck and still bears prominently on its front beam "To German Art 1871" (Lepik, 2000). Perhaps more convincing is the argument by one writer for *Die Zeit* that a half century of history cannot simply be undone with a return to an innocent before. Germans cannot all "meet again in the very far past" with the erasure of all separating uncomfortable history (Rauterberg, 2000).

World events in a century of extremes reverberated on Schloßplatz. Much has happened since 1871. While liberal Enlightenment ideals to be celebrated in a rebuilt castle are worth defending, more than ever the question has to be asked if the Schloßplatz proposal is not an act of cultural normalisation and amnesia taken too far. Presently a falsely reassuring reality of continuity presented by cosmetic urban design suture is preferred to the questions posed by the twentieth century "scar tissue". While President George W. Bush may have said in the sound bite of his speech to the German Bundestag in Berlin in May 2002, "the history of our time is written in Berlin", on Schloßplatz the legible traces are to be erased with statutory sanction at the highest level of the state. That any reassuring soporific story with a message that "all is well" could so easily provide a more comforting German national narrative is also, of course, at once preposterous. There is little danger of breaking Berlin's unique place identity on the rack of such high level urban planning. East German identity stubbornly persists with almost 30 per cent of the State of Brandenburg voting in September 2004 for the PDS, heirs to the party that constructed the Berlin Wall (Connolly, 2004). In his 1903 essay, *The Metropolis and Mental Life*, Georg Simmel suggested that from any point on the surface of existence one may drop a sounding into the depths of the soul. This was a principle shared by Walter Benjamin, a youthful follower of Simmel. In his own essay, *A Berlin Childhood around the turn of the Century*, Benjamin begins by challenging the dominance of the impulse to overt imageability and legibility in city planning (Lynch, 1960):

> Not to find one's way about in a city is of little interest. But to lose one's way in a city, as one loses one's way in a forest, requires practice…" (Benjamin, quoted Sontag, 1979, p.10)

Berlin still leaves plenty of space for losing oneself and for dropping a "plumb line" into the depths of its soul. Here the film *Berlin Babylon* continues to be suggestive.

The *Angel of History* Falls to Earth: Remembering the Past in the City of Remorse.

In Siegert's film following the chronicling of phases in the building of Potsdamer Platz and immediately following the invocation of the foreboding words of Benjamin's Angel, the musical sound track of the movie falls silent. We get a glimpse of the site close to the Brandenburg Gate set aside for the construction of the Memorial to the Murdered Jews of Europe before being transported to a journey through the nearby voids of Daniel Libeskind's newly constructed Jewish Museum. The voids represent the presence of the absence of the Jewish people and culture that were lost in Berlin during the Holocaust.

Berlin Babylon ends on a lingering view cutting an axial line southwest from the site of Albert Speer's city planning office on Pariser Platz beside the Brandenburg Gate[1] foregrounding the site for the Memorial to the Murdered Jews of Europe and with the new Potsdamer Platz rising in the background. Potsdamer Platz will always be overshadowed by what Habermas has called the "break in civilisation" during the Nazi period that cannot be easily dismissed from the German theatre of memory (Habermas, 1998, p.25). Any tendency towards escape by privileged urban splintering into the dreamy refuge of the consumption spaces of the network society (Graham and Marvin, 2001) will always be thwarted in Berlin by a special binding *genius loci*. Identity and meaning will continue to be sought in the particularity of place. It is no accident that the voluminous documentation cataloguing the process leading to the building of Berlin's "Holocaust memorial" is subtitled "a cross section through the soul of a nation" (Heimrod *et al*, 1999). The remainder of this chapter, amidst a sea of Third Reich memory project work both large and small in Berlin (Hattstein and Mecke, 2002), reviews the genealogy of Berlin's premier grand project of memory. This opened on May 8th 2005 and the tension in its interpretation between the representation of a "Null Stunde" in German identity construction and a place where a difficult past is laid to rest better enables an identity narrative of continuity.

The Memorial to the Murdered Jews of Europe
The late spring of 2005 saw the completion by the Federal Republic of Germany on a 19,000 sq metre site just south of the Brandenburg Gate of a "warning memorial" (Mahnmal) to the murdered Jews of Europe; 2,700 concrete pillars in a vast field of memory designed by the American architect Peter Eisenman will, in the words of the resolution passed by the German Bundestag on 25 June 1999:

> ... honour the murdered victims; maintain the memory of this unthinkable occurrence in German history and admonish all future generations to never again violate human rights, to defend the democratic constitutional state at all times, to secure equality before the law for all people and to resist all forms of dictatorship and regimes based on violence. (Foundation of the Memorial to the Murdered Jews of Europe, 2000)

This project has been a focus for fundamental debate over German identity and self-understanding since its genesis in a bottom up Citizens' Initiative dating back to 1988. Over the ensuing years and especially since 1995, when Chancellor Helmut Kohl vetoed the gigantism of a winning entry in a design competition for the project, national debate has involved politicians, historians, philosophers, novelists, journalists, artists, and architects amongst many others in what is a major place making set piece close to Berlin's main government quarter. Those charged with officially documenting the process leading to the Mahnmal decision acknowledge that the Mahnmal debate has stretched the patience of the German public beyond endurance but state:

> The debate has become a central discourse on political and historical self-understanding in the reunified Germany. The project is a point of crystallisation for the precarious ambivalence between the still valid onus of history and the desire for normality. With hindsight the debate around the concept and the design of the memorial for the Murdered Jews of Europe will probably be seen as a sharp break (Zäsur) in how the Germans look at their history after Auschwitz and in the new understanding of their role in Europe and the world on the threshold of a new century. (Heimrod, Schlusche and Seferens, 1999, pp. 7-8)

In giving his imprimatur to the final design concept in March 1999 as "the best alternative", Jürgen Habermas puts centrally the function of the memorial in making Germans think critically about their identity. Despite the 1995 intervention by Chancellor Kohl with his background preference for an identity narrative with a greater emphasis on continuity, the hope is expressed by Habermas that the memorial will be a sign stretching far into the future of the possibility of "a purified collective German identity … (where) the break in the continuity of our fundamental traditions is the condition to regain self respect" (Habermas, 1999).

The Berlin Mahnmal controversy has involved debate over why a memorial should be built, where it should be built and what it should look like. Concerning the first and most fundamental question of all, Lea Rosh, the leading campaigner who has seen the project through from inception to erection, is clear. The purpose of the monument is two-fold. It is about Germans "not forgetting but confronting the unique event in history involving the industrial murder of millions of Jews". Secondly, "it is a memorial erected by the perpetrators to their dead victims" (Rosh, 1999). Other major national memorials exist in central Berlin recalling the horror of war in general terms such as the landmark remains of the Kaiser William Memorial church dedicated as long ago as 1961. More recently Chancellor Kohl in 1993 had rededicated the Neue Wache in Berlin Mitte with the installation, at his personal selection, of a sculpture, *Mother and Dead Son* by the artist Käthe Kollwitz. Heavily criticised for being an overly sentimental and generalised memorial to "the victims of war and tyranny" Kohl's "gift to Berlin" has been seen as adding to the case for memorials to specific victim groups (Endlich, 1995). Rosh's arguments, however, for a specific memorial to the Murdered Jews of Europe have been met with honourable criticism. The question was inevitably raised as to why Germany should be unique in putting a national symbol of shame so publicly on display. As a forceful critic of "the Holocaust industry" points out, there is no memorial in Washington D.C. to the millions who died in the slave trade or to commemorate the extermination of Native Americans. Attempts between 1984 and 1994 to build an African-American museum on the Washington Mall, location of the US Holocaust museum were abortive (Finkelstein, 2000, p.72). As put by the liberal *Süddeutschen Zeitung*:

> ... Stone symbols are supposed to remind us of glorious moments in the past ... who wants to be reminded forever of the horror which will bind the descendants ad infinitum into a chain of collective liability. (SDZ, 1998)

Equally felt has been the fear that such a memorial could become a place of forgetting rather than remembering. In 1998 this view was expressed by Michael Naumann, spokesman on culture for the Social Democrats. Rather than addressing the black hole in German self-understanding, Naumann suggested that a memorial would communicate the message that the past could be overcome once and for all. It would stamp on the past an official seal of closure. In similar vein the urban planning voice of Peter Marcuse, who with his family was forced to flee Berlin as a child, has criticised Kohl's support for a Jewish Holocaust memorial as involving the "cleansing" of this part of Germany history (Marcuse, 1998, p.335). Michael Bodemann, a prominent academic tracker of how Germans are dealing with the memory of the Holocaust has likewise articulated the concern that the memorial could become a German "holy site" which one enters to be healed (Bodemann, 1998).

On the second rationale for the Mahnmal put forward by Rosh – that the descendants of the perpetrators and heirs of a common culture should erect a memorial to the dead victims – there have been equal reservations. Fundamental here has been the disquiet that there is perhaps something quite absurd, if not distasteful, in such a project given that a memorial in the land of the perpetrators would have quite a different meaning from, say, that of Yad Vashem in Israel where the Jewish state is presented as a deliverance from the catastrophe of the Holocaust (Korn, 1996). While Lea Rosh claims one quarter Jewish ancestry, the clamour for such a memorial has not come from Jews in Germany who quite naturally would find it awkward and have ambivalent feelings about asking the Germans for a memorial. Ignatz Bubis, former chairman of the directorate of the Central Council of Jews in Germany never publicly supported the idea of Jews "needing" a memorial from the Germans (Rosh, 1999). Hence, while acknowledging that the Holocaust for Germans is "constitutive" for the Federal Republic as "an ever present origin comparable to foundation myths", one writer points to the dilemma that memory must "take place for its own sake, not just as a tool for self betterment" (Ross, 1998) or as Habermas puts it, while the memorial will inevitably affect Germans' sense of identity, it is not the function of Auschwitz and the victims to "help Germans feel better about themselves" (Habermas, 1999). Moreover, the project of building a memorial specifically for the murdered Jews of Europe has raised the objection from Professor Julius Schoeps, head of the Mendelssohn Centre for European Jewish Studies at Potsdam University, that a "hierarchy of victims" will be created (quoted, Staunton, 1998). To this Rosh replies, echoing Ignatz Bubis on the issue (Bubis, 1997) that other victim groups such as the Sinti and Roma and homosexuals can legitimately expect memorials of their own, but to conflate the treatment of various victim groups is to belie the different stigmas and gradations of treatment meted out by the Nazis to each (Rosh, 1999), not to mention the fact that the Jews were the largest victim group marked out for extermination.

The officially designated site for the Berlin Holocaust Memorial is a large parcel of federally owned land promised to Lea Rosh by Helmut Kohl in 1992, lying just south of the Brandenburg Gate and formerly constituting the "gardens" for government ministries. While close to the centre of Nazi power, the site itself is not associated with any particular *genius loci* of its own. Counter proposals challenging the importance of this site for memory work arose in the course of the memorial debate. In March 1999 in the lead up to the federal government giving the official go-ahead for the Ministerial gardens location, the directors of seven concentration camp memorials (Belsen, Buchenwald, Dachau, Dora, Neuengamme and Ravenbrück, and Sachsenhausen on Berlin's doorstep) rebelled against such a centralised focus of memory. In an open letter they stated that: "Parliament is facing a fundamental decision – it is about how the Holocaust should be anchored in the cultural memory of Germany". Resources, it was argued, should be spent on the original camps so that visitors could see the real sites of the horror rather than an artistic representation (Boyes, 1999).

An objection of a different kind was raised by Salomon Korn, member of the governing board of the Central Council of Jews in Germany, in 1997. Korn, an architect with responsibility for articulating Jewish views on Jewish memorials, argued that the memorial site was not central enough. Being close to the former Chancellery and to Hitler's bunker, Korn argued, "binded the planned memorial to the Nazi past instead of to the federal republic's present which would be the case on a site close to the Reichstag." Even Lea Rosh, in rejecting the latter idea, is criticised as delivering the real message that "the Holocaust memorial is connected to past National Socialist history while the present centre of Germany history is untouched by the millennial crime, having to be kept clean for the future of the unified Germany" (Korn, 1996). Korn rather looked with favour on the radical idea for a deep trench in front of the main entrance to the Reichstag. This symbolism, recalling the "Zivilisationsbruch" of Habermas, would remind German legislators in an inescapable way of the historically conscious new beginning which the re-imaged Reichstag represented.

On the question of what Berlin's central Holocaust Memorial should look like, the aesthetic production of 528 entries for an artistic design competition in 1995 stoked a considerable furnace of national and international debate on how the awfulness of such an event could possibly be represented. Whether the Holocaust is conceived as a failure by Germany's political culture to adequately take on board the ideas of the European Enlightenment (Hohendahl, 1998), or in fact the reverse, a case of the worst expression of the narcissistic fantasies of omnipotence and superiority that haunt Western modernity as argued by the French post-modern philosopher Jean-François Lyotard (Huyssen, 1994), the question of the artistic representation of the Holocaust has always brought forth passionate views. While in the background lies Adorno's rightful wariness of aestheticising the unspeakable suffering of the victims, one contributor to a study of Holocaust memorials, based around an exhibition organised by the Jewish Museum of New York in the early 1990s, pointed out how much is at stake and not only to German identity:

> Fifty years after the notorious Wannsee Conference, at which the Final Solution was first given political and bureaucratic shape, the Holocaust and its memory still stand as a test case for the humanistic and universalistic claims of Western civilisation. The issue of remembrance and forgetting touches the core of a multifaceted and diverse Western identity …
>
> Perhaps post-modern culture in the West is itself caught in a traumatic fixation on an event which goes to the heart of our identity and political culture. In that case, the Holocaust monument, memorial and museum could be the tool Franz Kafka wanted literature to be when he said that the book must be the axe for the frozen sea within us. (Huyssen, 1994, pp. 10-17)

James E. Young, American author of a cultural history of Holocaust memorials (Young, 1994) and curator of the exhibition just mentioned has been an advisor to the Berlin memorial "sponsor group" since the mid-1990s. In general, Young argues that the Berlin memorial will "succeed", as is the case with all other memory sites within the fabric of a city, if it engages people in an active process of remembering. "Collected memory" around national memorials can even invest such places with a nation's "soul" (Young, 1993).

The German conundrum, as Young acknowledges, is how does a nation build a new and just state on the bedrock memory of its crimes that are to be memorialised in the heart of its capital city? (Young, 1994, p 35). As expressed by Young:

> ... Holocaust memorial work in Germany today remains a tortured, self-reflective, even paralysing preoccupation. Every monument, at every turn, is endlessly scrutinised, explicated and debated. Artistic, ethical, and historical questions occupy design juries to an extent unknown in other countries. In a Sisyphean replay, memory is strenuously rolled nearly to the top of consciousness only to clatter back down in arguments and political bickering, whence it starts all over again. (Young, 1993, p. 21)

The final memorial design has been the result of a process, described with prescience by Young, stretching back to 1994 and involving two design competitions, three discursive colloquia, extensive national debate and decisive political intervention along the way at the highest level. The first design competition in 1994/95 brought forth over 500 entries, the exhibition of which in central Berlin between April and May 1995, *Der Spiegel* was to call "an embarrassing parcours of hackneyed symbolism" (*Der Spiegel*, 1997). Responding to the large size of the site, many submissions went for gigantic monuments acknowledging the enormity of the Holocaust but also evoking memory of the gigantism of Nazi architecture. A handful of concept artists proposed to build nothing. A first prize awarded by the jury and favoured by Lea Rosh, was submitted by a group headed by the Berlin artist Christine Jacob-Marks. This proposed a vast 100 by 100 metre inclined stone slab in the style of a tombstone onto which would be engraved the names of all identifiable Jewish Holocaust victims. The proposed collection of money from the public to finance the inscribing of the names was described by Ignatz Bubis as enabling those with a bad conscience to buy indulgences, thus indicating how diametrically opposed meanings can be invested in the same object. The personal intervention by Chancellor Kohl in June 1995 in rejecting such gigantism has already been mentioned. This was to result in a second design competition organised by a new "Search Commission" two years later, where again, the intervention of Kohl, was to prove decisive. Of 19 submitted designs from invited contributors, two were short-listed by the Search Commission, those of Gesine Weinmiller from Berlin and Eisenman Architects with Richard Serra from New York. Any notion that a fair set of procedures and assessment criteria could ever exist and deliver a consensus result was dispelled when the sponsor group involving representatives from Berlin, Citizens' Initiative and federal government doubled the short-listed designs for the memorial project bringing in the entries of Daniel Libeskind of recent Jewish museum fame, and Jochen Gerz noted for his pioneering work in designing "anti-monuments" to the Holocaust which challenge the very premise of their being.

Following extensive debate in the media in late 1997, in January 1998 at a meeting between CDU Chancellor Kohl, Lea Rosh, Berlin's CDU mayor Eberhard Diepgen and president of the Bundestag, Rita Süssmuth, high level political consensus began to gel around a design based on the broad principles of Eisenman and Serra (Conradi, 1998). This took a step backwards on 18th March 1998 when Berlin's mayor publicly spoke out against the Mahnmal project giving the clearest of indications that memory debate in Germany, in terms of views and feelings held, crosses party lines. Diepgen, expressed the view that Berlin, in doing too much of the Republic's memory work, should not be turned into a "Capital of Remorse". Following discussions between Peter Eisenman and Chancellor Kohl, a modified memorial design was to emerge in the summer of 1998. The disorientating "waving" field of pillars with a cemetery motif was scaled down from 4000 to 2700 columns and the size of slabs reduced from a former 7 metres to 4 metres and less, lest the sense of fear be too intense. The prospect of disoriented and panic-stricken visitors in an architectural field of fear almost adjacent to the Brandenburg Gate would do little for the image of Berlin. The change Eisenman argued would "in no way diminish the idea of our monument" as "a place one feels alone and abandoned, a place without a beginning or an end, with no direction" (Eisenman, 1998; Eisenman quoted in Staunton, 1998). His collaborator Richard Serra disagreed withdrawing from the project on the grounds that artistic integrity had been compromised. In a situation where no "right" artistic solution can possibly exist, James Young, in August 1998, as a spokesperson for the Search Commission endorsed "Eisenman II":

>…this memorial comes as close to being adequate to Germany's impossible task as is humanly possible. This is finally all we can ask of Germany's national attempt to commemorate the Nazis' murder of European Jewry… By choosing to create a commemorative space in the centre of Berlin – a place empty of housing, commerce or recreation – the Chancellor reminds Germany and the world at large of the self-inflicted void at the heart of German culture and consciousness. [2] It is a courageous and difficult act of contrition on the part of the government. Because the murdered can respond to this gesture with only a massive silence, the burden of response must fall on living Germans – who in their memorial visits will be asked to recall the destruction of a people once launched in their name, the irredeemable void this destruction has left behind, and their own responsibility for memory itself." (Young, 1998)

With the Sisyphean "memory boulder" previously identified by Young almost at the top of the mountain, on 11th October 1998 it was to come crashing down again, but for the last time. In a public speech accepting a peace prize for his latest book, the prominent liberal novelist Martin Walser spoke out against the Berlin Holocaust memorial linking it to the strain of past disgrace which Germany should now move beyond. Conscience, he argued, should be a private matter and Germans should not foster a "cult of past guilt" where a nation is blamed forever (Ross, 1998). Walser's comments in fact echoed the concerns of James Young that while people should be "permanently marked" by a Berlin memorial they should not be "disabled by memory" (Young, 1997). Highlighting the fact that a consensus relationship to the Nazi past is fragile in Germany, the Walser intervention may be seen as having the opposite of its intended effect. With such sentiments exploited by far-right parties and with a condemnation of the remarks by Ignatz Bubis on the 50th commemoration of Kristallnacht, Gerhard Schröder as the new Chancellor, previously sceptical about a memorial, was galvanised into supporting yet another variant of the Eisenman design incorporating an information centre (Photograph 4.4).

Figure 4.4: Past and present: Memorial to the Murdered Jews of Europe as overlooked by Potsdamer Platz, 2005

Conclusion

Ultimately any assessment of how Germans and Berliners have coped with the necessary but impossible task of "dealing with" the legacy of the Nazi past and the Holocaust, in particular, must remain subjective. Yet for the most part it can be argued that the Nazi element of the *genius loci* in Berlin has been engaged with in a reasonably transparent and honest, if inevitably unresolved, way. While Chancellor Schröeder articulates a widespread view in Germany that after over half a century of democracy Germans should be able to face the world without being crippled by war guilt (Boyes, 2004), the charge can be too harshly made that memorialising is part of a process in Germany of laying memory to rest and forgetting, and that relationships between objects in the built environment are being required to do the memory work of people (Kramer, 1999). However, the process perhaps resembles more the reclamation of reason through recognition in memory work where, as the leading German Jewish activist Michael Friedmann has rightly said, Germans do not have the right to declare moral closure (Friedmann, quoted in Boyes, 2004). In the Memorial to the Murdered Jews of Europe being situated so close to the Brandenburg Gate, it may be suggested that none is sought. The nature of Germany identity wrapped up in memory work still remains "work in progress" dealing as it must with the brute intractability of the legacy of the Holocaust. Here no city is so much defined by the polarity of the embrace of a global networked future and a past that will not let go. The powerful reminder of the "writing on the wall" in Berlin represented figuratively by the grave slabs of the Memorial to the Murdered Jews of Europe will always, as in Babylon, endow this city of imagination with a frisson of foreboding.

Acknowledgement

This chapter is published with permission of *Planning Theory and Practice.*

Endnotes

1. Albert Speer's City Planning office and exhibition space is presently being preserved in the erection of a new Academy of Art building on the site designed by the German architect Guenter Behnisch, designer of Munich's 1972 Olympic Stadium.

2. The presentation of the site as a symbolic void by Chancellor Kohl risks exaggeration. The memorial site is on top of what was once the "death strip", an empty place for almost 30 years. However, to the East are major GDR housing developments, to the West the major recreational space of the Tiergarten and to the South the commercial redevelopment of Potsdamer Platz.

References

Ardagh, J. (1995) *Germany and the Germans*, London, Penguin Books.

Balfour, A. (1990) *Berlin: the politics of order*, New York, Rizzoli International Publications

Bartetzko, D. (1995) Synthesis of fragments, in A. Burg and S. Redecke (eds.) *Chancellery and Office of the President of the Federal Republic of Germany, International Architectural Competitions for the Capital Berlin*, pp.9-21, Berlin, Birkhaueser Verlag.

Bodemann, M. (1998) Neues vom Reichsopferfeld, *TAZ Berlin*, 19 Feb.

Boyes, R. (1999) Holocaust museums oppose memorial, *The Times,* 4 March.

Boyes, R. (2004) Red carpet cannot hide the rubble of war swept under it, *The Times*, 3 November.

Buruma, I. (1998) The rival spirits of Europe, *Sunday Times*, 29 November.

Bubis, I. (1997) Kommentar in Colloquium Dokumentation,. *Denkmal fuer die ermordeten Juden Europas*, pp.26-27, Senatsverwaltung fuer Wissenschaft, Forschung und Kultur, Berlin.

Caygill, H. (1992) The futures of Berlin's Potsdamer Platz, *Discussion Paper No. 9 in Public Choice and Social Theory*, Centre for Public Choice Studies, Norwich, University of East Anglia.

Connolly, K. (2004) Far Right surges as Schroeder feels fury of the East, *Daily Telegraph*, 20 September.

Conradi, P. (1998) Denkmal fuer die ermordeten Juden Europas, *Informationsbrief 7*, Mitglied des Deutschen Bundestages.

Cowan, R. (1989) The man who built the wall, *Architects' Journal*, 25 January, pp.50-52.

Craig , G. A. (1991) *The Germans*, Penguin Books , London.

Davied, N. (1996) *Europe: a history*, Oxford, Oxford University Press.

Deutsche Bahn AG (1998) *Publicity briefing in Info Box Catalogue*, Berlin, Nishen.

Easthope, A. (1997) The peculiar temporality of the national narrative, *Paper delivered at Time and Value Conference 10-13 April*, Institute for Cultural Research, Lancaster, Lancaster University.

Endlich, S. (1995) Der blick nach innen: denkmal zur erinnerung an die buecherverbrennung vom 10 Mai 1933, in *Architektenkammer Berlin*, Jahrbuch, Junius, pp.156-159.

Endlich, S. (1998) Naehe und ferne, in *Architektur in Berlin*, Jahrbuch, Architektenkammer Berlin, Junius, pp.156-159

Fessenden, H. (2002) Immigration in Germany, *Prospect*, September, pp.38-41.

Finklestein, N..G (2000) *The Holocaust industry: reflections on the exploitation of Jewish suffering*, London, Verso.

Foundation of the Memorial to the Murdered Jews of Europe (2000) *Das denkmal fuer die ermordeten Juden Europas*, Information Brief, Berlin.

Gillock, G. (1996) *Myth and metropolis: Walter Benjamin and the city*, Cambridge, Polity Press.

Grass, G. (2002) (in conversation with Pierre Bourdieu) The progressive restoration, *New Left Review*, 14, March-April, pp. 63-77.

Graham, S. and Marvin, S. (2001) *Splintering urbanism*, London, Routledge.

Guerra, M.W. (1998) Hauptstadtplanung als medium einer staedtischen identitaestsfindung, *69th Stadtforum Proceedings*, Berlin.

Habermas, J. (1998) *A Berlin Republic: writings on Germany*, Cambridge, Polity Press.

Habermas, J. (1999) Der Zeigefinger – Die Deutschen. und ihr Denkmal, *Die Zeit*, 31 March.

Hain, S. (2001) Struggle for the inner city – a plan becomes a declaration of war, in Neill, W.J.V. and Schwedler, H.U. (eds.) *Urban planning and cultural inclusion*, Basingstoke, Palgrave.

Hartung, K.(2001) Eine stadt hofft auf heilung, *Die Zeit*, 19 July.

Hattstein, M. and Mecke, B. (2002) *Spuren des Terrors*, Berlin, Verlagshaus Braun.

Heimrod, U., Schlusser, G. and Seferens, H. (ed) (1999) *Das denkmal: die debatte um das "Denkmal fuer die ermorden Juden Europas"*, Eine Dokumentation, Berlin, Philo.

Hohendahl, P.U. (1998) Introduction, in, Habermas, J, *A Berlin Republic: writings on Germany*, Cambridge, Polity Press.

Huyssen, A. (1994) Monument and memory in a postmodern age, in Young, J.E. (ed.) *The art of memory: Holocaust memorials in history*, Munich, Prestel-Verlag.

Ignatieff, M. (1995) *Blood and belonging: journeys into the New Nationalism*, London, Vintage.

Ignatieff, M. (1999) *The warrior's honor: ethnic war and the modern conscience*, London, Vintage.

Jencks, C. (1995) *The architecture of the jumping universe*, London, Academy Editions.

Korn, S. (1996) Der Tragoedie letzter Teil-das Spiel mit der Zeit, *Frankfurter Rundschau*, 13 September.

Kramer, J. (1999) Living with Berlin, *New Yorker*, July 5, pp.50-64.

Ladd, B. (1997) *The ghosts of Berlin: confronting German history in the urban landscape*, Chicago, University of Chicago Press.

Ladd, B. (2004) *The companion guide to Berlin*, Suffolk, Boydell and Brewer.

Lefebvre, H. (1991) *The production of space*, London, Basil Blackwell.

Lehrer, U. (2004) Reality or image? Place selling at Potsdamer Platz, in INURA (eds.) *The contested metropolis: six cities at the beginning of the 21st Century*, Basel / Berlin/ Boston, Birkhaeuser.

Lepick, A. (2000) Die Alte Nationalgalerie, in, Lepik, A. (ed.) *Masterplan Museumsinsel Berlin: Ein Europaeisches Projekt*. Bundesamt fuer Bauwesen und Raumordnung, Berlin, G und H Verlag.

Lynch, K. (1960) *The image of the city*, Cambridge, MIT Press.

Marcuse, P. (1998) Reflections on Berlin, *International Journal of Urban and Regional Research*, 22(2), pp.331-338.

Meier, C. (1997) Zweierlei Opfer, *Die Zeit*, 11 April.

Neill, W.J.V. (1997) Memory, collective identity and urban design: the future of Berlin's Palast der Republik, *Journal of Urban Design*, 2(2), pp.179-192.

Neill, W.J.V. (2004) *Urban planning and cultural identity*, London, Routledge.

Novick, P. (1999) *The Holocaust and collective memory: the American experience*, London, Bloomsberry.

Paulick, J. (2004a) East German architecture's second chance, *Deutsche Welle*, 13 September.

Paulick, J. (2004b) Memorial to victims of the Berlin Wall, *Deutsche Welle*, 1 November.

Rauterberg, H. (2000) Deutscher Nachlass, *Die Zeit*, 24 August.

Read, A. and Fisher, D. (1994) *Berlin: the biography of a city*, London, Pimlico.

Rosh, L. (1999) *Interview with the author,* 21 September.

Ross, J. (1998) Aus Auschwitz lernen? *Die Zeit*, 49, 26 November.

Range, P.R. (1996) Reinventing Berlin, *National Geographic*, 190(6), pp.96-117.

Reichhardt, H.J. and Schaeche, W. (1998) *Von Berlin nach Germania*, Berlin, Transit.

Richie, A. (1999) *Faust's Metropolis: a history of Berlin*, London, Harper Collins.

Selbourne, D. (2001) Why Europe is destined to fall apart, *Sunday Times*, 13 May

Sontag, S. (1979) Introduction to Benjamin Walter *One Way Street and other writings*, London, Verso.

Spiegel (1997) Die Zeit der Entscheidung, 46, Hamburg.

Spiegel (1998) Die Macht der Mauern, 22, 48-71

Staunton, D.(1998)Haunted still, *The Guardian*, 12 August.

Stern, R. (2002) Berlin: film and the representation of urban reconstruction since the Fall of the Wall, in Oakman, J. (ed.) *Out of Ground Zero: case studies in urban reinvention*, Munich, Prestel Verlag.

Sueddeutsche Zeitung (1998) Hauptstadt der Reue, 20 March.

Swoboda, H. (2002) Vorwort, *Internationale Expertenkommission. Historische Mitte Berlin,* Abschlussberisht, Bundesministerium fuer Verkehr, Bau-und Wohungswesen und Senatsverwaltung fuer Stadtentwicklung, Berlin.

Wilhelm, K. (2001) Demokratie als Bauherr, *Ueberlegungenzum Charakter der Berliner politischen Repraesentationsbauten*, Das Parlament Wochenzeitung, Bonn.

Wise, M.Z. (1998) *Capital dilemma*, New York, Princeton Architectural Press.

Young, J.E. (1993) *The texture of memory: Holocaust memorials and meaning*, New Haven, Yale University Press.

Young, J.E. (1994) The art of memory, in Young, J. E. (ed.) *The art of memory: Holocaust memorials in history*, Munich, Prestel-Verlag.

Young, J.E. (1997) *Memorial for Europe's Murdered Jews: the next stage*, Department of English and Judaic Studies, University of Massachusetts at Amherst.

Young, J.E. (1998) *Assessment of Peter Eisenman's revised design for Berlin's "Memorial for the Murdered Jews of Europe"*. Statement as spokesperson for the Findungskommission.

Section Two:

PERSPECTIVES ON REGIONAL PLANNING

From Undeveloped Areas to Spatial Strategies: Reflections on Irish Regional Policy

Thomas A. Boylan

Introduction

Notwithstanding the deep-seated rhetoric extolling the virtues and desirability of ruralism and regional identity in post-independence Ireland, the actual dynamics of Irish regional policy reflect an altogether more complex process of shifting emphasis and priority. While complexity is a feature of all areas of public policy-making, it is acutely evident in the domain of regional policy where, in addition to the difficulties of negotiating and balancing potentially conflicting aims, the tensions between the competing demands of place represent a unique and defining feature of regional policy. The specific period which is the focus of this chapter is the fifty-year period extending from the Undeveloped Areas Act of 1952 to the publication of the National Spatial Strategy in 2002.[1] These years have been characterised, in turn, by periods of commitment, retreat and more recently a pragmatic re-engagement with the issues of the spatial development of the Irish economy. The main concern is to decipher the informing principles that have shaped regional policy against the background of changing economic development over this period. More specifically the chapter will seek to identify the tensions and conflicts at both the policy-making and local levels that have influenced the aims and form of post-war regional policy. Within the confines of a short chapter it will not be possible to examine in detail the expanding volume of available empirical work, but where necessary reference will be made to the main results which it contains.

Regional Policy: From Designated Areas to Growth Centres

While there are many dimensions to regional policy, there is little disagreement among economists, a species not celebrated in the folklore for their ability to collectively agree on most things, that the motive force of regional change for most of the period under review here was based on industrial development, be it indigenous or foreign. As a consequence, regional policy, certainly in its more articulated form, was viewed as the spatial arm of industrial development. In context, while there is a compelling logic as to why this was the case – industrialisation dominated post-war development in both the developed and the less developed world – a number of interesting consequences followed from this development.[2] It arguably restricted, if not seriously fragmented our view of what constituted an adequate regional policy. Secondly, arising from the association within development thinking between industrialisation and urbanisation, it imparted an unwarranted 'urban bias' in the shaping of the strategic approach to regional policy.[3] Finally, it conferred a secondary or subservient role on regional industrial policy, if this was perceived as representing a constraint on national economic objectives. This latter tension, between national requirements and regional needs, has played a crucial role at critical junctures in the disposition of Irish regional policy. A brief examination of this experience over the early decades of this period will illustrate the pervasive presence of some or all of these influences on the formation of regional policy.

The passing of the Undeveloped Areas Act of 1952 may be taken as the introduction of a new phase of public policy towards the spatial development of the economy. Of historical interest here is the durability of the regional problem reflected here in that the Undeveloped Areas as defined in the 1952 Act coincided with the same areas identified by the Congested Districts Board of 1891. The spatial imbalance in the Irish economy was clearly a deeply embedded structural problem that posed a major challenge to the resources and creativity of the policy makers and planners.[4] However, in both its timing and the crudity of its policy instruments – basically a set of regionally differentiated industrial grants – the 1952 Act could not be expected to achieve any substantive transformation of the problem. It came in response to the alarming demographic scenario which was recorded in the 1951 Census of Population, which particularly affected the western counties. Circumstances were less than kind to this early post-war attempt at regional development. The following six years were characterised by extreme economic stagnation compounded by recurring balance of payments crises.[5] This was not a conducive environment to launching new policy initiatives in regional development. Notwithstanding these difficult circumstances the 1952 Act represented a fundamental commitment to addressing a persistent and deeply-rooted problem of regional imbalance within the economy through the dispersal of industry to the Designated Areas of the north-west, western, and south-western regions of the country.

The debate that emerged during the course of the 1960s highlighted the tensions between the perceived needs of the national economy and the form that regional development should take. Against the background of a reoriented strategy of economic development based on trade liberalisation, the requirements of regional industrial policy were increasingly made subservient to national economic objectives. These included the preparation of indigenous industry for the challenge of free trade and the attraction of foreign industry to provide the driving impetus for rapid economic development.[6] This led to a retrenchment in regional policy during the 1960s when the emphasis clearly shifted, as it was to do again in the 1980s, to the maximisation of national economic growth. While the tension between these two domains of public policy can be exaggerated, what is not in question were the consequences of prioritising the achievement of national economic growth for the form of regional policy to be adopted. The widespread dispersal of industry that was envisaged in the policy and legislative measures of the 1950s was now perceived as representing a constraint and a potential obstacle to the achievement of rapid economic growth. This was the line of argument that was vigorously articulated in some detail in Whitaker's *Economic Development* (1958), the seminal document of Irish post-war development thinking. It found additional support in a number of the influential advisory bodies of this time, in particular the Committee on Industrial Organisation (CIO) and the National Industrial and Economic Council (NIEC).[7] The case for the dispersal of industry to stimulate regional development was replaced by the argument for spatial discrimination in favour of a limited number of urban centres in order to reap the benefits of economies of scale and urban agglomeration. This was supplemented by an uncritical acceptance of the mechanism of 'trickle-down' from these selected urban centres.

In advocating the strategic centrality of selected urban centres as the epicentres for the spatial development of their adjacent regions, Irish policy-makers could be argued to have been very much in tune with the prevailing development thinking at this time. The idea of 'unbalanced growth,' driven by concentrated investment in leading sectors of industrial and economic activity, was central to development theory and practice. Allied to this was the preoccupation with both 'forward' and 'backward' linkages with the leading sectors of industrial activity.[8] These twin pillars of the development process – concentrated industrial investment and the mechanisms of industrial linkages – found spatial expression in the innovative theorising of the French economist Francois Perroux, whose work underlay the emergence of growth pole theory along with the functional and spatial linkage with adjacent activities and geographic areas.[9] If Irish policy makers at this time needed conceptual and theoretical validation of their proposals, then they would have found it in the extensive academic literature that was then available. They would also of course have found sceptical and analytically critical voices which pointed to the challenges of overcoming serious inter-regional imbalance. In the event the policy debate during the course of the 1960s polarised around the issue of 'dispersal' or 'selective concentration,' which culminated in the commissioning of the Buchanan Report.[10]

The Buchanan Report was an extensive and detailed empirical analysis of the Irish situation, which was charged with providing spatial scenarios for the Irish economy over a twenty-year period. These scenarios were to be consistent with achieving the maximal levels of economic growth at the national level within the context of a move toward free trade and predicated on potential membership of the newly established European Economic Community. The Report provided a number of options, but, consistent with the prevailing orthodoxy and based on its empirical analysis the preferred option was a limited number of growth centres within the existing regional structure for the country. The resulting debate arising from these proposals proved to be contentious and divisive. The hostility to the proposals for a limited number of growth centres was, when viewed in the light of hindsight, somewhat ironic in that the Buchanan Report's main recommendations had been well anticipated and in fact vigorously canvassed by the 'domestic' school of economic development, and this included its regional dimension, over the course of the previous decade. With the publication of the Buchanan Report certain policy parameters for national economic development became relatively clear: industrial development was viewed as the principal 'engine of growth' at both national and regional levels; the selection of a limited number of urban centres imparted a strong 'urban bias' to the form and structure that spatial development would have to adhere to; and regional development was acceptable, even desirable, to the extent that it did not act as a constraint on national development. The spectre of the classic trade-off between equity and efficiency with respect to regional policy was clearly haunting this debate, with the balance coming down in favour of viewing regional policy as an exercise in re-distribution to achieve regional stabilisation, as long as it did not inhibit or endanger the pursuit of national economic growth.

Regional Industrial Planning: The Rise and Decline of Regional Policy
The political sensitivity and ultimate unacceptability of the Buchanan proposals highlighted the urgency of producing a compromise. This was reflected in the government statement of May 1969, which expressed some difficulties in accepting the full array of the recommendations of the Buchanan Report, based on a shrewd evaluation of the political implications involved. The task of providing a compromise was given to the Industrial Development Authority (IDA) and in the Regional Industrial Plans 1973-77 this was deemed to have been achieved. The task given to the IDA was an unenviable one. On the one hand it had to translate into an operational set of policies an extremely broadly stated set of goals as contained in the government statements of 1969 and 1972, while at the same time negotiating a more nuanced variant of the

Buchanan proposals.

The informing principles of the IDA's strategy were predicated on two major premises: (i) the acceptance of the argument contained in the Buchanan proposals of the need for selectivity in establishing a small number of large urban (or growth) centres in each of the planning regions; (ii) the desirability and feasibility of achieving a greater dispersal of industrial activity and employment outside of the selected regional growth centres. This approach was seen as being complementary to, rather than in conflict with, the Buchanan proposals.

The compromise strategy proposed by the IDA was based on its capacity to influence the distribution of new industry, particularly new foreign industry, to locate in particular regions (inter-regional distribution) and within particular regions to locate in specific towns (intra-regional distribution). Within the proposed strategic framework, each of the nine planning regions, which had been established following the Planning and Development Act, 1963, were allocated a target number of jobs in manufacturing which were to be created within the period of the plan. In addition, each planning region was subdivided into 'town groups' consisting of neighbouring towns and villages, with each such group being assigned a manufacturing employment target over the period of the plan. This planning approach was essentially maintained for the IDA's second set of regional industrial plans, which covered the period 1978-82.[11]

Over the period of the two sets of Regional Industrial Plans (1973-82) substantial progress was achieved in the area of regional development. In a number of regions a new industrial base was established where previously little or no industry had existed, while in other regions older industries based on the traditional sectors were complemented by newer growth industries. In general the period from 1973-82 represented the most articulated phase of regional policy in Ireland, albeit its focus was predominantly industrial. Within its own terms of reference, and in the absence of any coherent thinking by way of a spatial or regional plan for other economic activities such as the service sector or agriculture, considerable success was achieved by the IDA, notwithstanding some disappointments and even failures. Measured by the criteria of meeting employment targets, the achievements during the period of the first set of Regional Industrial Plans (1973-78) were impressive. In a number of regions, such as the West and Midlands, the targets were surpassed, while in a number of other regions success rates of up to 85 per cent, as in the North-West and 86 per cent in the South-East were recorded. In contrast the East region, dominated by the emerging problems of Dublin City in the mid-1970s and the North-East region experienced net job losses in industrial employment.[12]

The same commitment to the regions was reflected in the second 1978-82 set of Regional Industrial Plans, though by this stage preoccupation with problems at the national economy level began to dominate. The predominant concern was the failure of indigenous industry to generate any substantial level of output or employment growth during the course of the 1970s. Consequently the later IDA plans had to address additional problems of restructuring of the industrial base of the economy, particularly that of the indigenous sector. At the same time, major changes were occurring in other sectors of the economy, particularly in the services sector. In the absence of an explicit policy addressed to the spatial dimension of service employment, there was a powerful momentum towards the concentration of service employment in the East region, particularly in Dublin. This process laid the basis for the problems that emerged later, as reflected in the over-concentration, congestion and traffic management problems that have characterised the 'Dublin experience' of the 1990s.

Post 1982 and the termination of the IDA's Regional Industrial Plans, along with the fact that no further set of plans were produced heralded a period of retreat from explicit regional policy issues, a situation that was to persist until the early 1990s. It is easy to see, however, why regional policy ostensibly retreated from the national agenda. From the 1970s and the absorption of two major oil crises in 1973 and again in 1978 and the decision to borrow our way out of the ensuing situation set the scene that was to dominate and oppress the economic landscape until the late 1980s, when radical corrective action was finally implemented to rectify the situation.[13] Allied to this the early 1980s witnessed a period of political instability which witnessed several changes of government in rapid succession, and was characterised by a period of delinquent political and economic management that threatened visitations from the global custodians of economic propriety, the IMF. Attention was clearly focused, of necessity, on national issues in the face of severe economic stagnation, which was more resonant with the decade of the 1950s albeit from a higher base of economic activity, than with the brave new world of our membership of the European Economic Community, although transfers from the latter provided an important medium of stability over this period.

Reference to the 1950s conjures up a decade of stagnation, along with economic and social loss to the economy and society, but it was also the decade that laid the conceptual critique of the then prevailing model of economic development and witnessed the implementation of a great deal of the legislative and institutional developments that facilitated later developments in the 1960s. While not exactly comparable in context, the 1980s was also a decade of interrogation and reflection on the future trajectory of industrial and economic development. The interrogation and self-reflection was not addressed to regional policy *per se*, but some of it had rather interesting implications for regional policy and spatial planning. One might reasonably have anticipated that in *Building on Reality 1984-1987*, the Coalition government's National Plan, published in 1984, something of interest pertaining to regional issues to have been included. But in the event regional policy did not feature. In the same year the Government's White Paper on *Industrial Policy* was published,[14] and while containing a mere eleven lines pertaining to regional policy they were of some interest. While regional development, it stated, "... will continue to be an important factor in our industrial development policies," the more interesting comment represented a shift in thinking on the strategy to be pursued. It stated that:

> Less emphasis will however be placed in future on job targets for individual town groups. The aim of policy is mobility and flexibility in the economy so industry must be where it can make greatest progress, rather than stick rigidly to job targets for particular town groups. (p. 47)

Clearly this represented a fundamental break with the compromise approach pursued by the IDA over the period 1973-83. The theme of flexibility was central to the thinking of the White Paper and elsewhere it stated that in future higher grants would be only for "clearly defined industrial sectors and limited periods" (p. 47). While the White Paper was sparse in the amount of space devoted to regional issues, three comments capture what we perceive to have been the significant implications for regional development in this document: (i) the priority of national development is clearly evident, reflecting one of the major tensions identified earlier. While understandable in the circumstances, national priorities were to be pursued at the expense of regional policy, certainly as it had been pursued in the recent past; (ii) the critical theme running through the White Paper was the need for flexibility in future industrial location policy, thereby pre-empting the demand of any one region or locality to inhibit the locational preference of industry; (iii) there was arguably a severing of the link between industrial and regional policies, in that the regional distribution of industry should not act as a constraint on industrial performance. Clearly this represented a shift in thinking in favour of locations that facilitated the needs of industry, particularly foreign industry. Taken in conjunction with the White Paper's emphasis on targeting selective high-technology industrial sectors, such as biotechnology, health-care products and the pharmaceutical industry, the number of locations that could meet their requirements were clearly limited. The reinstatement of a growth-centre strategy was, it is argued, contained in embryonic form at least, in the White Paper of 1984.

If further evidence was required for the shift in thinking in favour of a strategy of growth-centres it was contained in a report from the National

Economic and Social Council, published the following year, titled *Designation of Areas for Industrial Policy.*[15] The purpose of the Report was ostensibly to consider the establishment of objective criteria for determining designation status. While the Report does indeed address the issues of providing a metric to determine the status of designation, the sub-plot which becomes clearly evident later in the Report was to argue for the reintroduction of a growth-centre strategy as the basis for future industrial location policy. It is in effect an un-reconstructed re-run of the earlier arguments of the late 1950s and early 1960s, already referred to earlier in this chapter. The substantive difference in this report was that to ensure the implementation of a new growth-centre policy, objective criteria were recommended to delineate designated areas, arguably to minimise political interference.

This report proceeded on the basis of a distinction between a 'needs' approach to designation and a 'potential' approach. The needs approach was identified with the *status quo* approach to regional policy and interpreted as the identification of the worst off areas within the economy for special assistance or designation on a needs basis. However, the report was not interested in maintaining the *status quo* position and its main thrust was to argue for its abolition and to replace it with criteria for designation based on a 'potential' approach with a view to bringing regional policy into line with the reorientation of industrial policy as contained in the White Paper. The argumentation in favour of the shift to a potential approach to designation is worth quoting:

> The alternative scenario (i.e. the 'potential' approach) would be to depart somewhat from the regional policy emphasis and establish a new rationale for designation. This would result in a grant system being developed which would contribute to a maximisation of industrial growth in the economy. This would require that industry be actively encouraged to locate in the major population centres where viability and growth prospects would be higher and infrastructural development costs would be lower through the realisation of economies of scale. It is obvious that such a basis for designation would involve a substantial departure from the present pattern of wide dispersal of industry.

This report was clear that the issues at hand revolved around a distinction introduced earlier in this chapter. It argued that the basic conflict was between equity considerations which it associated with the 'needs' approach and efficiency which it linked to the 'potential' approach. To date in Ireland, it also argued, too much attention had been placed – in the context of industrial location policy – on equity considerations to the detriment of efficiency.

To reinstate efficiency in the spatial organisation of the economy required a serious reorientation towards a growth-centre strategy of development informed by such developments as: the locational requirements of the new high-technology industry particularly with respect to infrastructure, including physical, social and educational; the intense competition for foreign direct investment; and the emergence of new external developments in Europe, in particular the Single Act, which by this stage had emerged as a major policy issue.[16] As in the 1950s, an extremely difficult decade, similarly in the 1980s there emerged a number of documents which delivered a critique of existing policy and propounded a fundamental re-orientation of industrial strategy, with potentially significant implications for regional policy and spatial planning. Again as in the 1950s the critique and re-orientation of policies contained in these documents contributed in no small way to the achievement of the 'Celtic Tiger', though in the 1980s it was difficult to envisage the emergence of that particular scenario.

From Structural Funds to Spatial Strategies: The Rediscovery of Regional Policy

The rediscovery of interest in issues of regional policy in the 1990s was not born of a new-found enthusiasm to redress the retreat from this domain of public policy in the previous decade. It emerged almost exclusively from external sources emanating from European developments. The emergence of the Single Market agenda and more specifically the creation of the Structural Funds in the early 1990s forced the Irish government to make a number of important regional policy decisions in order to fulfil the requirements for drawing down the monies from these Funds. In 1994 eight new Regional Authorities were created which replaced the defunct Regional Development Organisations and reconfigured the existing spatial planning regions of the country. The statutory responsibilities of the new Regional Authorities were familiar in both their operational objectives and composition. However, it was events in the following year, 1995, which led to one of the most significant developments in Irish regional policy. In that year, five of the newly created Regional Authorities; Dublin, Mid-East, Mid-West, South-East and South-West, surpassed the income limits of Objective 1 status under the rules of the Structural Funds. What ensued was an intense period of negotiations with the European Commission in which the government attempted to retain parts of the Mid-West and South-West, specifically counties Clare and Kerry, as Objective 1 regions. These efforts were largely motivated by local political demands in these areas at this time and when they failed a pragmatic response emerged from the government. The country was divided into two regions, the Border, Midlands and West (BMW) region which qualified as an Objective 1 status region, and the South and East (S&E) region which qualified as an Objective 1 in Transition region according to the rules of the Structural Funds.

Two new Regional Assemblies were established in 1999, one for each of the newly established regions.

The period covered by the first tranche of Structural Funds covered the period 1994-1999, a period that will now be recalled as Ireland's second 'take-off,' to borrow Rostow's famous phrase, coming as it did thirty years after the first 'take-off' in the 1960s.[17] From 1994 the economy began to grow at annual average rates of 9-10 per cent and the 'Celtic Tiger' was born. As the decade progressed the infrastructural deficits, among other things were cruelly exposed and this constituted a domestic source of serious concern to policy makers which had serious regional implications. The situation in Dublin and its environs were particularly serious and the idea that the rest of the country, or selective parts of it at least, could alleviate the congestion problems in Dublin began to take shape. Regional policy was now identified as a means of alleviating the acute concentration and congestion in the Greater Dublin Area.

By the end of the decade, and the termination of the period of the Structural Funds, the government, in response to a European Union request, drew up the National Development Plan (NDP) to cover the period 2000-2006.[18] This would be the mechanism for drawing down further Structural Funds, though the basis of the financing of the NDP, which amounted to €47 billion, was different to the first tranche of Structural Funds. The NDP was organised around a number of Operational Programmes, which included four major economic and social programmes, along with two separate programmes for each of the two new regions. Under the plan the BMW region was to receive 30 per cent of total funding, with the S&E region receiving 70 per cent, though on a per capita basis the BMW region was to receive 15 per cent more than the national average, while the S&E would receive 5 per cent less. The NDP included the pursuit of balanced regional development as a national objective, and of "spreading the benefits of national economic development more widely across the regions" (National Development Plan, 2000, p. 44). The government requested the Department of Environment and Local Government to prepare a National Spatial Strategy (NSS)[19] as part of the NDP to cover a planning horizon from 2002-2020, and this was to provide the strategic means of achieving its objective of balanced regional development.

The presiding ideas that informed the NSS included the achievement of national competitiveness, and reflecting the line of argument of the National Economic and Social Council report discussed in the previous section, the achievement of balanced regional development would involve "developing the full potential of each area to contribute to the optimal performance of the State as a whole – economically, socially and environmentally" (National Spatial Strategy, 2002, p. 11). Clearly the shift from a 'needs' approach to a 'potential' based, as contained in the NESC report of 1985, would now appear to have been given official approval. Looked at more clearly the NSS was rather modest in its innovative thinking. The nomenclature had changed, but the content remained uncannily close to previous proposals.

In place of growth-centres, secondary centres and the smaller towns and villages, we have gateways, hubs and other towns and villages. The spinal chord of this approach is the centrality of urban hierarchy, as it was for the Buchanan Report over thirty years ago. Not that one wishes to crudely engage in an unfair or vulgar reductionist mapping of the NSS to the Buchanan Report. There are new features in the NSS, including the designation of four new gateways, Letterkenny, Sligo, Dundalk, and an innovative concept which includes the three towns of Athlone, Mullingar and Tullamore as constituting a new gateway. Similarly a total of nine hubs are identified, a number of them comprised of two linked centres, such as Tralee/Killarney and Castlebar/Ballina. The selection of the existing gateways, Dublin, Cork, Limerick, Galway, and Waterford, was based on their critical mass as urban centres, while the four new proposed gateways were to enhance the urban structure within their respective regions. The hubs are to support the role of the gateways by virtue of their interaction with their adjacent gateways. Similarly the other towns, villages and rural areas are envisaged as providing various complementary roles to adjacent hubs and gateways.[20]

What should have been a major development in the evolution of Irish regional policy has been disappointing both in its arrival and impact to-date. It is of course much too early to evaluate what the consequences of the NSS will be, whether seen or unforeseen. But the fact that its arrival was almost three years into the life of the National Development Plan – the NSS was launched in November 2002 – did little to enhance its status. This delay was preceded by a series of announcements informing of its continued postponement.

More disappointing, if not more worrying, has been the lack of debate following the launch of the NSS. This response to both its arrival and the absence of debate, critical or otherwise, may indicate either satisfaction with the many compromises struck with respect to competing demands within the NSS, or alternatively it may reflect a certain indifference to the urgency of regional issues in Ireland. We referred earlier to the pragmatic response by government following their failure in negotiations in 1995 with the European Commission to reconfigure counties Clare and Kerry as Objective 1 status regions. The division of the country into two regions, complete with their Regional Assemblies may well be viewed as both a pragmatic and even tactically ingenious manoeuvre to maximise the draw down of Structural and Cohesion Funds. There is a thin line between pragmatism and a healthy scepticism in this context, in that one could be allowed a justifiable scepticism, some might say cynicism, in response to the government's decision to configure the country into the BMW and S&E regions. This from an administration that had staunchly refused to engage any concession to the devolution of any powers to the regions. The conventional line, which was propagated and steadfastly adhered to on all possible occasions, particularly since our entry into the European Economic Community in 1973, revolved around two lines of argument. One involved an internal dimension that invoked the dangers of dispute, dissention and disagreement within and between the regions if power was conceded. The spectre of a belligerent localism was clearly anathema to the mandarin class. A second line of argument, which had a much higher public profile, as to why Ireland could not even contemplate the idea of regional devolution was an external one in relation to our bargaining power in Brussels. Ireland as a single region was a mantra, bordering on the sacrosanct, that provided the rationale for the excessive centralisation of the administrative system.

Space does not permit an extended analysis of the missed opportunity that the publication of the NSS presented to address a number of major issues pertaining to the spatial or regional dimension of Irish economic, social and administrative policy. A large complex and involved agenda centres around each of the following issues: the continued and clever management of the NSS within the NDP by the central authorities, reflecting the excessive, if not obsessive, disposition of a centralised mind-set, notwithstanding a European commitment to the principles of subsidiarity;[21] the opportunity to revisit and examine the future reform of local government, a long-standing agenda with deeply embedded problems of structure and process;[22] and the opportunity to seriously reconsider, as distinct from tinkering with the existing situation, the geographic divisions of the country considered in both their functional and administrative dimensions.[23] Any one of these issues contains an extensive and challenging agenda; taken together they constitute the material for an urgent national debate, allied to the need for equally extensive analytical research that should inform this debate. In the event the publication and the preparatory work leading to what should have been a major exercise in social, strategic and public choice within the framework of the NSS was missed. It reflects on balance the view that has, with the exception of brief interludes, dominated the official view of regional policy as being of secondary importance.

Conclusion

This short chapter has attempted to survey a half-century of Irish regional policy in the post-war period, from its modest beginnings in 1952 to the publication of the National Spatial Strategy in 2002. The dynamics of its unfolding is complicated, reflecting the innate difficulties of public policy formation and implementation. The argument is that it has revolved around a small number of critical tensions or trade-offs, such as that between the requirements of national growth and regional development, the equity-efficiency balance in framing one's view of the role of regional policy, and the responses to external circumstances, in this chase towards the European dimension but increasingly to the demands of an intensifying globalisation. In a short chapter it is not possible to do justice to either the complexities of the policy issues involved, of which the ones identified above constitute a sub-set rather than a comprehensive list, nor to provide the full and intricate narrative of events surrounding the formation of such policy. Notwithstanding the constraints of space, it is hoped that this chapter has conveyed something of the richness of the debate, the difficulties involved, and the challenging implications for the economy and society in a policy domain that for too long has been treated as the 'Cinderella' of Irish public policy.

Endnotes

1   Our interest is the economic dimension of regional policy. For a historical survey of physical planning in Ireland, see Bannon (1989).

2   See Hunt (1989) for a comprehensive overview of the main theories of economic development that emerged in the post-war period.

3   See Lipton (1977) for an elaboration of this relationship.

4   Boylan (1974).

5   See Kennedy (1986, 1988).

6   Boylan (1984).

7   See *Economic Development* (1958); Committee on Industrial Organisation (1963); and National Industrial and Economic Council (1969).

8   For the theoretical debate on balanced and unbalanced growth and forward and backward linkages see the seminal texts by Nurkse (1953), Myrdal (1957) and Hirschman (1958).

9   His classic paper is Perroux (1955), available in English in Livingstone (1971).

10   Buchanan (1968).

11   See Johnson (1981) and Ross (1978).

12   For an examination of the West region, see Boylan (1985, 1996).

13   For an 'insider' overview of this period and the ensuing economic boom of the 1990s, see MacSharry and White (2000).

14   White Paper on Industrial Policy (1984).

15   National Economic and Social Council (1985).

16   On the re-orientation of industrial policy and its implication for regional policy see Boylan and Cuddy (1984).

17   For an analysis of the role of the Structural Funds see Bradley and Fitzgerald (1989) and Matthews (1994).

18   National Development Plan (1999).

19   The National Spatial Strategy (2002).

20   For the most recent empirical work on regional policy issues, see Boyle, McCarthy & Walsh (1998); O'Leary (1997, 2001) and the interesting collection of essays in O'Leary (2003).

21   See Murray (2004) for an interesting discussion of the potential role of the European Spatial Development Perspective

22   See Forde (2005)

23   See OECD (2002)

References

Bannon, M. J. (ed.) (1989) *Planning: the Irish experience 1920-1988*, Dublin, Wolfhound Press.

Boylan, T.A. (1974) *Regional policy in contemporary Ireland,* Paper presented to Annual Conference of the Economic and Social History Society of Ireland, University College Galway, September 1974.

Boylan, T.A. (1984) The drive to industrialise, in W.J.L. Ryan (ed.) *Irish industry in the eighties*, Dublin, Helicon Press.

Boylan, T.A. (1985) Industrial location in the West: how should future non-farm employment be distributed? in *Conference Proceedings*, Dublin, Agricultural Research Institute.

Boylan, T.A. (1996) Rural industrialisation and rural poverty, in C. Curtin, T. Haase and H. Tovey (eds.) *Poverty in rural Ireland: a political economy perspective*, Dublin, Oak Tree Press, in association with Combat Poverty Agency.

Boylan, T.A. & Cuddy, M.P. (1984) Regional industrial policy: performance and challenge, *Administration*, 32(3), pp.255-71.

Boyle, G., McCarthy, T. and Walsh, J. (1988/9) Regional income differentials and the issue of regional income equalisation in Ireland, *Journal of the Statistical and Social Inquiry Society of Ireland*, xxviii (1), pp.155-211.

Bradley, J. and Fitzgerald, J. (1989) The EC Structural Funds and economic growth, in *Medium Term Review: 1989-1994*, Dublin, Economic and Social Research Institute.

Buchanan, C. and Partners (1968) *Regional Studies in Ireland*, Dublin, An Foras Forbartha.

Committee on Industrial Organisation (1963) *Fourth Interim Report: Industrial Grants*, Dublin, Stationery Office.

Economic Development (1958) Dublin, Stationery Office.

Forde, C. (2005) Participatory democracy or pseudo-participation? Local Government reform in Ireland, *Local Government Studies*, 31(2), pp.137-48.

Hirschman, A. (1958) *The strategy of economic development*, New Haven, Yale University Press.

Hunt, D. (1989) *Economic theories of development: an analysis of competing paradigms*, Hemel Hempstead, Harvester Wheatsheaf.

Johnson, J.J. (1981) Republic of Ireland, in H.D. Clout (ed.) *Regional development in Western Europe*, New York, J. Wiley and Sons.

Kennedy, K.A. (ed.) (1986) *Ireland in transition: economic and social change since 1960*, Cork, Mercier Press.

Kennedy, K.A., Giblin, T. and McHugh, D. (1988) *The economic development of Ireland in the Twentieth Century*, London and New York, Routledge.

Lipton, M. (1977) *Why poor people stay poor*, Cambridge, Cambridge University Press.

Livingstone, I. (ed.) (1971) *Economic policy for development*, Harmondswork, Penguin.

MacSharry, R. and White, P. (2000) *The making of the Celtic Tiger: the inside story of Ireland's boom economy*, Cork, Mercier Press.

Matthews, A. (1994) *Managing the EU Structural Funds in Ireland*, Cork, Cork University Press.

Murray, M. (2004) Strategic spatial planning on the island of Ireland: towards a new territorial logic?, *Innovation: The European Journal of Social Science Research*, 17(3), pp.227-42.

Myrdal, G. (1957) *Economic theory and underdeveloped countries*, London, Duckworth.

National Industrial and Economic Council (1969) *Report on physical planning*, Report No. 26, Dublin, Stationery Office.

National Economic and Social Council (1985) *Designation of areas for industrial policy*, Report No. 81, Dublin, National Economic and Social Council.

National Development Plan 2000-2006 (1999) Dublin, Stationery Office.

National Spatial Strategy 2002-2020: people, places and potential (2002) Dublin, Stationery Office.

Nurkse, R. (1953) *Problems of capital formation in underdeveloped countries*, Oxford, Blackwell.

OECD (2002) *Redefining territories: the functional regions*, Paris, Organisation for Economic Cooperation and Development.

O'Leary, E. (1997) The convergence performance of Ireland among EU countries: 1960-90, *Journal of Economic Studies*, 24(1-2), pp.43-58.

O'Leary, E. (2001) Regional divergence in the Celtic Tiger: the policy dilemma, *Irish Banking Review*, Spring 2001.

O'Leary, E. (ed.) (2003) *Irish regional development: a new agenda*, Dublin, The Liffey Press.

Perroux, F. (1955) La nation de pole de croissance, *Economie Appliquee*, 8 (1-2).

Ross, M. (1978) Comprehensiveness in regional policy, in B.R. Dowling and J. Durkan (eds.) *Irish economic policy: a review of major issues*, Dublin, The Economic and Social Research Institute).

White Paper on industrial policy (1984) Dublin, Stationery Office.

Chapter 6

The Irish BMW Region – Towards Convergence or Divergence?

Michael J. Bannon

Introduction

This chapter draws extensively upon a case study of the Border, Midland and Western (BMW) Region prepared by this author in 2003. This case study was one of twenty-eight regional case studies undertaken as part of the preparatory work for the European Commission's third report on economic and social cohesion - *New Partnership for Cohesion: Convergence, Competitiveness, Cooperation* (European Commission, 2004). The chapter also draws upon some post 2003 material, which has now become available. The BMW Region is examined in its national context and its changing relative economic and social position is documented and assessed. New administrative arrangements for the region are also discussed.

Work for the EU case study required the preparation of time-series data on monetary transfers into the BMW Region over the decade 1992 to 2002. Some of the more important of these data findings are presented below, including the scale of investment proposed under the *National Development Plan 2000-2006* (Government of Ireland, 1999). The performance of the region since 1996 is discussed both in terms of the region itself and relative to the overall performance of the State. The potential of the *National Spatial Strategy, 2002-2020* (Department of Environment and Local Government, 2002), if implemented, to transform the role of the BMW region is also discussed. The chapter concludes with an assessment of the adequacy or efficacy of regional policy for the BMW Region.

The BMW Region's Administrative Context

For more than twenty years the Republic of Ireland had been classified as a single Objective I region with all parts of the State equally eligible for regional aid. The regionalisation arrangements negotiated by the Irish authorities in the context of the Agenda 2000 agreement resulted in the designation of the State into two regions for Structural Funds purposes. The two NUTS II regions are the Border, Midland and Western Region (Figure 6.1) which has retained

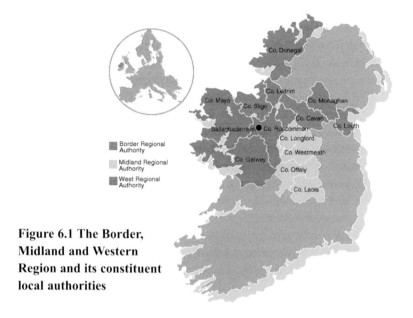

Border Regional
Authority

Midland Regional
Authority

West Regional
Authority

**Figure 6.1 The Border,
Midland and Western
Region and its constituent
local authorities**

Objective 1 status for the purpose of Structural Funds for the full period up to 2006, and the Southern and Eastern Region (S&E Region) which qualified for a six year phasing out regime for Objective 1 Structural Funding up to the end of 2005. Following this designation, two new Regional Assemblies were established and came into effect on the 21st July 1999 under the Local Government Act, 1991 (Regional Authorities) (Establishment) Order, 1999. The main functions of each Regional Assembly are broadly similar and, in the case of the BMW Region, the functions of the Regional Assembly are to:

- manage the BMW Regional Operational Programme under the *National Development Plan 200-2006*;

- monitor the general impact of all E.U. Programmes under the *National Development Plan / Community Support Framework* in the Border, Midland and Western Region;

- promote the co-ordination of the provision of public services in the Region, which comprises three contiguous NUTS III regions and thirteen county/city authorities, as well as a number of smaller urban authorities (Table 6.1). In addition to the constituent local authorities in the region, Udaras Na Gaeltachta, plays a developmental role in the Irish language speaking parts of Counties Donegal, Galway and Mayo.

Table 6.1: Administrative structures within the BMW Region

Level (NUTS) II Region	Level (NUTS) III Region	Local Authorities
Border Midland and Western Region	Border Region	Cavan Donegal Leitrim Louth Monaghan Sligo
	Midland Region	Laois Longford Offaly Westmeath
	West Region	Galway City & County Mayo Roscommon

The Physical, Demographic and Economic Dimensions of the BMW Region

The BMW Region is sparsely populated and essentially rural in character. The Region covers an area of 33,276 sq. kms., which is approximately twice the size of the average EU NUTS II region (15,684 sq. kms). The BMW Region accounts for 47.4 percent of the State's landmass, but it only contained 26.5 percent of the total population of the State in 2002 (BMW, 2003; Fitzpatrick et. al., 1999) With the exception of its eastern parts, the BMW region is characterised by a relatively difficult topography, poor quality land, relatively high rainfall levels, an over dependence on small farm agriculture, poor physical and information infrastructures, low levels of urbanisation and innovation and a lack of adequate off-farm employment. While parts of the eastern counties of Louth, Westmeath, Offaly and Laois are increasingly influenced by the overspill of the Dublin agglomeration, much of the BMW Region has been classified in the *National Spatial Strategy, 2002-2020* as consisting of large areas described as either being "weak" or "remote" (NSS, p.54).

The BMW Region is largely rural with a widely dispersed population and a heavy reliance on small-scale and dispersed employment sectors. Virtually all of the land in the Region is classified as "severely handicapped" or "less severely handicapped". Consequently, the Region is very dependent on locally-provided and locally maintained infrastructures. Roads are generally of poorer quality and they are predominantly non-national roads. All but two of the country's significant commercial ports are outside the BMW Region. In general, investment in telecommunications and related infrastructures in the BMW Region lags significantly behind levels in the State's other NUTS II region, the S&E Region. This adverse situation is highlighted by the reality that the BMW region accounts for only 21.0 percent of the total Gross Value Added (GVA) of the State well below its share of territory or population. While the BMW Region retains Objective I status up to 2006 under the current EU Community Support Framework, the Region faces a major task in reaching a standard of development comparable to that in the S&E Region of the State or that of the Greater Dublin Area (GDA), in particular.

As a consequence of the BMW Region's relatively poor physical endowment, its past history of over population and its limited urban growth, almost all parts of the Region have experienced lengthy and persistent out-migration of population, at least up to the 1990's. While the population of the State increased by 554,000 (or + 18.7 percent) between 1926 and 1991, the population of the BMW Region actually declined by 168,000 (or –15.0 percent) over the same period. During this sixty-five year period the region's share of the population of the State declined from 37.6 percent in 1926 to 26.9 percent in 1991. Over much of the period from 1926 up to the 1990s, population decline was both persistent and widespread across almost all of the Region. In contrast, between 1926 and 1991 the population of Ireland's S&E Region has increased by almost the equivalent of the BMW's total 1991 population. The demographic balance of the country was shifting in favour of the S&E Region, and towards the GDA in particular. Such a transformation of the patterns of population gave rise to repeated calls to "save the west" and to political intervention to assist declining areas.

Between 1961 and 1991 the BMW Region's population grew by a mere 7.4 per cent (from 883,455 to 948,945 persons), mostly in and around the Region's larger urban centres, while the Region's share of the total population of the state continued to decrease. As can be seen in Table 6.2, the three NUTS III regions which constitute the BMW Region all experienced strong growth between 1991 and 2002, with the BMW Region population increasing 89,066 persons, or by 9.4 percent.

Table 6.2: Population change in the BMW Region, 1991 – 2002

NUTS III Regions	1991	1996	2002	Percentage Change 1991-2 002
Border	402,987	407,295	432,366	+7.3
Midland	202,984	205,542	225,588	+11.1
West	342,974	352,353	380,057	+10.8
Total BMW	948,945	965,190	1,038,011	+9.4
BMW as % of Total State	26.9	26.6	26.5	

The rate of growth increased during the latter part of the period, although even this proved insufficient to enable the region to increase its share of the population of the State. The Region's growth performance remained significantly behind that of the S&E Region over the same period; population growth was largely driven by urban expansion both from within the Region's urban centres, as well as through overspill from the GDA.

During the 1991 – 2002 period there occurred a significant restructuring of the population of the BMW Region. Growth took place in and around the larger towns with a particular tendency "to take the town into the countryside", while large tracts of the more remote rural areas continued to decline. Growth was largely confined to urban areas, particularly Galway, Mullingar, Drogheda and Letterkenny (Table 6.3).

Table 6.3: Population change in larger urban centres, 1996 – 2002

City/Town	1996	2002	Population Increase	
			Number	Percentage
Galway City	57,363	66,163	8,800	15.3
Dundalk	30,195	32,505	2,310	7.7
Drogheda	25,282	31,020	5,738	22.7
Sligo	18,509	19,735	1,226	6.6
Athlone	15,544	15,936	392	2.5
Mullingar	12,492	15,621	3,129	25.0
Letterkenny	11,966	15,231	3,265	27.0
Portlaoise	9,474	12,127	2,653	28.0
Castlebar	8,532	11,371	2,839	33.3
Tullamore	10,039	11,098	1,059	10.5

Between 1996 and 2002 two-thirds of total population increase took place in the 'aggregate town' areas of the Region, with much of the remainder accounted for by increasingly long distance commuting from the eastern parts of the Region, particularly from within counties Laois, Louth and Westmeath, as residential locations for people working in the GDA. The BMW Region is increasingly driven by its urban economy, as well as by overspill from Dublin, which in turn, reflects the changing nature of work open to the residents of the Region.

A significant restructuring of the BMW regional economy has taken place in the ten years between 1992 and 2002 (Table 6.4). One of the most obvious features of Table 6.4 is the continued serious regional decline of employment in agriculture, which lost over one quarter of its employment between 1992 and 2002. However, the decline in employment in the BMW Region should not cloud the fact that the agricultural sector remains important to the productivity of the Region and this sector continues to make a large contribution to its GVA.

Table 6.4: Estimated persons at work by sector, BMW Region 1992 – 2002

Sector	1992	2002	Change	
			Number	Percentage
Agriculture, Forestry and Fishing:	68,100	49,700	-18,400	-27.1
Production, Building and Construction:	85,800	137,100	+51,300	+59.8
Services:	146,500	252,000	+105,500	+72.0
Total Employed	300,400	438,800	138,400	+46.1

Source: CSO Labour Force Survey, 1992 (adjusted) and 2002 data from CSO.

Employment in the industrial and construction sectors increased by 60 per cent, changing the BMW Region's share of total employment in this sector from 26.6 per cent in 1992 to 28.3 per cent in 2002. But it was employment growth in the service sector that accounted for over three-quarters of all net new job creation between 1992 and 2002. This expansion included new jobs in education, health, professional services, local administration and recreation or personal services. Many of these sectors are likely to have concentrated in and around Galway – the largest urban centre in the Region with the only university in the BMW Region. Galway has developed as a major tourism focus and the city has become an established centre for professional services.

The result has been a slight increase in the regional share of total service employment by 2002. But, overall, the Region's share of total employment in the State dropped slightly from 25.8 per cent in 1992 to 25.1 per cent in 2002.

While the interpretation of data on GDP or GVA remains the subject of debate, the available data assists in determining the trends over time and in assessing comparative regional performance. Table 6.5 presents GVA data for the years 1995 to 2002 for the BMW Region, for its component NUTS III regions and for the State as a whole. The data show that per capita GVA for the BMW Region in 1995 was at 74.9 percent of that for the State; by 2000 that share had declined to 71.2 per cent of the total, with a further decline to 69.1 percent by 2002. While there was little variation in GVA per person at the NUTS III level within the BMW Region, there were stark contrasts for the year 2002 between the BMW's GVA index level at 71.2, the S&E Region's at 111.1 and the NUTS III Dublin region with a score of 128.9. While the contribution of the *Agriculture, Forestry and Fishing* branch of the economy has been especially important in the case of the BMW Region, the composition of regional GVA for 2002 indicates a significant change in the importance of services in the BMW accounts. The variations in regional GVA patterns are further mirrored in the 2002 data on disposable income per person, with a difference of 11.2 per cent between the BMW and S&E Regions, and almost a 20 percent difference between income levels in Dublin and the BMW Region, although the income gap is narrowing over time.

Table 6.5: Gross value added per person at basic prices, 1995–2002 in €.

NUTS III Regions	1995	2000	2002
Border Region	10,174	16,571	20,851
Midland	9,047	15,172	18,565
West	9,867	18,999	20,716
Total BMW Region:	9,823	17,149	20,305
Total State:	13,111	24,072	29,371

Source: CSO Regional Accounts for the years 1995 to 2002.

Selected European Union Transfers into the BMW Region

Over many decades, initially under the Congested Districts Board and then under the *1952 Undeveloped Areas Act,* most counties within the territory of the BMW Region benefited from various forms of regional aid, designed to alleviate poverty and congestion and to transform and modernise the economy and social structure of the area. Over the past quarter century various forms of

EU supports, most especially agricultural supports and regional aid, have further assisted in the transformation of what had been one of the most seriously disadvantaged regions of the EU. Improved data sources enable an examination of the scale of some of these payments over a ten year period and an assessment of their relative importance. This section provides data on a number of the principal EU schemes and transfers, using data for the decade 1992 to 2002.

Agriculture payments into the BMW Region, 1992-2002
Agriculture represents one of Ireland's most important export industries and is considered important in terms of both its economic role and as an essential component of rural development, protecting the rural way of life. The agriculture sector has been a major beneficiary of transfers from the European Commission under both the Common Agricultural Policy and the EAGGF. Table 6.6 summarises the principal agriculture related programmes, the levels of payments under each and the share of such transfers going to the BMW Region, with most of the data covering the ten years 1992 to 2002. The Table documents a total of €4,241.6 million going to the various schemes operating in the Region. This amount represents 45.1 per cent of the total payments to the State over the period 1992-2002, a figure broadly commensurate with the BMW's share of the territory of the State. Those programmes designed to support the intensification of agriculture as an industry generally contribute smaller shares to the BMW than programmes designed to assist more marginal agriculture through compensatory measures or environmental initiatives. The share of payments to the BMW Region under the Rural Environmental Protection Scheme is notable, as is the increased share of total funding received by the Region for the year 2002.

Table 6.6: EU agriculture payments to the BMW Region, € Millions.

Programme	Total Payments BMW 1992 – 2002	Average annual Payment	Expenditure in 2002	Percentage of State	
				1992 – 2002	2002
Suckler Cow Premium	996.7	87.9	125.1	54.1	54.8
Ewe Premium*	387.2	55.3	53.8	54.1	54.9
Special Beef Premium*	622.6	89.0	104.1	37.9	38.8
Slaughter Premium*	131.4	18.8	46.5	35.8	36.9
Compensatory*	766.0	69.7	143.4	62.4	60.1
Arable Aid*	169.9	24.3	26.5	20.3	20.7
Extensification *	346.5	49.5	0.0	48.8	0.0
Early Retirement Scheme**	166.2	18.5	22.0	28.1	27.8
Rural Environment Protection Scheme**	655.1	72.8	101.8	58.6	58.9
Total EU Payments	4,241.6	–	623.2	45.1	47.4

Source: Data supplied by Department of Agriculture, Food and Rural Development.
* Data for1996 to 2002; ** Data for 1994 to 2002.

The Cohesion Fund for Ireland

Ireland was one of four Member States to benefit from the Cohesion Fund which was established at the Edinburgh summit in1993. The Cohesion Fund has made an important contribution to the improvement of Ireland's infrastructure over the ten years up to the end of 2002, involving a total investment of almost €2 billion in Irish based projects since its inception in 1993 (Table 6.7).

Table 6.7: Cohesion Fund commitment distribution, 1993 – 2002 (€ Millions)

1993	1994	1995	1996	1997	1998	1999	2000	2001	2002
141.9	167.7	190.7	219.6	245.4	258.6	271.9	188.6	127.4	184.9
Total: €1,996.8									

Source: Data supplied by the Department of Finance, Dublin.

Data on the Cohesion Fund is available on a project basis rather than by region. An examination of the project payments shows that a relatively small share of the fund's allocations have been invested in the BMW Region. Apart from works on the M1 Dublin to Belfast road in County Louth, the major road works within the BMW Region which received Cohesion funding were the Longford By-Pass (€9.1 million); the Curlews By-Pass on the N4 route to Sligo (€31.3 million); the Collooney–Sligo road (€41.5 million) and the Galway Eastern approach road (€9.9 million). Approximately fifteen water supply and wastewater schemes throughout the Region, including those serving the urban centres of Dundalk and Drogheda, have received a total of €366.4 million from the Cohesion Fund up to the end of 2002. There has also been some allocation for the improvement of the Dublin to Galway rail line, some conservation funding and two river catchment studies. However, it has to be noted that none of the €561.1 million allocated for the years 2000 to 2003 inclusive had been explicitly allocated to projects or locations within the BMW Region by early 2003.

Funding for the Region's fishing industry
Since around 1990 there has been a concerted effort to develop the Irish fishing industry. This has been undertaken within the framework of Ireland's National Development Plans, and involving Irish public and private sector assistance, together with EU support from the Fisheries Guidance Fund, the European Regional Development Fund (ERDF), the European Social Fund (ESF) and contributions from both the EU INTERREG and PEACE programmes. In turn, the fishing industry has made an increasing contribution to Irish development over the years, with the value of fishery product exports increasing from €240 million in 1992 to almost €400 million in 2002. Fisheries development is especially important in many of the remoter areas of the BMW Region, where alternative sources of economic activity and employment have been limited.

The PESCA Community Initiative 1994-1999 was important for Ireland and provided funding and an integrated approach to the development of the industry. The Initiative had a total forecast expenditure of €183.5 million, with two of its four implementation zones being within the BMW Region.

In 1998 the Government launched the Whitefish Renewal Programme to assist in the provision of equipment and the modernisation of the existing fleet. A total of 700 projects around the country have been assisted under this programme. By mid 1993 a total of €5.7 million had been paid in grants to the industry under the programme, with 56.0 percent of the total payments going to assist developments in the coastal counties of the BMW Region, principally in the counties of Donegal, Galway and Louth. In *the National Development Plan, 2000-2006* a further sum of €64 million has been earmarked for the continued development of the marine sector through research, technological development and innovation, with €18 million earmarked for investment in the BMW Region as of mid 2003.

ESF contribution to FAS training initiatives
The *Community Support Framework for Ireland 1994–1999* allocated €2,203 million from the European Social Fund for human resource development over the six years of the Programme, while *the National Development Plan 2000 – 2006* assigned an expenditure of €12.6 billion for employment and human resource development, of which just under 30 percent is allocated to the BMW Region. Expenditure in the years 2000 and 2001 by FAS, the Irish Employment and Training Authority, shows a 34.7 percent share of their ESF expenditure going into the BMW Region (Table 6.8).

Table 6.8: ESF expenditure through FAS, 2000 – 2001 (€ Millions)

NUTS III Regions	2000	2001	Total BMW	Region Share of National Total
Border	10.266	10.635	20.901	16.4
Midlands	5.157	5.596	10.753	8.4
West	6.044	6.554	12.598	9.9
Total BMW:	21.467	22.785	44.252	34.7

Source: Data supplied by FAS, the Irish Employment and Training Authority.

Other EU transfers to the BMW Region
The LEADER I and LEADER II Community Initiatives operated in Ireland with considerable success from 1992 to 2000. From 2000 to 2006 the LEADER programme is being delivered in two ways. The LEADER+ Initiative, with a public contribution of €73.7 million, is in place in 22 localities throughout the country, of which 10 are in the BMW Region. Alongside these groups there are some thirteen Area Based National Rural Development Programme Groups, of which seven are in the BMW Region. These groups, together with three Collective Bodies, are to receive a total of €75.6 million as part of the Regional Operational Programmes. The general impression is that the funds are widely distributed and that allocations have more regard for per capita and local needs, rather than strategic considerations.
    INTERREG can be regarded as one of the most significant Community Initiatives affecting the BMW Region. Under the cross-border INTERREG II programme a total of €274 million was invested by the EU in the Region,

particularly under its sub-programme 5 where the EU spent €159 million on Environmental Protection measures. The INTERREG IIIA cross-border programme 2000 – 2006 has a total financial allocation of €180 million.

It is anticipated that the PEACE II programme will provide approximately €700 million for project development in the relevant territories of Northern Ireland and the Republic. The share of total funding going to the Republic is of the order of 20.0 percent.

Over the past quarter century, particularly since 1992, the EU has made a significant and diverse contribution to the funding of programmes across the State. In general these programmes have been seen as part of Ireland's national development process and they have promoted the national objectives of supporting the development and modernisation of the economy and the infrastructure of the BMW Region. As such, they have played an important part in the modest turn around of this Region in the 1990s, which has experienced sustained population and employment growth since 1991.

Regional transfers to BMW Region under national policies
Over the fifty years since 1952 Ireland has operated a range of regional policies, which through time have become increasingly national in scope, but with higher levels of assistance allowable in "disadvantaged" regions. All such regional aid payments have been increasingly regulated under EU competition rules and are to be phased out from 2006. In the Irish case such regional assistance has been regarded as an important factor in attracting industry and some service enterprises into the disadvantaged areas, including much of the BMW Region. The principal state aids relate to industrial and tourism development supports, as well as infrastructural developments. The following sections of this chapter look at some of the more important of these regional aids.

State aid to industry: payments by the principal agencies, 1992 – 2002
In total, a sum of €3,063 million has been invested in encouraging and assisting enterprises to develop or to locate in the State between 1992 and 2002, with just under €750 million given to support enterprises locating in the BMW Region, i.e. 24.5 per cent of the overall total. These figures represent the payments by all the principal development agencies of the State; in the case of the BMW Region these include the Industrial Development Authority, Enterprise Ireland and Udaras Na Gaeltachta. Table 6.9 provides an overview of direct payments to companies for the eleven years 1992 to 2002, totalling €746,480,000. The percentage share of the total being invested in the BMW Region has varied from year to year, being highest at 31.0 percent in 2000 and lowest at 20.6 percent in the year 2002. Of the €1,515 million invested by the IDA in enterprise supports in the State over the 1992-2002 period, the amount

Table 6.9: Direct payments to companies (all principal agencies) 1992 – 2002, (€000s)

	1992	1993	1994	1995	1996	1997	1998	1999	2000	2001	2002
All Agencies											
Border	21,716	27,953	26,479	27,632	29,950	34,461	31,871	32,199	44,215	19,744	23,760
Midlands	8,756	8,813	8,680	6,476	6,263	8,790	11,122	5,923	7,020	8,451	6,760
West	18,823	17,198	24,542	29,003	35,722	42,507	37,955	33,508	45,088	37,431	17,669
Total BMW €000	49295	53964	59701	63111	71935	85758	80948	71630	96323	65626	48189
BMW % Share	25.8	23.5	30.2	25.1	21.7	24.6	23.4	21.1	31.0	23.4	20.6

Source: Data supplied by Forfas. Includes relatively small amounts paid by FAS, Shannon Development and An Bord Bia.

going to the BMW region was €270 million or 17.8 percent of the total, predominantly in Galway and the remainder of the West Region. In the case of Enterprise Ireland, charged with indigenous development, the total invested in the State was €1,162 million, of which €312 million or 26.9 percent of total assistance went into the BMW Region, predominantly into the Border Region. Within the BMW Region, the Midlands (NUTS III) Region received a relatively small share of the total funding going into the BMW Region under this heading. Finally, Udaras Na Gaeltachta, the development authority for Irish speaking areas, spent a total of €178 million in the years 1992-2002, of which 87.6 percent was invested in the BMW Region, in firms in Donegal, Galway and Mayo. Apart from the agricultural payments made to the Region over the 1992-2002 period, these direct payments to companies represent the next single major source of support.

The National Development Plan approach
Ireland is now more than half-way through the implementation of the third of its National Development Plans, covering the years 1989 through to 2006. The *National Development Plan, 1989-1993* detailed an investment and expenditure programme in excess of £9,110 million (€11,567), of which 31.9 percent (€ 3,690.1 million), was allocated in respect of an area approximately the same as the current BMW Region. The *National Development Plan, 1994-1999* was developed around an expenditure programme of £16,668.6 million (€21,164.8 million), of which 29.8 percent (€6,301.8) was earmarked for the BMW Region. The *National Development Plan, 2000-2006* is based on an expenditure programme of €51,535.9 million. This programme of action is detailed in Table 6.10 in terms of the funding for each Operational Programme and the share of investment proposed for each of the two NUTS II regions.

Table 6.10: National Development Plan, 2000-2006 expenditure levels by Operational Programme and NUTS II Region (€millions)

Programme 2000-2006	Total Expenditure	EU Contribution		Expenditure in BMW	
		Amount	% Share	Amount	% Share
Economic & Social Infrastructure	22,360.1	1,412.0	6.3	5,958.5	26.6
Employment and Human Resources	12,562.7	880.0	7.0	3,595.0	28.6
Productive Sector	5,724.2	418.0	7.1	2,100.0	36.7
BMW Regional O.P.	2,646.1	375.0	14.2	2,646.1	100.0
S&E Regional O.P.	3,791.4	538.0	14.2	–	–
PEACE Programme	127.0	106.0	83.5	127.0	100.0
Total Programme:	47,212.4*	3,729	7.9	14,426.6	30.6

*CAP Rural Development Programme of € 4323.5 million excluded from regional Table. See Table 2 above.

Almost half of the total expenditure under the *National Development Plan 2000-2006* is devoted to the Economic and Social Infrastructure Operational Programme, with a 26.6 per cent share of this investment proposed for the BMW Region. The next largest Operational Programme is that for Employment and Human Resources with a budget of €12.6 billion over the period of the plan and a 28.6 share of the investment proposed for the BMW Region. These figures include proposed investments in roads and other forms of transport infrastructure. They also include proposed investment levels for tourism developments in the country and the BMW Region. An important component of *National Development Plan* expenditure is in environmental improvement works, which have been calculated to account for €18.3 billion of expenditure under the plan (Clinch, 2001).

Implications for the future of the BMW Region: discussion of key issues
The BMW Region continues to lag behind the national average, and the Dublin NUTS III region, in terms of productivity, wealth and employment diversity and growth. The principal strengths of the Region lie in natural beauty, its potential for tourism development and its capacity to benefit from

the marine endowment. Eastern parts of the Region benefit from having better quality land, closer access to the Dublin labour market and the GDA in general, while County Louth has the further economic advantage of being a key location on the Dublin – Belfast corridor. The weaknesses of the BMW Region stem from its relatively high scores on a wide range of indicators of multi-dimensional disadvantage. These arise from the Region's physical environment for development, its relative remoteness, poor infrastructures, limited urbanisation and relatively few opportunities for graduates. But, perhaps, the greatest disadvantage lies in the highly centralised nature of this small state, where the BMW Region is seen as a classic peripheral region largely run by the centralised system. The positive outturns for the Region in the 1990s, as measured in terms of population, employment and income levels, are in stark contrast to the long history of economic and social decline which has affected much of the Region for the previous century and a half. The chapter concludes with a review of some pressing issues.

Regional boundaries – the influence of Dublin
Welcome as the Region's growth performance since 1990 has been, it has not been of a sufficient scale to increase the Region's share of the total population or employment in the State. The BMW Region has remained largely peripheral to the Dublin centred "Celtic Tiger" phenomenon. While the BMW Region has been ranked high relative to most other Objective I regions across the former fifteen member EU (Southern & Eastern Region 2003), the Region's growth has failed to keep pace with that of the S&E Region, especially with the rapid growth of the Greater Dublin Area. Analysis of the BMW Region's performance is made difficult by the fact that the boundaries of Irish regions, both at NUTS II and NUTS III levels, have little regard for functional realities or for modern urban spheres of influence. As a result, it is difficult to determine accurately the extent to which the BMW Region's growth has been attributable to endogenous factors from within, or fuelled by the exogenous expansion of the Greater Dublin Area and the developments along the Dublin to Belfast corridor in Co Louth.

Impact of monetary transfers – a diminishing resource
This chapter has also devoted considerable attention to improved time-series data in respect of both EU and nationally funded transfers and investments into the BMW Region, mostly from 1992 to 2002 inclusive. These monetary transfers, most notably under the Common Agriculture Policy have done much to improve living standards across the Region. Other programmes, such as the Cohesion Fund, have assisted in improving aspects of the Region's infrastructure, while Direct Payments to Companies through the work of the Irish development agencies have helped to generate new enterprise,

employment, innovation and structural change. A disconcerting feature of these direct payments has been the relatively small share of the total investment going into the BMW Region over time – 23.4 percent of funding as against the Region's 26.5 percent share of population and its 47.4 percent of the territory of the State. Another important feature of a number of the monetary transfers since1992 has been their increasing emphasis on environmental considerations as seen in the REPS scheme and in environmental improvement expenditures under the *National Development Plan 2000-2006.*

Need for strategic investment over "fair share" mentality
While it can be seen that Irish direct payments to companies favoured the S&E Region and especially the Greater Dublin Area, the wider reality is that generally Irish planning policy has been repeatedly frustrated by political pressures to insist on a "distributional bias" in regional investments and to insist that each area or each group receives its "fair share". Such tendencies militate against strategic choices, as does the actions of politicians and their advisers who "shirk the task of prioritising" (O'Leary, 2002). O'Leary puts the blame for the failure of the BMW Region to grow more rapidly on those who have not shown "much appetite for to make the necessary trade-offs in the selection of growth centres" and thus have failed to provide an environment in which internationally competitive enterprise might be embedded in Ireland's regional economies. Such was the fate of the 1969 *Regional Studies in Ireland* regional growth centre strategy (Buchanan and Partners, 1969) and, to-date, public authorities have shown little enthusiasm to channel investment into the Gateways and Hubs proposed in the *National Spatial Strategy 2002-2020* (NSS). Thus, the 2004 Enterprise Strategy Group Report paid little attention to the NSS strategy other than to recommend that the government should "invest in infrastructure ahead of demand in key locations" (Forfas, 2004). The devolution of decision-making functions into regional centres or the decentralisation of key public bodies to Gateway locations was argued as a crucial policy lever to promote the strategic aspects of the NSS. The decision of the government to propose a widespread dispersal of public sector work in December 2003 to fifty-three locations, mostly neither Hubs nor Gateways, raised questions as to the commitment of government to the key elements of the NSS. Rather than laying the basis for a competitive national urban strategy, the dispersal of public sector work as proposed, and if implemented, "is likely to further enhance the dominance of Dublin and the east of the country as a business and enterprise location" (Bannon, 2003). This will be carried out in the absence of any real understanding of the economies or diseconomies attaching to such a centralised and mono-centred strategy (Bannon, 2000).

Need for new model of governance?

For the future, there arises a serious issue of governance in relation to the BMW Region and the State as a whole. As flows of funding from either the EU or from national programmes continue to wither or diminish, regions will have to rely increasingly upon their own resources and to become increasingly self sufficient. This transformation will pose a challenge for Ireland's traditionally centralised form of administration, inherited from the ideology of the Home Rule era and repeatedly re-enforced by successive governments (Ferriter, 2004). The establishment of the BMW Regional Assembly in 1999 represented a modest innovation in the domain of Irish governance, an innovation which might be built upon and further developed. How different might be the story of the west of Ireland or the performance of the BMW Region if the principle of local and regional subsidiarity had become the norm? What would be the present patterns of Irish development if the development agencies had been based in Galway or Sligo rather than in Dublin?

Higher education in regional development

In terms of regional self reliance, the role of higher education provision and research is likely to become a key driver of regional development in the future. The BMW Region contains one University and five Institutes of Technology. Since 2002 the Programme for Research in Third Level Institutions has allocated a total of over €560 million in funding to the various Colleges in the State; almost €73 million of this funding has been allocated to institutions in the BMW Region, with the vast majority of these funds (€67.5 million) going to the National University of Ireland, Galway. If the BMW Region is to develop as a location for high technology firms and advanced service functions, then the role of higher education institutions, particularly the university sector, will become even more crucial.

References

Bannon, M. J. *et. al.*(2000) *Development restraint and urban growth management*, A research report prepared for the National Spatial Strategy Team, Dublin, Department of the Environment and Local Government.

Bannon, M.J. (2004) *Irish urbanisation: trends, actions and policy challenges*, PEP Working Paper series, No.04/03, Dublin, University College.

Border, Midland and Western Regional Assembly (2003) *Submission to An Taoiseach on "Balanced regional development in the BMW Region"*, Ballaghaderreen,BMW Assembly.

Border, Midland and Western Region (2000-2003) *Monitoring, progress and various reports*, Ballaghaderreen, BMW Assembly.

Buchanan, C. and Partners (1969) *Regional studies in Ireland*, Dublin, An Foras Forbartha.

Clinch, P. (2001) *Reconciling rapid economic growth and environmental sustainability in Ireland*, Environmental Studies Research Series, W.P. 01/01, UCD.

Department of Environment and Local Government (2002) *The National Spatial Strategy 2002-2020*, Dublin, Stationery Office.

European Commission (2004) *A new partnership for cohesion: convergence Competitiveness and cooperation*, Luxembourg, EU.

Ferriter, D. (2004) *The transformation of Ireland 1990 – 2000*, London, Profile Books.

Fitzpatrick Associates *et. al.*(1999) *Border, Midland and Western Region Development Strategy 2000 – 2006*, Prepared for the Regional Authorities.

Forfas Enterprise Strategy Group (2004) *Ahead of the curve: Ireland's place in the global economy*, Dublin, Forfas.

Forrestal, C. (2002) *Balanced regional development: an inter-regional perspective*, M.Econ. Thesis, National University of Ireland, Galway.

Government of Ireland (1999) *National Development Plan 2000 – 2006*, Dublin, Stationery Office.

O'Leary, E. (2002) *Sources of regional divergence in the Celtic Tiger: Policy responses*, Paper delivered to the SSIS of Ireland, Dublin, ESRI.

Southern & Eastern Regional Assembly (2003) *The Southern and Eastern Region – comparisons with other NUTS II Regions*, Internal discussion paper, Waterford, S&E Assembly.

Chapter 7

Spatial Planning Frameworks for Ireland: Critical Reflections on the Dublin – Belfast Corridor

James A. Walsh

Introduction

The National Spatial Strategy (NSS) for the Republic of Ireland and the Regional Development Strategy (RDS) for Northern Ireland are policy documents of potentially immense importance for the long-term development of different parts of the island of Ireland. Both documents provide spatial frameworks that are of direct relevance to the implementation of actions in many areas of public policy, and which can also significantly influence the geographical distribution of investments by the private sector. While each strategy is primarily concerned with issues related to the promotion of more balanced regional development within their own jurisdictions, there are of course also opportunities for achieving enhanced outcomes through greater coordination of the two territorial planning frameworks.

This chapter reviews the wider policy context within which the NSS and the RDS have been formulated and explores some of the barriers that need to be overcome in order to achieve more coherent spatial development in the Dublin - Belfast corridor. Specific consideration is given to two issues: the relationship between strategic spatial planning and theories of regional development, and implementation and capacity building in the sphere of strategic spatial planning.

The Context for the NSS and the RDS

The preparation of the NSS and the RDS must be viewed as part of a more general orientation towards new approaches to spatial planning in many European countries and also at EU level. A major catalyst in inserting strategic spatial planning firmly into the public policy arena was the process that culminated with the publication of the European Spatial Development

Perspective (ESDP) in 1999. The publication of the ESDP (European Commission, 1999) is widely regarded as a very significant milestone in the history of spatial planning which has introduced new perspectives, policy aims and concepts that are currently being further elaborated, for example, within the context of the ESPON research programme.

The ESDP was the culmination of a lengthy preparation process that gained momentum in the 1990s as the EU sought to devise a new geography that would be of assistance in the pursuit of the higher level goals of the Community, especially that of improving competitiveness in global markets. Three policy guidelines inform the ESDP:

- the development of a balanced and polycentric urban system and a new urban-rural relationship,
- securing parity of access to infrastructure and knowledge, and
- sustainable development, prudent management and protection of natural and cultural heritages.

Taken together they provide a basis for reconsidering traditional patterns of territorial and spatial relations and, in particular, they identify opportunities where co-operation and coordination between regions could lead to enhanced outcomes. Such ideas are clearly relevant in the context of the Dublin – Belfast corridor given the nature of its urban structure, the relationships between metropolitan and rural areas, and the presence of the Border.

The specific local contexts from which the NSS and the RDS emerged are also important. The National Development Plan (NDP) for Ireland, published in 1999, identified the promotion of balanced regional development as a core strategic objective and included a commitment by the Government to prepare a national spatial strategy. This was a significant departure from the strategic goals and objectives of previous National Development Plans. The case for a spatial planning framework had been made in a number of influential reports, including the Sustainable Development Strategy, the White Paper on Rural Development, and studies by the Economic and Social Research Institute and the National Economic and Social Council. The NDP chapter on regional development outlines the government's objective for regional policy as follows:

> To "achieve more balanced regional development in order to reduce the disparities between and within the two regions (the Border, Midland and Western Region, and the Southern and Eastern Region) and to develop the potential of both to contribute to the greatest possible extent to the continuing prosperity of the country. Policy to secure such development must be advanced in parallel with policies to ensure that this development is sustainable with full regard to the quality of life, social cohesion and conservation of the environment and the natural and cultural heritage". (NDP, 1999, p.43)

This is a rather formidable statement of objectives with a strong emphasis on development based on harnessing potential rather than on relying on redistribution between regions, and also on regional policy being advanced in parallel with other policies. This approach does not explicitly recognise the need for an overall coherent spatial framework that would be adopted by all government departments and public agencies. Later there is further evidence of caution, which is repeated in the NSS, in statements such as "a prerequisite for implementation of the (regional) policy is the achievement of the macroeconomic objectives on which the Plan is based so that the necessary resources can be made available" (NDP, 1999, p.46). Thus it can be seen that regional policy and the NSS are contested political, and indeed administrative, constructs which need to be nurtured over the medium to long term. The consultation processes that were employed in the preparation of the NSS helped to secure a high level of political and administrative support which needs to be maintained by ensuring that the implementation programme and structures have the support of all government departments.

Given the contextual origins of the NSS it is clear that any discussion of the potential of the Dublin – Belfast corridor must also take account of the tensions between maximising the overall level of development (usually measured by GDP per capita) and the relationship with the remainder of the island. The primary economic objective of the Government is to maintain or enhance the level of international competitiveness of goods and services produced in Ireland so that there can be a continuation of economic growth. It is vitally important that the level of priority attached to balanced regional development and spatial planning in the current National Development Plan, which was formulated during a phase of unprecedented levels of economic growth, will be maintained in future NDPs even though the rates of economic growth may be lower.

The RDS for Northern Ireland also had a lengthy preparation process that lasted almost four years with extensive consultation and discussion (Murray and Greer, 2002). Here the process had the added dimension of seeking to secure a consensus on future development patterns against a background of social divisions and distrust. Indeed the commitment to prepare the RDS was a component of the Good Friday Agreement in 1998. The detail of the final strategy represents a number of compromises that were achieved via the participatory processes that were employed at different stages, including a public examination into draft strategic policies.

The outcome from the contrasting preparation models is that while the broad structural components (gateways, hubs, regional/local urban centres, radial and linking transport corridors) are similar, there are a number of significant differences. Firstly, the NSS is more skeletal in that it provides a framework that is to be elaborated in more detail via regional planning guidelines and later via statutory local development plans. By contrast, the RDS is more detailed as it is a regional strategy, though of course it is not part of any UK level framework for spatial development as there is not yet any such framework. This is a potentially serious constraint given the extent to which Northern Ireland is linked to the rest of the UK.

Secondly, the strategies differ in the extent to which they each refer to the remainder of the island of Ireland. Thus, in recognition of the current political realities, the RDS juxtaposes references to cross-border cooperation with discussion of linkages with Scottish regions. The point is most aptly illustrated by the truncated representation of 'key transport corridors' in the RDS maps. By contrast, the NSS provides more explicit recognition of the inter-dependencies between the North and the South. This is evident in the manner in which the transport proposals are depicted and also in the selection of Dundalk and Letterkenny as strategic frontier gateways with potential for much further development based in part on developing stronger linkages with Newry and Derry respectively. The NSS also identifies the potential offered by the ports by Belfast and Larne.

The lesson to be drawn from these comparisons is that the concept of a Dublin - Belfast corridor is not particularly strongly nor coherently articulated in the two strategies. While this may be a disappointment to some, it is important to recognise that any attempts to devise an integrated spatial planning framework along the east coast of Ireland, which may fit comfortably with the discourse underpinning the ESDP, will be essentially a long term project. The reflections of Professor Faludi, one of Europe's foremost thinkers on spatial planning, are pertinent here. He has noted that among the challenges of strategic planning are those of 'shaping the minds of those involved in spatial development, rather than shaping spatial development as such' (Faludi, 2001). It is against this contextual background that the chapter now considers some key issues that are pertinent to achieving the goals of the spatial strategies, and in particular the shared quest for a Dublin – Belfast corridor.

Spatial Planning and Regional Development Theory

The NSS and RDS both seek to promote more balanced regional development. A fundamental issue relates to the interpretation of this objective. For some, usually located outside the core regions, it is viewed as achieving a more equal sharing of opportunities and more equalisation of rewards. This perspective has been largely rejected in both strategies and replaced by a focus on harnessing regional potential through, in part, the realisation of critical mass in the supply of various development factors. The strategies also recognise the critical role of the metropolitan centres for international linkages and as bases for competitively producing internationally tradable economic output.

The strategies opt for a settlement framework consisting of gateways and hubs which are connected by radial and linking corridors. Special roles are also identified for small settlements and for rural areas. But there is a risk that in a conceptual sense the NSS and the RDS will be regarded as little more than updated versions of the plans produced in the 1960s and 1970s when 'growth centres' were in vogue. It would be a serious mistake to equate gateways with regional growth centres of the type envisaged in the 1960s. The reason for this is that the earlier growth centres were based on theories of regional development that are no longer considered satisfactory. Economically successful regions today, which include both urban and rural areas, are characterised by many diverse sets of factors including a blending of indigenous and externally driven enterprise strategies, by strong institutional capacity which is enhanced by intensive networking involving diverse sets of actors, and also by a strong commitment to innovation. There is a very extensive literature on the role, variety and potential of territorial or spatial innovation systems. Over recent years there have in fact been considerable efforts to build national or regional innovation systems. However, as argued by international theorists such as Professor Edward Malecki, a focus on territorially bounded innovation systems such as those organised by national or regional agencies may be too restrictive. Instead he proposes (Malecki, 1997; Oinas and Malecki, 2002) the concept of spatial innovation systems that consist of overlapping and interlinked national, regional and sectoral systems of innovation which are all manifested in different configurations in space. Thus the spatial innovation system approach seeks to highlight the complex and evolving integration at different levels of local, national and global forces. In order to promote development on an all Ireland basis, and more specifically within the Dublin - Belfast corridor, it will be necessary for spatial planning coordination to be supported by coordination of other key strategic objectives, for example, innovation. The concept of all Ireland spatial innovation system would benefit from further exploration.

The NSS and RDS provide the physical planning frameworks within which development may occur in the future. In order to capitalise on the opportunities presented by the two strategies it is essential that a deeper understanding of the dynamics of development in the regions of Ireland is promoted and that sectoral and regional policies take account of such dynamics and incorporate best practice models from regions in other countries. It is also important to note that the transfer of best practice from other regions is not unproblematic and will usually involve local adaptations. In relation to the Dublin - Belfast corridor there are opportunities to achieve higher levels of critical mass in a number of key areas through coordinated actions. Improvements in transport infrastructure, the possibilities offered by ICT, and the improved political context certainly offer the prospect of much increased interaction between the two cities and for enhanced development especially in a linked gateway consisting of Dundalk and Newry.

However, such optimism must be tempered by a consideration of the legacy of partition. The reality is that the histories of economic development in Northern Ireland and the Republic of Ireland are very different and, therefore, the preconditions that are usually required for enhanced levels of economic integration are weak. These include complementarities in production systems, strong and dynamic institutional linkages, excellent transport and communications infrastructures, and effective information dissemination. Hamilton (2001) identifies three sets of issues that have hindered, either directly or indirectly, the pace of economic integration between the North and the South. Firstly he draws attention to the legacy of the Border. This includes physical infrastructure systems (transport, waste management, public utilities, etc) that have been developed with little attention to coordination on an all Ireland basis. The Border has also created internal peripheries and artificially distorted the hinterlands of regional centres such as Dundalk and Newry. Secondly, Hamilton identifies major contrasts in the industrial structures of the Republic of Ireland and Northern Ireland. In summary, manufacturing in Northern Ireland is much more reliant on traditional sectors which are characterised by lower productivity levels; its service sector is much more oriented towards the non-market or public sector. Thirdly, and to a large extent related to the previous factors, the patterns of trade are very different. Not surprisingly North/South trade is very low as a percentage of total imports/exports for both the North and the South and is mainly confined to agricultural and traditional low technology manufacturing.

These structural differences are very significant and are unlikely to change substantially in the short to medium term. A convergence in industrial structures and a greater integration of the Northern Ireland economy into the global as distinct from the UK economic systems, as has occurred in the Republic, may not necessarily lead to much closer economic integration in the form of North/South trade. However, convergence might lead to more opportunities for sub supply firms to operate on an all Ireland basis, or to greater labour mobility among highly skilled workers, and more importantly to enhanced prospects for knowledge transfers, specialist business networks with a strong international orientation and, more generally, social capital formation. The factors just listed have been identified in many studies as crucial ingredients in sustainable regional development. It has also been well established that geography has a role in the transformation of regions. There is a large body of international evidence that supports the role of urban centres as locations that drive regional development. In an all Ireland context, and bearing in mind emerging trends towards polycentricity in other parts of Europe, the Dublin – Belfast Corridor represents a geographical as well as a political, economic and cultural space that merits much more attention in relation to how it might be transformed from its current position of weakly integrated components into a region consisting of several overlapping activity spaces. The frameworks set out in the NSS and RDS can help policy makers and others to make this transition if the analytical framework is extended beyond considerations of purely physical planning.

Implementation and Capacity Building in the Area of Strategic Spatial Planning

There is an urgent need to strengthen the capacity for strategic spatial planning as an on-going activity in the context of the implementation of the NSS and the RDS. While administrative structures have been put in place to oversee implementation it is imperative that systems are developed to ensure that the practice of strategic spatial planning becomes an on-going rigorous and robust process that will be able to effectively support the ambitious goals of the strategies as spatial frameworks to be adhered to by all government departments and development agencies. Critical issues that need to be addressed in this respect are (1) coordinated development of digital spatial databases, (2) development of expertise in spatial modelling so that alternative scenarios can be developed and evaluated and so that crucial evidence can be produced in support of claims for resources to achieve the strategic goals, and (3) mechanisms to ensure on-going dialogue between policy makers in both the political and administrative arenas, the diverse range of actors involved in activities related to regional and local development, and researchers on an all Ireland basis, so every opportunity is used for cooperation and coordination of actions in support of the long term goals and objectives of the strategies.

Take, for example, the issue of data assembly and dissemination in a coordinated manner. Both the NSS and the RDS provide the basis for requiring a very strong territorial focus in the design and delivery of a wide range of public policies. More significantly, each strategy recognises the need to co-ordinate strategic territorial planning between the North and the South, and especially in the Border zones. Meeting the diverse needs of policy makers, local and regional development organisations, private sector actors, political leaders, educators and others at this time can be most efficiently and effectively addressed through the development of an integrated and dynamic approach to collation, analysis and dissemination of digital spatial data.

There is now an urgent need for a broadly based initiative in this area. There are a number of key stakeholders who already have some statutory responsibilities in this area. The Ordnance Surveys (North and South) have responsibilities in relation to the collection, management, storage and dissemination of data recorded at a variety of geographical scales. They also guarantee the quality of the data and ensure that the practices in Ireland are in conformity with international standards. The Department of the Environment,

Heritage and Local Government in Dublin has recently been assigned responsibility for developing a National Spatial Data Infrastructure. This initiative is very timely even though it is primarily concerned with data provision in the Republic of Ireland.

On a practical level, over the short to medium term, a cross border structure needs to be established, perhaps under the auspices of the North South Ministerial Council, that will be responsible for developing an integrated and dynamic approach to the collation, analysis and dissemination of digital spatial data. The structure might include representatives of the ministries with responsibility for spatial planning in Belfast and Dublin, the two Ordnance Surveys, the Central Statistics Office Dublin and the Northern Ireland Statistical and Research Agency, the regional and local authorities, other agencies with responsibility for collection and management of spatial datasets, the GIS user groups, and researchers in spatial analysis. The structure could provide assistance at two levels. At the high level of strategic policy development it could assist government officials in Dublin and Belfast in the preparation of policies to guide the long term development of digital spatial data infrastructure for the island of Ireland. At an operational level it could oversee a range of actions to be undertaken by the main stakeholders with responsibility to:

- establish a data management and integration system for spatial datasets
- develop an integrated virtual Spatial Data Archive consisting of generalised spatial datasets;
- co-ordinate the development of metadata across partner institutions on an all-Ireland basis;
- develop and implement data transfer protocols to communicate with the data archive;
- investigate ways of identifying, measuring and communicating geographic data quality indicators;
- provide an advisory service to researchers in order to encourage and facilitate greater usage of spatial datasets and spatially referenced databases;
- promote greater usage of spatial data for analyses undertaken by researchers and among policy makers through the development of a web interface for users, production of promotional literature and organising workshops/seminars and conferences;
- maintain promotional material on an on-going basis; and
- co-ordinate as a medium term project the production of a multi-thematic digital *Atlas of Ireland* that will be a major resource for researchers and for informing wider audiences on spatial aspects of the economy, society, environment and culture. It will also be a major promotional tool for all of the agencies engaged in the collection and processing of spatial data.

On a practical level a first module in the production of a multi-thematic Atlas of Ireland could be a comprehensive spatial analysis of the data from the Censuses of Population taken in Northern Ireland in 2001 and in the Republic in 2002 with comparisons back to the 1991 data. This is a major project that will have to overcome substantial technical issues related to differences in definitions, the geographical scales at which data are provided, and for mapping purposes unharmonised digital boundary systems. Nevertheless, it is imperative to develop as quickly as possible a thorough understanding of the spatial trends that emerged over the last decade and for these trends to be examined on an all Ireland basis using micro level data so that the extent of spatial imprints can be more clearly identified.

The tasks outlined above are fundamental building blocks for a new and more rigorous approach to spatial planning, not least in the Dublin – Belfast corridor. While accepting the limitations of quantitative data analysis and quantitative models, there is an urgent need for more sophisticated tools to assist the promotion of spatial planning. There is a need to develop a comprehensive spatial model that will be able to explore the interactions between economic, social and environmental indicators and provide alternative scenarios to guide policy formation. This is a very large task that will require a number of years to accomplish, partly due to the paucity of data to calibrate any model. However, there are possibilities to learn from experience in other parts of Europe. For example, in the Netherlands comprehensive models have been constructed to assist in the preparation of strategies for the next 25 to 30 years. The current reality is that much of macroeconomic and sectoral planning is guided by models that permit investigation of different scenarios and which are also used in the bargaining process with the Finance ministries to secure public resources. Without a similarly rigorous approach to spatial planning there is a risk that the aspirations in the NSS and the RDS will be assigned lower priority than sectoral or other objectives. The pursuit of an integrated and coherent approach to territorial cohesion as envisaged in the NSS and RDS frameworks could be frustrated from the outset.

Conclusion

The National Spatial Strategy and the Regional Development Strategy are important starting points for a new era of comprehensive spatial planning at a time when the broader political and economic contexts are more supportive of an approach towards a coherent development strategy for the island while recognising that policies must in the first instance be formulated within each of the jurisdictions. They represent the beginnings of a process that will need to be supported on an on-going basis over the long term. A crucial part of the process is that explicitly spatial goals are maintained as core objectives of all development strategies in the future and that the frameworks established by the Strategies are adhered to, subject to adjustments following rigorous periodic reviews. Responsibility for spatial planning and the pursuit of goals related to territorial cohesion must be shared by all government departments and public agencies, while accepting that one Department must take on the lead role in each jurisdiction.

This chapter has highlighted a number of areas where further work is needed in order to advance the spatial planning agenda. These relate to the need to incorporate into spatial planning a deeper understanding of the dynamics of spatial development and especially of the interactions that occur at, and between, different geographical scales so that the regional perspective can deal with locations and spatial units in a relational as well as in an absolute sense. There is also an urgent need to develop more sophisticated methodologies to support strategic spatial planning on an all Ireland basis.

The Dublin - Belfast corridor, whatever its extent, undoubtedly has the potential to become a significant axis of development within the framework of northwest Europe. However, this will be a long-term process as there are significant legacies to be overcome. The NSS and RDS provide a basis for a more coherent development strategy along the east coast of Ireland. While a vigorous approach to supporting development in the corridor may pose a threat to other parts of the island this need not be the case. Rather, greater inter-regional competition may provide a springboard to support more radical long-term proposals involving the other major urban centres on the island of Ireland.

References

Department for Regional Development (2001) *The Regional Development Strategy for Northern Ireland*, Belfast, Department for Regional Development.

Department of the Environment and Local Government (2002) *National Spatial Strategy: people, places and potential*, Dublin, Stationery Office.

European Commission (1999) *European Spatial Development Perspective: towards balanced and sustainable development of the territory of the European Union*, Luxembourg, Office for Official Publications for the European Communities.

Faludi, A. (ed.) (2001) *European spatial planning*, Cambridge, Mass., Lincoln Institute of Land Policy.

Hamilton, D. (2001) Economic integration on the island of Ireland, *Administration*, 49(2), pp.73-89.

Ireland: National Development Plan 2000 –2006 (1999) Dublin, The Stationery Office.

Malecki, E.J. (1997) *Technology and economic development: the dynamics of local, regional and national competitiveness*, London, Addison Wesley Longman.

Murray, M. and Greer, J. (2002) Participatory planning as dialogue: the Northern Ireland Regional Strategic Framework and its public examination process, *Policy Studies*, 23(4), pp.283-294.

Oinas, P. and Malecki, E.J. (2002) The evolution of technologies in time and space: from national and regional to spatial innovation systems, *International Regional Science Review*, 25(1), pp.102-131.

Section Three:

PERSPECTIVES ON RURAL PLANNING AND DEVELOPMENT

The Social Shaping of Rural Vernacular Housing

Ken Sterrett and Jayne Bassett

Introduction

The term *vernacular dwelling* is commonly used by planners and policy makers to describe some sort of historically valid architectural model that contemporary rural designers are encouraged to interpret and employ in the design of new rural houses. In addition to this focus on traditional building forms, policy makers and lobby groups also point to what they consider to be a natural visual relationship between traditional rural settlement form and the countryside; that is, between all the elements of the external appearance of a building and site, and its landscape context. Accordingly, this chapter explores a number of important questions. Firstly, are there legitimate rural vernacular traditions in the northern part of Ireland, and if so, what are they? Secondly, what socio-economic and cultural forces shaped those traditions? And thirdly, what value does the so-called vernacular tradition have for contemporary rural housing development.

The Origin and Development of Rural Vernacular Housing

Alan Gailey's seminal text on rural housing presents not only a detailed account of the development of vernacular houses in the north of Ireland but also offers an understanding of the socio-cultural and economic circumstances that shaped their physical form and siting characteristics. For Gailey the traditional building in the Irish countryside 'was the outcome of an ecological situation in which the cultural expectations of its occupants, the potentialities of their surrounding physical environment, and economic factors were dominating factors' (Gailey, 1984, p.7).

Although there are many variations of vernacular form, all traditional rural dwellings in Ireland share some common characteristics (Figure 8.1). For Gailey and others traditional dwellings are normally one room-deep with a pitched roof spanning from front to back; the gables do not usually contain openings except where small windows are used to throw light into an attic floor. In addition, chimneys are normally situated on the ridge, to accommodate the axial location of the internal hearths. Gailey also recognises that for the most part, vernacular dwellings are single storey. Most of the 'pioneering studies' of Irish rural vernacular architecture focused on the single storey dwelling because it was the predominant form in the nineteenth century. Where two storey houses were developed they were normally based on the traditional ground floor plan of the single storey.

Figure 8.1: Traditional rural dwelling, County Cork

Although there were many variations of what might be termed the vernacular house, Gailey identifies two derivations (Figure 8.2). One he calls the direct entry dwelling and the other the hearth-lobby dwelling. The origins of the direct entry dwelling, which in some areas of the northern part of Ireland was the only house type, can be traced back to the byre-dwelling. This simple building form was used to house people as well as animals and is not peculiar to Ireland.

Figure 8.2: (i) Direct-entry dwelling, County Donegal
(ii) Hearth-lobby dwelling, County Fermanagh

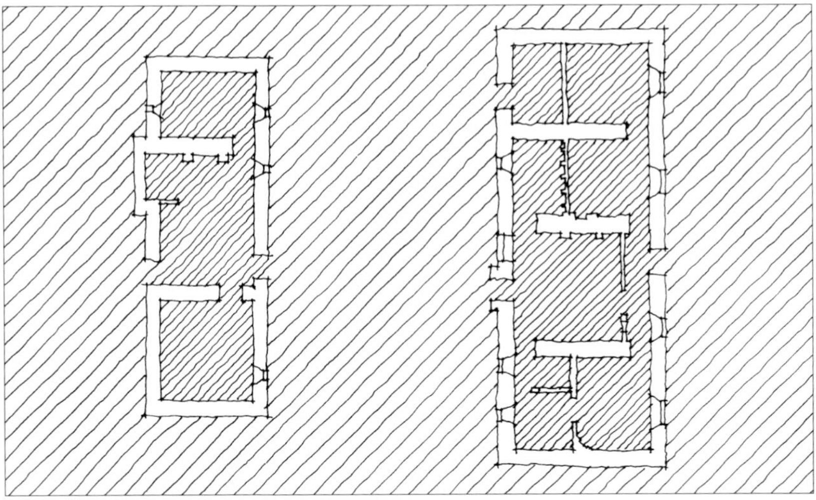

Source: after Gailey, 2004

Estyn Evans traces this simple building form back to at least the early Celtic period, and notes that it was 'best suited to the needs of a society dependent on a pastoral economy and closely attached, with magical as well as practical purpose, to livestock' (Evans, 1981, p.53). Arguably, therefore, the byre-dwelling was the 'natural' built form for an Irish peasantry whose economy and very existence depended on the well-being of its cattle. The nineteenth century saw the development of the single unit byre-dwelling into two and three unit buildings allowing separate rooms within the house as well as separate accommodation for animals. Significantly, though, Gailey records that for many poor families, particularly during the period of population growth before the Famine, the single kitchen unit cabin was commonplace (Gailey, 1984, p.148).

The second distinguishable vernacular house type – the hearth-lobby or lobby-entrance dwelling – was probably introduced by English settlers. Both its arrival in history without any obvious indigenous derivation, and its distribution across those areas settled during the early seventeenth century, suggest English rather than Scottish origins (ibid, p.187).

Of course what is now regarded as the vernacular tradition in rural northern Ireland can be understood as an amalgam of both dwelling forms. Significantly, though, Gailey is of the view that a particular northern Irish vernacular rural architecture 'does not exist'. Rather, and as already suggested, local dwelling types developed within a wider Irish and British context. In addition, Gailey makes the distinction between what he calls 'formal or academic architecture' where the architect or professional designer is involved in a process of considerations including aesthetic concepts and client specification. The large Georgian houses of the landed gentry, quite common in the Irish countryside were the outcome of such processes. The vernacular house on the other hand was 'constructed to accord with locally accepted tradition'.

Importantly, there is significant evidence that the so-called rural vernacular tradition was influenced by the formal architecture of the 'big house'. In rural northern Ireland this was achieved in a number of ways (Figure 8.3). The adoption of Georgian-style sash windows became quite common in the nineteenth century cottages, as did large gate pillars at the entrance to farm houses; the latter 'inspired by the grand estates created by landlords'. Most interestingly too, from a contemporary concern, the design of the vernacular dwelling was influenced by the symmetrical arrangement of elements typical of the Georgian or neo-classical grander houses. Pfeiffer and Shaffrey note that the Palladian principles were often 'disseminated through pattern books like Richard Morrison's *Useful and Ornamental Designs in Architecture (Villas),* which offered designs for a range of needs such as 'the Parsonage or Small Farmhouse' or 'A Temporary Residence for a Gentleman whose Principal Residence is in England' (Pfeiffer and Shaffrey, 1990, p.20).

Figure 8.3: Formal façade of hearth-lobby farmhouse, County Fermanagh

Source: after Gailey, 2004

As already noted, the development of vernacular dwellings in terms of their form, internal and external design, and indeed their siting in the landscape was the outcome of socio-economic and cultural forces both within Ireland and from Great Britain. Perhaps one of the determining factors in the evolving historical context of rural Ireland was the series of plantations during the seventeenth and early eighteenth centuries. There is, it might be fair to suggest, a general view among historical commentators that the new British settlers appropriated the more productive parts of the northern lowlands for their small farms, pushing the indigenous population into the less fertile hills and bogs. Evans in rather romantic language seeks to capture the relationship that developed between the chosen environment of the settlers, largely drumlin terrain, and their imported Presbyterian culture. 'The landscape has a charming intimacy. Roads winding their way through bushy hollows among the little hills bring constantly changing views, but think of the moulded drumlins as moulding, in turn, the outlook of the farmers who dwell among them. Much of the drumlin country is Orange country... The deep drumlin soils, previously utilised mainly for grazing, responded to the labour of a Protestant people who saw virtue in hard work' (Evans, 1981, p.29). He notes too that the farm holdings were smaller than the average in the rest of Ireland. It was recorded in Armagh, for example, that in 1841 the average farm was only one and a quarter acres.

If there was an identifiable pattern of Protestant and Catholic settlement, it is relevant to enquire how this affected the development of vernacular dwellings. In broad terms it seems that the affecting forces were social rather than cultural. As previously noted changes to the vernacular forms came mostly from the formal architecture of the houses of the higher classes. Gailey's research on this suggests on the one hand that the rural Protestant dwellers were inclined to borrow the symbols of the 'socially superior', presumably because they represented a social aspiration. Consequently changes to the elevation of vernacular houses such as the attempts to achieve symmetry on the facade, started in the east of the region 'among relatively prosperous farmers', but eventually permeated almost all of rural society including the 'rural landless' (Gailey, 1984).

During the nineteenth century the north of Ireland remained largely rural. Although minor innovations in housing form and layout were occurring, overall the conditions of the rural population were very poor. On the eastern side of the region, the relative prosperity of Protestant farmers facilitated the development of the parlour and what might be called a 'reception area'. Other largely ornamental developments followed, including entrance porches and painted-on quoin stones to imitate the formal corner structures of the grand houses. It is interesting to note how the colourful decoration of the imitation quoin stones is now celebrated almost as 'primitive art'.

Location and Siting

A key concern of contemporary policy makers relates to the location and siting of new dwellings in the landscape. Evans reminds us that urbanisation 'hardly touched most of Ulster until the seventeenth century' (Evans, 1981, p.32) and it remained largely a rural society until the latter part of the nineteenth century. The pattern of settlement in the countryside was of scattered farmhouses and cottages connected by a matrix of laneways. Of course scattered here refers to the spatial distribution of buildings in the countryside and not their number. Indeed the number of people living and working in the countryside in the eighteenth and nineteenth centuries was at least three times the current population. In addition to the scattered dwellings of small farmers and landless labourers, as already noted, many clachan developments existed, particularly in the west. These were widespread, as Evans notes (ibid, p.55), in the period before the Great Famine, and are associated with the 'rundale' or infield/outfield system. Clachans were generally composed of 10-20 houses arranged in a seemingly formless cluster and provided accommodation for normally related families. The infield was an area of good arable land that was 'shared' by the inhabitants. Although 'egalitarian' in a sense, it was, as Evans notes, 'complicated by the subdivision among co-heirs and in former times by the periodic reallocation of the holdings, which were scattered in many plots so that all shared land of varying quality' (ibid, p.60). This attachment to land and, more especially, to its ownership and use, has a sustained relevance for contemporary rural culture. The outfield comprised land for grazing outside the settlement.

Gailey records that within these clusters of houses very little privacy existed. 'Distinctions between 'inside' and 'outside' were blurred, inevitably so when cattle, which belong to 'outside', were taken into the internal family space' (Gailey, 1984, p.225). The break-up of the clachan system, according to Evans, was already well under way by the time of the 'Great Famine'. The system's very purpose of providing a communal arrangement and subsistence was under pressure from a growing market economy characterised by individualism. Significantly too, as Mitchell and Ryan note, the early nineteenth century saw a massive growth in the population brought about by a range of causes including improved medicines, and better food, particularly the easily cultivated potato. 'Within a balanced community, ... (the clachan) system was viable and could stand limited expansion. More potatoes could come into the arable field and the productivity of the outfield could be raised. But once population-growth exceeded a certain rate, the system had to collapse (Mitchell and Ryan, 1997, p.337).

In terms of the physical layout of buildings the rationalisation of the clachans system brought about separate holdings with separate houses (Figure

8.4). Evans notes that in Gweedore the greatest objection from tenants to the break-up of the system was to the 'house-scattering'. There were, he comments, 'complaints about the solitary grandeur of the new dwellings, though they were neither solitary nor grand. Even on the new squared farms they were rarely more than 100 or 200 yards apart, and on the narrowest strip farms were separated by no more than a few yards' (Evans, 1981, p.96). It seems too that where clachans were dispersed into a new system of holdings at the behest of landlords, new dwellings were built to replace the byre-type clachan cottage. The new dwellings and the new siting arrangements, it was believed would negatively affect the communal folk culture that had sustained impoverished communities.

Figure 8.4: Murphystown clachan, County Down

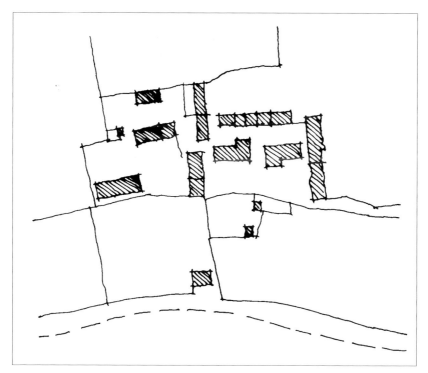

Source: from *An archaeological survey of rural County Down*, 1966

The historical change from a rural society based on communality to a more individual based culture was already underway, according to Gailey at the beginning of the seventeenth century (Gailey, 1984, p.226). The process of change, however, was relatively slow. Traditionally the siting of cottages in the countryside sometimes took account of prevailing winds and local topography, so that for example, the entrance would be sheltered from the elements and the byre situated on the lower part of a sloping site. Glassie records that a concern with orientation was one of three traditions of siting evident in the Ballymenone district of Fermanagh. 'On ridges like Drumbargey Brae, houses line the crest, each fronting the sunrise with its blank back to prevailing winds from the west, (however) on domes in the terrain of Sessiagh, houses circle the peak, down the slope from the top, parallel to the rise and looking downhill, no matter what winds pound their faces' (Glassie, 1982, p.334). Interestingly, he also notes evidence which indicates that 'townlands were formed first upon the hilltops, then grew downhill as population expanded.' It would seem too, that siting characteristics were also influenced by superstition, so that traditional builders would normally 'not build to the south or east of a house.' Blocking the sun and warmth to a house would, it was believed, bring bad luck.

However, new social aspirations began to compete with traditional functional and superstitious concerns. The more prosperous farmers, particularly in the east and in those areas colonised by British settlers in the previous century, sought out more private locations for their dwellings. Farmhouses were set back from the roadside and accessed by a laneway and were often surrounded by trees. Gailey records that in the 1830's Ordnance Survey compilers commented on the occurrence of this phenomenon in some of the most prosperous parts of south Antrim (Gailey, 1984, p.226).

The layout of buildings within the farm holdings in northern Ireland varied considerably from place to place and also over time. Separate outhouses for keeping animals or equipment usually were added to the lower end of the dwelling, creating a continuation of the building along the main axis. The need for additional space increased as new economic activities were introduced such as weaving. Moreover, growing social pressures to provide separate rooms for family also contributed to this.

However, the rectangular arrangement of dwelling and outhouses which is often the preferred building layout of contemporary policy makers was not common in Ulster. Gailey comments that the relatively small number of outhouses in the Ulster farmstead did not facilitate this arrangement. The rectangular layout was more common in Leinster, Munster and east Connaght and in Scotland. Again though, the formal arrangements of the farmyards of the wealthy within localities did provide another symbol for the small farmers to aspire to. Consequently two-sided and occasionally three-sided lay-outs began to flourish among 'the upwardly mobile' (ibid).

Glassie notes how work and home, once united in the same linear building form, began to occupy separate spaces in the nineteenth century. 'The organic mixture of domesticity and industry that formed the interior and facade of the old house was displayed frankly before it, along the street, in a zone that incorporated working dependencies, dairy and cartsheds, as well as a strip of "lawn" and patches of flowers' (Glassie, 1982, p.384). New arrangements saw the 'working parts' moved to the rear to allow the dwelling to present its facade and domestic decoration to the community.

The Contemporary Design Debate

Although the romanticisation of the countryside was already occurring in the 'high' culture of the nineteenth century, it was not until the Matthew Plan in 1963 that a conservationist ethos was formally introduced into Northern Ireland planning policy. This initiated a debate that in turn became a political contestation between the state on the one hand and the rural development lobby on the other, over the meaning and use of the countryside. In addition, what might be called the 'amenity lobby', that is those lobby groups which champion the preservation of the countryside, increasingly exerted pressure on the state to tighten control over both the number and the design of houses in the countryside.

Since the Matthew Plan there have been three significant attempts by the state to create a rural design agenda. The first was the introduction of 'Location Siting and Design' (LSD) standards in 1987. This represented the state's first direct attempt to impose aesthetic control over single house developments in the countryside. A number of points can be made about this initiative. Firstly, the design advice was not so much based on replicating or re-interpreting tradition, but rather focused on aesthetic appreciation. It might even be argued that a didactic approach to aesthetic appreciation was employed. The document sought, on the one hand, to inform the 'design decision makers' about how to make an aesthetic judgement based on pictorial composition and on key aesthetic concepts such as form, scale, relationship and proportion. On the other hand, it explained how 'inappropriate' and 'intrusive' elements could disrupt a composition.

Three years after publication of the LSD standards the House of Commons Environment Committee listened to a critical commentary by a number of environmental lobby groups which included comments on siting and design as well as on the number of houses being built. One referred to 'the peppering of Spanish style and other inappropriate new buildings throughout the countryside, and a disastrous 'ribbon' type development pattern along roadways' (House of Commons Environment Committee, 1990, p.157). Another spoke of the minimal effect of the LSD standards and suggested that the initiative did 'nothing to address the real problem which is quantity' (ibid, p.177). However, while the environmental lobby's evidence showed some appreciation of 'the fierce attachment to land' in rural areas, it arguably failed to comprehend the deep rural cultural heritage. Commenting on the replacement dwelling category in rural policy, for example, the Ulster Society for the Preservation of the Countryside asked why there is an insistence 'in keeping an old settlement pattern (ibid, p.185). In a similar vein, the Historic Buildings Council decried the loss of thatched cottages in the countryside and commented that 'at the moment, negative social attitudes seem to prevail in Northern Ireland towards old vernacular buildings (ibid, p.157).

In September 1993, and following an extensive consultation exercise as well as direct discussions with local councils, the Department published a new and more comprehensive set of policies for rural areas known as 'A Planning Strategy for Rural Northern Ireland' (Department of the Environment, 1993). Two of the key issues raised in the strategy document have particular relevance for this chapter. One refers to 'the amount of housing development which has already taken place' in the countryside as well as continuing development pressures, and asserts the need to establish 'the extent to which future development can be accommodated ... without detriment to the environment'. The second, reflects the amenity lobby's concern about 'the quality and impact of much recent development in the open countryside and about the standards which should be applied to ensure that new development is satisfactorily integrated into its rural setting' (ibid, p.17). Put simply, the first is about density and capacity, while the second refers to siting and design standards.

The policy response to more specific issues of siting and design standards is set out in 'Des 5 Buildings in the Countryside'. The language is stronger and more assertive than before and combines an almost romantic adoration for the vernacular tradition, or at least for its external visual form, with an imperative to preserve the scenery of the countryside. In relation to the former, there is some recognition that vernacular style was influenced by formal architecture. Indeed the policy now promotes this: - 'some (traditional) buildings were altered over time and they may show the influence of a more formal architecture. Indeed there are many rural houses of a formal design which could act as appropriate models for modern houses in the countryside' (ibid, 128). In relation to the latter, more forceful direction is provided on how to blend a new house into the countryside:

> 'A new building in the countryside will be acceptable if, when viewed from these surrounding vantage points, it meets all of the following criteria:
> * it blends sympathetically with landform;
> * it uses existing trees, buildings, slopes or other natural features to provide a backdrop;
> * it uses an identifiable site with long established boundaries, which separate the site naturally from the surrounding ground; and
> * it does not spoil any scenic aspect or detract from the visual appearance of the countryside.' (ibid, p.126)

Arguably, the imperatives underpinning this approach aim to sustain the notion of the countryside as aesthetic composition. To put it rather crudely perhaps, from the 'vantage point' a new house and its site, should either look as if it is 'naturally' part of a romanticised version of nineteenth century countryside scenery, or else it should be camouflaged by existing 'natural' features. The key concept is 'natural'. Any new development in the landscape should not disturb its 'natural' quality. Traditional houses, outbuildings, trees, vegetation and field patterns are considered to be 'natural'; to be either part of nature or to be an integral part of an unaffected rural idyll.

The publication the following year of 'A Design Guide for Rural Northern Ireland' (Department of the Environment, 1994) represented the first region wide illustrated guide for rural house development. The initiative was guided by a steering group comprised of representatives from what was regarded as the key institutions of professional influence: the Royal Society of Ulster Architects, the Institute of Landscape Architects, the Northern Ireland Housing Executive and the Ulster Folk and Transport Museum. A Belfast based architectural practice was responsible for the preparation of the document. The composition of the steering group is reflected in an approach which fuses architectural methodology with references to vernacular tradition. Interestingly too, there is explicit recognition of those who actually practice design in rural areas. In other words the guide is targeted at 'designers' who are not architects and who normally use a standard set of suburban house plans for rural sites. Again too, the approach is educative and steers the designer / applicant through a process of analysis from site selection, to site and building design. The rationale underpinning this is now more dependent on the aesthetic merits of traditional design. It is almost implied that traditional builders / designers selected sites and building forms for aesthetic reasons, or at least their functional concerns coincided with appropriate aesthetic outcomes: buildings tucked into the folds of the hillside to avoid the wind; finding a sheltered site among the trees; and selecting building materials and forms that were plain, simple, even austere (Figure 8.5).

On reflection, it might be argued that rural design policy to date has employed two rationales. The first has attempted to apply a nostalgic cleaned-up notion of the vernacular heritage, while the second has used what can be called a Kantian aesthetic (see Bourdieu, p.85) approach to the contemplation of composition and form. The two rationales have been fused in places, but have been consistently presented in terms of an aesthetic which is superior to the garish uneducated design choices of the rural population.

Some Contemporary Dilemmas

The number of houses being built in the northern Irish countryside continues to increase. Recent figures suggest that over 50% of all new houses being built

Figure 8.5: Contemporary vernacular expression

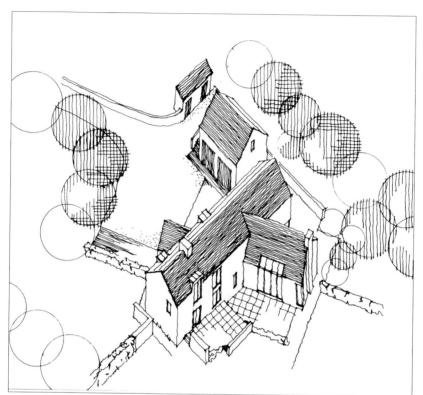

in Northern Ireland are single houses in the open countryside. In its Planning Policy Statement Issues Paper on Sustainable Development in the Countryside, the Department for Regional Development records that the numbers of single new dwellings approved has increased from 1,790 in 1991/92 to 5,628 by 2002/03 (Department of Regional Development, 2004, p.4). It notes, moreover, that 'on-going pressures for new rural development, particularly new dwellings, create a need for high standards of siting, layout, design, construction materials and integration into the landform to reflect local traditions'. The key question for the Department, therefore, is 'how could the issues of rural design quality be more effectively controlled, improved and implemented?' (ibid, p.7).

The issue is not simply about design or the effectiveness of the development control processes, but is also about understanding the single house in the countryside phenomenon. Although very little, if any, research has been undertaken to discover who is building in the countryside, it may be that what is emerging are two rural constituencies. The first is centred on the need to sustain indigenous rural communities, while the second captures a significant number of people who have moved to the countryside for lifestyle reasons and are buying into locations that are within travelling distance of the major urban employment centres.

There is a sense too that the gulf is widening between urban and rural culture, or at least between urban and rural perceptions. During public consultations on a regional strategy for Northern Ireland (Queen's University et al, 1998), there was evidence that the unacceptability of both the number and design of new houses in the countryside had spread from the elite groups that make up the amenity lobby, to a wider urban population.

One suggestion about the 'housing in the countryside' dilemma coming from a number of the amenity lobby groups, is to adjust rural policy to promote the refurbishment of derelict dwellings rather than replacing them. An exploration of this rationale highlights some of the key differences of view in the countryside debate.

Replacement policy applies specifically in 'policy areas'; this includes Green Belts and Countryside Policy Areas where applicants have to prove 'a need' to live there. The only exception to this is to replace an existing vernacular house with a new one. In fact replacement dwellings are the largest category of housing development in policy areas (Department of the Environment, 1993, op. cit., p.48). Although current policy promotes the re-use of the traditional building, this seldom happens. Indeed this was anticipated in the policy: 'In general the continued use, with adaptation if necessary, of existing houses, especially those of traditional design, will be encouraged in preference to replacement but this is not always the preferred solution of the applicant' (ibid). The proposed policy adjustment would require the refurbishment of the existing dwelling and would not normally allow replacement.

Pressure from the amenity lobby to achieve this policy change had its fullest expression at a UAHS conference in 1998, titled 'Bliss or Blitz' and in an accompanying television programme of the same title. The theme of the conference was set out in the 'proceedings publication' (Ulster Architectural Heritage Society, 1998). 'Planning Policy since Cockroft has allowed a liberal number of new homes to be built and there are many who see the unique and special character of the countryside disappearing beneath swathes of new bungalows, straight lines of 'Castlewellan golds' and suburban gardens. In parallel to that, the traditional, vernacular, buildings of the countryside, simple in form, using local materials and sited intuitively and snugly into the landscape, are being abandoned and lost (ibid, p.5).

For the most part conference speakers aimed their venom at the DoE's Planning Service and at the Northern Ireland Housing Executive (NIHE). One line of argument focused on the 'serious vulgarity' of modern houses in the countryside, using descriptions such as 'the Country and Western school of architecture' and 'the aluminium and PVC house'. New dwellings, replete with contemporary ornamentation and elaborate site designs were compared with the simple, almost austere minimalism of traditional buildings. This argument about the inappropriateness and vulgarity of contemporary rural designs was twinned with a concern about the ongoing loss of traditional dwellings. Research undertaken by Maguire showed that '49 per cent of vernacular buildings which had existed in 1909 had completely gone, and most of the rest were so altered that only 12 per cent survived with their features more or less intact' (ibid, p.19). A number of state policies were deemed to be responsible for this decline. The loss of character of those traditional buildings which had survived was largely due to NIHE Improvement Grant policy which eschewed traditional building methods and required modern improvements which were incongruous with the vernacular form. The complete loss of traditional buildings was the outcome of a number of policies including, NIHE's Replacement Dwelling Grant, DoE Planning Service's Replacement Policy and current VAT policy which taxes repairs at 17.5 per cent but exempts newbuild. In the NIHE view however, Replacement Grant for single houses in the countryside was designed to be both cost effective and to provide modern amenities for rural people. NIHE research showed that 'of the five hundred buildings which had currently been approved for replacement grant but had not yet claimed it, 80 per cent of them had originally sought a replacement grant, and only 12 per cent indicated a preference for improvement grant (ibid, p.13). Moreover it was argued that the internal condition of many vernacular dwellings which old people and sometimes young families were living in, was socially unacceptable. Such conditions included different floor levels, low ceilings, uneven damp walls and dark smoky interiors. Not only would the cost of a so called sensitive repair be high, but in many cases necessary structural changes and improvements would destroy the aesthetic of the traditional form that such an initiative was designed to conserve. In the NIHE's experience, rural people wanted modern amenities like their urban counterparts; their attachment is to the land not to the buildings.

The main thrust of the conference papers though was to be scornful of the popular aesthetic and to celebrate the aesthetic quality of the rural vernacular form. In relation to the latter, the focus was very much on the external form of the building and site and on the craftsmanship involved in its production. This was presented as the view of the educated, the view of those who had a superior understanding of what was right aesthetically as well as morally. Again there was little attempt to comprehend the contemporary needs of the rural community.

An additional argument employed by some, and one that is gaining ground in this 'period of peace', was that relating to the needs of the tourist industry.

Stelfox for example, noted that 'people came to Ireland for its cultural and natural heritage, but we were in danger of attracting tourists hoping to find scenic beauty and never returning after finding only a mundane international landscape' (ibid). On a similar theme McLaughlin on behalf of Rural Cottage Holidays Ltd. (an initiative set up by the Northern Ireland Tourist Board), referred to a number of neo-vernacular rural cottage schemes which had proved to be very successful holiday accommodation for those seeking a 'rural experience'. Even more 'authentic' however were a number of cottages her organisation had restored in the Glens of Antrim. This recent trend to holiday in neo-vernacular or restored rural cottages is being paralleled by a trend to live in similar dwellings in close proximity to the Belfast urban area. Although the evidence is anecdotal at this stage, there are indications of an increasing number of neo-vernacular and restored vernacular dwellings appearing in the countryside within the Belfast travel to work area. These architect designed 'traditional cottages' offer an authentic rural appearance but with all the conveniences needed for working in the city and living in the countryside.

What is potentially interesting about this emerging neo-vernacular phenomenon is its sociological significance. While the rural community, particularly in the west and south of Northern Ireland, continue to prefer a suburban aesthetic replete with as much ornamentation as the planners will allow, a small but increasing number of (obviously) affluent, urban people are keen to embrace a vernacular aesthetic. There are some possible explanations for this. Firstly, those who are holidaying in the restored cottages in the Glens of Antrim or who are buying or building neo-vernacular cottages on the shores of Strangford Lough are likely to be urban people with no immediate connection to rural culture. In other words they are one or two generations removed from a rural past. This allows a certain romanticisation of what it means to be rural. The countryside as a passive, 'beautiful and tranquil setting' for 'a traditional style four bedroom cottage' is arguably, wholly inauthentic. The countryside was seldom considered in such terms by rural people, and a 300 square metre four bedroomed traditional cottage would not have been possible.

A second possible and related explanation, is that a new class is emerging from within the middle classes which seeks to distinguish itself through a different lifestyle. Featherstone's comments (Featherstone, 1991, p.86) about how postmodern culture promotes lifestyle as a distinguishing project has some relevance here. Distinction is a vital part of the lifestyle project and is realised through visually transmittable goods and activities such as home, car and social activities. Bourdieu's notion of taste as the key classifying category of the habitus supports this observation (Bourdieu, 1986). The new vernacular houses are distinctively different from suburbia both in terms of location and design. They offer a country lifestyle complete with stables and outhouses.

There is ample room for the 'Range Rover' and the 'Aga'. Significantly too, the cottages lack an obvious pretension, and indeed that is their appeal. Their single storey minimalist exteriors suggest 'peasant rural' rather than 'landlord rural', and in a subtle way also convey architect design rather than 'off the peg' speculative developer design. This is consistent with the superior aesthetic promoted by the state, UAHS and others. The cleaned-up family of vernacular forms arranged as modest farmyard and simultaneously as an architectural composition of forms, meet both of the aesthetic objectives discussed before.

Conclusion

A question posed at the beginning of this chapter asked if there are legitimate rural vernacular traditions in northern Ireland. The short exploration of Gailey and others' work would suggest that the contemporary image of a rural vernacular dwelling is largely a sanitized and hybrid version of the nineteenth century cottage. Contemporary interpretations of rural vernacular form are significantly different to the 'wattled houses' found in Armagh around 1600 or the sod built cabins of the landless labourers common in Ireland up until the eighteenth century. The components of vernacular form that are presented in current policy guidance are a mix of the formal and informal, the 'architectural' and the 'traditional'.

Possibly more interesting, is the question about the forces that shaped the design and siting of an 'evolving vernacular tradition'. In many respects the same social forces were at work in the nineteenth century as are apparent today. The social aspirations of even the most modest rural dwellers were given expression in rural house design or alteration. Choices made by rural dwellers to attempt a symmetrical facade design, for example, were not made through contemplative aesthetic pondering, but rather were the expression of what they perceived to be the superior taste of a higher social class. Bourdieu's famous phrase that 'taste classifies and it also classifies the classifier' (Bourdieu, 1986, p.6) is a reminder that choices which are seemingly subjectively made, are in fact made within taste communities; that is, the lifestyle communities of our postmodern world. Moreover, choices reflect values and values reflect cultural heritage, social position and aspiration. Design, in this context, is about social communication not aesthetic contemplation.

What value then do the so-called vernacular traditions have for contemporary rural housing development? Arguably the development and reworking of a sanitized rural vernacular plays to people's social psychology and to their romance with the countryside and the landscape (Figure 8.6). This is particularly important for urban dwellers, for tourists, and for people who have long since stepped away from their rural heritage, in other words, those who are now in a position to romanticise about the meaning of the rural and what they expect to see in the countryside. Design can never be a panacea for the dilemmas challenging rural policy makers. However, it might offer a temporary, albeit superficial response, to the ontological difficulties facing an increasingly urbanised Irish society.

Figure 8.6: The contemplative northern Irish landscape

References

An archaeological survey of rural County Down (1966) HMSO.

Bourdieu, P. (1986) *Distinction: a social critique of the judgement of taste*, London, Routledge.

Department of the Environment for Northern Ireland (1987) *Location, siting and design in rural areas*, Belfast, Department of the Environment for Northern Ireland.

Department of the Environment for Northern Ireland (1991) *What kind of countryside do we want?* Belfast, Department of the Environment for Northern Ireland.

Department of the Environment for Northern Ireland (1993a) *Summary of submissions received in response to the consultation exercise*, Belfast, Department of the Environment for Northern Ireland.

Department of the Environment for Northern Ireland (1993b) *A planning strategy for rural Northern Ireland*, Belfast, HMSO.

Department of the Environment for Northern Ireland (1994) *A design guide for rural Northern Ireland*, Belfast, HMSO.

Evans, E. (1981) *The personality of Ireland: habitat, heritage and history*, Belfast, Blackstaff Press.

Featherstone, M. (1991) *Consumer culture and postmodernism*, London, Sage.

Gailey, A. (1984) *Rural houses of the north of Ireland*, Edinburgh, John Donald Publishers..

Glassie, H. (1982) *Passing the time*, Dublin, The O'Brien Press Ltd.

House of Commons Environment Committee (1990) *Environmental issues in Northern Ireland*, London, HMSO.

House of Commons Northern Ireland Affairs Select Committee (1996) *The planning system in Northern Ireland*, London, HMSO.

Kennedy, B.P. (1993) The traditional Irish thatched house: image and reality 1793-1993, in Dalsimer, A.M. (ed.) *Visualising Ireland: national identity and the pictorial tradition*, London, Faber and Faber.

Maguire, C. (1998) *The changing vernacular landscape, research undertaken under the Alan Gailey Fellowship in 1996-97*, Belfast, Institute of Irish Studies, The Queen's University of Belfast.

Mitchell, F. and Ryan, M. (1997) *Reading the Irish landscape*, Dublin, Town House.

Pfeiffer, W. and Shaffrey, M. (1990) *Irish cottages*, Weidenfeld and Nicolson.

The Queen's University of Belfast, The Urban Institute of University of Ulster, The Rural Community Network and Community Technical Aid (1998) *Shaping our future: public consultation on a regional strategic framework for Northern Ireland*, Belfast, The Stationery Office.

Ulster Architectural Heritage Society (1998) *Bliss or blitz: the proceedings of a conference on the future of rural buildings in Ulster*, Belfast, Ulster Architectural Heritage Society.

Chapter 9

Preserving Character in the Towns and Villages of Northern Ireland

Karen Latimer

There is a house with ivied walls,
And mullioned windows worn and old,
In blazing brick and plated show,
Not far away a villa gleams
(Thomas Hardy, written1902).

Introduction

Further study of Hardy's poem *Architectural Masks* (in Johnston,1979, p.222) reveals that all is not as it seems. But the issue that Hardy touches on, of the old versus the new and the perceptions of both, remains pertinent today. Indeed the issue of housing in rural areas is fraught with difficulties and contradictions. Numerous academics and policy makers have wrestled with the problem of balancing overdevelopment in areas of natural beauty with the need to provide housing to meet local demand and prevent the drift away from the countryside to the larger towns and cities. Often the need to meet modern standards and expectations seems to be at odds with retaining the traditional buildings that blend so unobtrusively into the landscape and give an area its sense of place. And then there is the debate about second homes in the countryside which has been such a burning issue, literally and metaphorically, particularly in Wales, but also in Scotland and Ireland. Holiday lets have rescued many an attractive old building from extinction. However, in some areas, notably on the smaller islands of the Inner Hebrides, there is barely a permanent household left. The crofts and estate houses of the past, although externally unchanged, are somehow soulless within, as families no longer go about their ordinary everyday chores and fill these homes with purpose.

Paddy Shaffrey, architect, planner and long-time perceptive commentator on buildings in rural Ireland, noted thirty years ago that its towns and villages changed hardly at all until after 1960 when the rate of development began to increase dramatically. He observed that "in the process the character of towns has suffered badly" and that this would continue "unless there is a fresh and imaginative approach to urban development" (Shaffrey, 1975, p.16). Nearly half a century later the pressure of change continues to pose problems. Different patterns of working, demographic change, architectural innovation and shifting expectations have an impact on rural areas whether it be buildings in the towns and villages or in the surrounding countryside. This chapter looks at a number of approaches, in particular that of Hearth Housing Association and the Revolving Fund, to preserving those buildings of character which contribute so much to our architectural heritage, our sense of identity and our enjoyment of town and country.

Change and Preservation
In 1976 two little booklets were published, one on each side of the border, which addressed the issue of rural living. Sean Rothery argued that the "Irish traditions of stone buildings and carving, of shop front lettering and the adventurous use of colour on facades are all traditions to be studied and learned again before our marvellously varied Irish towns and villages become anonymous and faceless" (Rothery, 1976, p.1). In the same year the Ulster Countryside Committee commented that "we must try to blend the new with the old, and attempt to strike a balance between the need to develop and the need to conserve the best features of our natural heritage" (Ulster Countryside Committee, 1976, p.5).

This was all very positive stuff but some twenty years later the Ulster Architectural Heritage Society held a conference in Belfast entitled *Bliss or Blitz* which looked at the future of rural buildings in Northern Ireland. Frank McDonald, the outspoken environment correspondent of the *Irish Times* and author of a series of articles highlighting the poor design of many new houses in the Irish countryside, did not pull his punches and railed wittily and tellingly against the "serious vulgarity" of much modern rural housing (UAHS, 1999, p.9). At this same conference, Donal Boyle reported on the Environment and Heritage Service's townland survey carried out in Northern Ireland in 1996-97. Some 900 sites in 49 townlands were visited. The results highlighted the serious loss of traditional buildings: 49 per cent of the buildings recorded in 1909 had gone, a further 39 per cent survived only in an altered form, and only 12 per cent had survived complete with correct roofing and detailing (UAHS, 1999, p.11). This important conference identified four areas for attention. These were: legislation - notably The Planning Order, The Housing Order and VAT measures; economic issues including sustainability and the need to take account of the value to the economy of a distinctive and attractive vernacular built heritage; the maintenance and development of traditional skills; and education to raise awareness of the rural and vernacular heritage. John Greer in reviewing the proceedings of this conference pointed out that "reconciliation between rural development and conservation interests is long overdue" (Greer, 2000, p.40). Seven years on from this conference the debate rages on, barely unchanged. Oram and Stelfox (2004), writing on the historic development of traditional buildings, point out the persistent presence of derelict properties and the less than flattering contrast of old and new. They argue that a "wholesale change in the rural built environment is taking place without any debate as to the consequences, whether they be the loss of distinctiveness, national or regional, the loss of history and cultural values, or the sustainability issues arising from energy and material losses …" (p.2).

Another commentator on the changing character of buildings in the countryside, Caroline Maguire, has highlighted the loss of both the quality and quantity of traditional housing in a study carried out when she was the Alan Gailey Fellow at the Institute of Irish Studies, Queen's University Belfast. This study (Maguire, 1999) pointed out the damage done to buildings under the umbrella of the Northern Ireland Housing Executive's improvement grant schemes. These so-called improvements included the removal of traditional features such as doors, windows and rainwater fixtures as well as changing the external render from lime-based to cement-mixed, now widely recognised as poor conservation practice. An even greater threat to traditional buildings in the countryside was identified as the Replacement Dwelling Grant Scheme. Clearly a balance has to be found between retaining the old and embracing the new. No-one advocates a return to the past, but equally most buildings are capable of sympathetic restoration. Maguire also noted "the continuum of extending and adapting traditional buildings until relatively recently" and urged "the promotion of positive schemes for the practical reuse of these buildings which remain very much part of the landscape" (p.40). It is such schemes that are examined next in this chapter.

Conserving the Past in the Present

Hearth is an organisation that was set up in 1972 under the driving force of Charles Brett as a joint initiative of the Northern Ireland Committee of the National Trust and the Ulster Architectural Heritage Society. Marcus Patton in his history of Hearth, *Conservation at the Coal-face,* recorded the ambitions of those establishing Hearth as:

> an eleventh-hour attempt to rescue at least some remaining examples of Ulster's architectural character which are disappearing fast as a result of redevelopment and neglect. If this effort fails, and does not inspire imitators, most of the buildings which give character to the towns and villages of Northern Ireland will vanish. (Patton, 2003, p.75)

Happily the effort did not fail and imitators were inspired to act. Hearth's two sister organisations, Hearth Revolving Fund and Hearth Housing Association, have restored over 120 dwellings between them (Hearth, 1999). This is a modest contribution numerically, perhaps, but it is one that has had a significant impact on many towns and villages. By demonstrating the art of the possible, it has prompted others to follow. Hearth's role is twofold. Firstly, it aims to bring back into use, often for social housing, threatened and often derelict historic buildings with a minimal loss of fabric. Secondly, it aims to encourage others to restore neighbouring buildings, or to influence planners and others to hold the line rather than allow the demolition of buildings of interest that are in poor condition.

Hearth Revolving Fund (HRF) was formed in 1972 to facilitate the purchase and restoration of dwellings for resale. It is non-profit-making and has charitable status. The Revolving Fund acts as a Building Preservation Trust and works on the principle that a relatively small amount of capital can be used over and over again to buy, restore and sell successive properties. Hearth Housing Association (HHA) was formed in 1978 and is registered under the Housing (NI) Order 1976. It is also non-profit-making and has charitable status. It is a member of the Northern Ireland Federation of Housing Associations and provides a wide range of housing units. Houses and flats are allocated to applicants under the Housing Selection Scheme approved by the Department of the Environment and administered by the Department for Social Development. HHA manages and maintains the properties and rents are set each year broadly in line with public sector rents. Funding for projects restored by HHA comes mainly from public housing grants.

Both wings of the organisation focus on buildings at risk which for one reason or another have not been considered financially attractive as investments by private developers. The Housing Association must, of course, take into account local housing need before embarking on a project. It is this requirement that usually informs the decision as to which route Hearth will go down, Revolving Fund or Housing Association, when attempting to rescue a derelict historic building.

One of the earliest and most visible of Hearth's schemes is the group of almshouses in Seaforde, County Down (Photograph 9.1). Seaforde is a proposed Conservation Area. It is very vulnerable to unsympathetic development and was even more so when, in the early 1970s, the Forde family agreed to sell property to Hearth. The almshouses had been built in 1828 by Colonel Forde as acommodation for six people and the village courthouse. These small but attractive Regency Tudor buildings were restored in 1979-80, each pair of houses now forming one new house. One door in each porch was converted to a window and new kitchen and bathroom extensions were added to the rear. Granite fire surrounds in the almshouses were kept, as was the red sandstone plaque in the gable of the central house recording the date the buildings were erected. Many other details were retained. The relationship of the almshouses to the 18th century parish church and the demesne walls of Seaforde House makes for a harmonious grouping. The houses now provide attractive and comfortable accommodation for a number of longstanding tenants. Indeed, it is hard to imagine Seaforde without them, but they could so easily have been demolished. All over Northern Ireland many similar simple little buildings have gone and as a result the character of our towns and villages has been diminished. In 1983 Hearth carried out a further restoration scheme on the estate workers' houses in Seaforde's Main Street. Again the old houses were combined two-into-one with some doors converted into windows and new gables added at the back. Unfortunately, new housing in Seaforde is less than sympathetic in style, scale and siting and thus further development needs to be carefully monitored if Seaforde is to retain its character as a small, coherent, estate village.

Photograph 9.1: Almshouses at Seaforde

Glenarm in County Antrim is another village of great charm and character where Hearth has carried out restoration work. In the early 1970s the Antrim Arms Hotel was bombed and the building remained vacant for a number of years. Since the building was one of the largest along the main street (Toberwine Street), its restoration was very important to the village. Although no longer offering Bed & Breakfast at 12s 6d per night, the building now provides a mixture of flats and houses. Its outbuildings to the rear have been demolished and replaced by a terrace of five pensioners' cottages designed along traditional lines. Shortly after completing the Antrim Arms project, Hearth took on the restoration of the schoolhouse in Castle Street. Described by Brett as a "most attractive little T-shaped building of random blackstone with red sandstone dressings, some square windows with dripstones, and some tall paired pointed windows" (Brett, 1971, p.17), it too plays an important part in the social and architectural history of Glenarm. Conversion involved extensive internal changes but externally the building remains virtually unchanged and provides two very desirable two-bedroomed houses. A pleasing corollary to the tale of Hearth's work in Glenarm is the recent restoration of the Barbican gate lodge beside the schoolhouse by the Irish Landmark Trust, about which more later. A less pleasing endnote is the current debate about development at both ends of the Glenarm Conservation Area which continues to highlight the need for adherence to the worthy aspirations of *Planning Policy Statement 6: Planning, Archaeology and the Built Heritage*, published by the Department of the Environment in 1999.

Over the years Hearth has gained expertise in certain building types. One of the earliest HRF schemes was the Drumbeg lockhouse beside the River Lagan, a chunky little building designed about 1760 by Thomas Omer for the Lagan Navigation with a wonderfully robust Gibbsian doorcase and a pleasing combination of rubble stonework and sandstone detailing (Photograph 9.2). This building is well known to the many who walk the Lagan Towpath. It was particularly pleasing, therefore, to be able to demonstrate the viability of such a small but historically, aesthetically and environmentally important building. Some ten years later (and almost twenty years after negotiations opened) Hearth took on the restoration of another Omer lockhouse, this time upriver at Ballyskeagh. Had the Department of the Environment not refused listed building consent, this distinctive and evocative building would have been replaced by a bungalow.

Photograph 9.2: Drumbeg Lockhouse

Another building type and one that poses its own challenges when it comes to reuse, is the gate lodge. Dean in his comprehensive study of the gate lodges of Ulster (Dean, 1994) pointed out that more than half the gate lodges that he identified have been lost completely and many more have been so unsympathetically remodelled as to have lost all architectural integrity. Dean argued that gate lodges "offer picturesque variety, skilled craftsmanship, scholarly design, and simple delight to Ulster townscape and countryside" (p. vi). Hearth has undertaken a number of exemplary gate lodge restoration projects. In 1997 it restored the much vandalised Alexandra Park gate lodge in Belfast and it has just recently completed work on the lodge to Castle Upton in Templepatrick, designed by Edward Blore of Crom Castle fame (Brett, 2005). This scheme, which won a Commendation Award at the Royal Institution of Chartered Surveyors conservation awards ceremony in 2005, was described in the seventh catalogue of *Buildings at Risk* as being "a clever and discreet extension in sympathy with the original structure" (BAR, 2005, p.xxxv). Another recently completed scheme involved the two unlisted but contextually crucially important gate lodges at Wallace Park, Lisburn. Built in 1884 these two identical single-storey red-brick structures have been rescued from dereliction to provide two two-bedroomed homes of modern standards while retaining their distinctive character and enhancing the park. In Ballymena another gate lodge project is under way in 2005.

Hearth has restored only one thatched cottage to date, Curry's Cottage at Derrylin in County Fermanagh (Photograph 9.3). This simple but highly attractive mud-walled cruck cottage is very important as there are only a few surviving examples of such structures in their original location. This was a technically demanding project and the eventual solution involved providing modern facilities in a new and adjacent free-standing annex while allowing the original cottage to be restored as the living room for the house. The original cottage remains very much the focal point of the farmstead. The owner, who has lived there all of his 70+ years, stokes up the open turf fire and boils up the kettle on it every morning. He had wanted an improvement grant for the cottage but, because it was considered unfit, the only grant available was for a replacement dwelling. Fortunately, after much negotiation, the Northern Ireland Housing Executive agreed to waive the requirement to demolish the original dwelling. The old building still retains its integrity while the new annex provides the requirements for 21st century living. It is a happy ending for a structure that could so easily have been knocked down.

Photograph 9.3: Curry's Cottage with its new annex, Derrylin

One of Hearth's most unusual projects is Turnly's Tower in Cushendall, County Antrim (Photograph 9.4). This quirky building was built about 1820 as a folly or eyecatcher in the village. John Cornforth, the architectural historian, described it as "a distinctively individual house for someone not only good at stairs but with thin friends" (Cornforth, 1994, p.63). In keeping with the

Photograph 9.4: Turnly's Tower, Cushendall

character of the building, a number of eccentric individuals have lived here and Marcus Patton has described a number of them elsewhere (Patton, 2003) including the one-legged inebriate and the unorthodox DIY specialist who made his own fake old glass out of heated and flattened corrugated Perspex!

The above are only a few examples of Hearth's work in the towns and villages of Northern Ireland. Other schemes include distillery workers' terrace houses in Comber, the almshouses at Annahilt and a terrace of 19th century houses in Castlederg which looked like being one of Hearth's easier projects until the buildings were wrecked by a 500lb bomb left outside the police station opposite. Fortunately no-one was injured but it was business as usual for Hearth with full restoration required. Hearth has also carried out projects in Moira, Newtownards, Downpatrick, Holywood, Glenoe and Gosford Forest Park as well as a number of major restoration schemes in Belfast and Armagh. There are just too many to mention but, cumulatively, they are an impressive testament to Hearth's founding fathers and a small, dedicated and enthusiastic staff led by its Director, Marcus Patton.

Hearth's involvement in preserving the character of our towns and villages and saving buildings at risk is just one approach and others have emerged. In 1992 the Irish Landmark Trust was founded in Dublin and in 1996 it was incorporated as a charitable trust in Belfast. The Trust restores buildings, without altering their original character, for use as short-term, self-catering holiday homes. It currently has four properties in Northern Ireland – Ballealy Cottage near Randalstown, the Blackhead Lightkeepers' houses, Drum gate lodge at Bushmills and the Barbican gate lodge at Glenarm which was referred to earlier. A comparable project, Rural Cottage Holidays, set up by the Northern Ireland Tourist Board and for which Hearth had carried out a number of restoration schemes in the Glens of Antrim converting traditional farmhouses into holiday accommodation, is no longer developing schemes.

An innovative area-based strategy for addressing the issue of traditional buildings at risk is provided by the Mourne Homesteads Scheme. It is an initiative of the Mourne Heritage Trust, formed in 1997, with the Homesteads Scheme being launched in May 2000. Its aim is "to identify, repair and bring back into use a number of traditional dwellings of different styles and sizes for full time use by local people" (Devlin, 2004, p.3). The target is to renovate up to ten traditional dwellings in the Mourne and Slieve Croob Area of Outstanding Natural Beauty. So far only one project has been completed, at Rock Cottage in Castlewellan, but further projects are due to commence on site under the next phase of the scheme. A very successful part of this project is the education and training programme in traditional building skills which has been undertaken in advance of the actual restoration work. This has included general courses on vernacular building and more specific courses on lime, stone masonry, Irish thatch and thatching, dry stone walling and hedge laying. Just as Hearth initially drew its inspiration from the National Trust for Scotland's Little Houses Scheme in the fishing villages of Fife, the Mourne Heritage Trust learnt from Cadw's experience with the small rural dwellings of the Llyn peninsula in north Wales (Cadw, 2003). It is interesting to note that the success of the Cadw scheme lay in the fact that it was operating in an area of severe rural deprivation and that little change had occurred to the buildings or, indeed, to the landscape.

The Building Preservation Trust movement, to which all of the above organisations belong for at least some part of their activities, is growing fast in Northern Ireland. Some Building Preservation Trusts are revolving funds whose capital turns over from project to project but most are single project trusts set up to rescue and manage specific buildings. They work to high standards and can often lever loans and grants not available to conventional developers or individuals because they do not set out to make a profit. In 1996 there were only two such trusts and there are now over twenty with a geographical spread across Northern Ireland. These trusts have attracted funding of over £9 million from the Heritage Lottery Fund in the last ten years.

Conclusion

This chapter has looked at one small part of the overall conservation picture by mainly examining the work of one small organisation and its attempt to set an example for others to follow. However, this is not an organisation working in isolation. In Dublin, the Department of the Environment, Heritage and Local Government (2004) has published a set of comprehensive guidelines on protecting our architectural heritage. In the opening paragraph it states:

> The built heritage consists not only of great artistic achievements, but also of the everyday works of craftsmen. In a changing world, these structures have a cultural significance which we may recognise for the first time only when individual structures are lost or threatened. (p.13)

In Northern Ireland, the Department of the Environment's Planning Policy Statement 6 links conservation and economic prosperity, promotes sustainable development and clearly states that the presence of historic buildings "adds to the quality of our lives, by enhancing the familiar and cherished local scene and sustaining the sense of local distinctiveness which is such an important aspect of the character and appearance of our cities, towns, villages and countryside" (p.6).

Fine words indeed, but why then are only some 100 of the 30,000 traditional thatched cottages that were standing in the 1950s intact in 2005 (SAVE, 2001, p.32.)? Why is it that "the number of single dwellings currently approved in rural Northern Ireland is approaching treble that approved annually in England, Scotland and Wales combined" (Department for Regional Development, 2004, p.4)? Are we failing to translate words into action? Are we failing to make our policies deliver? Every age undergoes change but perhaps for those of us dealing with historic buildings it is happening faster and on a wider scale than ever before. As Oram and Stelfox (2004) point out, it is happening "not because these older buildings can no longer serve a useful purpose, it is because ... we, as a society, do not need to count the cost. How future generations will judge us we can only guess" (p.2). We are not only changing the landscape, but with the loss of buildings of character, we are wiping out layers of social and cultural history. Policy document after policy document, politician after politician invoke the greatness of sustainability, but again as the old saying goes, 'fine words don't butter parsnips'. Where is the evidence that we do really care about the legacy we pass on to future generations? Hellman, cartoonist for the *Architects' Journal*, devised a spoof exam paper for the proposed A-Level in Architecture. It read as follows: "Discuss current ecological concerns while limiting the use of the word sustainable to thirty times" (Hellman, 2005). Hearth, at least, needs to mention the word only once, along with integrity, imagination and social responsibility.

References

Brett, C.E.B. (2005) *Towers of Crim Tartary: English and Scottish architects in the Crimea, 1762-1853*, Donington, Shaun Tynas.

Brett, C.E.B. (1971) *Historic buildings, groups of buildings, areas of architectural importance in the Glens of Antrim*, Belfast, UAHS.

Buildings at risk Northern Ireland. Vol.7 (2005), Belfast, UAHS & EHS.

Cadw: Welsh Historic Monuments (2003) *Small rural dwellings in Wales: care and conservation*, Cardiff, Cadw.

Cornforth, J. (1994) Keep Hearth's fires burning, *Country Life,* 188(11), p.63.

Dean, J.A.K. (1994) *The gate lodges of Ulster: a gazetteer*, Belfast, UAHS.

Department of the Environment, Heritage and Local Government (2004) *Architectural heritage protection: guidelines for planning authorities*, Dublin, Stationery Office.

Devlin, H. (2004) *Traditional buildings within the Mourne and Slieve Croob Area of Outstanding Natural Beauty,* Unpublished thesis, Belfast, RSUA.

Department of the Environment (1999) *Planning Policy Statement 6 – Planning, archaeology and the built heritage*, Belfast, Department of the Environment.

Department for Regional Development (2004) *Planning Policy Statement 14 – Sustainable development in the countryside: issues paper*, Belfast, Department for Regional Development.

Environment and Heritage Service (1998) *A sense of loss: the survival of rural traditional buildings in Northern Ireland*, Belfast, Department of the Environment.

Greer, J. (2000) Review of Bliss or blitz, *Heritage Review*, 3, p.40.

Hearth (1999) *Hearth: a review of projects*, Belfast, Hearth.

Hellman, L. (2005) A-level architecture, *Architects' Journal*, 221(15), p.20.

Johnston, T. (1979) *Poems by Thomas Hardy*, London, Folio Society.

Maguire, C. (1999) The changing vernacular landscape, in UAHS (ed) *Bliss or Blitz*, pp.27-40, Belfast, UAHS.

Oram, R. and Stelfox, D. (2004) *Traditional buildings in Ireland: home owners' handbook*, Newcastle, Mourne Heritage Trust.

Patton, M. (2003) Conservation at the coal-face: a short history of Hearth, in T. Reeves-Smyth and R. Oram (eds.) *Avenues to the past*, pp.75-103, Belfast, UAHS.

Rothery, S. (1976) *Everyday buildings of Ireland*, Dublin, Department of Architecture, College of Technology.

SAVE Britain's Heritage (2001) *Blink and you'll miss it: Northern Ireland's heritage in danger*, London, SAVE.

Shaffrey, P. (1975) *The Irish town: an approach to survival*, Dublin, O'Brien Press.

UAHS (1999) *Bliss or blitz: proceedings of a conference on the future of rural buildings in Ulster, held at the Waterfront Hall, Belfast on 20 March 1998*, Belfast, UAHS.

Ulster Countryside Committee (1976) *Building in the countryside*, Belfast, HMSO.

Chapter 10

Consultation, New Countryside Housing and Rural Planning Policy in Northern Ireland

Michael Murray

Introduction

The imperative of stakeholder consultation is now at the heart of contemporary public policy formation. Central government departments, devolved administrations, public agencies and local authorities are all on this treadmill of inviting comment on the content of draft policy papers. The aim is to enhance public policy responsiveness to service constituencies through a variety of citizen involvement mechanisms. There is almost a universality of application as evidenced by the publication in 2001 of the OECD handbook *Citizens as Partners* that seeks to give best advice on information, consultation and public engagement practices (Gramberger, 2001).

Within the United Kingdom the Government has published a raft of advice on the need for consultation and has also given guidance on methods to be adopted. Thus, for example, in 1998 the Cabinet Office issued *An introductory guide: how to consult your users*. This was followed in 1999 by *Involving users: improving the delivery of local public services* and in November 2000 by *A code of practice on written consultation*. The alleged benefits of consultation include: helping to plan services better to give users what they want and expect; helping with the prioritisation of services and making better use of limited resources; helping set performance standards relevant to users' needs and associated monitoring; fostering a working partnership with users so that there is understanding of the problems being faced and how they can help; providing speedy alert to problems so that there is a chance to put things right before they escalate; and symbolising a commitment to be open and accountable.

It is now commonplace for guidelines to specify the period of weeks that is desirable for a consultation engagement, to outline methodologies for large group interactions, to caution against the risks of consultation burn-out, and to offer suggestions on how to reach the most excluded or vulnerable people and groups in society. Information technology is advanced as being an appropriate conduit for providing details of existing consultations, notification about forthcoming consultations and the results of completed consultations. A call has even been made for the electronic publication of a comprehensive consultation register to which all UK government departments and agencies would be required to submit details of their consultations in a compatible format (Consultation Institute, 2003).

In Northern Ireland the Office of the First and Deputy First Minister (2003) lists not fewer than ten features of 'good policy making' all of which are denoted by a dependency on consultation. Policy formulation should be forward looking, outward looking, innovative, evidence based, inclusive, joined-up, based on lessons learnt, communicative, and draw on evaluation and review. In short, the context presented by public managers is one of openness, an earnest willingness to learn and a need for policy messages to be heard.

Information gathering, analysis and dissemination have thus become crucial elements for managing the 'hollow state' (after Howlett, 2000). This reflects the structural transformation of government behaviour which increasingly obliges it to steer rather than row (Osborne and Gaebler, 1992), to work within a complex framework of policy communities (Rhodes, 1997), to support the managerialist revolution of charters, market testing and contracting out (Theakston, 1998), and to embrace a multiplicity of organisational partnerships for delivery (Lowndes and Skelcher, 1998). Accordingly, consultation is deeply embedded in working through the shift from government to governance whereby the latter can be defined as a process of participation constructed around networks of engagement that attempt to embrace diversity in society, that promote greater responsiveness to service users, and that seek to reshape accountability relationships (Lovan *et al*, 2004).

Within the specific sphere of town and country planning there is a long tradition of stakeholder engagement. But all too often a professional style, fashioned under an arrogance of 'knowing best', has relegated the role of citizens to a position well beneath the highly technocratic prescriptions of the planning expert. More than thirty years ago Friedmann (1973) in his transactive model of planning recognised that inputs are required from both technical experts and civil society. The former, he argued, brings valuable theoretical concepts and analysis, processed knowledge, new perspectives, and systematic search procedures for the resolution of problems. Civil society, on the other hand, has a more intimate knowledge of local context and challenges, a better feel for realistic alternatives and a greater capacity to prioritise needs and make feasibility judgements. This participatory approach, premised on interaction, is more demanding than any quick-fix planning solution. But if it leads to a relationship of mutual obligation and reciprocal trust between all parties, then planning policies will be more firmly embedded and stand a healthier chance of successful implementation, not least through enduring political support.

It is within this context of popular support for stakeholder engagement as an important element of participatory planning processes that this chapter reviews the contribution made by consultation to the moulding of planning policy for new countryside dwellings in Northern Ireland. Four prominent and sequential consultation processes are examined in this case study: an independent review committee convened by Government in 1977, a key stakeholder-led consultation as an input into a new planning strategy for rural Northern Ireland in 1991, the use of a public examination forum as part of the preparation process of a regional spatial strategy in 1997, and a write-in, issues-based consultation connected with the preparation of a Planning Policy Statement in 2004. Reflections on these experiences draw out important matters of wider interest. These revolve around the extent to which citizen participation through different forms of consultation can function as an effective policy-making tool, and the scope for future consultation action that may help reduce the longstanding contestation between the countryside dwelling policy preferences of planning bureaucracy and rural communities.

Countryside Housing and Rural Planning Policy

The sustained consultation engagement by policy-makers in Northern Ireland on the matter of new countryside dwellings and rural planning policy since the 1970s reflects the existence of a most wicked planning problem. The background to this debate is rehearsed by Caldwell and Greer (1984) who trace the derivation and subsequent evolution of rural planning policy back to the Matthew Plan of 1963. This gave emphasis to curtailing the expansion of the Belfast Urban Area and establishing a suite of growth centres principally within the city region, but with a number of key centres for industry elsewhere in Northern Ireland. Caldwell and Greer argue that the rural dimension received little attention and that as a result:

> Physical planning for rural areas therefore got off to an inauspicious start in this period of intense Government effort and concern for development. There prevailed little perception of the personality of the countryside and its people, save a somewhat inconsistent, negative and regulatory attitude to amenity and preservation of the landscape; a seeming unawareness of the unique and complex inheritance of history and culture and above all a lack of understanding of the consequences of the persistent drift from the land, particularly in peripheral rural areas, where the agricultural base was in severe decline. (p.4)

General planning principles set out by Matthew in his Interim Report comprised: restriction of scattered development; restriction of ribbon development; preservation of best agricultural land and natural amenities; economy of development costs; convenience in relation to communications and places of employment; convenience to social and commercial facilities; and general planning suitability. While not designed for rural areas, these were subsequently refashioned in 1964 as Circular guidance to planning authorities in Northern Ireland to be applied to all rural developments, but principally new countryside dwellings. Four prominent consultation processes with rural stakeholders since the 1970s have sought to fashion an appropriate responsiveness by rural planning policy.

(1) The Cockcroft Committee
On the 1st October 1973 the Department of the Environment for Northern Ireland became the sole planning authority for the region following the removal of planning responsibilities from the then newly established District Councils. New guidelines for rural planning policy were subsequently published by the Department of the Environment in 1974. These recognised that the demand for rural housing could come from people who must live in the countryside, from people who would like to live in the countryside, and from people who believed they had a strong claim to live in the countryside because of kinship ties and other personal circumstances. This represented the first official statement in this policy area since 1964. It defined a range of circumstances in which individuals would be given special consideration in respect of receiving planning permission for a dwelling in open countryside. At the same time, work was being advanced on preparing a regional development strategy for Northern Ireland and following the publication of a Discussion Paper with a range of spatial options, the Government issued its Regional Physical Development Strategy 1975-1995 in May 1977. It gave prominence to what was known as the District Towns Strategy, involving a greater dispersal of resources to 23 urban centres across Northern Ireland. The proposed dynamics of change were such that while the District Towns were expected to grow by 34 per cent over the planning period, compared with an increase of 2.8 per cent for Northern Ireland as a whole, the population in rural areas was anticipated to decline by an average of 5 per cent and by as much as 10 per cent in the more remote districts. The application of complementary rural planning guidelines, updated in 1976, reaffirmed the need for strict residential development controls in the countryside.

Policy opposition by District Councils became much more vocal in the wake of this perceived indifference to rural living by Government planners. Crisis led to the appointment in May 1977 by Mr Ray Carter, Parliamentary

Under-Secretary of State, with responsibility for the Department of the Environment, of a five persons Committee to review the Department's rural planning policy, chaired by Dr W H Cockcroft, the then Vice Chancellor of the New University of Ulster. The Committee convened its first meeting in June 1977 and moved quickly to advertise an invitation for both written submissions and oral representations. The Committee indicated that it would travel widely to receive evidence and by January 1978 a total of 81 bodies and persons had participated in the consultation process, including not fewer than 23 District Councils. Analysis of the evidence submitted, and now available at the Public Record Office of Northern Ireland, reveals an overwhelming plea for greater flexibility in the application of rural planning policy as it related to countryside dwellings. Even elements of the landscape conservation lobby recognised the need for policy change as illustrated by an oral representation made by the North Regional Committee of the Ulster Society for the Preservation of the Countryside and which is minuted as follows:

> The present policy was much too inflexible and planning applications were determined without regard to the social, educational and other needs of the people in rural areas. Decisions regarding the building of new houses and schools were being taken in isolation and on economic grounds rather than as part of an overall integrated social policy. (ENV1/1A/23 Public Record Office of Northern Ireland)

Considerable anecdotal evidence was submitted to the Committee; indeed that is to be expected in a consultation process such as this. There is no denying, however, that the opportunity taken by consultees to vent strong emotions greatly influenced its deliberations. In short, the thrust of argument unleashed by the consultation process indicated perceived major shortcomings of the then present policy. In his submission and oral evidence, John Greer concluded that firstly, it was a blanket policy which did not recognise differences between those areas under development pressure and those at risk from rural depopulation, and secondly, it was derived, without further analysis, from the rural settlement policies which have been devised for the densely populated and highly urbanised areas of lowland Britain. What was required was a policy that reflected the particular condition and problems of rural life in Northern Ireland, and that this could only really be achieved by closer study and research (Public Record Office of Northern Ireland ENV1/1B/42).

The report of the Cockcroft Committee was submitted to Government in March 1978 and was published in June of that year along with an invitation to interested parties to submit their views. Essentially the Committee accepted that the strict system of planning controls on new countryside dwellings were not consistent with the long-term well being of rural communities. As reported by the Department of the Environment a wide cross section of inputs was received including those from District Councils, statutory bodies, conservation groups and professional bodies and indeed "overall reaction to it was favourable". Rural planning policy in Northern Ireland was also debated in Parliament on 3rd July 1978 and support was expressed for a change in direction. In November 1978 the Department of the Environment introduced a new and more relaxed rural planning policy for housing and other development in the countryside.

(2) A Planning Strategy for Rural Northern Ireland
In September 1991 the Minister with responsibility for the Department of the Environment for Northern Ireland issued a consultation leaflet titled *What kind of countryside do we want? Options for a new planning strategy for rural Northern Ireland.* The leaflet identified four key issues: changes taking place in the rural economy and the trend towards rural economic diversification; the building of some 25,000 dwellings in the Northern Ireland countryside over the previous decade and the emergence of pockets of semi-urban development where the rural scene is dominated by buildings; less than expected development going into the 120 settlements across Northern Ireland in the population range 500-5,000, principally because people have opted to live in the countryside; greater public awareness of environmental issues and growing support for conservation, not least the visual appearance of the landscape. This initiative was launched on foot of a report into environmental issues affecting Northern Ireland that had been prepared in 1990 by the House of Commons Environment Committee. It had expressed concern about indiscriminate development in the countryside and had recommended that the Department of the Environment for Northern Ireland undertake a review of the effects of its rural planning policies.

This consultation came at a time, therefore, when the legacy of the Cockcroft Committee induced reforms were perceived by Government as unwelcome. But at the same time a new area of public policy was emerging in the form of broad based rural development under the leadership of the Department of Agriculture for Northern Ireland (Murray and Greer, 1993). The establishment of the Rural Development Council and Rural Community Network to carry forward action in the most deprived rural areas gave prominence to the role of community-led initiatives in the villages and open countryside. A host of local development strategies identified the sweep of necessary interventions across, for example, enterprise and tourism, social infrastructure and housing. With so much energy, and not least considerable funding going into rural projects, rural planning policy, it could be argued, could not afford to remain disconnected from that wider developmental agenda.

This review of rural planning policy was, therefore, the first of its kind since 1977 – 1978, the importance of which prompted three organisations (the Rural Development Council, Rural Community Network and Community Technical Aid) to undertake a collaborative consultation exercise with rural community groups. The Planning Service of the Department of the Environment agreed to take an active role in the process, not only by part funding the consultation programme, but also by sending a planner from Headquarters and the relevant Divisional Planning Office to each of the meetings arranged. Twenty venues were selected on the advice of a Steering Committee established to oversee the consultation. Clinics in the form of group discussions took place between 23rd October 1991 and 12th December 1991. Total attendances comprised some 750 people. Minutes from the sessions were used to prepare a draft report that was forwarded to local community organisers and, following amendments, the final community consultation document in two volumes (Community Technical Aid, 1992) was submitted to the Department of the Environment for Northern Ireland in January 1992.

Some principal insights from this consultation process usefully locate the issue of countryside dwellings within a broader rural development context:

- rural Northern Ireland extends far beyond the agricultural sector, with the number of people owning land or having access to it through kinship being much greater than the number employed in farming;
- the family farm in most cases does not provide sufficient income to maintain all the members of the household and thus off farm incomes are important in maintaining a reasonable standard of living;
- farm diversification projects, while being promoted by agriculture and rural development policies, very often do not receive support from Planning Service;
- new business development in the countryside and villages, including rural tourism, is part of the rural development portfolio which rural planning policy must embrace;
- many parts of the countryside can absorb and need to accommodate more people and more dwellings than they currently have in order to ensure their survival as living rural communities;
- local towns and villages do play an important role in rural areas and thus there should be high standards of amenity, housing and services. But the growth of towns and villages should reflect natural increase and the voluntary migration of people from the countryside, rather than the push impact of planning restrictions on countryside dwellings;
- while rural dwellers appreciate the value of environmental protection, the

human dimension should not be overlooked; and

• the perceived bureaucracy of Planning Service must be altered to make it more approachable, accountable and proactive in its dealings with rural people.

The Department of the Environment published *A Planning Strategy for Rural Northern Ireland* in September 1993 in which it noted having received a total of 109 consultation responses including the report from Community Technical Aid. Not fewer than 900 separate suggestions were made by consultees for improving rural planning policy, practice or procedure. At first sight the language of the *Planning Strategy* appeared to be conciliatory to all these rural interests. On the positive side the Department of the Environment recognised for the first time the spatial reality of dispersed rural communities, supported farm diversification, abandoned a rigid hierarchy of settlements, promised generous development limits around smaller settlements and promoted rural regeneration in circumstances of economic and social disadvantage. But it quickly became very apparent that this document with its 117 policies, some quite detailed in nature, would increasingly be used to frame planning permission refusals. Moreover, these Strategy policies would inform the preparation of Area Plans and provide for their defence at public inquiries, not least in relation to the designation of extensive Countryside Policy Areas and Green Belts where the presumption is against housing development. All this is unfortunate since there was a real opportunity at that time, in the context of the enthusiasm for rural development, to give rural planning a new set of credentials which would have allowed it to rise well above the 'trench warfare' of countryside dwellings development control. When it is recalled that there is a high correlation between high amenity areas and those experiencing disadvantage, the pivotal importance of land use planning becomes all the more evident. Grounded as it is in environmentalism, it serves to militate against rather than enable development. Physical planning policies for rural Northern Ireland needed to be informed by a broader and deeper understanding of rural society and economy and their dynamics, if planning is to be more than a negative regulatory mechanism, wedded to the environmental agenda.

It is scarcely surprising that strong opposition to this policy prescription was spawned. A subsequent House of Commons Northern Ireland Affairs Committee scrutiny of the planning system in Northern Ireland in 1996 weighed in behind that criticism and prompted the Department of the Environment to respond that the *Rural Strategy* will be progressively withdrawn and replaced by new guidance to be set out in a series of planning policy statements.

(3) Shaping Our Future

The process of preparing a new regional strategy for Northern Ireland, to replace the earlier Regional Physical Development Strategy, commenced in mid 1997 and was given significant profile by the publication in the following November of a discussion paper titled *Shaping Our Future: Towards a Strategy for the Development of the Region.* The Discussion Paper proposed a daunting (and with the benefit of hindsight, impossible) timetable for completion of the process through to December 1998 and linked with which there were to be considerable inputs by way of public involvement. When concluded this had comprised a number of features:

- a total of 116 direct consultations by the Department of the Environment with District Councils, political parties, other parts of Government and regional organisations;
- a total of 207 formal submissions from District Councils, political parties, elected representatives, business organisations and public sector bodies;
- the appointment of a research consortium from Queen's University, Belfast, The Urban Institute at University of Ulster, Community Technical Aid and Rural Community Network which facilitated consultation with 477 community and voluntary groups;
- the convening of 2 conferences attended by some 600 young people which resulted in the submission of a Northern Ireland Youth Council Report.

Nonetheless, on a conceptual spectrum of citizen participation which ranges from information dissemination, to opinion gathering, to active involvement in decision making, through to delegated authority, it is clear that these processes of engagement were located at its lower end. In contrast, a proposed Public Examination which formed the cornerstone of consultation on the draft strategy lay more within the domain of active involvement in the policy formulation process albeit that the setting of the agenda and the subsequent determination of policy preferences were to be overseen by the Department for Regional Development and the Northern Ireland Assembly.

But the planning process also created the opportunity for the establishment of a new sub-regional alliance within Northern Ireland as evidenced by the insistence of five neighbouring District Councils to respond collectively to consultative invitations by the Department of the Environment. Under the compact of the West Rural Region these District Councils took the view that any meaningful rural input into a Northern Ireland strategy could best be represented through a collective voice. The Councils were in addition mindful of other policy frameworks being devised at that time within the context of

Well into 2000 by the Department of Health and Social Services, an *Economic Strategy for Northern Ireland* by the Department of Economic Development, and a new EU Structural Funds bid by the Department of Finance and Personnel. Accordingly, the Councils commissioned staff at Queen's University, Belfast and University of Ulster, under the leadership of John Greer, to (1) facilitate discussion among elected representatives, public sector officials and stakeholders from the business, community and voluntary sectors, (2) assist with the preparation of an audit of the West Rural Region and, (3) help identify development principles and themes which could go beyond conventional land use planning and have relevance for these additional policy areas. Intensive work sessions with elected representatives over a period of 4 months were rotated around each of the Council offices and, at the insistence of the Councils, a highly symbolic consultative plenary meeting, rather than 5 separate sessions, was convened with planners from the Department of the Environment.

The important point here is that the analysis by the West Rural Region probed much deeper into the living and working patterns of rural people than was attempted by the Department of the Environment in its Discussion Paper. The local authorities outlined a suite of measures that are designed to strengthen communities, develop business and invest in people. It is not appropriate to dwell on the detail within the limitations of this chapter except to note that these measures fitted well with the Government's intention to go beyond land use planning, to create joined-up policy initiatives and to engage an active citizenry in the quest for growth and development in Northern Ireland as a whole. These measures also captured the essence of what rural development should champion. Accordingly, physical planning and transport policy were exhorted to promote locational choice and accessibility thereby respecting the distinctiveness of the dispersed settlement pattern and cultural diversity of the territory. In short, a primary aim of this submission was to strengthen an internal consensus across 5 District Council areas about the desired shape of a shared future and to contest the rather minimalist consideration of this area by the Department of the Environment in its Discussion Paper. The geographical scale of this collective criticism and advocacy was without parallel in Northern Ireland and did succeed in putting pressure on the regional planning team to rework its preliminary proposals.

The draft Regional Strategic Framework (RSF) for Northern Ireland was subsequently published in December 1998. It is not surprising that the content and tone are, were at first sight, much more conciliatory to rural interests. For example, there was fresh recognition of the "Rural Community" and "Rural Northern Ireland". Of particular significance was the articulation of not fewer than 30 draft strategic planning guidelines (SPG). These ranged widely from the global to the local and from urban to rural, but essentially were written as 'feel good headlines' that could be expected to attract little criticism. For example: SPG 9: *To sustain a living and working countryside.*

A total of 169 representations in relation to the draft regional strategy were received from District Councils, political parties, organisations and individuals by the Department of the Environment following its publication through to April 1999. Within the West Rural Region the draft RSF was welcomed as a significant advance in thinking compared with the Discussion Document of November 1997. Nevertheless, elected representatives voiced a number of reservations in their collective submission to the Department of the Environment. The West Rural Region took the view that the draft Strategy as a whole did not sufficiently respond to the challenge of joined-up government, especially in regard to rural development, education and health care provision and indeed had tended to stay clear of important, though controversial, areas of policy formulation work. The submission concluded by pressing for the opportunity to further debate concerns at the forthcoming Public Examination.

A Public Examination is designed to provide information through informed public discussion of certain matters relevant to policy decision-making. It provides an arena within which different stakeholders can present facts and arguments to an independent panel whose task, in turn, is to make recommendations on the basis of the evidence to the sponsoring authority. Within Great Britain the Examination in Public tool has long been associated with the preparation of Structure Plans and has been adopted to test the content of draft Regional Planning Guidance. But within Northern Ireland, that tradition of policy deliberation has not been a feature of physical planning which has tended to rely on the conventional, adversarial public inquiry process to deal with land use and development issues associated with statutory development plans. The decision to include a Public Examination in the programme for the preparation of a Northern Ireland regional strategy can be viewed, therefore, as a welcome innovation. From the perspective of rural planning and development this is particularly relevant since the *Rural Planning Strategy for Northern Ireland*, discussed above, was not made subject to public scrutiny when it was published in 1993 and, as such, its contents retained the status of unsubstantiated planning doctrine.

The Public Examination into the draft RSF was convened over a 5 weeks period during October and November 1999. Prior to that the appointed Panel of 3 members, along with its secretariat, had:

- made themselves familiar with the GB Examination in Public experience;
- reviewed all 169 submissions received by the Department of the Environment in relation to the Draft RSF;
- selected and revised, following additional consultation, the matters to be

included in the Public Examination;
- selected the participants;
- invited written statements from participants on the selected matters;
- convened 2 public meetings to provide procedural information;
- agreed different venues across Northern Ireland to hold the Public Examination; and
- conducted a pre-meeting on the central issue of housing projections.

Over 170 different participants attended the Public Examination on behalf of a wide range of invited organisations drawn from central government departments and agencies, district councils, the business, community and voluntary sectors, and representative bodies. Their input was organised by the Panel to be in line with their previously expressed concerns and expertise, and while a number of organisations appeared at more than one debate, any single debate did not usually have more than 24 participants. Thus, for example, the West Rural Region attended a total of 11 sessions out of the 14 separate listed matters. Its spokespersons consisted solely of district council elected representatives and chief executives who, following a division of labour, were then delegated to speak on behalf of the compact as a whole. The formation of strategic alliances was very much encouraged by the panel and resulted, for example, in several community organisations concerned, *inter alia*, with protection of the Belfast green belt coming together under the umbrella of the Belfast Metropolitan Residents Group.

The report of the Panel which conducted the Public Examination into the draft RSF was subsequently published in February 2000. It ran to 130 pages and contained some 110 recommendations. A follow-on response by the Department for Regional Development (DRD), which assumed responsibility for regional planning following devolution in December 1999, appeared in April 2000 and, over its 35 pages, comprised a series of statements which indicated acceptance of, a willingness to take note of, or an undertaking to give further consideration to these recommendations. The chapter in the report of the Public Examination Panel dealing with rural Northern Ireland comprised a most incisive critique of public policy within this spatial arena. The sub-headings phrased by the Panel for its analysis demonstrated an empathy with rural issues which went far beyond the tone and content of the draft RSF and were warmly welcomed by the West Rural Region. These included: threats to rural society; a fragmented Government response; sustainable development in rural areas; the need for integrated rural policy making and co-ordinated action; promotion of diversity - the urgent case of the rural economy; positive planning measures in rural service centres; problems of access and disadvantage; supporting community participation; and the need for a coherent planning statement on rural social issues. This independent analysis had successfully located the central issue of rural housing in its wider rural development context.

The response of the DRD, in contrast, was somewhat disappointing in that there was no unequivocal support for the preparation of a White Paper on rural planning and development as called for by the Panel. On the other hand a commitment was given to include a new chapter in the final strategy which would acknowledge different development pressures and the need for different planning responses as between the Belfast Travel to Work Area and the rest of rural Northern Ireland. When the completed strategy was eventually published in September 2001 rural Northern Ireland was positively promoted through a combination of rural development objectives, specific strategic planning guidelines and a spatial framework for future development. But arguably the real chill on the warm rhetoric of the Regional Development Strategy in this sphere is the promise of a Planning Statement on the Countryside to deal with the perceived cumulative impact of 'inappropriate single house development' in the countryside. Accordingly, the publication in 2004 of an Issues Paper, connected to the preparation of Planning Policy Statement 14, set in train the fourth and most recent consultation process on rural planning in Northern Ireland.

(4) Planning Policy Statement 14: Sustainable Development in the Countryside

Within the United Kingdom Planning Policy Statements (PPS) set out government policies on land use and related matters They act as a material consideration in the determination of planning applications and assist with the preparation of development plans. They have been steadily introduced in Northern Ireland over the period since 1996 by the Department of the Environment working in conjunction with the Department for Regional Development and are designed to replace comparable planning policy guidance set out in the *Planning Strategy for Rural Northern Ireland*. It is usual practice for draft PPS to be published for public consultation and, thereafter, to move to a final statement. However, in the case of rural planning and new countryside dwellings the Department for Regional Development as the lead authority proceeded more cautiously by publishing an Issues Paper in June 2004 to capture stakeholder comments at an early stage. This PPS, of course, has long been promised, and thus the Issues Paper approach could also be interpreted as a necessary response to a difficult delivery commitment within the Department's corporate plan. As the discussion, thus far, has shown, the rural planning challenge undoubtedly remains one of the most contested planning issues in Northern Ireland. Indeed the overall tone for the consultation process is captured by the data presented in the Issues Paper to the effect that the number of single new dwellings being approved in the countryside has increased from 1,790 in 1991/92 to 5,628 by 2002/03 and that these approvals in Northern Ireland are treble that approved annually in England, Scotland and Wales combined.

At the time of writing (June 2005) the draft PPS 14 has not yet been issued, but it has been possible to obtain, as a result of the Freedom of Information Act 2000 and the Environmental Information Regulations 2004, the consultation input to the Department for Regional Development arising from that Issues Paper. In all, there were 77 responses through and beyond the consultation period ending 4th October 2004 of which 18 were from District Councils. The submissions once again expose the longstanding dialectic of landscape protection and rural community development with a wide range of organisations from each side offering opinions, evidence and proposals in relation to a range of questions oriented in the main to countryside housing. A summary analysis written by the Department for Regional Development concludes as follows:

> The general split in opinion on this issue is also a microcosm of the broader argument between those who live in the countryside and their elected representatives, including those with a vested business interest, and those bodies / agencies whose primary remit is the protection, preservation or conservation of the countryside. These competing interests or divisions are not new, (and) should be of no surprise. (p.9)

The data, it is pointed out, illustrate a broad 50/50 split on the question regarding a presumption in favour of development in the open countryside; some 78 per cent of consultees favour the proposition of tailoring policies to areas in line with differential pressures and needs, while 77 per cent favour the introduction of some form of 'local needs' criteria in respect of single dwellings. Improved design standards are overwhelmingly endorsed, as also is the strengthening of services provision to rural communities. However, what is interesting is that the overwhelming majority of respondents, including key rural community stakeholders, hold the opinion that the countryside is under pressure from housing development.

What makes this consultation input to the policy process especially useful is that it stands in marked contrast to the depopulation tone of much of the evidence submitted to the Cockcroft Committee back in 1977. But, when set alongside a general perception of development pressure in the countryside, it points once again to the serious structural defect in the way that rural planning and rural development policies have been formulated and delivered for some considerable time. Each policy domain has operated independently without any interactive understanding and shared vision of the type of rural society that is desirable and how that can be jointly secured at local levels. Unfortunately the thrust of the PPS 14 Issues Paper compounds this limitation in that the rural challenge, notwithstanding the title *Sustainable development in the countryside,* is seen only as a new housing in the countryside problem and thus sits somewhat uneasily with the hard-won and more extensive advocacy of the rural throughout the Regional Development Strategy preparation process. The final part of this chapter picks up on this worrying disconnection and how it may begin to be addressed.

Conclusion

This chapter has explored the contribution made by four major consultation processes over the period 1977 to 2004 to the formulation of rural planning policy in Northern Ireland. Each wave of policy investigation has been able to draw on the criticisms of rural stakeholders and the concerns of powerful parliamentary oversight. On the basis of the evidence reviewed, the substantive content of the rural planning debate has shifted quite markedly from alarm at the prospects of unremitting population decline, to the consequences of unbridled housing construction in the countryside. Consultation has provided a significant mechanism to uncover the changing texture of popular feeling by seeking information about 'how things are on the ground', by floating possibilities for policy adjustment, and by engaging important interests in policy debate.

While the instruments used over time do vary, they nonetheless offer interesting insights into the behaviour, learning and adaptation of public policy managers. Thus, it could be argued that the openness of the independent Cockcroft Committee to an alternative developmental narrative compares quite favourably with the willingness of the Public Examination Panel of the Regional Development Strategy to confidently articulate new thoughts about the rural. Each has attempted to understand and embrace the wider rural development context for new countryside housing. It is also significant that the reports of the Cockcroft Committee and the Public Examination Panel commanded independent status and were not tied by the dogma of the professional planning regime. On the other hand, the formulation of the Rural Planning Strategy for Northern Ireland without a draft version for open debate and the painfully slow emergence of Planning Policy Statement 14 point to a more direct exercising of authority by an uncertain bureaucracy.

Accordingly, the externally driven consultation mechanisms can be seen as illustrative of situations where policy is searching for a *rapprochement* with an emergent political and citizen consensus around the rural, while the more internal processes can be seen as being representative of difficult policy-making in more deeply contested arenas. Expressed in this way, consultation provides for varying levels of responsiveness and manipulation in order to deliver some legitimacy to the levers of cautious control. There can be little doubt that the importance placed on consultation is circumscribed by this pragmatism. Thus the stated unwillingness of the Department for Regional Development in Northern Ireland to subject the forthcoming draft Planning Policy Statement 14 to the equivalent of an open Public Examination process, with independent scrutiny of all cases being stated, points to the operation of a more constrained contemporary framework for rural planning policy than might be thought.

In Northern Ireland the enormous profile given to the latest phase of front-ended, but internally structured, consultation may ultimately serve only to mask the true desire by Government planners in Northern Ireland for top-down compliance on the matter of new dwellings in the countryside. Of course the pursuit of that model of planning managerialism runs the considerable risk of speedy alienation, political discomfort and policy breakdown. The fracturing of the pre-1978 rural planning guidelines, the fate of the subsequent 1993 *Rural Planning Strategy for Northern Ireland*, and the transformative intervention of strategic alliances at local government level in the lead up to and during the regional strategy Public Examination, as discussed above, collectively provide important lessons from recent history.

But at a broader level within Europe the current policy landscape for rural planning is also very different, not least because a concern for the overall wellbeing of rural areas is now much more deeply embedded in national, regional and local governance structures. Area-based and community-led approaches to the delivery of change in rural areas are commonplace and there is now greater capacity and willingness by rural citizens to negotiate local futures which rural planning policy ignores at its peril. This different form of dialogue, the equivalent of consultative interaction, while challenging the orthodoxies of technical calculus, nonetheless constitutes a major opportunity for achieving a more durable rural planning policy succession. In short, there is a need to go beyond mere conformity with consultation obligations and to embrace the boundary-spanning and empowering potential of a collaborative engagement between planners and rural people on a locality basis.

To conclude, the time is right to take forward a considerable programme of action research on the island of Ireland that will develop and test new participatory and collaborative methodologies for finally integrating rural planning and rural development. The principal focus of this work should be to marry local preference for new countryside dwellings with environmental responsibility. It should seek to contextualise through local involvement the long-running single house in the countryside issue, described in this chapter, within a robust analysis of rural settlement patterns and their economic, social and cultural dimensions. Innes and Booher (1999) argue that the most important consequences from this form of shared learning occur not at the end, but during the discussion process itself. How well these rural planning challenges are dealt with will depend on how a different approach to the

References

Caldwell, J. and Greer, J. (1984) *Physical planning in rural areas of Northern Ireland*, Occasional Paper No 5, Belfast, Queen's University, Belfast.

Community Technical Aid (1992) *Rural planning strategy review: a community consultation response*, Belfast, Community Technical Aid.

Consultation Institute (2003) *The Consultation Institute's preliminary response to the Draft Code Of Practice on Consultation*, Orpington, The Consultation Institute.

Cookstown District Council, Dungannon District Council, Fermanagh District Council, Omagh District Council and Strabane District Council (1998) *The West Rural Region: A strategy for people, partnership and prosperity*, Cookstown, Cookstown District Council.

Department of the Environment for Northern Ireland (1977) *Northern Ireland Regional Physical Development Strategy 1975-95*, Belfast, HMSO.

Department of the Environment for Northern Ireland (1978) *Review of rural planning policy: report of the Committee under the Chairmanship of Dr W H Cockcroft MA, DPhil, FIMA,* Belfast, HMSO.

Department of the Environment for Northern Ireland (1978) *Review of rural planning policy*, Belfast, HMSO.

Department of the Environment for Northern Ireland (1993) *A planning strategy for rural Northern Ireland*, Belfast, HMSO.

Department of the Environment for Northern Ireland (1998) *Shaping our future – the family of settlements report*, Belfast, Department of the Environment for Northern Ireland.

Department for Regional Development (2001) *Shaping our future: Regional Development Strategy for Northern Ireland 2025,* Belfast, CDS.

Department for Regional Development (2004) *PPS 14: Sustainable development in the countryside: Issues paper*, Belfast, Department for Regional Development.

Friedmann, J. (1973) *Retracking America: a theory of transactive planning*, New York, Anchor Press.

Gramberger, M. (2001) *Citizens as partners: OECD handbook on information, consultation, and public participation in policy making*, Paris, OECD.

Howlett, M. (2000) Managing the hollow state: procedural policy instruments and modern governance, *Canadian Public Administration*, 43(4), pp.412-431.

Innes, J. E. and Booher, D. (1999) Consensus building and complex adaptive systems: a framework for evaluating collaborative planning. *Journal of the American Planning Association*, 65 (Autumn), pp.412-423.

Lovan, W. R., Murray, M. and Shaffer, R. (eds.) (2004) *Participatory governance: planning, conflict mediation and public decision-making in civil society*, Aldershot, Ashgate.

Lowndes, V. and Skelcher, C. (1998) The dynamics of multi-organisational partnerships: an analysis of changing modes of governance, *Public Administration*, 76 (Summer), pp.313-333.

Matthew, R. (1963) *Belfast regional survey and plan: recommendations and conclusions*. Cmd 451, Belfast, HMSO.

Murray, M. and Greer, J. (eds.) (1993) *Rural development in Ireland*, Aldershot, Ashgate.

Office of the First and Deputy First Minister (2003) *A practical guide to policy-making in Northern Ireland*, Belfast, Office of the First and Deputy First Minister.

Osborne, D. and Gaebler, T. (1992) *Reinventing government: how the entrepreneurial spirit is transforming the public sector*, New York, Plume.

Rhodes, R. (1997) *Understanding governance: policy networks, governance, reflexivity and accountability*, Buckingham, Open University Press.

Theakston, K. (1998) New Labour, new Whitehall, *Public Policy and Administration*, 13(1), pp.13-34.

Chapter 11

Connecting Rural Dwellings with Rural Sustainable Development

Mark Scott

Introduction

The background to this chapter is the increasing difficulty that is being experienced in addressing the issue of housing development in the Irish countryside and the vexed relationship that exists between planning policy and many rural communities. This has been an issue for many years, but the debate surrounding housing in rural areas has become increasingly contentious and polarised between community and conservation interests. This is due to an increasing pace of development, the changing population dynamics of rural areas, and the increased pressure to include environmental considerations in the land-use planning process. Central to this debate is the concept of sustainability and its interpretation and application in rural areas. In recent years, the concept of sustainable development has become central in the formulation of spatial plans throughout Europe. Indeed, as recorded by Briassoulis (1999), sustainable development is now commonly cited as the ultimate planning goal, although what it means is not usually specified exactly nor how it is to be achieved. In general, participants in planning processes agree that sustainability is concerned with the simultaneous satisfaction of three objectives – environmental protection, social equity and economic development (Lindsey, 2003); in other words, creating a positive-sum strategy embracing these three policy goals (Albrechts *et al.*, 2003). In this regard, the planning system (and specifically the development plan), is a "key arena within which economic, social and environmental issues come together with respect to the spatial dimensions of management of environmental change" (Healey and Shaw, 1993, p.770).

The objective of this chapter is to evaluate the different interpretations and contested meanings of rural sustainability surrounding the housing in the countryside debate in the Republic of Ireland. The chapter argues that sustainable development has become a flag of convenience for those involved in the rural housing debate, leading to selective interpretations of sustainable management of housing in the countryside. Within this context, the planning system offers a potential arena to deliberate between conflicting objectives for managing rural housing and to formulate holistic approaches to rural sustainable development. However, at present the planning system appears to be failing to reconcile these different perspectives and values. Accordingly, this chapter is structured as follows: firstly, the nature of rurality and sustainability in Ireland will be discussed; and secondly, planning policy for rural areas will be outlined. Then, two local case studies in the west of Ireland will be outlined before conclusions are developed that are relevant to developing holistic approaches to the sustainable management of rural housing.

Rurality and Sustainability in Ireland
Few places in Europe are so closely identified with the 'rural' as Ireland (McDonagh, 2001). Despite growing industrialisation and urbanisation throughout the country, few places outside the cities of Dublin, Cork, Limerick, Galway and Waterford are referred to in any other context. In the most recent census in 2002, 40 per cent of the State's population lived in settlements smaller than 1,500 people or the open countryside. However, Ireland's rural communities are undergoing rapid and fundamental changes: the agricultural sector continues to restructure; the economic base of rural areas is diversifying; new consumer demands and practices have emerged; there is a growing concern for the environment and increased pressure to include the environmental dimension in decision-making; and some rural communities are under intense pressure from urbanisation, while other areas continue to experience population decline. Within this context of change and new demands on rural space, rural sustainable development has become a highly contested and divisive concept. For example, housing in the countryside, environmental directives for landscape protection, potential wind-farm development, access to farmland for recreation, and the Government's decentralisation programme for civil service departments, have all been marked by high profile and polarised debates in the popular media. As McDonagh (1998) argues, in this era of what is increasingly being referred to as a 'post-agricultural' society, there is an urgent need to question the understandings of the term 'rural' in Ireland and whether there is a coordinated policy direction for the changing future of rural areas.

The Irish Government is committed to sustainability principles (for example, *Sustainable Development – A Strategy for Ireland, 1997)* and since the enactment of the Planning and Development Act 2000, sustainable development is now central to the planning system. Local authorities must ensure the proper planning and sustainable development of their areas.

However, an absence of a working definition of sustainable development has led to the use of the concept of sustainability without any agreement as to its meaning. Practice from elsewhere suggests that, at the level of generality the imperative of sustainable development seems unquestionable, but its elaboration within policy permits potentially conflicting and, therefore, selective interpretations of what constitutes sustainable planning practice (Owen, 1996). Managing rural housing in Ireland provides a useful case study of the difficulties in developing holistic approaches to sustainable development as (drawing on Hajer, 1995) various and conflicting 'discourse coalitions' have emerged with actors grouping around specific and often selective 'storylines'. Therefore, policy development is critically dependent on specific social constructions of rural sustainable development, and is underpinned by latent social conflicts.

Planning Policy for Rural Settlement
Dispersed rural settlement growth over the past thirty years is a distinctive feature of many rural areas of Ireland (McGrath, 1998) and recent years have witnessed increasing difficulties in addressing the issue of housing development in the countryside. Rural settlement patterns are predominantly comprised of single dwellings in the open countryside with residents usually unconnected to agriculture, but who often have family roots in the locality and a strong attachment to place. The proliferation of dispersed single dwellings (or one-off housing) in the countryside has been an issue for many years. Indeed, commentators such as Aalen (1997) and McGrath (1998) have argued that the planning system is unable to respond effectively to rural settlement growth. In a critique of rural planning, both commentators suggest policy is driven by the priorities of a few individuals, an intense localism, and the predominance of incremental decision-making. Similarly, Gallent *et al.* (2003), in a review of rural housing policies throughout Europe, classify rural planning in Ireland as a laissez-faire regime, suggesting that: "the tradition of a more relaxed approach to regulation, and what many see as the underperformance in planning is merely an expression of Irish attitudes towards government intervention" (p. 90).

The debate surrounding dispersed rural settlement has become increasingly contentious both at a local and national scale. Analysis undertaken during the preparation of the National Spatial Strategy suggests that between 1996-1999 over one in three houses built in the Republic of Ireland have been one-off housing in the open countryside, and highlights that the issue of single applications for housing in rural areas has become a major concern for most local planning authorities (Spatial Planning Unit, 2001). This increased scale and pace of development has resulted from a number of factors including: the demographic recovery of many rural areas; a cultural predisposition to living in the countryside (Duffy, 2000) and a perception of the quality of life in urban areas; the relative lower costs associated with developing a one-off house (Clinch et al., 2002); increased mobility; and a desire for living in a rural environment, in particular with good accessibility to urban centres (Spatial Planning Unit, 2001). In essence, the rural housing debate is characterised by contestation and the development of two bodies of opinion (Lynch, 2002). One that represents conservation interests, the planning profession and local authority management, proposes severe restrictions on dispersed rural housing as a means to protecting landscapes and reducing car dependency. The second body of opinion represents rural communities, local political representatives and agricultural interests, who favour more liberal policies to enable greater social vitality and to protect against the further loss of rural services. Indeed, the issue of granting planning permission for housing in the countryside raises fundamental questions surrounding the politics of planning in rural Ireland, including the relationship between national and local planning policies and spatial strategies; the relationship between planning policy and development control decisions; and the noticeable worsening in relations between local authority planning officials and elected representatives evident in recent years.

Managing housing in the countryside is a complex and multi-dimensional issue and, in this context, the media portrayal of a 'one-off housing' debate is perhaps misleading. Rather than a singular rural housing debate, in reality the generators of rural housing, development pressures, environmental and community contexts vary widely across space – in other words, housing in rural North Mayo, with a declining population, is a different issue than housing in Fingal's countryside, where urban sprawl is a real threat. Also, the term 'one-off housing' itself has been criticised as it suggests that rural housing is disconnected from place and community and ignores the reality that the countryside is also a social space. The key issues surrounding rural housing can be summarised as follows:

- distribution and intensity;

- environmental costs;

- public health and safety (related to groundwater pollution and road access for housing);

- infrastructural implications;

- siting and design issues; and

- settlement patterns and community vitality.

Current Policy Context

Given the rapidly changing dynamics of rural areas and communities in the Republic of Ireland, the National Spatial Strategy (NSS) published in 2002, provided a timely opportunity to formulate a national framework for managing rural settlement growth. The NSS outlines four broad objectives as a basis for a sustainable rural settlement policy framework (p.105):

- to sustain and renew established rural communities and the existing stock of investment in a way that responds to various spatial, structural and economic changes taking place, while protecting the important assets rural areas possess;
- to strengthen the established structure of villages and smaller settlements both to assist local economies and to accommodate additional population in a way that supports the viability of public transport and local infrastructure and services such as schools and water services;
- to ensure that key assets in rural areas such as water quality, the natural and cultural heritage and the quality of the landscape are protected to support quality of life and economic vitality; and
- to ensure that rural settlement policies are appropriate to local circumstances.

Encouragingly, the Strategy calls for different responses to managing dispersed rural settlement between rural areas under strong urban influences and rural areas that are either characterised by a strong agricultural base, structurally weak rural areas and areas with distinctive settlement patterns, reflecting the contrasting development pressures that exist in the countryside. This is further developed in the Strategy with the distinction made between urban and rural generated housing in rural areas, defined as follows (p.106):

- urban-generated rural housing: development driven by urban centres, with housing sought in rural areas by people living and working in urban areas, including second homes; and
- rural-generated housing: housing needed in rural areas within the established rural community by people working in rural areas or in nearby urban areas who are an intrinsic part of the rural community by way of background or employment.

In general, the Strategy outlines that development driven by urban areas (including urban-generated rural housing) should take place within built up areas or land identified in the development plan process and that rural-generated housing needs should be accommodated in the areas where they arise. As a more 'sustainable' alternative to dispersed single housing in the countryside, the Strategy places considerable emphasis on the role of villages in rural areas. The NSS suggests that villages have a key role to play in strengthening the urban structure of rural areas (for example, in supporting local services and public transport) and as providing an important residential function for those seeking a rural lifestyle.

While the NSS is careful to avoid detailed policy prescription on rural housing (and thus avoid additional political controversy at the time of publication), more recently the Department of Environment, Heritage and Local Government has produced Guidelines for Sustainable Rural Housing (finalised in April 2005)), ensuring that dispersed rural housing in the countryside is to remain a high profile issue and a deeply contested feature of the planning policy arena. The Final Guidelines suggest that the Government is shifting to a less restrictive position on housing in the countryside. In summary, the guidelines provide that: (1) people who are part of and contribute to the rural community will get planning permission in all rural areas, including those under strong urban-based pressures, subject to the normal rules in relation to good planning; and (2) anyone wishing to build a house in rural areas suffering persistent and substantial population decline will be accommodated, subject to good planning. In this context, it is worth noting that the term 'good planning' refers to issues surrounding siting, layout and design, rather than planning in a strategic or spatial sense.

Spatial Planning and Rural Sustainable Development
At a local level, planning policy and, in particular, the local authority development plan potentially could provide an important arena for developing horizontal linkages between economic, social and environmental objectives. Local authorities in the Republic of Ireland are required to review or prepare a new development plan every six years, and both the procedures for preparing the development plan and its content are outlined in legislation. A key feature of the recent Planning and Development Act was the enhanced role of public participation in the development plan process, particularly at the 'pre-draft' stage. At a basic level, the purpose of the development plan is broadly to provide a spatial framework for the regulatory control of land-use and development and, therefore, concerned with the amount and location of development, and with its characteristics. The written statement of the development plan generally should fall into two sections: the first relates to a strategy for development over a 20 year period, and the second is concerned with the detail, and contains policies and objectives for implementation of the plan over a 6 year period.

In theory, the planning system, and in particular development plans, should provide a key statutory spatial framework for managing rural change, for example: in outlining the future location of housing, services, identifying sites for economic opportunities; landscape management; and balancing conservation and development interests. In addition, public participation in the preparation of the development plan suggests a potential for the planning process to produce consensus-driven development strategies or to mediate between conflicting conservation and development goals. This suggests that the development plan can perform a key role in 'place making', and as Healey (1998) argues, to generate enduring meanings for places which can help to focus and coordinate the activities of different stakeholders and reduce levels of conflict. Furthermore, the involvement of local elected representatives provides a political and democratic legitimacy for managing spatial change. Therefore, there appears to be considerable potential for planning policies and development plans to provide key instruments in developing integrative and multi-dimensional approaches to rural sustainable development in partnership with rural communities and other key stakeholders.

The findings outlined below form part of a research project titled *Spatial Policy in Rural Ireland: The Interaction of Statutory Land-use Planning and Rural Development Programmes*, funded by the Irish Research Council for Humanities and Social Science (IRCHSS). A component of the research is to investigate the formulation of local goals for rural sustainable development at a local authority level, including planning policies and strategies promoted by local development partnerships relating to rural development, enterprise development and community development. A key conflict to emerge surrounds the issue of rural housing and how this connects to wider debates concerning rural sustainability, and the interplay between economic, social and environmental policy objectives. The overall research project involves two case study local authorities in peripheral areas of Ireland – County Mayo and County Donegal. These case studies involve primarily undertaking a series of semi-structured in-depth interviews with elected representatives (county councillors), local authority planning officials and representatives from local LEADER groups, local development partnerships, the Irish Farmers' Association, umbrella community organisations (representing local community groups), the County Enterprise Board and the County Development Board (n = 35).

Local Case Studies: Mayo and Donegal
Both case study areas are predominately coastal counties, located on the western periphery of Ireland (Figure 11.1). Mayo is the third largest county in the Republic of Ireland (roughly 10 per cent of the state's land mass), but accounts for only 3 per cent of the state's population. At the last census in 2002, Mayo had a population of 117, 400, which was an increase of 5 per cent from the previous census in 1996 compared to an 8 per cent increase for the state's population as a whole. This recent increase in population, however,

should be placed in a broader historical context. Similar to most western counties, Mayo experienced considerable population loss for most of the last century. In 1901 the population of the county was approximately 200,000; this declined to under 150,000 in 1951 and by 1971 this had further decreased to 110,000. This was followed by a period of modest increase to 115,000 by 1986, again followed by decline in the in the 1986-1991 period. The recent population increase, moreover, masks uneven population change across the county, with more remote areas continuing to decline in population. The most recent statutory land-use development plan for the county council area was formally adopted in 2003 and covers a six-year period. This is the county's first development plan since the latest Planning Act and also the publication of the National Spatial Strategy.

County Donegal is located in the north-west of the island of Ireland with a population of 137,600. Not only is the county geographically peripheral, politically there is also a sense of isolation due to the presence of the Northern Ireland border. The economy of the county has been traditionally dominated by small agricultural holdings and fishing, both of which are increasingly economically unviable. A third pillar of the local economy has been textile manufacturing, but recent years have been marked by a number of high profile closures as production has shifted to regions with cheaper labour costs in Eastern Europe or developing countries. Donegal's population has remained fairly static over the last decade or so. However, the population has become increasingly concentrated in or nearby the county's largest town, Letterkenny. Moreover, as the border with Northern Ireland has become progressively more demilitarised as a result of the peace process, a significant trend has emerged where the housing market of Northern Ireland's border towns have effectively expanded into Donegal as people have taken advantage of the relative strength of the UK Sterling against the Euro currency (Paris, 2005). Donegal County Council has recently begun to undertake its statutory duty to review and replace its Development Plan, and at the time of writing a draft plan was expected in mid-2005.

The remainder of this chapter will focus selectively on three aspects of policy formulation for managing rural spatial change, particularly relating to rural housing and the role of planning policy in promoting rural sustainable development: (1) framing rural problems/issues; (2) rural sustainable development goals and policy outcomes; and (3) the development plan as tool for rural sustainable development.

Figure 11.1: Map of County Mayo and County Donegal case study are 95

1. Framing rural problems and issues

This refers to the manner in which rural policies are framed by analyses of rural sustainable development issues, the scope of rural discourses and assessment and construction of rurality by the various local agencies and groups involved in rural sustainable development. In relation to planning policy, a central theme identified as a key issue in the development plans of both case study areas relates to the quality of the landscape and the need for protection. Indeed, both plans contain a fairly comprehensive analysis of the landscape, undertaken as part of central government's landscape assessment planning guidelines. The landscape is framed as a key asset to be exploited for economic development, particularly related to the potential of rural tourism and is illustrated in the development plan extracts below for County Mayo:

> The outstanding quality of the Mayo landscape is one of its main strengths. The landscape is under constant threat from inappropriate development pressures particularly over the last 5-6 years. (p.10)

> Large parts of the rural areas and coast of the county contain some of the most outstanding landscape and seascape in the world and are designated as areas of high amenity in terms of their scenic and visual quality. Such areas are vital to the tourism economy and as such could contribute to the diversification of the economy of these areas as traditional agriculture declines in economic importance. (p.22)

In this case, the environment is treated as a commodity, a stock of assets which are to be exploited or packaged for visitors – an approach termed by Davoudi *et al.* (1996) as a 'marketised utilitarian' approach to the environment, common in the UK in the 1980s.

However, a number of tensions can be identified with this analysis of the rural landscape, with all stakeholders interviewed from a community/economic development perspective interpreting the landscape in different terms, particularly related to housing development in the countryside. In general, landscape policies were viewed with scepticism and as a method for introducing restrictive planning policies in rural areas. For example, one community development representative commented that:

> It's rubbish to have restrictive policies [for rural housing]. No one visits most of the rural areas anyway…What do they [visitors] want from the countryside? This landscape is man-made and man-managed anyway. (interview with community development representative)

It was further suggested by another stakeholder, this time from an enterprise development perspective, that:

> Landscape protection will turn this area into a national park. Do they [planners] want rural people to live in thatched cottages so that people can come out to rural areas for the weekend to the see the community here like they're visiting a zoo? (interview with enterprise development representative)

This interview extract is also indicative of a key tension as to whom landscape policies are directed. A particularly strong theme to emerge from both elected representatives and local development representatives was the perception that landscape protection is aimed at tourists and visitors rather than the local community:

> Our emphasis [in local development] is locals first and visitors second. If tourists like what we do, then that's fine, but it's not a key priority. We need to be responsible to the people who live here 365 days a year. (interview with community development representative)

> Who do you legislate for? The people who live here and have lived here all their lives, or the tourist who drives by once in their life? (interview with elected representative)

In this sense, there was considerable conflict over the new demands for rural space as farming continues to decline, particularly between residential use and tourism and recreation. Both demands are indicative of the consumption countryside with a 'locals versus visitor' attitude, and related to the increasing shift to the rural as a post-productivist space. In contrast to the local authority development plan, the countryside was constructed as a living and working environment, for example:

> We've got to maintain a living countryside and it has got to include people …we're under-populated in rural areas as it is. Good housing can enhance a landscape …The landscape should be seen as functional spaces. (interview with community development representative)

Throughout the interviews with local stakeholders, the central narrative of the rural to emerge was imagery surrounding depopulation and out-migration, particularly in County Mayo. Countering long-term depopulation trends is regarded as the key rationale for rural sustainable development actions in the area. Stabilising the population levels is viewed as central in maintaining social and community infrastructure and local services. One area in east Mayo is commonly referred to in interviews and strategy documents as the 'black triangle', renowned for its extraordinarily high levels of sustained out-migration. The impact of this trend is highlighted in IRD Kiltimagh's forthcoming local development strategy:

> The manifestation of this problem was evident in the town [Kiltimagh] and its hinterland. Whole townlands had been wiped out, denuded of their population by death of the old and emigration of the young. The decaying, derelict and overgrown houses and farmyards were clearly visible in the countryside. In the town the problems were equally apparent. Over 40 per cent of the buildings in the town were derelict.

This 'framing' of out-migration is central in the subsequent formulation of rural development strategies, discussed further below. In summary, key problems/issues experienced in rural Mayo and Donegal, identified in interviews with local stakeholders included: decline of farming; out-migration of young people; economic and enterprise development; access to services, transport and jobs; isolation and rural transport; lack of infrastructure; and affordable housing. No environmental issues were raised by elected representatives or economic or community development groups, apart from the context of housing in the countryside.

2. Rural sustainable development goals and policy outcomes
Although both local rural development actors and the local authority development plan are concerned with rural sustainable development, the research suggests that rural sustainable development goals are poorly integrated, conceptually and in delivery. This tension appears to relate closely with the approach to 'framing' rural issues and varying interpretations of both rurality and sustainability. Although sustainable development involves the reconciliation of economic, social and environmental considerations, various policy documents and stakeholders tend to give emphasis to a particular aspect. Given the core narrative of the rural among community development and economic development stakeholders related to depopulation and out-migration, unsurprisingly this provided an important direction for local development initiatives. Therefore, local development programmes were generally focused on: enterprise development and job creation; workspace programmes; social inclusion initiatives; affordable housing schemes; and village enhancements. Rather than view planning policy as a useful mechanism to address these issues, planning was often described as a barrier, particularly in relation to settlement policies:

> Our organisation is concerned mainly with out-migration. In the past, three-quarters of our young people were leaving the area to find work. But as these people try to return, they face barriers from planning through planning refusals for housing in the countryside. (interview with local development representative)

> Rural Ireland was cleared out in the 1950s. It's hard to imagine that when people wanted to return that they would be denied planning permission for building in the countryside…If you're going to have rural development, you need people living in rural areas! (interview with LEADER group representative)

Dispersed rural housing proved to be the most contested aspect of both development plans. In the case of Mayo, in the initial draft plan planning officials had originally included restrictions on dispersed rural housing in favour of locating housing in clusters and villages, considered to be more 'sustainable settlement patterns'. The draft plan outlines, from a planning perspective, the negative environmental impacts of rural housing on the landscape and rural amenities and suggests that other negative impacts include:

> ...Demands for uneconomical extension of infrastructure and services and negating of past investment, dependence on the private car and commuting, loss of agricultural land, increase in land prices, and conflict with farming activities and the development of certain natural resources. (extract from Mayo Draft County Development Plan, p. 26)

Similar to Owen's (1996) critique of planners in rural areas of England, this suggests that planning officials had a fairly narrow interpretation of sustainable settlements, focusing on landscape impacts, car dependency and the economic costs of dispersal, and excluding concerns related to sustainable livelihoods and viable rural communities. However, through the development plan process, a shift in policy emerged through political pressure from local councillors, whereby restrictive policies were replaced with more liberal guidelines (except in high amenity areas). In Donegal, rural housing policy was based largely on the classification of rural areas into three landscape character types, based on scenic quality. In this example, limited reference is given to local social and economic contexts in the formulation of housing policies.

3. The development plan a tool for rural sustainable development
Although both local rural development programmes and the local authority development plan are concerned with rural sustainable development, the research suggests that rural development and planning goals are poorly integrated, conceptually and in delivery. A key issue to emerge throughout the interviews with the LEADER groups and other local development partnerships was the strong perception that the development plan was not a relevant policy instrument for their organisations. This was perhaps surprising as the majority of the groups interviewed were involved in programmes with a clear spatial emphasis, such as village enhancements (including producing physical development strategies); developing and providing workspace for local enterprise; rural transport initiatives; and environmental schemes such as developing a coastal zone management strategy. Rather than a tool for managing spatial change, the development plan was viewed primarily as a technical document and a regulatory instrument. This is illustrated by the following interview extracts:

> The development plan is a document that should have an impact on our work, but up to now it hasn't ...Planning policy seems to be about what you can't do and this is a bad place to start. Maybe they [planners] could start from what you

can do. (interview with community development representative)

> We weren't involved [in the development plan process], but we did make a written submission. It's not something that would impinge on our work. It seems strange to say that, but we wouldn't see it as pertinent. (interview with local development representative)

One possible explanation for this perception may relate to the style of discourse adopted by planning officials. The development plan was thought of as a technical document, written by 'experts'. As one community development representative contended:

> The council's plan is very much about engineering, services and physical infrastructure …The National Spatial Strategy was much more interesting – it was more conceptual and not too focused on specifics but more the general. (interview with community development representative)

In the case of Mayo, there was a clear sense that the development plan was not related to rural development initiatives and few interviewees had read or referred to the county's plan. A common criticism of planning has been that 'plans are produced by planners for planners' (Healey, 1996). This suggests that local planning initiatives should attempt to create a new discourse and as Healey argues, this process should explicitly explore 'new storylines' for shaping attention and for possible actions.

Therefore, the development plan was largely perceived as a negative tool – in other words, 'planners stop things happening in rural areas'. Instead, rural development stakeholders stressed the need both for planners to adopt a more positive approach to planning for rural areas and also for the development plan to evolve into a more proactive strategy – as one interviewee commented: 'planning is a negative tool trying to do something positive' (interview with County Enterprise Board representative). A key theme to emerge from the interviews was the sense that there was a conflict of rural sustainable development goals between the planning authority and local rural development interests. Rural development groups, community groups and enterprise development agencies commonly described their goals in terms of 'ensuring a living and working countryside' or 'to maintain a rural population while providing economic and social opportunities for rural dwellers'. In contrast, planning officials expressed their goals in terms of landscape protection, reducing car dependency and strengthening the urban structure of the county. In this context, the development plan in both case study areas failed to reconcile economic, social and environmental objectives, and instead selectively focuses on environmental and restraint policies.

Unsurprisingly, the most commonly cited example of conflict between planning and rural development interests related to tensions surrounding dispersed housing in the open countryside. Whereas planning officials favoured restraint policies for rural housing and a preference for rural housing to be located in villages/service centres, rural development stakeholders contended that dispersed rural housing is the traditional settlement pattern in the Irish countryside. Therefore, increased rural housing was viewed as an indication of a healthy or successful rural community. Furthermore, planning officials were criticised for basing their settlement policies on landscape quality criteria, while ignoring the social and economic context of rural communities. In particular – as both case studies are remote rural areas with significant pockets of depopulation – rural development interests urged planners to be 'flexible when faced with decline' (interview with LEADER group representative).

From this assessment of the role of the statutory development plan, there appears to be a gap between planning and rural development objectives. In this context, the role of the development plan in managing rural space is at risk from being marginalised as an increasingly regulatory tool, with investment driven rural development programmes developed in partnership with rural communities setting the agenda. However, it is unclear if planning officials are currently in a position to formulate a spatial vision for rural communities, often related to resource restraints and daily work priorities:

> We're [planners] responding to crisis after crisis – I know it's a lame excuse. The amount of creative thinking in planning is at a very low ebb. The explosion of economic development [in Ireland] has left us struggling behind. We're simply struggling with our statutory responsibilities – we don't have time for that thinking which is critical … We're just muddling through. (interview with senior planner)

This quote suggests that planning officials are currently unable to articulate a wider spatial vision for rural areas and that the reality of day-to-day planning actions is a preoccupation with development control and incremental development, rather than 'big picture' strategies.

Conclusion

Although this chapter represents work in progress, with a further two local case studies to be undertaken, a number of tentative conclusions can be developed. At both national and local level, formulating agreed rural sustainable development policies in relation to housing in the countryside remains an elusive and contested policy goal. To understand these conflicting arguments and positions, examining the various social constructions of rurality and sustainability proved a useful exercise, particularly as non-agricultural interests become more central in processes shaping rural space. The dominant narrative of the rural 'problem' from a pro-development perspective was related to depopulation and out-migration; the loss of the traditional rural way of life and culture; and interference in individual rights. In contrast, from a planning perspective and pro-conservation position, the image of the rural portrayed is one of the countryside under pressure from extensive and inappropriate development. This perspective stresses the importance of the public good rather than individual interests. Both these conflicting 'storylines' of the rural problem have led to increasing difficulties in attempting to develop a consensus surrounding housing in the countryside. In this context, the term 'sustainable development' has proved too vague, enabling all parties to claim that their position achieves sustainable development goals.

Furthermore, the research suggests a clear need to develop integrated, holistic and multi-dimensional approaches to rural sustainable development. For example, in relation to environmental sustainability (usually cited as a rationale for a more restrictive approach), can more environmentally-friendly house designs minimise the impact of rural housing in terms of landscape and energy emissions? Perhaps more significantly, the rural housing debate has increasingly been viewed as a single issue – however, a multi-dimensional and integrative approach suggests that this issue should not be divorced from wider discussions surrounding rural development and a future vision for rural Ireland. This includes the need to consider the economic and social health of rural settlements as aspects of sustainability alongside the environmental dimensions, and to address the evident 'disconnect' between environmental and spatial policy goals and economic and social issues in local policy-making. As Healey (1998) argues, this process should explicitly explore 'new storylines' and attempt to create a new discourse for rural policy through collaborative action.

In this regard, the planning system should provide a key statutory spatial framework for managing rural change with the potential to produce consensus-driven development strategies or to mediate between conflicting conservation and development goals. However, at present, the role of the planning system as a discursive arena appears limited. Key rural stakeholders at national and local level, in general, view the planning system as a technical and regulatory process, with planners as 'gatekeepers' of change in rural areas. In addition, rural development interests often describe planning officials as 'urban planners' who demonstrate limited affinity with rural communities. This represents a considerable challenge for planners. However, as Murray and Greer (1997) suggest, this challenge can also be viewed as an opportunity to engage in a more interactive style of statutory plan-making with rural communities, linked to interest group mediation and the building of trust-relations.

Acknowledgement

The author would wish to gratefully acknowledge the financial support of the Irish Research Council for Humanities and Social Sciences for the research

References

Aalen, F. (1997) The challenge of change, in Aalen, F, Whelan, K. and Stout, M. (eds.) *Atlas of the Irish rural landscape*, Cork, Cork University Press.

Albrechts, L., Healey, P. and Kunzmann, R. (2003) Strategic spatial planning and regional governance in Europe, *Journal of the American Planning Association*, 69, pp.113-129.

Briassoulis, H. (1999) Who plans whose sustainability? Alternative roles for planners, *Journal of Environmental Planning and Management*, 42, pp. 889-902.

Central Statistics Office (2003) *Volume 1, Population by area (Census)*, Dublin, CSO.

Clinch, P., Convery, F. and Walsh, B. (2002) *After the Celtic Tiger, challenges ahead*, Dublin, O'Brien Press.

Davoudi, S., Hull, A. and Healey, P. (1996) Environmental concerns and economic imperatives in strategic plan making, *Town Planning Review*, 67, pp.421-436.

DOEHLG (Department of the Environment, Heritage and Local Government) (2005) *Sustainable rural housing, Guidelines for planning authorities*, Dublin, Stationery Office.

DOELG (Department of Environment and Local Government) (2002) *The National Spatial Strategy 2002-2020, people, places and potential*, Dublin, Stationery Office.

Duffy, P. (2000) Trends in nineteenth and twentieth century settlement, in T. Barry (ed.) *A history of settlement in Ireland*, London, Routledge.

Gallent, N., Shucksmith, M. and Tewdwr-Jones, M. (2003) *Housing in the European countryside: rural pressure and policy in Western Europe*, London, Routledge.

Government of Ireland (2000) *Planning and Development Act*, Dublin, Stationery Office.

Government of Ireland (1997) *Sustainable development – a strategy for Ireland*, Dublin, Stationery Office.

Hajer, M. (1995) *The politics of environmental discourse*, Oxford, Oxford University Press.

Healey, P. (1998) Collaborative planning in a stakeholder society, *Town Planning Review*, 69, pp.1-21.

Healey, P. (1996) The communicative turn in planning theory and its implications for spatial strategy formation, *Environment and Planning B: Planning and Design*, 23, pp.217-234.

Healey, P. and Shaw, T. (1993) Planners, plans and sustainable development, *Regional Studies*, 27, pp.769-776.

Lindsey, G. (2003) Sustainability and urban greenways: indicators in Indianapolis, *Journal of the American Planning Association*, 69, pp.165-180.

Lynch, C. (2002) Capacity and community – The balance between the social and the environmental in a specific cultural context, Paper presented to the *6th Annual Conference of the Nordic Scottish Network*, Sustainability in Rural and Regional Development.

Mayo County Council (2003) *County Development Plan*, Castlebar, Mayo County Council.

McDonagh, J. (1998) Rurality and development in Ireland – the need for debate? *Irish Geography*, 31, pp.47-54.

McDonagh, J. (2002) *Renegotiating rural development in Ireland*, Aldershot, Ashgate.

McGrath, B. (1998) Environmental sustainability and rural settlement growth in Ireland, *Town Planning Review*, 3, pp.227-290.

Murray, M. and Greer, J. (1997) Planning and community-led rural development in Northern Ireland, *Planning Practice and Research*, 12, pp.393-400.

Owen, S. (1996) Sustainability and rural settlement planning, *Planning Practice and Research*, 11, pp.37-47.

Paris, C. (2005) From barricades to back gardens: cross border urban expansion from the city of Derry into Co. Donegal, in Moore, N. and Scott, M. (eds.) *Renewing urban communities: environment, citizenship and sustainability in Ireland,* Ashgate, Aldershot, pp. 114-131.

Spatial Planning Unit (2001) *Rural and urban roles – Irish spatial perspectives,* Dublin, Department of the Environment and Local Government.

Chapter 12

The Rural Economy: Value Added Creation, Market Sustainability and the Limits of Policy Measures

Michael P. Cuddy

Introduction

Economic resources and the exploitation of these resources through the interplay of market forces is what creates "value added"[1]. The amount of this value added created will determine the combination of both the level of economic wellbeing and number of people sustained at the particular level in any geographic area, which may be termed market sustainability. This chapter explores the creation of value added in a specific geographic space, namely rural space. It explores the market processes which dominate the value added creation activity there. It highlights the limitations on the efficient functioning of the market in rural space and the various factors which operate in or characterise rural space and influence the value added creation activity. Finally, it looks at the main strands of public policy, which are implemented to redress the deficiencies of the rural economy.

Rural space is occupied by individuals, households and families, who co-operate and interact to form rural communities. Although recognising that one can view different facets of rural society through different windows or lenses, the orientation of this chapter is economic. While an attempt is made to address issues of rural, in general, rural Ireland is used specifically as the focus to give expression to concrete examples.

The chapter is laid out as follows: first, the term rural or rurality is addressed, moving from the more colloquial to the more critical distinguishing features; second, the emerging policy context is explored where the major policy instrument which was concentrated on rural society, the Common Agricultural Policy (CAP), has broadened its focus from farm activities to also include non-farm activities; third, the creation of value added is examined, its precise meaning is articulated and the process is illustrated; fourth, the concept of market sustainability is reviewed, addressing, initially, the market requirements and, subsequently, the factors influencing the efficiency of the market; fifth, the reason for policy intervention in rural areas, the broad strands of policy intervention and their impact are explicated; and, finally, some concluding remarks are offered.

Rural

Rural or rurality defies definition for two reasons. The first is that rural does not stand alone but is an integral part of continuous space, which is artificially fragmented for administrative purposes. It is always linked both physically and functionally to ever-larger spatial entities, which include lower to higher urban centres. Second, rural can take on different definitions depending on through whose eyes it is being viewed, for example, the farmer milking his cows or harvesting hay, on the one hand, or the city dweller, on the other, who has come to take in the scenery, the fresh air or walk the open spaces.

Nevertheless, despite its arbitrariness, there are certain characteristics which might be associated with rural space: the physical landscape, the natural resources, the environment, the spatial aspect, the market integration and social integrity or cohesion. "The country" stands in opposition to the city, while countryside immediately throws up the physical landscape with mental images of open green fields, woodlands and hillsides, which in turn invoke the more poetic or romantic notions of rustic, bucolic or pastoral scenes.

The countryside has natural resources, which can be exploited for the creation of economic wellbeing. Traditionally, this has been the exploitation of the land, the forests, the waters and the mines. Because of the extent to which the land was exploited for food to the population within and beyond the rural area, and the extent to which farmers were able to organise themselves as an interest group, the country and countryside economic activity became synonymous with farming. However, public and private services have become increasingly important with increasing affluence and the attempts by the state to provide services and direct payments in order to realise a certain level of social equity. Manufacturing industry and construction have also become increasingly important. In particular, industry has been able to feed off the continuing labour surplus in agriculture.

The rural environment is receiving increasing attention. The environment is understood to be that which surrounds us. It encompasses the air, water and soil and the physical landscape which it produces. Environmental awareness has also been a product of affluence. It is related in the first instance to health and the impact which the pollution of these elements might have. It is important to recreation and the impact of the quality of the environment on the use of rural space, particularly, by tourists and urban dwellers. The "public good" aspect of the rural environment (where, in principle, everyone can benefit without affecting the welfare of others) has come to the fore in recent times and, in particular, the interrelationship between the landowners and the quality of the environment.

One of the dominant distinguishing characteristics between urban and rural is the spatial dimension. Rural is associated with dispersed population or small settlement size and low density of population. However, as we move between large settlements and small settlement, what is the turning point between urban and rural? This divide is quite arbitrary and it depends on who is making this distinction and for what purpose. Social scientists and statisticians in Ireland have arbitrarily divided up geographic space into urban and rural, where the latter includes settlements of less than 1,500 people. However, at the local level in daily life, the inhabitants of settlements of even much smaller sizes are considered to be "townspeople" both by themselves and by those living in the countryside.

Urban centres are generally more integrated into the market economy than rural areas, because of proximity to transaction points and the availability of alternative goods and services. However, if one believes in efficiency being associated with specialisation in production and trade, then the greater the level of integration into the market economy, the greater the likelihood that the economic wellbeing of the rural community is being optimised.

Sociologists draw a clear distinction between social relationships in urban and rural areas. This distinction centres round the degree of social interaction and co-operation. This is presumed to be greater in rural communities for a number of reasons. It arises out of the stable historical structure of rural communities, despite significant out-migration, extended family connections and the significant trust established over a long time period; it arises from the need for co-operation given the nature of production activity and from the overall necessity for community self reliance due to limited availability of market and public services.

The Emerging Policy Context
Rural development as a focus of research enquiry and policy initiative is well established internationally. The importance of rural society in Ireland and in the European Union, from a policy perspective, has evolved steadily with the long and gradual overhaul of the Common Agricultural Policy. This overhaul commenced in the early 1980s, coinciding with the emergence of agricultural surpluses and the increasing budgetary burden in disposing of them. It was also recognised that, in general, the improvement of the wellbeing of rural inhabitants was not commensurate with the budgetary outlay, while the transfers were very unevenly distributed, leading to significant financial waste and social inequity. First, transfers were made to farmers through an administered price mechanism, which maintained high prices to the consumer and what the European Union consumer did not want was sold into

"intervention" at the administered price. The proportion of rural labour relying on agriculture for their livelihood was rapidly declining and in most rural communities no longer constituted a majority of the rural labour force[2]. Second, the transfers were linked to production and, therefore, privileged the larger producers, located mainly in the more economically advantaged regions (Commission of European Communities, 1981). Although a more enlightened approach to promote and support rural development (widening the definition of rural to include the non-farming community) was well articulated by the European Commission (1988), it took much time and painstaking negotiations (and finally the enlargement and its potential explosive impact on the budget without CAP reform), to reform, re-structure and re-orient CAP toward a more effective instrument of rural development (European Commission, 2002, 2004a, 2005). Although the final solution has not yet been achieved, the tramlines are put in place toward achieving the necessary overhaul.

The essence of the new direction is that the link is broken between the support for farmers and agricultural production. That means that agriculture must now compete in a world market economy. Consequently, due to low margins, only large-scale production units can give an acceptable livelihood to fulltime farmers under the traditional production systems. Direct income support, which has an upward limit, will, in part, compensate for the divergence between the administered price and the market price. This, however, is likely to be a sort of transition measure, which is likely to decline over time. The rural development aspect of CAP has been significantly strengthened with the setting up of a European Agricultural Fund for Rural Development (EAFRD), embracing four axes (European Commission, 2004a):

- Axis 1: Improving competitiveness of the agriculture and forestry sector
- Axis 2: Improving the environment and the countryside
- Axis 3: The quality of life in rural areas and diversification of the rural economy
- Axis 4: LEADER

Axis 3 is directed at supporting value added creation beyond the farm gate, while Axis 4 directs that a minimum of 7 per cent of the Fund be managed and implemented by local LEADER groups.

In parallel with the CAP reforms, enlargement has taken place, which has created a new lower tier of European regions, which will absorb the majority of EU Structural Funds in future planning rounds. Rural areas in the more advanced regions will thus be constrained to dependency on their national governments to provide whatever supports they are financially and politically capable of delivering.

The upshot of all of this is that rural areas will be increasingly obliged to compete in the global market place, not just for agricultural produce, but for all its tradable production. The level of market activity, which determines value added creation, will be constrained by natural endowments, on the one hand, and the natural disadvantage in the workings of the market in rural areas and the extent to which this disadvantage is ameliorated by policy intervention. The level of this activity or the potential level of this activity may be defined here as sustainable market activity. The rest of this chapter is an exploration of the workings of the market or rather the limitations of the market in sustaining value added creation in a rural context and the extent to which policy intervention can mitigate these limits.

Value Added Creation
Value added creation is the main source of economic wellbeing in rural society. Public and private transfers also add to this level of economic wellbeing. The creation of value added in a rural community and the economic transactions surrounding it can best be understood using a Leontief input /output framework (Table 12.1). The "economic sectors" are at the heart of the activity. The "output" from a particular economic sector can be used as "input" into the sector itself or into other economic sectors (shown in the cells as you move, from left to right, along the row of the particular sector) and indicated by the light shaded area in the upper-left quadrant; it can, also, be purchased locally for consumption or investment, or it can be exported out of the local area as indicated by the dark shaded area in the upper-right quadrant. The "inputs" into the production of a particular sector consist of "input" from the sector itself, inputs from other sectors (shown in the cells as you move down the column of the particular sector) and indicated by the light shaded area in the upper-left quadrant, imports and the inputs of labour and capital. The value of the labour and capital inputs is measured by the wages paid to labour and the profit accruing to capital. However, part of the income accruing to labour and capital goes to the government by way of taxes. The income generated, namely, taxes, wages and profits, indicated by the dark shaded area in the lower-left quadrant, is the value added created. The value added retained is what contributes to local economic wellbeing. The local value added is augmented by government transfers like pensions, unemployment benefits, direct EU farm payments and private pensions and remittances from family members away from the community. (These transfers are included in the cells of the rows and columns in the light shaded area in the lower-right quadrant).

Table 12.1: Leontief input/output framework

Output Inputs	Economic sectors			Local consumption (Public and private)	Local investment (Public and private)	Exports	Total Output
Economic sectors	X	X	X	X	X	X	X
	X	X	X	X	X	X	X
	X	X	X	X	X	X	X
Imports	X	X	X	X	X	X	X
Taxes	X	X	X	X	X	X	X
Wages	X	X	X	X	X	X	X
Profit	X	X	X	X	X	X	X
Total inputs	X	X	X	X	X	X	X

Market Sustainability

Value added in a rural community is created primarily within a market framework, where competitiveness, in an essentially global market environment, is the essence of business survival. Thus the extent to which economic activity can be generated and value added created within that framework determines the level of economic wellbeing which can be sustained in a particular community. This level of economic wellbeing, which a rural community can sustain through economic activity and the associated value added creation, may be called the level of market sustainability.

Meeting the market requirements. Three broad sets of markets, which can be related to the Leontief input/output flows (Table 12.1), operate in rural economies. There are markets for goods and services, which are traded as inputs into the production process, for final use in public and private consumption, public and private investment and for export. There are markets for labour, which is used in the production of goods and services, and there are the markets for capital to provide the finances for the production assets and working capital.

Resources will be efficiently utilised only if markets exist for each of the goods and services required and if there is an adequate number of buyers and sellers on all markets, so that a competitive equilibrium of quantity and price can be achieved. Thus in each of the three market sets – goods and services, labour and capital - an adequate number of buyers and sellers is an essential requirement.

The demand for goods and services is determined by local demand for intermediate and final goods and services and external demand (exports). This latter depends on access to external markets and the marketing effort. The supply of goods and services will depend on the natural resources available, local entrepreneurial capacity on and off-farm, the availability of finances to acquire the physical and working capital, the local labour supply and the various physical and service inputs for the production process.

The demand for labour will depend on the level of production activity being generated. The supply of labour will depend on the population level and its demographic structure, labour mobility, information flow, education and training and the general social support system.

The demand for financial capital will depend on the market opportunities for goods and services, the availability and quality of entrepreneurs to exploit those markets and the physical and working capital needed in the production process. The supply of finances will depend on the projected profit flow and the capacity to repay capital and costs, the level of risk involved, the opportunity cost of investing elsewhere and the efficiency of the information flow.

The major problem in the rural economy is the thinness or non-existence of markets, the imperfect performance of markets and information flows. The principal issue in the goods and services market is the low level of local demand. When local demand is below the enterprise viability threshold, the good or service is not produced. Although most goods can be imported, when the local quantity demanded is low, the unit cost of importing and stocking is too high, so a limited choice of goods is available locally. Thus for certain goods and services there are no markets. This limits consumer choice, which has a negative impact on quality of life, and thus makes the rural location less attractive to live in. It also curtails value added creation activities when certain critical inputs into the production process, either goods or services are not available.

The local demand for labour is limited by the level of value added creation activity locally. The local labour surplus is obliged to commute to the nearest town where employment is available or to migrate. A common problem in the rural economy is the "single factory" phenomenon, where a single employer or few employers can exploit their market strength against the employees, where the opportunity cost of the latter is close to zero. Although alternative opportunities may exist by migrating, very often this is not an option due to family responsibilities or other mobility constraints.

On the labour supply side, the low concentration of population and labour means that large-scale industrial activity, which can exploit scale economies is unlikely to emerge. Similarly, niche market value added creation activity is unlikely to emerge, since the skilled labour pool locally is unlikely to be adequate to meet the demand. Allied to this is the common problem of inadequate training due to out-migration of the more skilled and the normal deficiencies in training facilities locally.

Capital markets also function badly in rural areas, because the general problem of "asymmetric information"[3] associated with the capital market is accentuated. The, normally, small size of loan transactions and relatively high risk in rural areas leads to a relatively high unit cost. The upshot of this is that the opportunity cost to banks of lending for rural investment is higher and, therefore, lending is more attractive in urban areas leaving funds for investment in rural areas difficult to access.

Factors influencing the efficiency of the market. There are many factors according to the literature in regional economics and economic geography (apart from the basic requirements for efficient market transactions, outlined above), which influence the workings of the market and thus the competitiveness of enterprises in a particular location. Rural space is a special type of geographic space to which these factors readily apply. They may be the result of external forces; they may be determined exogenously by nature or they may be determined endogenously through the interplay of economic and social forces and the physical environment. It is not easy to clearly classify these factors as they are often part determined externally and part internally, or part exogenously and part endogenously. A snapshot of these factors (by no means exhaustive), roughly classified into external and internal factors, is presented in Figure 12.1.

Here attention is turned to how these factors may be incorporated into the neoclassical market framework and to see how they influence the competitiveness of business in rural communities.

The *general economic conditions* internationally are determined through the interaction of demand and supply conditions of all economic space, which makes up the global economy. Since most of the production from the tradable sectors in Ireland is sold into international markets, general economic conditions in the rural economy in Ireland are set by international forces. International economic demand for tradable goods and services stimulates the production of those firms, which are capable of producing for the international market. Thus strong general economic conditions internationally, generate demand for local production of goods and services. If local entrepreneurial skills are able to take advantage of this opportunity, demand for labour and capital is expanded and additional value added is created generating income for labour and capital. A downturn in general international economic conditions will have the opposite effect.

The level of *market integration*, however, will determine the extent to which rural firms can take advantage of the expansion of international markets and the corresponding expansion of Irish markets beyond local markets. Although there are some internal factors, which influence the integration into external markets, including the ingenuity of the enterprise manager and staff, there are other factors, which are primarily of an external nature. These include national and international institutional structures and processes such as the euro zone, international agreements and international law. Access infrastructure, including alternative transport modes and telecommunications, is an essential component of the architecture of market integration.

Figure 12.1: Factors influencing the market sustainability of rural communities

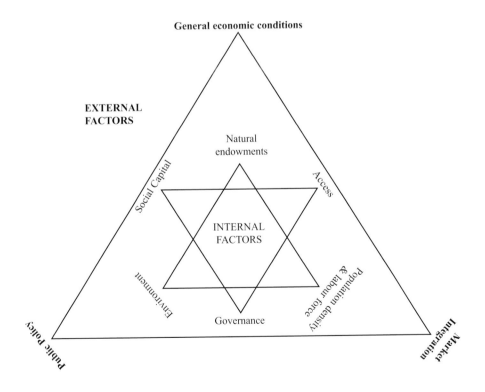

Public policy is enacted, primarily, by the national parliament. However, in the Irish context it has been strongly influenced by EU membership and EU policy. Public policy has a direct and indirect impact on rural enterprises. The most important policy impact on rural society since 1973 has been the Common Agricultural Policy (CAP). The reform of this policy will have a singularly important impact on rural society. However, policies with regard to competition, labour, capital, innovation, knowledge management, environment, transport and telecommunications also have significant impacts on the rural economy. They can lower costs, which can encourage expansion of supply or raise costs, which can contract supply. Various measures addressing all of these issues have been implemented under different rounds of the Structural Funds in Ireland.

The *natural endowments* are an important determinant of the sectoral economic activities of a rural area. The extent and quality of farmland, forestry, waters and mines determine the potential of the primary sector to contribute to the local economy. Alternative uses of agricultural land, whether it is used intensively or extensively, will contribute differently to the value added created. The CAP has had a powerful influence in raising the intensity of production in Ireland, which, in turn, has had a negative impact on the environment, particularly water quality. However, the recent reform is likely to see a return to more extensive production, since direct payments to farmers will be no longer linked to actual levels of production and agricultural prices will be determined, primarily, by international market forces. Fresh water and seawater, in addition to being exploited for traditional fishing allied to the tourism industry, have been used for fish farming in Ireland, although there are environmental limits to this activity. Limits have been placed on the sea fishing because of Common Fishery Policy restrictions.

Heavy dependency on the primary sector has implications for relative incomes and under-employment. Since incomes in the primary sector are normally significantly below those in other sectors, rural communities, which are heavily dependent on the primary sector, are likely to have incomes which are inferior to the national average. This has implications for population migration and economic and social stability. It also has the positive implication of making labour available for other economic activities in the community, if that labour can be employed by alternative enterprises. Indeed, this has been the pattern of evolution of the Irish rural economy, induced by the positive general economic environment.

One of the most significant characteristics of rural areas is the low *density of population and labour force*. This has two major impacts: first, low density of population means that local demand will be low and so benefits cannot be obtained from scale economies and, second, the production externalities created by "agglomeration", which reduce costs, are not present.

Consequently, the economic activity in rural communities is linked, in the first instance, to the exploitation of natural resources, in agriculture, forestry, fishing and mining, for direct sale, for processing and for the tourist industry associated with the local environment.

Traditional employment in rural communities is also provided by public services, funded by the state and by industrial and service employment in large towns for those rural communities within short commuting distance. Commuting to work from rural communities to the large towns has become a spectacular phenomenon associated with recent Irish economic growth. For those rural communities, which lie within the influence of large towns, out-migration has been considerably replaced by commuting to work. The vibrancy of these communities is noticeably enhanced by the population growth and spending power, which increases demand for local services, thus generating increased value added locally.

Access to markets, both markets for inputs into the production process and markets for outputs, is critical to all economies. It is normally a problem in rural economies because they are distant from markets. Transport and telecommunications infrastructure are the means to ameliorate the distance barrier and reduce the access costs. However, very often this infrastructure is inadequate in terms of quality and alternative modes of transport and communications. The latter is becoming increasingly important with the explosion of the "knowledge' economy. Distance from markets adds to costs and reduces competitiveness. There is the cost of travelling to meet customers in the market place and the cost of transporting in inputs and the cost of delivering output to the market. Telecommunications, whether through the traditional telephone and facsimile, or through the Internet, is the means to access knowledge. Knowledge is a means of lowering unit cost, whether through making the labour market or goods and services markets more efficient, or through accessing new ideas, which can alter the product mix or the production process. Costs arising from transport and telecommunications lower the value added created leaving a lower return to capital and labour. Since capital is more mobile than labour, however, labour is obliged take a lower return if production is to continue. The breaking point comes when labour decides that the opportunity cost of staying locally is too high and it migrates to an alternative labour market location.

A healthy *environment,* which one normally associates with rural communities, can be both an asset, to be exploited for value added creation, for example, in the case of quality food products or tourism, and a cost where the production activity leads to a deterioration of the environment. In the past the "polluter" did not pay but rather society paid by absorbing this negative externality. Now, due to the new environment legislation most negative externalities must be internalised, which increases the private cost of production. Due to CAP induced intensification of production, there have been increasing tensions between farming interests and other rural community interests. Farming has been responsible for water pollution, which has infringed on the tourist and fishing industry. However, EU environmental legislation is redressing this distortion, which will increase costs and reduce the private value added created in the farming sector and increase it in the tourism sector. An opportunity, however, is created for farmers to adopt a positive approach toward the environment by engaging in organic production. There is, however, considerable inertia in moving in this direction due to both formal institutions and informal institutions. The existing institutions are more geared to the traditional kind of production. For example, if legislation with respect to residues of antibiotics and pesticides in food products was more strict or more strictly enforced, then organic production, which has a higher unit cost, would be more competitive. Also, the existing norms have a greater affinity to the traditional production activities and it will take time to adapt to the required norms for this new kind of production.

Membership of the European Union has brought with it a more effective *governance* structure based on the concept of "subsidiarity", where decision-making is decentralised down to the lowest possible level. LEADER groups[4] now take decisions on local policy measures, which are also implemented at that level. These measures are more effective in addressing the local constraints on enterprise formation and growth than similar measures formulated and implemented at central or local government levels. Thus cost of production is reduced and value added creation is increased.

Fukuyama (1999) describes *social capital* as "an instantiated informal norm that promotes cooperation between two or more individuals". This is familiar activity in rural society between pairs of farmers or groups of farmers for mutual benefit. It is less familiar between non-farm enterprises. However, it is precisely this type of inter-enterprise co-operation, enterprise/government agency co-operation and enterprise/research institution co-operation, which is at the heart of knowledge sharing and knowledge management toward the dissemination and adoption of innovation ideas. These innovation ideas originate in and permeate through an "innovation system" with its national and international dimensions. They lead to new products and processes and new ways of doing things, which lower costs and enhance competitiveness. Networks at many different levels – inter-enterprise, inter-institutional, enterprise-institutional, worker-worker – are also important in knowledge sharing, which lower the cost of the various business transactions. These networks are weak between and within rural areas. Strengthening these partnerships and networks would lower unit cost and increase rural community value added creation.

Policy Intervention

There are at least three reasons why government intervenes to enhance the value added creation activity in rural areas: to bring unused or underused economic resources into production in order to raise overall national production; to provide access to rural residents to higher levels of economic wellbeing in the interests of social justice and social cohesion; and to curtail the social inefficiency resulting from persistent labour flows from rural to urban areas, leading to overburdening of the social infrastructure, on the one hand, and leaving it unused or underutilised, on the other. The various limitations or constraints of rural areas in creating value added immediately invoke specific policy measures to release these limitations, which may be grouped under three broad headings: enhancing the *market environment*, enhancing the access *infrastructure* and supporting and promoting *endogenous development*.

It is generally assumed that the institutional environment, like legislation and regulation, is favourable in the more established market economies, which is not the case, for example, in transition economies. The principal *market environment* problem concerns thin or non-existent markets. The general policy action is to increase local demand for goods, services, labour and capital by linking smaller urban concentrations together through the creation of urban networks or gateways (Government of Ireland, 2002). The market size issue can also be addressed through e-commerce and through the integration of the local market into national and international markets. Support for high-speed telecommunications and greater marketing action become the focus of policy intervention here. Services, which are critical to business expansion, may also be supported in order to prime development. Providing training support and upgrading information flows are well recognised measures for increasing labour market efficiency. Lowering the cost of capital, including the lowering of interest rates, sharing risk and even publicly supported specialist lending institutions are familiar initiatives in the arsenal of public support measures in enhancing the market environment for rural development.

Providing the *access infrastructure* in order to ameliorate the cost of distance is one of the more traditional approaches to rural development, providing or upgrading the various transport modes and telecommunications. There are practical and financial limitations to providing the necessary infrastructure to all rural areas. It is a question of reducing access costs as much as possible, but regardless of how much they are reduced, economic actors in rural areas will always be faced with costs, above those in central locations, in terms of time and service charges to reach markets. The extent to which this cost gap can be bridged, is a question of social choice and financial capacity.

Promoting and stimulating *endogenous development* has been a less traditional approach to rural development, but has now become the principal focus for policy instruments. Of course this assumes that issues like access and market environment have already been addressed. Creating development corridors, gateways and hubs, in addition to providing a greater local demand, is also addressed at providing agglomeration effects or positive externalities, which reduce costs and increase competitiveness. Bringing decentralisation down to local level, makes decision making and policy measures more place specific and more effective in addressing local issues. Creating partnerships and networks toward achieving common objectives can be effective between private businesses in a whole host of areas, for example, in upgrading skills, marketing and overcoming common local obstacles to enterprise development; between businesses and state institutions in addressing legislation issues, in providing critical services which are not available or in short supply; between businesses and research institutions in knowledge generation and management toward innovation and its diffusion; and between different levels of public administration and local actors in identifying and mitigating local obstacles to development, for example, in the case of LEADER.

Natural resource endowments are no longer fixed in terms of quality or use; the challenge is to increase the capacity of existing resources to create greater value added. The reform of the CAP with the price of conventional farm commodities being set by global markets, means that smaller production units must find higher value added production opportunities. These opportunities can be had in activities like organic farming, rural tourism or product-branding in association with a clean environment. This means that in moving from intensive traditional production with its negative environmental impact to more environment friendly activity where the quality of the environment itself is an input into the creation of value added, the quality and capacity of the natural resources have been enhanced.

Public policy, driven primarily by EU policy initiatives, since joining the Common Market in 1973, but more especially since the initiation of the Structural Funds in 1989, has had a significant influence on value added creation in rural areas in Ireland. This has come through considerably expanded public expenditure on agriculture in the form of the CAP, which has gradually widened its rural focus beyond farming to the other rural actors. It has come through the Structural Funds, which combined public funds (European Union and Irish Government) and private funds for expenditure on infrastructure, human resources, business and tourism development and environment. However, this influence on value added creation has also been effected by changes in the institutional environment: the more rigorous programming (over a five to six year period), planning, implementation and monitoring of policy measures; the integration of plans from local to regional to national level; the integration of efforts by the various agencies and authorities and especially the initiation, elaboration and now the mainstreaming of the LEADER programme, which has brought decision-making to the local level.

Despite the enhancement of value added creation in rural areas, and despite the fact that there has been a convergence between the income per capita in EU Member States (European Commission, 2004b), the extraordinary expenditure of EU funds has failed to bring about a convergence of GDP/capita between the regions of the EU (Rodriguez-Pose and Fratesi, 2004). This is because growth has been urban centred and urban driven and regions without significant urban centres or which have relatively large rural areas, have failed to grow as quickly as the more urban dominated regions. The clear implication here is that despite significant public policy intervention, market forces have been the dominant force in the spatial allocation of value added creation activity.

Conclusions

There is a continuum of rural situations where some or all of the parameters which are associated with rurality apply to varying degrees. Nevertheless, regardless of the particular situation, unless a rural community can create value added within an environment where market forces dominate, then it is not sustainable as a viable community. The evolving direction of CAP strengthens the dominance of the market in determining the fate of rural communities. The major market weakness in rural areas in the efficient exploitation of local resources is the thinness or non-existence of markets. In addition, a number of factors, which characterise the rural economy, combine to limit the level of value added created there. Despite the very significant input of finances and a substantially improved institutional environment, the income per capita of regions, which are strongly rural, has failed to converge with that of the more urbanised regions.

It is necessary to understand the market processes in the creation of value added and to recognise the limits of rural communities in their capacity to reach desired levels of economic wellbeing. It is also necessary to understand, particularly for policy makers, that there are limits to which policy measures can enhance further the value added creation activity in rural areas. At least, there are diminishing returns. If it is the wish of society that rural regions, which fail to achieve the desired value added creation, are sustainable, then direct income payments might be economically more efficient than further policy measures.

Endnotes

1   This term is explained and elaborated on, later in the chapter, but it may be generally understood as income generation.
2   The average share of agriculture in the rural labour force in areas with less then 150 persons per square kilometre had fallen to just 11.3% (Meredith, 2004)
3   Lenders and borrowers are working with different information sets leading to market transactions, which are less than Pareto efficient.
4   A sub-county level of community organisation, which operates in partnership with national and local government and non-government bodies in formulating and implementing development measures at this local level.

References

Commission of the European Communities (1981) Regional impact of The Common Agricultural Policy, *Studies Regional Policy*, 21, Brussels.

Government of Ireland (2002) *National Spatial Strategy 2002 – 2020: people, places and potential*, Dublin, Government Publications Sales Office.

European Commission (1988) *The future of rural society*, Com(88) 501 final/2, Brussels.

European Commission (2002) *Mid-Term review of the Common Agricultural Policy*, COM(2002) 394 final, Brussels.

European Commission (2004a) *Council Regulation on support for rural development by the European Agricultural Fund for Rural Development (EAFRD)*, COM(2004)490 final, Brussels.

European Commission (2004b) *A new partnership for cohesion: convergence, competitiveness, cooperation*, Third Report on Economic and Social Cohesion, Brussels.

European Commission (2005) *Tomorrow's Rural Development policy: broader, simpler, responding better to citizens' concerns*, Press Release, IP/05/766, Brussels.

Fukuyama, F. (1999) *Social capital and civil society*, Paper read to the Conference on Second Generation Reforms, IMF, November 8-9, Washington, D.C.

Meredith, D. (2004) *European rural regions: current trends, future prospects*, Paper read at workshop on Improving living conditions and quality of life in rural Europe, May 31-June 1, Westport, Ireland.

Rodriguez-Pose, A, and Fratesi, U. (2004) Between development and social policies: the impact of European Structural Funds in Objective 1 regions, *Regional Studies*, 38(1), pp.97-114.

Section Four:

PERSPECTIVES ON
THE PLANNING SYSTEM

Chapter 13

Planning Methodology and the Rational Comprehensive Paradigm

Patrick L. Braniff

Introduction

This chapter explores planning methodology, the search for synergy in physical planning and the contribution that this search can make towards the enrichment of the planners' tool kit. While the academic discipline and the professional practice of planning demand a sufficient knowledge of a wide range of topics, the subject of planning methodology must be recognised as holding a unique importance since it supplies not only the basic skills which constitute the tools of the planners' trade, but also the broader conceptual framework required for their effective deployment.

In planning, as in any art or science, consistent performance is necessary. Repeatability is important, not only within the field of scientific experimentation, but also within artistic performance. Yet repeatability cannot be left to chance. Chance is an inconsistent ally and will yield differing results from time to time. The proven way to ensure repeatability is to fully understand the complete process and also the techniques used in implementation. Hence two things are necessary: firstly, a commitment to the overall process and its successful conclusion, and secondly, an interest in and mastery of the techniques necessary for implementation. In short, these two facets are inextricably linked. Planning, therefore, is focussed upon relationships and involves complexity. As Abercrombie observed over 60 years ago:

> The touchstone of what constitutes a planning scheme is this matter of relationship, the accommodation of several units to make a complete but harmonious whole. The juxtaposition of independent units, however perfect in themselves, which remain distinct, does not produce a planning scheme; nor does the concourse of units, however large, which makes a mere mass or muddle. (Abercrombie, 1943, pp.11-12)

Physical planning requires political will for the commitment of resources. It also needs some systematic approach that will help it to achieve its purpose. Again as Abercrombie pointed out:

> Peddling improvements without any plan or policy behind them are worse than useless: they are similar to sticking bits of sticking plaster upon the sore places of a body permeated with disease. The patches - if anything, cause a deeper festering of the local wounds. A diagnosis in the form of a survey of the most searching nature is necessary. (Abercrombie, 1943, pp.154-155)

Hence, any discussion about planning inescapably requires talking about the processes which enable the will to plan to be implemented. It is interesting, therefore, to consider the relationship between planning methodology and the overall planning process as it has evolved over time. This chapter reviews that context and gives particular attention to the prominence of the rational comprehensive model in the delivery of European Union Structural Funds expenditure.

Context

A key characteristic of the early planners was their perception of need. They clearly saw that the environment, both built and natural, needed to be cared for. They saw the need for forethought in dealing with this environment. They struggled for comprehensiveness in their overall approach and they understood many of the key relationships between society and environment, between function and hardware.

In their reaction to perceived need, the primary attribute of the early planners was their determination to plan. Armed with these positive attitudes, they eventually developed a broad methodological perspective, commonly referred to as the rational comprehensive approach. This approach was, in turn, the procedural refinement of the methodology of "Survey, Analysis and Plan" advocated by the profession's founding fathers. In the heady days of economic growth in the 1960s, this model was unquestioned. At that time, problems were perceived as being primarily related to the provision of better environmental hardware – hardware to facilitate existing functions. The function was the focus. However, the long wave of economic growth faltered in the 1970s and ended with the OPEC oil price rises in 1979. A new era was born in which the relationship between the planners and the market was fundamentally changed. The resources for neo-Benthamite benevolence were no longer available.

The focus for planning shifted to social and economic problems, many of which were perceived to have an environmental dimension. And there was also the slowly growing awareness of the fragility of the natural environment.

An entirely new "green" constituency emerged and this resulted in new political pressures, organizations and institutions. Within this shifting context, problems were less easy to define, harder to anticipate and more difficult to remedy with the result that some degree of reorientation was forced upon planning. Most planners were puzzled as to how to proceed, but some like Field and MacGregor (1987), took a positive approach to the new challenges:

> It is not just the transformation of the planning process which has promoted the rational decision making approach; planning has become more systematic in a second important respect, namely it is now based on the use of more formal replicable methods of analysis at each stage within the overall process, as compared with the informal 'rules of thumb' which characterized planning practice in the immediate post-war period. In this respect, the planners' lexicon or 'tool kit' has changed quite markedly as the techniques of quantitative analysis have been brought to bear in the study of the structural relationships among the variables within the system. (Field and MacGregor, 1987, p.11)

It must be admitted, albeit with regret, that such commentators were in a minority in the development of professional thinking and practice. As evidence of this statement, it is interesting to consider the results of a key word search of the titles of the articles published in *The Planner* between 1971 and 1990 (the year for which the last index is available). The key words selected for the search were "methodology", "method", "analysis", "technique" and "system" (with their plurals). The results were disappointing: out of more than 10,500 article titles, only 74 included any of these key words. While this survey does not purport to tell the whole story of planners' preoccupations, it is interesting to find that, in the largest circulation planning journal in the United Kingdom and Ireland, only 0.70 per cent of articles seem to have been focussed on methodology over the 1971 -1990 period. An equivalent search of the successor publication, *Planning*, over the more recent period 2003 to 2005 yielded a result of 5.4 per cent; however, the vast majority of the key word occurrences were found in the context of news stories rather than substantive academic articles.

Skills and the Rational Comprehensive Model
Accordingly, there has been a worrying separation between theory and practice to the extent that theory is now seen by many non theoreticians as irrelevant. The relevance and applicability of the early theoreticians is easily seen and judged. For example, those interested in Robert Owen can reflect on his philosophy by visiting New Lanark. Those seeking the influence of Patrick Geddes can inspect his work from Scotland to India. Those wishing to assess the value of Sir Patrick Abercrombie's theories can judge their concrete worth by visiting urban centres from Dublin to Doncaster. Unfortunately, most of

today's leading theoreticians have left little in the way of physical concretisation of their theoretical constructs. This makes it difficult to arrive at a fair assessment of their worth. Where theoreticians have sown the seeds of doubt and demoralisation has been in their treatment of procedural planning theory. For too long it has been fashionable to attack the rational comprehensive approach on the basis that its effective implementation is impossible. It has been alleged that the information demands, and the information handling demands, of the rational comprehensive approach are impossible to fulfil and that hence the approach should be discarded. Nothing could be more damaging to professional morale. Some writers have highlighted that in important areas of professional work, there is considerable self-questionning about the value of technical knowledge and skill:

> Even planners themselves doubt whether they have the developmental and financial training for the jobs they now see as relevant. Where their work involves policy issues, there are doubts about whether there is any role for technical knowledge and skill. (Healey et al., 1982, p.14)

Often, the rational comprehensive approach has been misrepresented as constituting an effort to regress to the era of the old "master plan" concept of the 1950s. It is no such thing. It is rather, a style of, or approach to planning – that is all. Indeed few planners would wish to be less than rational or less than comprehensive in the exercise of their professional skills. After all, the unique core of planners' skills relates to their ability to handle comprehensiveness and synthesis. While many techniques used by planners, such as projection and evaluation, are commonly used by other professions, the skills of analysing, understanding and orchestrating complexity within the sphere of physical planning are the unique domain of the professional planner. Although planning methodology introduces students to these skills, some influential planning theorists have proclaimed them to be useless, naive and impossible to implement. But as Batty quite elegantly put it:

> Planning must move back to educating what is needed with respect to town and country, it must reinvigorate its idealism and it must provide the skills necessary to enable such idealism to be achieved. (Batty, 1983, p.67)

Europe, Synergy and the Resurrection of the Rational Comprehensive Model

There has, however, been a considerable opportunity in European Union regional policy to develop, test and apply rational comprehensive techniques in the pursuit of effective plan making. The Commission constantly reviews and updates the methods for implementing the Structural Funds. Over the past two decades it has explored specific methodologies for improving the effectiveness of its regional development measures. The "Programme Approach" and the "Integrated Approach" are mutually complementary manifestations of these efforts. The identification of operational problems has resulted in recognition of the need for a specific methodology to facilitate the implementation of integrated planning. In this regard the European Commission's approach to integrated planning has been adopted in an effort to ensure that the grant aid disbursed by the Structural Funds achieves the maximum in terms of the defined goals of the Union:

> The basic idea underlying an Integrated Development Operation is better coordination of resources and procedures with a view to greater effectiveness. The idea has all the more immediate importance since the resources available are still limited. (Economic and Social Committee of the European Parliament, 1982, p.9)

A major impetus for the development of an operational methodology for integrated planning was the reform of the Structural Funds following the signing of the Single European Act. The move away at that time from a management by project approach and the stated preference for funding effectiveness and programming demonstrated well the Commission's desire to develop the concept of an integrated approach:

> An integrated programme would seek to achieve synergy between different measures and to ensure regional convergence of the effects of different partners with different backgrounds and different responsibilities. (Commission of the European Community, 1988, p.4)

This situation has presented planning methodologists during the interim with two challenges. The first is to develop broad procedural models that will help with the clarification and implementation of the integrated approach and the second is to develop individual techniques to deal with the detailed problems of integrated analysis and integrated programme generation. The general concept of integrated planning has evolved through a number of manifestations. Initially conceived as a rational approach to the restructuring of third world rural economies, it has been adopted and adapted by the European Commission to serve a variety of purposes. Especially important has been the widely felt need to increase the impact of Community and national interventions, particularly in regions affected by serious problems. The general objectives of the approach were set out in the Commission Document COM(86) 401 final/2, as follows:

> Where appropriate, the Integrated Approach is a preferred Commission formula for structural interventions. The Commission will seek to facilitate

and encourage the access of all Member States to the Integrated Approach; the initiative can come from the Commission or from a Member State. Their implementation will become progressively more feasible as Community, national, regional and local authorities gain from the experience of working together in such a framework. (CEC, 1986, p.1)

The same general integrated approach has been applied to both urban development programmes and to rural programmes, the latter under the banner of integrated rural development. There have been, of course, additional and important considerations related to administrative structures. For example, as Greer (1984) pointed out, this is particularly the case at national government level where administrative changes are often necessary to ensure that development programmes are introduced on a broad and unified front rather than being left in the hands of ministries and departments each of which usually has its individual functional interest.

It is appropriate, therefore, to now turn to the challenges confronting integrated planning and the possible methodological response. Within the field of integrated planning, the concepts of integration and synergy require careful consideration and demand that some attempt at definition should be made. In earlier work, I developed the QUBIST model for the European Commission, which used cross-impact methodology to identify, measure and evaluate the spatial relationships between actions funded under the Structural Funds. Here, I provide a short account of the conceptual approach but a more detailed version is set out in the MEANS COLLECTION, the EU framework for monitoring and evaluating Regional Policy (CEC, 1999). Ideally, the proposals forming a development programme should have a strong positive relationship to each other. This positive relationship can only be judged to be positive within the context of goals that are either explicitly stated or implicitly recognized. The specific goals for an integrated programme will emerge from study of the facts discovered by relevant survey, within the context of the Commission's general philosophy of integration. Examination of the facts in this light will identify problems and opportunities. In turn, solving the problems and capitalizing upon the opportunities will constitute the programme goals.

The positive relationship between proposals may relate to the functional character of the proposals (e.g. a fruit cannery development and a fruit growing scheme). It may relate to the location of the physical development that is to be brought about by the proposals (e.g. an industrial factory complex and a new motorway access). The positive relationship between proposals may depend upon the timing involved (e.g. proposals to provide transport services the operations of which are timed so as to facilitate interconnections). Of course, two proposals could complement each other by having a positive relationship of more than one kind.

A simple one-dimensional relationship between two proposals forming part of a programme can be described as complementarity. However, to achieve synergy, the relationships must be more than one-dimensional. A one-dimensional relationship can be such that activity A contributes to activity B, without any degree of reciprocity and without any resulting contribution to other activities. Such a relationship, or linkage, is good, but it is a simple one-way link that constitutes complementarity and falls short of generating synergy. To achieve synergy, a higher complexity of beneficial interrelationships between proposals is necessary. This higher complexity of interrelationships will involve multiple complementarities at many levels and from a number of perspectives. These interrelationships can only be judged to be positive within a given goal context. For example, a proposal to erect housing beside a busy motorway interchange could be considered to be positive within the context of a goal such as "to minimize the time taken by the journey to work" but would be considered negative within the context of a goal such as "to maximize the quietness of the environment in residential areas". The benefits that derive from a well integrated programme are twofold. Firstly, there will probably be financial savings in the implementation of the development. Secondly, and more importantly, there will be benefits accruing from improved general functionality. By this I mean not the particular functioning of any individual proposed project, but the general collective functioning of the programme's proposed projects, taken as a whole.

In normal English usage, "synergy" means "combined or correlated action of a group of bodily organs (as nerve centres, muscles etc.) hence of mental faculties, of remedies etc." (Oxford English Dictionary). However, when specialist technical dictionaries are consulted, the results are more illuminating. The Concise Chemical and Technical Dictionary defines "synergy" as "united action" and its derivative "synergism" as "co-operative action of discrete agencies or substances whose total effect is greater than the sum of their separate effects". The Condensed Chemical Dictionary, while not defining "synergy", defines "synergism" as "a chemical phenomenon (the opposite of antagonism) in which the effect of two active components of a mixture is more than additive, i.e. it is greater than the equivalent volume or concentration of either component alone".

Within the field of integrated planning, the concepts of integration and synergy require equally careful consideration and demand that some attempt at definition should be made. Any development plan consists of a programme of proposals to be implemented over time. Proposals can be of two types - either investment proposals (which involve capital investment in the built environment) or policy proposals (which involve the implementation of policies and their associated regulatory and current expenditure provisions). The proposals forming a development programme may owe their origin to a variety of sources and pressures. It is, indeed, quite possible that some organisations could put forward proposals which run counter to the proposals advanced by other organisations. When the spatial aspects of physical planning are considered, the likelihood of such circumstances arising can all too easily be appreciated.

Integration describes the relationship between the proposals forming a programme, while synergy describes the process or activity jointly generated by the proposals once they are implemented. Looking again at the definitions of synergy and synergism, discussed earlier, it is clear that this improved functionality or enhancement of functional performance amounts to synergy as we would wish to use the term. Synergy does not derive from the effective design of an individual proposal; it is the complex and multi-directional interaction between the proposals which generates it.

Despite the problems, the future for the Integrated Approach seems bright. It was initially adopted by the European Commission as a philosophy without a methodology. But within the legislative and administrative arenas, the methodology has seen rapid refinement. Even within the technical sphere, some of the most recent studies show improvement and, significantly, the latest round of the Structural Funds has taken the project of integration much more seriously than in previous programming periods (Roberts, 2003). The guidelines set out for monitoring and evaluating interventions highlight the need to think about integration between sectors and actions in order to unlock stubborn area-based problems (CEC, 2000). Similarly, the guidance established for complying with Structural Funds regulations and criteria also emphasise the importance of *connected programmes*, that are embedded within local policy and which use financial interventions to *lever* other resources in regeneration initiatives. Chorianopoulos (2002), for example, has demonstrated how the generic principles of vertical and horizontal integration have found their way into the EU URBAN II Community Initiative Programme 2000-2006. Vertical linkages relate to the relationship between European, national and local policies and the need for these to be working in mutually reinforcing and complementary ways is deemed vital for success. Horizontal linkages emphasise the connections between programmes operating in a single area and across Europe, and there is an increasing awareness of the need for local government and governance structures to facilitate such relationships in practice. Elaborating on this, Van den Berg *et al.* (2004) make the crucial point that integrated programmes rely on political and administrative structures that overcome silo thinking, policy disconnections and professional rivalries.

Conclusion

If planning is to be comprehensive, then it must develop the skills and procedures for dealing comprehensively with spatial problems and development opportunities. It must develop these skills to the utmost, since there is no such thing as being semi-comprehensive. If planning is fact-based and rational, then it must pay great attention to its data and their analysis. This has many implications for the refinement of specific techniques, particularly computer-based techniques. Again, this must be done because there is no alternative. There is no benefit in being semi-rational. In offering her or his contribution, the professional planner must attempt to shed light upon the factual situation within the subject environment. Unfounded generalizations will be of little help.

There is now comforting evidence that the current period can amount to a renaissance for planning methodology in general and the rational comprehensive model in particular. Firstly, there are technical developments in information technology taking place not only within computing, but also within those related fields that affect the ease and accuracy of data acquisition. Such developments will undoubtedly strengthen planning's capacity for analysis and, in particular, integrated analysis. Secondly, there is the rebirth of regional planning, largely under the auspices of the European Commission. As competing regions present their cases for subventions from the Structural Funds, it is now accepted that strong argument is strengthened by solid fact. And thirdly, within the profession there is increasing awareness of the value of evidence-based policy across government, but especially in land use planning and urban development programmes, where expensive mistakes have been made in the past (Rhodes *et al.*, 2003). In conclusion, I would argue that the professional planner has little hope of surviving without a toolkit. Planning will prosper only on the basis of its ability to perform useful work for society and, to do this, it must strive to improve the unique skills and insights which justify its existence as a profession.

References

Abercrombie, Sir Patrick (1943) *Town and Country Planning*, London, Oxford University Press.

Batty, M. (1983) The reskilling of planning, *EPA Newsletter*, 12 (3), p.67.

Batty, M. (1990) How planning education can survive the future: thoughts about new curricula, *EPA Newsletter*, February, pp. 57-73.

Chorianopoulos, I. (2002) Urban restructuring and governance: north-south differences in Europe and the EU URBAN Initiative, *Urban Studies,* 39(3), pp.705-726.

Commission of the European Communities (1986) *COM(86) 401 final/2*, Brussels, Commission of the European Commission.

Commission of the European Communities (1988) *Back Up Policies: Reform of the Structural Funds, COM (88) 500 SYN 151/2,* Brussels, Commission of the European Communities.

Commission of the European Communities (1999) *The MEANS Collection: Evaluating Socio-economic Programmes*, Brussels, Commission of the European Communities.

Commission of the European Communities (2000) *Indicators for Monitoring and Evaluation in the New Programme Period 2000-2006: Methodological Working Paper No.3*, Brussels, Commission of the European Communities.

Economic and Social Committee of the European Parliament (1982) *Study of the Section for Regional Development on Integrated Operations, CES 916/80 fin WGN CHJ*, Brussels, 5th April 1982.

Field, B. and MacGregor, B. (1987) *Forecasting techniques for urban and regional planning*, London, Hutchinson.

Greer, J. (1984) Integrated Rural Development: reflections on a magic phase, *Pleanáil*, 1(4), pp.10-15.

Healey, P., McDougall, G. and Thomas, M.J. (1982) *Planning theory – prospects for the 1980s*, Selected papers from a conference held in Oxford, 2-4 April 1981, Oxford, Pergamon.

Rhodes, J., Tyler, P. and Brennan, A. (2003) New developments in area-based initiatives in England: the experience of the Single Regeneration Budget, *Urban Studies*, 40(8), pp.1399-1426.

Roberts, P. (2003) Partnership, programmes and the promotion of regional development: an evaluation of the operation of the Structural Funds regional programmes, *Progress in Planning,* 59(1), pp.1-69.

Van den Berg, L., Van der Meer, J. and Pol, P. (2004) Organising capacity and social policy in European cities, *Urban Studies*, 40(10), pp.1959-1978.

Chapter 14

Prizes and Pitfalls in Enforcement Planning

Stephen McKay

Introduction

The purpose of this chapter is to review planning enforcement in Northern Ireland, to highlight inherent weaknesses, and make suggestions as to how, through structural change, the system might be improved. This is important as enforcement in the United Kingdom (UK) has long been regarded as the weakest link in the planning system, characterised by technicality, complexity and lack of urgency (Dobry, 1975). Despite some tinkering with the legislative mechanisms, most notably as a result of recommendations made by Carnwath (1989), enforcement remains relatively ineffective (McKay, 2003). A review of planning enforcement in England by the Office of the Deputy Prime Minister (ODPM, 2002) has suggested additional changes to the legislative framework which aim to increase the effectiveness of the system. While a number of interesting suggestions have been proposed, none take into account the importance of understanding the structural factors which influence regulatory compliance at the everyday level. This chapter will look, therefore, not just at the prevailing Northern Ireland legislative framework, which provides a toolkit for planners to remedy unauthorised activities, but specifically at the relationship between planning practice and regulatory compliance. The objective is to identify strategies which may be worthy of consideration in attempting to improve the overall effectiveness of the enforcement system.

The Planning System in Northern Ireland

There are three key elements within mainstream planning: development planning or forward planning, development control and enforcement. Although the form and content of development plans vary widely, there appears to be a general consensus within Ireland and the United Kingdom that the key function of the development plan is to provide guidance as to the amount of development which may be expected and where it may best be located, within a specified area. Effectively these documents constitute a planning policy framework which is used to assist in the process of determining whether or not a particular form of development is likely to be acceptable. In contrast, development control is a process by which society regulates changes in the use and appearance of the environment. Decisions taken in the planning process have long-term consequences and well-considered decisions can enhance and enrich the environment. Poor decisions will be endured long after the decision-takers have died (Audit Commission, 1992). Development control is, therefore, a process which regulates development, mainly in the public interest. Proposals for new development are assessed, within the development plan policy framework, as to whether or not they constitute acceptable development and one of the key functions of development control is to ensure that unacceptable development does not take place (DOE, 1996).

The Northern Ireland system of development control is based on Article 12 of the Planning (Northern Ireland) Order 1991 which states that "planning permission is required for the carrying out of any development of land"(DOE (NI), 1992). Article 11(1) of the same legislation defines development as: "the carrying out of building, engineering, mining or other operations in, on, under or over land, or the making of any material change in the use of any buildings or other land"(DOE(NI), 1992). In order to establish a comprehensive understanding of the fundamental principles of mainstream planning practice it is essential to realise the distinction between "operations" and "use". The true meaning of the concepts can best be grasped through case law. Lord Parker (Cheshire CC v Woodward 1962) stated than an "operation" is some act which changes the physical characteristics of the land, or of what is under it, or of the air above it, "use" refers to the purpose to which the land and buildings are devoted. Lord Denning (Parkes v Secretary of State for the Environment 1978) made the comment that "operations" comprise activities that result in some physical alteration to the land which have some degree of permanence in relation to the land itself – whereas "use" comprises activities which are done in, alongside, or on the land but do not interfere with the actual characteristics of the land.

Taken together, the effect of Article 11(1) and Article 12 is that every minor operation or activity would require planning permission, for example the ploughing of farmland. Since such a degree of control would be unnecessary and indeed impractical to operate, the legislation provides for reasonable limits to be placed on the extent of control in two ways. Firstly, it excludes certain operations and uses from the definition of development (Article 11 (2)), and secondly it empowers the planning authority to make Development Orders which can exclude certain classes of development from the need to obtain planning permission (Article 13).

Under certain circumstances, such as, those specified in the Planning (General Development) Order (Northern Ireland) 1993 (as amended) planning permission is granted, in accordance with Article 3 (1), for specified classes of development, thereby avoiding the need for a planning application. Such developments are normally of a minor nature or represent changes of use from more to less significant forms of operation. Any other class of development is likely to require an application for planning permission. It is deemed to be the responsibility of would-be developers to take steps to ascertain whether such an application is required. For this purpose, the 1991 Order provides that developers may approach the planning authority for a determination. In order to ensure that unacceptable development does not take place it is essential to have a deterrent mechanism. Development control, therefore, necessarily involves measures for planning enforcement referred to under Part VI of the Planning (Northern Ireland) Order 1991.

It is not a criminal offence to carry out development without first getting planning permission, with a small number of exceptions. If, however, the development is deemed to be unacceptable, it is incumbent upon the offender to take remedial action. Failure to comply with such requirements may result in the initiation of enforcement procedures. The purpose of planning enforcement is therefore to protect the integrity of the planning system by enabling planning authorities to remedy any harm to amenity or "other interests of acknowledged importance" that may result from unauthorised development (DOE (NI), 1999). The nature of the system means that the decisions on whether to take enforcement action, and if so what action is best suited to particular circumstances, are matters for the planning authority's discretion. Indeed the three planning tasks, labelled "the planning trinity" by Millichap (1998), are all intimately related – none is more important than the other if the ultimate goal is effective use of the planning legislation's powers. Forward planning, development control and enforcement are all mutually dependent and mutually reinforcing. To deploy any of these mechanisms ineffectively is to undermine the legitimacy of the entire planning system.

Criticisms of the Enforcement System

While enforcement in the UK generally has often been criticised for ineffectiveness, most notably by Dobry (1975) and Carnwath (1989), the Northern Ireland system has frequently been subject to condemnation, not least from Government. On 29th March 1994 the Government appointed the Northern Ireland Affairs Committee, under Standing Order No 130, to "examine the expenditure, administration and policy of the Northern Ireland Office; administration and expenditure of the Crown Solicitor's Office; and other matters within the responsibility of the Secretary of State for Northern Ireland"(House of Commons, 1994). Two years later the Committee issued a report titled *The Planning System in Northern Ireland*. This report looked in detail at the working methods of, what was then called, the Town and Country Planning Service of the Department of the Environment for Northern Ireland. It analysed the activities of the Service under three main headings: administration, planning guidance and public control (House of Commons, 1996).

Two of the key areas that came under scrutiny were planning enforcement and planning conditions. With regard to the former the report made the following statement "the Planning (Northern Ireland) Order 1991 should be amended to provide for more effective enforcement of breaches of planning control" (House of Commons, 1996, p.22). It concluded that practice and procedure surrounding planning conditions represented "an important weakness in the current planning system" and overall that "the management of the Planning Service is dangerously complacent about this problem which must be addressed as a matter of urgency"(House of Commons, 1996, p.23).

Since 1996 the Planning Service has made significant progress in improving its enforcement system. It has introduced guidance through the publication of Planning Policy Statement 9: The Enforcement of Planning Control; it has introduced new legislative mechanisms including Breach of Condition Notices and Planning Contravention Notices; and it has introduced a network of dedicated planning enforcement teams across Northern Ireland. Nonetheless evidence suggests that the system remains reactive and compliance levels with planning conditions are relatively low (McKay, 2003). So how can the planning enforcement system be made more effective? Increasing the effectiveness of enforcement is not an easy task, but not an impossible one. Traditionally, reviews of planning enforcement have often been restricted to the nature and content of legislative mechanisms to the exclusion of the structural components which underpin the effectiveness of the system. In this context attention in this chapter will turn firstly to a consideration of regulatory frameworks, secondly to strategies pursuant to improved regulatory compliance, and thirdly to how such frameworks and strategies might foster effective planning enforcement in Northern Ireland.

Regulatory Frameworks
At the outset it is important to recognise that many and varied regulatory frameworks exist. The key questions are firstly, to which classification does our planning enforcement system belong and secondly, to which should it belong? It is surprising to find that, given the significance and high profile of environmental regulation, there is a dearth of specific theory on planning enforcement. Prior (2000) states that this means risking the adoption of new policy measures underwritten by an implicit model of regulation, based on traditional conceptions of relations between enforcer and enforced, and at

variance with current and anticipated operational conditions. Indeed, Baer (1997) in dealing with the problems of planning enforcement relates to the regulatory framework of Ingram and Schneider (1990) who draw upon theoretical perceptions of a number of academics and suggest that the design of regulations be considered on four levels. Each of these levels and their origin is now discussed.

1. The strong statute which removes discretion from the enforcement equation. This approach advocates that discretion over the elements in designs should be retained by the statutory designers. The statute should contain objectives and goals that are consistent, clear and specific. Under this approach participation is limited to those who are supportive of the goals. The statute should leave little uncertainty about relationships and causal theory should be adequate to link means to ends (Sabatier and Mazmanian, 1981). While it is apparent that the systematic approach of the strong statute is relevant to planning enforcement in Northern Ireland, it is true to say that there is a high degree of local discretion which is reflected in the second level of the typology put forward by Ingram and Schneider (1990) and referred to as the Wilsonian perspective.

2. The Wilsonian perspective is the same as the strong statute in relation to goal specificity but facilitates discretion by administrative agencies on other matters, including organisational structure and rules. The statute therefore retains complete control over policy goals and purposes while agencies are left to add the details providing the means for achieving the goals. This mirrors the Northern Ireland situation where a strong statute exists and a high degree of discretion is allocated to those who implement policy.

3. The grass roots approach, which advocates interpretation by the street level bureaucrats, is diametrically opposed to the strong statute perspective. Discretion over all elements of policy logic is given to the lowest level implementor or to the target populations themselves. The statute does little more than provide agents or citizens with the legal authority to act. Salamon (1981) indicated that this has been relevant in many policy areas in the United States, giving rise to citizen-initiated governance through special districts whereby the government establishes funds, but the discretion over the use of the public authority and the spending of public funds is often in the hands of one or another non-federal, often non-public, third party implementer.

4. The support-building approach emerges from the thesis of Stone (1988) that supports the assertion that the ends and means are achieved by consensus building and agreement. It places emphasis on how statutes influence values and participation patterns and how various groups reconcile their interests and there is limited emphasis on the achievement of instrumental goals. Similarly Lipsky (1980) advocated an approach underpinned by negotiation consensus building and agreement where the relationship between the regulators and the regulated is of paramount importance, while Hanf (1993) stressed the significance of the relationship between the regulator and the offender in achieving successful outcomes rather than the rigid implementation of a strong statute.

While it is clear that in a utopian society a bottom up approach driven by consensus compliance is ideal, it is likely to remain an unachievable aspirational goal in Northern Ireland society, that is unless, policy makers and street level bureaucrats turn their attention to successful developments which have taken place in other areas of society as a result of taking cognisance of theories of regulation pursuant to compliance.

Regulation Theory

Hutter and Sorenson (1993) defined regulation as the use of the law to constrain and organise the activities of business and industry. It is a state activity and contentious as it determines the degree to which governments intervene to protect particular groups. While this is perhaps a narrow perspective in the consideration of planning control, where often domestic disputes between individuals result in violations, it provides a useful starting point in the consideration of theories of regulation.

Yaeger (1991) distinguished between economic and social regulation. While the distinction between the two is not always clear cut and largely heuristic, economic deals with the regulation of financial markets and social considers laws protecting the environment, consumers and employees. In the case of planning, social regulation is particularly relevant as government attempts to regulate using legal sanctions and administrative measures such as licensing in the form of planning permissions.

Hutter (1997) highlighted how regulation theory can be divided into accommodative or consensual theories and conflict theories. Lowi (1972) defined the former as regulatory policies protective of public goods or populations. In terms of planning the activities of developers are, therefore, regulated to protect both the public and, on occasion, private interest. Conflict theorists such as Gunningham (1974) consider regulatory laws to have little impact and are designed to facilitate developers who themselves are major players in the formulation of regulations, a view which may go some way towards explaining why planning control has been largely ineffective and regulatory compliance levels poor (McKay, 2003).

Compliance and the Enforcement of Regulations

Compliance is a major consideration in all forms of enforcement but is particularly important in the regulatory context (Hutter, 1997). It is a complex process of defining responses to mandates that are often ambiguous. Edelman (1991) states how this occurs at field level and the level of policy making which can involve both standard setting and administrative guidance about how to comply with statutes and regulations and policy making about how to enforce these. Di Mento (1986) states this may be a reflexive process in which policy makers, field level inspectors and even the regulated feed their expectations and practices into each other and adapt accordingly. The result is that, with regard to planning, recommendations aimed at achieving compliance must recognise the varying and at times contradictory perceptions of rule violations and must take into account the complex processes that make for non-compliance.

Hawkins (1984) espouses the notion that regulatory legislation should be as much a process as an event. This is supported by Di Mento (1986) who argues that compliance should be seen as evolving from interaction among several groups over time while Bardach and Kagen (1982) feel this is the case, not only at the level of standard setting, but at the enforcement stage of the regulatory process. Manning (1988) in turn takes the view that compliance is the process of extended and endless negotiation. While this may seem strange to those not acquainted with law enforcement, a number of studies have suggested that negotiation is a significant characteristic of regulatory enforcement (Carson, 1970; Cranston, 1979; Hawkins, 1984; Hutter, 1988; Richardson *et al.*, 1983). Indeed Hutter (1997) has suggested that the tendency to deal with breaches of regulations through informal techniques centred on negotiation has established the term compliance to denote a whole enforcement system.

Over the last two decades authors including Richardson *et al* (1983) and Hawkins (1984) have examined in detail how regulators apply legislation to reach their goals. Such research has demonstrated that enforcement of the law does not relate only to legal action but a series of mechanisms including education, advice, persuasion, and negotiation. For example, Scholz (1991) advocates that a cooperative strategy can increase enforcement effectiveness. It is argued that potentially effective administrative strategies frequently impose problems of control thus making effective strategies less attractive to policy supporters than safer, more controllable strategies. A binary model of enforcement styles has been used to facilitate the understanding of law enforcement processes. One of the most important elements of this model approximates to Richardson's (1983) *accommodative* or Hawkins' (1984) *compliance* strategy of enforcement. The key objective of the strategy is to achieve compliance through the remedy of existing problems and prevention of new ones (Reiss, 1984). The most effective way to achieve compliance is perceived to be via cooperative and conciliatory methods which tend to be long term and underpinned by negotiation and persuasion. The imposition of punitive measures is perceived to be a last resort when all other options have been exhausted. This reflects the work of Hanf (1993) which is underpinned by the assumption that the enforcement of regulations occurs through bargaining rather than the consistent, even handed application of general decision rules (Prior, 2000).

The second element of the binary model is characterised by a penal style of enforcement and has been termed the *deterrent* model (Reiss, 1984) and the *sanctioning* strategy (Hawkins, 1984). While the objective of both models is to prevent the occurrence of violations Hawkins believes the approach is primarily concerned with delivering retribution which may have several objectives ranging from inflicting punishment to utilitarian aims.

Hutter (1997) has refined the binary model to include two strategies which provide the framework for discussing approaches used in dealing with breaches of planning control within the context of this research. The first of these is the *persuasive* strategy which is akin to the accommodative or compliance model of enforcement and is based upon informal procedures including educating and persuading offenders to comply with regulations. Braithewaite *et al* (1987) used a similar approach to classify regulatory agencies. The second is an *insistent* strategy which is 'less benevolent and less flexible' than the first. Under this scenario regulators are reluctant to embark on long-term negotiation preferring to implement legislative action when faced with resistance to comply. Hutter (1997) stresses that, unlike the sanctioning approach (Hawkins, 1984), the ultimate objective is to gain compliance and not effect retribution whereas Reiss (1984) states that this characterises situations where violations are unpredictable and preventative actions are not possible.

A third approach of direct relevance to this chapter is that identified by Braithwaite *et al* (1987) that complements Hutter's (1997) model. Falling somewhere between the persuasive and insistent strategies it is typified by regulators being flexible in their interpretation of the rules and willingness to instigate legal action, thus mirroring the *'flexible enforcement'* ideal of Bardach and Kagan (1982).

The Facilitative Approach

While the above concepts can be drawn upon in pursuit of an optimum approach to achieving regulatory compliance it is also important to take into account the facilitative holistic approach advocated by Burby *et al* (1998). They present two choices in considering which enforcement actions are *most effective*. The first focuses on whether to increase the capacity to enforce, or enhance the commitment of developers to comply voluntarily with regulatory provisions. The second choice is whether to adopt a systematic or a facilitative philosophy for dealing with regulated entities. However, the preferred option supported by Burby's research is one that supports fostering regulated entities commitment to comply and of facilitating willingness to comply among developers. This strategy is underpinned by the belief that the reasons for failure to comply with regulations are not limited to calculations of the cost of sanctions against the benefits of non-compliance (Kagan and Scholz, 1994). McKay *et al.* (2003) agrees and concludes that many of the key reasons for non-compliance in the Northern Ireland planning system are similar, for example, ignorance of the regulations, incompetence, negligence and disagreement with conditions attached to planning application approvals. The approach suggested to deal with violations includes a number of elements: using general, flexible guidelines when assessing compliance; explaining the provisions violated and advising how to fix them; using incentives such as relaxed inspection schedules and leniency when violations are detected to reward those who endeavour to comply; and providing technical assistance to regulated firms and individuals.

Burby's approach is not confined, however, to facilitative strategies but recognises the need for a number of traditional supporting mechanisms which include: an adequate number of technically competent staff; strong proactive leadership; adequate legal support; and a consistently strong effort to check building and development plans, and inspect buildings and development sites. The work of Burby *et al.* (1998) suggests that some movement towards the lower thresholds of Ingram and Schneider's hierarchy just might be achievable with the application of appropriate facilitative strategies. So how does this sit with the Northern Ireland planning enforcement system?

Conclusion

Legislative considerations are not a panacea for the malaise of planning enforcement. If a cure is to be established, it can only evolve through research into the structural factors underpinning the system. In this context it is clear that the discretionary regulatory framework is the foundation upon which the enforcement system is constructed. While Ingram and Schneider (1990) have examined patterns of allocating discretion at four levels, it is apparent that planning enforcement in the UK can be configured to conceptualise implementation options for compliance with planning regulations and enforcement tactics across a more definitive spectrum. The extreme right is autocratic, non-discretionary and there is strict liability. The statute is clear and explicit permitting legislators to confront disagreements in democratically accountable arenas as opposed to leaving crucial decisions to bureaucrats. Attitudes mellow with movement towards the centre and, although a strong explicit statute remains, discretion to apply the law to its full effect is passed to agencies and street level bureaucrats who use skills, local knowledge and balanced judgement to achieve the goals. On the extreme left of the spectrum discretion over all aspects of policy logic are allocated to street level implementers who facilitate collaborative agreement. It is a support-building approach that concentrates on the policy process rather than the outcomes. The political resolution of conflict is deemed to supersede policy substance. The planning process becomes a partnership with all stakeholders involved. Specifically, planners and developers concur with all aspects of proposals prior to commencement of works through education, negotiation and collaboration with an aim of signing up to an agreed programme of action underpinned by self-regulation.

Where on the regulatory spectrum UK enforcement stands at any time is a matter of balance. The evidence from this research would suggest that, presently, it sits to the right of centre though whether this is the optimum location is dubious. The preferred position is, perhaps, one where self-regulation, peripheral in Northern Ireland planning, is a significant factor. The enforcement equation is, however, complex and it would be naive to suggest that such a strategy would resolve the problems *per se*.

Approaches weighted towards balanced judgement, which are regularly employed by planning enforcement officials, comfortably facilitate both the accommodative (Richardson, 1983) and sanctioning (Hawkins, 1984) strategies, but to adopt one or other of these would be oversimplistic. As Ayres and Braithwaite (1992) state 'to reject punitive regulation is naïve; to be totally committed to it is to lead the charge of the light brigade'. The trick of successful regulation is to establish a synergy between punishment and persuasion accommodating different styles and techniques in pursuit of the appropriate position on the regulatory spectrum. To seek out this location it is, however, important to recognise the contributions made by Burby *et al.* (1998). It is clear that many enforcement departments are in urgent need of adequate numbers of technically competent staff, strong leadership, support from the judiciary in the application of sanctions when prosecutions are successful and monitoring teams to facilitate moving from a reactive to proactive stance (McKay *et al.* 2003). If these components were in place there may be merit in taking enforcement to a new level by investigating the potential to implement a facilitative philosophy where delegated discretion is paramount and self-regulation can be introduced without compromise to regulatory goals. This may presently be a utopian aspiration, but with the provision of appropriate human and physical resources, in tandem with the implementation of a tailored legislative framework, it may become an achievable goal. At that point our rudimentary knowledge of regulatory control in planning will finally begin to evolve.

References

Audit Commission for the local authorities and the National Health Service in England and Wales (1992) *Building-in quality: a study of development control*, London, HMSO.

Ayres, I. and Braithwaite, J. (1992) *Responsive regulation,* New York, Oxford University Press.

Baer, W.C. (1997) Towards design of regulations for the built environment, *Environment & Planning B: Planning & Design*, 241, pp.37-57.

Bardach, E. and Kagan, R. (1982) *Going by the book: the problem of regulatory unreasonableness,* Philadelphia, Temple University Press.

Braithwaite, J., Grabosky, P., and Walker, J. (1987) An enforcement taxonomy of regulatory agencies, *Law and Policy* 9, pp.323-51.

Burby, R., May, P. and Paterson (1998) Improving compliance with regulations: choices and outcomes for local government, *Journal of the American Planning Association*, 64(3), pp.324-334.

Carnwath, R. (1989) *Enforcing planning control*, London, HMSO.

Carson, W.G. (1970) Some sociological aspects of strict liability and the enforcement of factory legislation, *Modern Law Review*, 33, pp.396-412.

Cheshire CC v Woodward (1962) 2 Q.B. 126.

Cranston, R. (1979) *Regulatory business: law and consumer agencies,* London, MacMillan.

Department of the Environment (1975) *Investigation into planning enforcement: the Dobry Report*, London, HMSO.

Department of the Environment for Northern Ireland (1992) *The Planning (Northern Ireland) Order 1992*, Belfast, HMSO.

Department of the Environment for Northern Ireland (1999) *General Principles, Planning Policy Statement 1,* Belfast, The Planning Service.

Department of the Environment (1996) *Statement on the Government Response to the Select Committee Report on The Planning System by T.W. Stewart,* Belfast, The Planning Service.

DiMento, J.F. (1986) *Environmental law and American business: dilemmas of compliance,* New York, Plenum Press.

Edelman, L.E., Petterson, S., Chambliss, E., and Howard, S.E. (1991) Legal ambiguity and the politics of compliance: affirmative action officers' dilemma, *Law and Policy,* 13(1), pp.73-97.

Gunningham, N. (1974) *Pollution social interest and the law,* London, Martin Robinson.

Hanf, K, (1993) Enforcing environmental laws: the social regulation of co-production, in M. Hill (ed.) *New agendas in the study of the policy process,* London, Harvester Wheatsheaf.

Hawkins, K. (1984) *Environment and enforcement: regulation and social definition of pollution,* Oxford, Clarendon Press.

House of Commons (1994) *Standing Order No.130,* March, London, HMSO.

House of Commons Northern Ireland Affairs Committee (1996) *The planning system in Northern Ireland,* March, London, HMSO.

Hutter, B.M. (1997) *Compliance: regulation and environment,* Oxford, Clarendon Press.

Hutter, B. and Sorenson, P. (1993) Business adaptation to legal regulation, *Law and Policy,* 15 (3), pp.169-78.

Ingram, H. and Schneider, A., (1990) Improving implementation through framing smarter statutes, *Journal of Public Policy,* 101, pp.67-88.

Kagan, R.A. and Scholz, J.T. (1984) The criminology of the corporation, in Hawkins, K. and Thomas, J.M. (eds.) *Enforcing regulation,* Boston, Kluwer-Nijhoff, pp.134-138.

Lipsky, M. (1980) *Street-level bureaucracy: dilemmas of the individual in the public sector,* New York, Russell-Sage.

Lowi, T. J. (1972) Four systems of policy, politics and choice, *Public Administration Review,* 32, pp.4-14.

Manning, P.K. (1988) Review of Braithwaite, J., To Punish or Persuade, *British Journal of Criminology*, 28 (4), pp.559-61.

Mc Kay, S. (2003) Sheriffs and outlaws: in pursuit of effective enforcement, *Town Planning Review*, 74(4), pp.423-443.

McKay, S., Berry, J. and McGreal, S. (2003) Planning enforcement: lessons for practice and procedure, *Planning Theory and Practice*, 1(3), pp.325-344.

Millichap, D. (1998) *Planning ghosts - past, present and future*, London, Linklaters.

Office of the Deputy Prime Minister (2002) *Review of the planning enforcement system consultation paper,* Norwich, HMSO.

Parkes v Secretary of State (1978) 1 W.L.R. 1308.

Prior, A. (2000) Problems in the theory and practice of planning enforcement, *Planning Theory and Practice*, 1(1), pp.53-69.

Reiss, A. (1984) Selecting strategies of social control over organisational life, in Hawkins, J. and Thomas, J.M. (eds.) *Enforcing regulation*, Boston, Kluwer-Nijhoff.

Richardson, G.M., Ogus, A.I. and Burrows, P. (1983) *Policing pollution: a study of regulation and enforcement,* Oxford, Clarendon Press.

Sabatier, P.A. and Mazmanian D.A. (1983) Policy implementation, in Nagel, S.S. (ed.) *Encyclopedia of Policy Studies,* New York, Marcel Dekker.

Salamon, L.M. (1981) Rethinking public management: third-party government and the changing forms of government action, *Public Policy,* 29(3).

Scholtz, J.T. (1991) Cooperative regulatory enforcement and the politics of administrative effectiveness, *American Political Science Review*, 85, pp.115-136.

Stone, D. (1988) *Policy paradox and political reason*, Glenview, Scott, Foreman and Company.

Yeager, P.C. (1991) *The limits of the law: the public regulation of private pollution*, Cambridge, Cambridge University Press.

Chapter 15

Retailing Theories – Attempts to Explain an Ever Changing Industry

Anthony M. Quinn

Introduction

The retail system is comprised largely of three components – the retail institution, the retail product and the retail entrepreneur. The interplay of these three retail components has resulted in changes in retail organisation, retail location and retail technique that have led to the creation of large retail formats that are more suited to out-of-centre locations and which offer an extensive range of both retail and non-retail goods and services. This pattern of change has been characterised by the concentration of shopping provision into fewer, bigger businesses, resulting in a concomitant decline in the number of independent outlets (Davies and Kirby, 1980). The marked polarisation in the structure of retailing between large-scale multiple retailing and small-scale independent shopping began at the end of the nineteenth century and intensified significantly towards the end of the twentieth century (Shaw,1992).

Changes to this system are caused, both in the long run and the short run, by the interrelationship between mutually dependent external drivers of supply and demand on the one hand (Scott, 1970) and internal competitive forces of product and service innovation on the other (Agerard *et al*, 1970). The role of the external drivers is sometimes theorised as environmental determinism, while the contribution of internal innovation by the retail institution and retail entrepreneur has been conceptualised under cyclical and conflict theories. This chapter provides a brief overview of these theories, namely the theory of environmental determinism, cyclical theories and conflict theories with a view to helping planners better understand the nature of change in an extremely dynamic industry.

Environmental Determinism and Retail Change

External drivers of supply include economic, technological and political change, while external drivers of demand embrace demographic, social and lifestyle changes that impact upon the retail system. Although they are inextricably linked and in many respects mutually inclusive, each of these external drivers of change is now considered separately for ease of comprehension.

Economic driver of supply

The demonstrable link between retail investment and the state of the economy was most apparent in the mid 1970s, when retail development nose-dived during the economic downturn precipitated by the oil crisis (Guy, 1995). In contrast, the demand for additional retail development usually increases during a period of sustained economic growth as developers/retailers compete to translate 'increasing incomes' into 'increasing floorspace' (Gayler, 1984). For example, the peace-related improvements to the economy in Northern Ireland during the latter half of the 1990s help account for the phenomenal rate of retail investment during this time. Not surprisingly, therefore, Benson and Shaw (1992) assert that the economic driver of supply is the most pervasive influence upon retail systems by virtue of its all encompassing capacity to induce significant changes to the other drivers of change discussed below.

Technological driver of supply

Advances in technology, most notably in the field of computerisation and electronics, continue to have sweeping modernising impacts on the retail system, spanning the entire production-consumption continuum. Digital linkages from EPOS (Electronic Point of Sale) are able to integrate all arms of retail administration spanning management, accounts, marketing, stock control, distribution and supply. This technological progress, coupled with advances in mechanisation, has allowed for the intensification of production and an increase in labour productivity (Wrigley, 1988). On this point, some research findings suggest that the retail output received from an investment of one pound in information technology is equivalent to the output obtained from ten pounds worth of investment in labour (Reardon *et al*, 1996). Allied to these developments, the storage role of refrigeration as a technological driver of supply should not be understated. It has encouraged the development of larger stores in two ways. In the first instance, in-store refrigeration by the retailer has allowed for the expansion of chilled product lines and ready-made meals (Rogers,1987). Secondly, domestic refrigeration enables shoppers to purchase goods in bulk, which has the effect of encouraging retailers to stock more products within a larger floor area.

More recently, the impact of the computer via the Internet has also made a huge impression on the supply of retailing. The Internet exploded onto the commercial stage from the mid-1990s, with the development of consumer friendly software packages. Its manifestations include online shopping, electronic shopping, remote shopping, e-tailing, and e-shopping. E-tailing is either conducted by new retail companies, known as 'pure play' businesses, that have been formed specifically to transact trade through this medium, or, by established retailers, referred to as 'clicks & bricks' retailers, that utilise the new technology alongside their mainstream retailing operations. Amazon.com is an example of a pure play retail company, while Tesco leads the way in developing the clicks and bricks approach.

Demographic driver of demand
There is a clear positive correlation between population growth and the increase in the provision of retail facilities as there are more mouths to feed, bodies to clothe and homes to furnish. However, as population growth stagnates in many developed countries, demographic change continues to impact on the retail system in other ways through declining household size and the ageing of the population.

The trend towards smaller household size has increased the demand for suburban housing and the decentralisation of new retail facilities (Rogers, 1987). The attendant rise in home ownership has also swollen the demand for household durables and the provision of retail warehouse parks from which to purchase such items. Furthermore, the breakdown of the traditional family household and the formation of single person households contribute significantly to the increasing popularity of ready-made meals. As noted above, it has been found necessary to build bigger stores to accommodate this growth in chilled product lines.

Added to the decline in household size, the ageing of the population, which could see a fifth of the customer base in the UK aged over 65 by the year 2011 (Mintel International Group Limited, 2001) may yet have an impact on the localised need for retailing by promoting a greater demand for convenient and accessible neighbourhood facilities. Overall, therefore, it is clear that the demographic driver of demand will continue to have an enduring impact on the nature of retailing.

Social / lifestyle driver of demand
Changing consumer lifestyles, increased female participation in the workforce and increasingly demanding work schedules reduce the time available for shopping, strengthen the demand for bulk buying and, therefore, increase the need for convenient and accessible retail facilities. Combined with the benefits of refrigeration, these factors encourage people to undertake fewer shopping trips. This in turn exerts pressure to provide larger stores with expansive commodity ranges capable of facilitating bulk purchases (Jefferys

and Knee, 1962). The growth in female employment and in time spent at work has also prompted the retailer to adopt flexible trading hours and to stay open longer. In 1998, the new Sainsbury store at Forestside, Belfast became the first supermarket in Northern Ireland to open on a 24-hour basis (Belfast Telegraph, 1998).

The growth in bulk shopping has a strong correlation with the rise in car ownership. Since 1960, car ownership levels in Northern Ireland have quintupled creating a situation whereby 70 per cent of households in the region now have access to a car (Department for Regional Development, 2001). This rise in car borne shopping and bulk buy trips has encouraged the development of spacious stores equipped with wider aisles and commodious circulation space for the needs of the trolley shopper (Neafcy, 1987).

The social/lifestyle dimension to consumer demand is becoming ever more complex and is underpinned by greater diversity and sophistication of consumer tastes. The need to customise supply necessitates the expansion of product lines and, ultimately, a proportionate increase in selling space from which to supply such items (McGoldrick, 1987).

Political driver of supply
Unlike other branches of the economy such as industry and transport, no specific government department exists to oversee the functioning of the distributive trades. This state of affairs arises from a general perception that, due to the importance of the consumer for their existence, the distributive trades will regulate themselves in the public interest (Davies, 1984). Retail sales from shops in Northern Ireland account for 30 per cent of the region's Gross Domestic Product (InterTradeIreland, 2001) and thus in view of its centrality to the welfare of the economy, political influence on the retail sector is very real. In the United Kingdom and Ireland this is mainly administered via the statutes of town and country planning legislation, which are discharged by planning authorities at both the central and local government level. This form of intervention is justified on the grounds that planning can influence and press for positive impacts on the environment as a whole through active public policy making, while preventing negative impacts through the development control process. Positive action at the local scale may include the proactive assembly of town centre land for retail development while the prevention of negative impacts normally involves the refusal of retail applications that threaten adverse impact on existing town centre traders (Guy, 1995). To help planning authorities assess applications for new retail build, cognisance is taken of the relevant policy documents and findings of the technical methods of retail assessment (commonly referred to as Retail Impact Assessments).

Apart from land use planning, other direct ways in which government can influence retail change include price control and anti-monopoly legislation (Breheny, 1988). However, with increasing liberalisation in the market place and globalisation in the retail economy (Wolf, 2000) the relevance of the former has waned, while the latter struggles to make an impact. Today, retail prices are private sector driven and are determined by company policy, having regard to wholesale and manufacturing costs, store size and the socio-economic profile of the catchment (Davies, 1976). However, up until the middle of the 1960s, manufacturers, with government acquiescence, still commanded considerable influence on pricing policies through the mechanism of Resale Price Maintenance. Resale Price Maintenance (RPM) is an instrument of vertical price control that was devised by manufacturers to obtain guaranteed prices for retail goods (Department of the Environment and Local Government, 2000). Guaranteed fixed margins in retailing meant that small independent retailers were able to co-exist alongside large multiples (Wrigley and Lowe, 2002). With its abolition in 1964, larger retail organisations, which could absorb short-term profit downturns for improved long-term market share, pursued a policy of price reductions, thereby significantly undermining competition from the independent sector. The advance of the retail multiples, at a time when the manufacturing base was in retreat, strengthened their hand when negotiating price concessions from producers and suppliers (Wrigley and Lowe, 2002). Accordingly, the abolition of RPM for many products ensured that the multiple retailer, rather than the manufacturer, would become the supreme driving force in the retail market place. This was especially the case in respect of the grocery/convenience sector. As a driver of change, therefore, McGoldrick (1987) recalls the abolition of Resale Price Maintenance (RPM) as providing a watershed date from which the prominence of the multiple chains in the retail field can be charted.

According to Rogers (1987), all the above drivers of retail change have culminated in ensuring that the customer has become a more complex entity, with the means of retail supply having to be constantly reinvented and expanded to cater for the idiosyncrasies of demand. Both the retail institutions and the retail entrepreneurs have sought to innovate in line with this ever changing reality and it is their contribution to the retail dynamic that some scholars have chosen to highlight under cyclical and conflict theories.

Cyclical Theories of Retail Change
Four different cyclical theories have been popularised by commentators under the headings of retail accordian theory, the wheel of retailing, the theory of spiral movement and the retail life cycle. This section of the chapter considers each in turn.

Retail accordian theory

First noted by Hower in 1943 (Hower, 1947) and elaborated upon by Hollander in 1966 (Hollander, 1966), this theory postulates that the retail dynamic is characterised by retail institutions switching from general retailing to specialist retailing over time, involving the expansion and contraction of product lines. According to this perspective, the centrifugal forces underpinning the broadening of product lines that can give rise to scrambled merchandising are reciprocated by the centripetal forces that lead to specialisation. Both forms of retailing have their own perceived advantages and disadvantages. Although scrambled merchandising allows for a greater degree of trading flexibility, both product knowledge and service expertise may be lost (Knee and Walters, 1985). Conversely, the advantages of exclusivity and strong customer service appeal associated with retail specialisation are counterbalanced by a loss of trading adaptability (Hollander, 1981).

As in the case of all marketing theories, the accordion hypothesis has no spatial grounding and is specific to the actions of the retail institution. However, the ability of the institution to make the switch from general retailing to specific retailing and vice versa requires the sustenance of a critical mass of expenditure normally only found in urban areas. Accordingly, the retail accordion theory has been applied to the American situation to explain the historical shift from general stores to department stores and then speciality stores (Cox and Brittain, 2000). It also has an explanatory relevance for the expansion into non-food lines by superstores in Britain since the 1990s.

Wheel of retailing

The wheel of retailing has as its central thesis the proposition that as retail institutions trade-up and mature a trading vacuum is created which is typically filled by lower cost modes of retailing (McNair, 1957). Hence, as shops trade up and modernise in the pursuit of increased profits, the no-frills discount outlets move to fill the gaps left in the market place. Trading up by Tesco and other superstores from the late 1970s and the simultaneous arrival of discount chains in the UK can be quoted as one applied illustration of the wheel theory (Alexander, 1999). Similarly, in Northern Ireland, the wheel of retailing was characterised by Tesco's modernisation of no-frills outlets like Westside Stores and Crazy Prices, which created a market void from the late 1990s that was filled by discount stores like Lidl. However, by trading up, retail institutions also run the risk of becoming more vulnerable to new competition and innovation. This is markedly exemplified by Marks and Spencer's decision to upgrade its stores and sell high-cost designer fashion brands (Finch, 2000) thus creating a scenario whereby the competitiveness of its clothing arm is now sandwiched between the ongoing inventiveness of branded outlets such as Gap and the cheaper apparel lines on offer by discounters (Marchand, 2000).

The widespread applicability of the concept of low cost institutions stepping into the slipstream of high cost operators can be called into question having regard to modern retail trends. Department stores, shopping centres and boutiques do not start up as low margin outlets with few services (Mason and Mayer, 1990). Moreover, mergers and the desire for market domination now enable retail institutions to acquire different positions on the wheel at the one time. The pervasive saturation of the market at different segments essentially ossifies the wheel, creating conditions in which the new entrants are often confronted with the task of competing against established businesses with established trading pedigrees (Rosenbloom, 1981). In the light of these caveats, the theory of spiral movement has been conceived as an adjustment to the wheel of retailing.

Theory of spiral movement

Traced to the work of Agerard, Olsen and Allpass (Agerard, *et al*, 1970) the theory of spiral movement argues that as stores trade up and leave behind a market vacuum, the new entrant to the market will tailor the business to reflect rising living standards and increasing consumer expectations. The theory of spiral movement, therefore, acknowledges the impact of a changing environment and recognises that retail institutions are able to join the wheel at an advanced stage.

Retail life cycle

The final theory to fall under the cyclical umbrella is the retail life cycle. According to this perspective, the evolutionary stages of retailing can be likened to the anthropomorphic events of birth, growth, maturity and decline. It postulates that retail institutions become the victims of their own good fortune. As they grow and mature, their success gives rise to imitations, and competition from these new challengers eventually leads to the decline of the trend-setting institution. Moreover, refurbishment and expansion costs incurred in attempts to compete more effectively with the newcomer can also exacerbate the demise of these established retailers (Davidson *et al*, 1976). The inevitability factor attached to the life cycle theory has been criticised for devaluing the role of entrepreneurialism and innovation in countering the decline of retail institutions, the importance of which is underscored in conflict theories (Dhalla and Yuseph, 1976).

Conflict Theories of Retail Change

As opposed to cyclical theories, conflict theories maintain that it is inter-institutional competition and entrepreneurial skills that are the driving forces behind retail change and innovation. As such, the human factor is more strongly asserted in the roots of these theories. Developing upon the notion of economic man, conflict theories embrace the Newtonian principle that a force is always met by an equal and opposite counter force. This need to imitate and the compulsion to adapt also resonate with Darwinian Theory and its focus on the struggle between species. In this regard, parallels can be drawn with the retail life cycle concept in that innovation shown by the established institution will almost certainly lead to imitation by the newcomer and vice versa. An example of the latter was provided by Asda's introduction in the United Kingdom of its discount operation in the early 1990s in response to the competition from incoming discount chains (Alexander, 1999). This imitation aspect to conflict theories was also reflected in the activity of the Co-operative Society in Northern Ireland. It unsuccessfully attempted to pitch its business at the superstore level by creating three such stores across the region.

Although the rationale for conflict theories is closely aligned to capitalism and free market forces, they also accord with Marxian and dialectic theory, which have an emphasis on the rejection, in part or whole, of previous stages of retail change. Within this context, Gist's dialectical theory espouses a rather simplistic 3-stage process governing retail change (Gist, 1968). The first stage is known as the 'thesis' phase and refers to the introduction of a particular form of retailing. The second stage describes the emergence of a new form of retailing and is referred to as the 'antithesis' stage. Finally, the third stage involves combining the old with the new and is referred to as the 'synthesis' stage. Bearing these three stages in mind, it can be postulated that the rise of self-service represents the 'synthesis' of trading modes adopted by independent grocers (thesis) and by supermarkets (antithesis). In the same way, there is strength in the contention that the emergence of co-operative societies reflects the synthesis of independent control (thesis) and multiple retail organisations (antithesis) (Dawson, 1979). Mason and Mayer (1990) quote the example of Kmart in America, whose operations are viewed as comprising an amalgamation of the strengths associated with department store trading and discount shopping. In the same way, it could be argued that Supervalu, the wholesaler-sponsored retail entrant into Northern Ireland, represents the synthesis of vertical integration and independent operations.

Developing upon work by Fink, Baek and Taddeo (Fink *et al*, 1971), Stern and El Ansary (1977) liken this conflict to a stimulus-response mechanism involving the four stages of shock, defensive retreat, acknowledgement of the threat and adaptation to change. Chesterton (1991) has focused upon this analogy, in conjunction with the retail life cycle concept, to explain the development pattern of multiple retail organisations. This pattern has been termed a 'food share market cycle' and consists of 4 stages:

- the opening of a single foodstore (Introduction Stage);
- the opening of other foodstores (Expansion Stage);
- acknowledgement of a saturation point and need for reassessment of provision (Characterisation Stage); and
- closure or relocation of existing stores (Rationalisation Stage).

In recent times, the pace of change in retailing, involving takeovers and mergers, has blurred the clear identification of these stages to such an extent that the use of the word 'stage' could be construed as a misnomer, given that all four stages can occur almost simultaneously.

These theories of retail change have been criticised for being geographically limited to the American experience and chronologically restricted to events in the first part of the twentieth century (Savitt, 1989). From a practical level, the absence of a spatial basis to these theories accounts for their lack of appeal to planners (Davies, 1976). However, notwithstanding the above criticisms, the advantages of marketing theories lie in their illuminating insights into the dynamics of the distributive trades (Davies, 1984). By acquiring a clearer appreciation of the theoretical fundamentals of change in retailing, the planner is better informed to develop spatial theories and models upon which to plan for future changes. In this respect, both cyclical and conflict theories should be recognised as useful 'conceptual devices' (Brown, 1984) in an era when consumer-friendly text and glossy productions dispense with the more complex theoretical underpinnings of the subject matter.

Conclusion

Ultimately, when seeking to develop theories to explain the ever changing retail reality it is perhaps prudent to embrace Brown's assertion that cyclical and conflict theories can be intertwined against a background of environmental determinism to provide a framework for understanding the retailing industry (Brown, 1984). In short, the retail system and its component parts – the retail institution, the retail product and the retail entrepreneur – are all subject to external impacts or drivers of change. These external drivers of change induce the dynamism of the retail development process, the effects of which are best conceptualised using the analogy of circular motion, and which are internally sustained by competition-driven institutional and entrepreneurial conflicts (Brown, 1987).

References

Agerard E., Olsen P.A., and Allpass J. (1970) The interaction between retailing and the urban centre structure: a theory of spiral movement, *Environment and Planning*, 2, pp. 55-71.

Alexander, N. (1999) *International retailing,* Oxford, Blackwell Publishers Limited.

Belfast Telegraph (1998) Forestside on target, Business Supplement, October 20, p.9.

Benson, J. and Shaw, G. (eds.) (1992) *The evolution of retail systems 1800-1914,* Leicester, University Press.

Breheny, M. (1988) Practical methods of retail location analysis, in Wrigley, N. (ed.) *Store choice, store location and market analysis,* pp. 39-86, London and New York, Routledge.

Brown, S. (1984) *Retail location and retail change in Belfast City Centre*, Unpublished Ph.D. thesis, Belfast, Queen's University.

Brown, S. (1987) Institutional change in retailing: a review and synthesis, *European Journal of Marketing*, 6, pp. 3-36. Cited in Sampson, S. D. and Tigert, D. J. (1994) The impact of warehouse membership clubs: the wheel of retailing turns one more time, *The International Review of Retail Distribution and Consumer Research,* 4 (1).

Cox, R. and Brittain, P. (2000) *Retail management,* Harlow, Pearson Education Limited.

Davidson, W.R., Bates, A.D. and Bass, S.J. (1976) The retail life cycle, *Harvard Business Review*, 54 (November-December), pp. 89-96. Cited in Brown, S. (1984) Retail location and retail change in Belfast City Centre, Unpublished Ph.D. thesis, Belfast, Queen's University.

Davies R.L. (1976) *Marketing Geography*, University of Newcastle upon Tyne, Retail and Planning Associates, pp. 288-293.

Davies, R.L. (1984) *Retail and commercial planning,* Kent, Croom Helm.

Davies, R.L. and Kirby, D.A. (1980) Retail organisation, in Dawson, J.A. (ed.) *Retail Geography*, London, Croom Helm.

Dawson, J.A. (1979) *The marketing environment.* London, Croom Helm.

Dawson, J. A. ed.(1980), *Retail Geography,* London, Croom Helm.

Department of the Environment and Local Government (2000) *Retail planning guidelines for planning authorities*, Dublin, The Stationery Office.

Department for Regional Development (2001) *Shaping Our Future: Regional Development Strategy for Northern Ireland 2025*, Belfast, Corporate Document Services.

Dhalla, N.K. and Yuseph, S. (1976) Forget the product life cycle concept, *Harvard Business Review*, 54 (January – February), pp.102-112. Cited in Brown, S. (1984) Retail location and retail change in Belfast City Centre, Unpublished Ph.D. thesis, Belfast, Queen's University.

Finch, J. (2000) M & S prices get the couture touch, *The Guardian*, February 5, p. 28.

Fink, S.L., Baek, J. and Taddeo. (1971) Organisational crisis and change, *Applied Behavioural Science*, (1), 1971, pp. 15-37. Cited in Brown, S. (1984) Retail location and retail change in Belfast City Centre, Unpublished Ph.D. thesis, Belfast: Queen's University.

Gayler, H.J. (1984) *Retail innovation in Britain: the problems of out-of-town shopping centre development*, Norwich, Geo Books.

Gist, R.R. (1968) *Retailing: concepts and decisions*, New York, Wiley & Sons. Cited in Brown, S. (1984) Retail location and retail change in Belfast City Centre, Unpublished Ph.D. thesis, Belfast, Queen's University.

Guy, C. (1995) *The retail development process: location, property and planning*, London and New York, Routledge.

Hollander, S.C. (1966) Notes on the retail accordion, *Journal of Retailing*, 42 (Summer), pp. 29-40. Cited in Brown, S. (1984). Retail location and retail change in Belfast City Centre, p.85. Unpublished Ph.D. thesis, Belfast, Queen's University.

Hollander, S.C. (1981) Retailing theory: some criticisms and some admiration, in Stampfl, R.W. and Hirschmann, E.C. (eds.) *Theory in retailing, traditional and non-traditional sources*, pp.84-94, Chicago, American Marketing Association.

Hower, R.M. (1947) *History of Macy's of New York 1858-1919: Chapters in the Evolution of the Department Store*, Cambridge, Harvard University Press. Cited in Benson, J. and Shaw, G. (eds.) (1992) *The evolution of retail systems 1800-1914*, Leicester, University Press.

InterTradeIreland. (2001) *Ireland: a £2 billion plus retail market*, Belfast, Local Enterprise and Development Unit.

Jefferys, J. B. and Knee, D. (1962) *Retailing in Europe: present structure and future trends*, London, MacMillan and Co Ltd.

Knee, D. and Walters, D. (1985) *Strategy in retailing: theory and application*, Oxford, Philip Allan Publishers Ltd.

Marchand, R. (2000). M&S tailspin continues despite its revamps, *The Sunday Business Post*, August 13.

Mason, J.B. and Mayer, M.L. (1990) *Modern retailing: theory and practice*, Boston, BPI Irwin.

McGoldrick, (1987) Trends in retailing and consumer behaviour within the UK, in Davies, R.L. and Rogers, D.S. (eds.) *Store location and store assessment research,* Chichester, John Wiley and Sons Ltd.

McNair, M.P. (1957) Significant trends and developments in the post-war period, in Smith, A.B. (ed.) *Competitive distribution in a free high level economy and its implications for the university,* pp. 1-25, University of Pittsburg. Cited in Brown, S. (1984) Retail location and Retail Change in Belfast City Centre, Unpublished Ph.D. thesis, Belfast, Queen's University.

Mintel International Group Limited (2001) *Online shopping (Irish Series),* Belfast, Local Enterprise and Development Unit.

Neafcy, E. (1987) The impact of the development process within the UK, in Davies, R.L. and Rogers, D.S. (eds.) *Store location and store assessment research,* Chichester, John Wiley and Sons Ltd.

Reardon, J., Hasty, R. and Coe, B. (1996) The effects of information technology on productivity in retailing, *Journal of Retailing,* 72 (4).

Rogers, D.S. (1987) Trends in retailing and consumer behaviour within North America, in Davies, R.L. and Rogers, D.S. (eds.) *Store location and store assessment research,* Chichester, John Wiley and Sons Ltd.

Rosenbloom, B. (1981) *Retail marketing,* New York, Random House. Cited in Brown, S. (1984) Retail location and Retail Change in Belfast City Centre, Appendix 3.1. Unpublished Ph.D. thesis, Belfast, Queen's University.

Savitt, R. (1989) Looking back to see ahead: writing the history of American retailing, *Journal of Retailing,* 65 (3), pp.326-355.

Shaw, G. (1992) The European Scene: Britain and Germany, in Benson, J. and Shaw, G. (eds.) *The evolution of retail systems 1800-*1914, Leicester, University Press.

Scott, P. (1970) *Geography and retailing,* London, Hutchinson and Co (Publishers) Ltd.

Stern, L.W. and El Ansary, A.I. (1977) *Marketing channels,* Englewood Cliffs, Prentice Hall. Cited in Brown, S. (1984). Retail location and Retail Change in Belfast City Centre, Unpublished Ph.D. thesis, Belfast: Queen's University.

Wolf, M. (2000) Why this hatred of the market? in Lechner, F.J. and Boli, J. (eds.) *The globalisation reader,* Oxford, Blackwell Publishers.

Wrigley, N. (1988) Retail restructuring and retail analysis, in Wrigley, N. (ed.) *Store choice, store location and market analysis,* London and New York, Routledge.

Wrigley, N. and Lowe, M. (2002) *Reading retail: a geographical perspective on retailing and consumption spaces,* London, Arnold.

Chapter 16

The City of the Black Stuff: Belfast and the Autism of Planning

Geraint Ellis

Introduction

It must be acknowledged that Belfast has had a troubled past and that historically there have been times when planning of the city has been undertaken under severe economic and political constraints. During the 1970s and 1980s, Belfast must have been a most difficult environment in which to work as a planner and while other UK cities were innovating with radical forms of community planning (e.g. Sheffield, see Montgomery and Thornley, 1990) or experimenting with market-led planning (e.g. London Docklands, see Imrie and Thomas, 1993), Belfast planners were forced to keep their heads down and be grateful for the slightest whiff of development. But things are, or should be, very different now. Admittedly there are many areas still facing acute problems of deprivation, but eleven years on from the paramilitary ceasefires, seven years on from the 'Good Friday' Agreement and with economic conditions vastly improved from the dark days of the Troubles, Belfast has many more opportunities to develop in a sustainable and prosperous way. There are also plenty of enlightening examples of how planning and urban regeneration can be used in imaginative and empowering ways, such as the Masterplan for the rebirth of Barcelona, the environmentally-driven development of Freiburg and the inspirational public transport system of Curitiba. Yet when one surveys the state of Belfast and considers the way planning continues to intervene in the urban environment, there is something lacking. It just appears to be too unimaginative and overly bureaucratic, reactionary rather than progressive, and, above all, does not seem to be primarily aimed at enhancing the long term interests of the city's citizens. This chapter suggests a few reasons why this may be so.

The Operation of the Planning System

We start, however, with something that Belfast should be proud of. Many discerning urbanists and architects have noted the desirability and art of combining indigenous materials and local craftsmanship in the construction of the built environment. Europe has many examples of such tradition, from the slate villages of North Wales, the marble work in Italian cathedrals and the granite city of Aberdeen. Belfast has a vernacular tradition that reflects its broader cultural heritage. Indeed, it can be argued that what now most characterises the built form of the city ironically brings together the road-building expertise of the Irish (Catholic) navvy with the liberal use of tarmac, invented by Scottish (Protestant and freemason) John MacAdam from Ayr. Indeed, of all cities in these islands, Belfast is the one where the road is really king. For example, taken per head of population, Northern Ireland has 2.2 times more miles of road than elsewhere in the UK (Fawcett, 2000) and Belfast has been noted as being "the most car dependent city in Europe" (Cooper *et al*, 2001), with 81 per cent of people travelling to work by car compared to 70 per cent in the UK as a whole. Indeed, the figures related to road transport are quite startling: 84 per cent of spending on transport in Northern Ireland has been on roads, and only 16 per cent on public transport, walking and cycling (Fawcett, 2000). Traffic continues to grow in Northern Ireland at twice the rate of the UK (DoENI/DRD 1991- 1998) and there is much less integration of sustainable transport and land use planning than in most other European regions (McEldowney, 2000). Yet the city's planners refuse to take any action that is likely to substantially alter this situation. While comparable cities, like Dublin and Nottingham are seeing a new generation of trams glide through the city streets, residents of inner city Belfast prepare for the bulldozers to move in to widen its urban motorways and like 'Nero fiddling while Rome burns', the Government toys with the idea of closing part of the rail network that serves the region. Indeed, the dominance of the car has left a deep topographic imprint on the city as exemplified by the vast acreage of road surface at the Bridge Street / Ravenhill Road junction, the pedestrian desert around Yorkgate, and the *cordon sanitaire* created by the Westlink between the city centre and the inner neighbourhoods of west Belfast. Even the unfulfilled aspirations of the transport planner haunt the city, as demonstrated, for example, by the 'urban park' alongside the Dublin Road Movie House, created by the need to protect the corridor of a new stretch of urban motorway, blighting and threatening the Sandy Row and Markets communities for over 20 years. This all leads to the conclusion that we should typify Belfast as 'the city of the black stuff', not Guinness, but Tarmac.

This *roadfest* could be seen as an admirable objective if one wants to awe at the dull aesthetic of the highway, or if the explicit aim of the planning system is to improve the short-term mobility of the most affluent sections of society. However, this proves disastrous if measured against any other economic, social and environmental variable. Take, for example, the fairness of this planning approach for the 44 per cent of all Belfast households that do not have access to a car, which rises to 70 per cent in inner city areas which have to bear the brunt of commuter traffic. Does such an approach take into account the trauma caused by the death or serious injury of 1400 people in road accidents in Northern Ireland every year and hundreds others that die as a direct result of air pollution caused by road transport? A planning approach based on the car is also economically regressive as a large proportion of transport spending is not circulated back to the local economy by paying for bus drivers, building cycle lanes or maintaining trains, but is siphoned off to central government, the multinational oil magnates and car manufacturers. The way in which planning for the car has been given prior importance over the long term well-being of Belfast's citizens and economy acts as a powerful metaphor for the way in which the city has been shaped in recent decades. Before we explore why this may be so, it is worth highlighting a number of other examples from the city where transport planning has failed in the expectation that it will deliver for the community.

Consider first the E-way project proposed as a part-solution to congestion in the east part of the city. The E-Way has been proposed as a rapid transit project (i.e. a segregated bus lane) linking the Newtownards Road in inner east Belfast with the outlying suburbs of Dundonald and eventually out to Comber. While the proposal offers some modest rise in the expectations of public transport, it also highlights the failure to appreciate the scale of urban disfunction and illustrates how the urban planning process is gripped by a timid professional conservatism unmatched to tackling the scale of the traffic and environmental problems faced by the city. The main reason that the E-Way has been proposed for this route is that it can be implemented without much disruption to car users by using the old Comber railway line. It is, therefore, an easy way to show that *something* is being done, not necessarily because it is the most effective way to tackle congestion, or optimise other environmental or social objectives. Rather than planning a route that could best be coordinated with new development, maximise displacement of car use or open up the more deprived parts of the city to regeneration opportunities, the E-Way would actually have the opposite effect by opening up further greenfield areas to lucrative suburban development. Thus, while Belfast needs drastic action to combat road congestion, the best that is proposed is a glorified park and ride scheme. While other cities are offering bold gestures to tackle transport (e.g. congestion charging in London, Luas in Dublin), this timid effort has been put forward as a pilot project, just in case we mistake it for a new comprehensive approach to transport in the city. A further example of how the planning system is failing to get to grips with the critical relationship between accessibility and other social, economic and environmental objectives is in the area around Central Station, the area most well connected by public transport in the whole of Northern Ireland. Many other cities would realise the benefits of such connectivity to stimulate regeneration and attract those land uses that could best exploit such accessibility as a way to reduce overall car use (e.g. major retail, leisure or office development). What we find, however, is an area largely devoid of development and indeed, in the case of the few key sites that have been built upon, their transport advantages are simply squandered – so that the site right opposite the main entrance to the station has recently been developed as a multi-storey car park, sucking even more cars into the city centre and suggesting a permanent two fingered salute to any notions of public transport-led planning and the benefits this could bring. Similar examples occur elsewhere. We have two airports where the railway lines do touch the airport perimeters, yet neither has a rail link. Indeed, in the case of the City Airport there was ample opportunity to secure such a link during its recent redevelopment. In any city with a transport system such as in Belfast, the first thing on the planner's shopping list would be a public transport link in return for planning permission, but this appears to be a low priority. Similarly, the Odyssey Arena, despite its potential to attract thousands of people into the city every night, remains isolated from the public transport network and as such has to be surrounded by acres of sterile car parking rather than using the attraction to stimulate a cluster of cultural and job-creating activities on neighbouring sites. It should be noted that these examples are not historic remnants of an age when we could not conceive of future rates of car use or understand the local and global consequences of car dependency. They have all been developed in the last five years, during which there has been a global consensus on sustainable development and many examples of innovative urbanism across Europe. Unfortunately, these mistakes are repeated across Belfast and collectively heap further transport misery on the city as they result in more pollution, less incentive for getting the public transport system right and adding to the unremitting erosion of quality of urban life.

The critical point of these examples is not to highlight the transport issue itself, but to suggest what they infer about the broader operation of the planning system. The interpretation offered here is that planners do not, or are unable, to see their primary role as one to improve the well being of Belfast's citizens, tackling its social problems or inching the city towards sustainable development. These are all critical issues in achieving a prospering urban culture. At a very basic level, the governing town planning legislation defines the key objective of the system to deliver the 'orderly and consistent development of land', which does not provide much in terms of guidance on how planning can be used to improve the quality of urban life. This is combined with an institutional framework that, almost uniquely amongst European cities, places planning responsibility within central government rather than a local authority, thus depriving planners of critical local political leadership to guide its objectives. This has entrenched planning within in a civil service culture, based on bureaucratic regulation and obsessive impartiality rather than professional creativity and politically-driven innovation. The planning system is thus staffed by officers who have only a remote relationship with the communities they serve and who are constantly caught in the tension between being independently-minded professionals and small cogs in the government machine. As a result, planning in Northern Ireland has become a technocracy, through which the city is primarily seen in cold objectivity, as if it is a machine to be tuned by crude technical fixes (like road widening), rather than appreciating Belfast from the more messy, human perspective, in which people's hopes and aspirations are realised and dashed. One symptom of this is that the planning system has consistently hid behind a defence of impartiality by excusing poor planning outcomes as having been implemented on behalf of the "public interest" (Benvenisti, 1983; Boal, 1996; Ellis, 2000; 2001). The culture of technocratic neutrality adopted by Belfast's planners, which was a critical tactic to promote stability and overcome sectarian discrimination during the Troubles, is now increasingly being perceived as aloof and insensitive to the particularity of place. Indeed, Bollens (1999) suggests that 'neutrality is associated with unequal outcomes, poor public perception, and ineffective uplifting of Belfast's economically deprived' (p.268).

Such an approach does not lend itself well to citizen-centred planning. Indeed, although largely anecdotal, one hears many tales of frustration about the interaction of people with the planning system. For many, the planning system appears to offer only problems and comes across as being self-absorbed with its own internal bureaucratic problems: planners grumbling about the pressures of work, the friction with other government departments, the unrealistic demands of the public, or why the profession has such a bad image. Has any one come across a public sector planner lamenting the fact they cannot do enough to address urban problems or enhance the quality of life? This culture is exemplified by the common retort of the Planning Service to the comments made by the public during the current consultation process for the new generation of Area Plans where they state that they do not have a statutory remit to tackle many of the issues the public expects them to address. Nor do they suggest ways in which these could be resolved by other agencies.

The Autism of Planning
These observations have led to the suggestion that it may be helpful to envisage Belfast's planning system as being *autistic*, in the same way as the term has been applied to the discipline of economics (see www.paecon.net). This term is used cautiously and advisedly and it is not intended to depreciate those individuals with disorders associated with Asperger's Syndrome (which is part of the wider autistic syndrome, see Wing 1996), nor to imply that

individuals working in the planning system harbour learning difficulties, nor indeed question the abilities of individual planners. Although there is danger of taking this analogy too literally, it offers a new way of pinpointing the causes of some of the institutional failures of planning in Belfast, as outlined above. The Oxford English Dictionary definition of autism as characterising those who are 'morbidly self-absorbed and out of contact with reality' is immediately transferable to the planning system. A more refined understanding of what this means is seen in the *Triad of Impairments* (Wing and Gould, 1979), which sees autism reflected in:

• impairment of social interaction;
• impairment of social communication; and
• impairment of social imagination and flexible thinking.

Furthermore, most of the diagnostic criteria that have been applied in psychology to Asperger's Syndrome (after Wing, 1981 and taken from Cumine *et al*, 1998) can be seen as afflicting planning in Belfast:

• *impairment of two-way social interaction and general social ineptitude;* i.e. the failure of the planning system to listen to what the public really wants, and to explain the reason for particular policy responses in a way in which the public can easily identify;
• *language that is odd and pedantic, stereotyped in content*; i.e. a retreat into legalistic and over professionalised, technocratic jargon;
• *resistance to change and enjoyment of repetitive activities*; i.e. an inability, or fear, of approaching issues in more challenging and innovative ways or to adapt to changed political, economic and environmental conditions;
• *circumscribed special interests and good rote memory*; i.e. a fetish over the importance of economic interests and the promotion of individualism where collective responses are more appropriate; and
• *poor co-ordination;* i.e. failures to link pressing social issues (e.g. health) and global issues (e.g. climate change) with the outcomes of the planning system, and to fully coordinate with initiatives by other government departments (e.g. those responsible for transport, urban regeneration, housing).

These are potentially complex issues that cannot be done justice here and can be further explored through the concept of the planning system being a learning institution (see, Robinson, 2004; Romme and Dillen, 1997). However, by conceptualising the problems of planning in terms of autism rather than say, professional competence, lack of political accountability or poor institutional organisational capacity, it opens new vistas on potential avenues for reform. For example, Tantam (1987) notes that Asperger's

Syndrome is 'quintessentially a disorder of human relationships' and thus it may be appropriate to view the failures of planning in the same way. In the case of a child displaying symptoms of autism, the first and most important intervention educational professionals can offer is to understand the function and purpose of any discordant behaviour *from the point of view of the child*. This would be a fruitful perspective when applied to planning, not only for critics to understand the constraints acting on individual planning officers (and thus perhaps lead to alternative organisational structures, such as neighbourhood planning offices or the loosening of bureaucratic constraints), but also for planners themselves to reverse the diagnosis and see how the planning system intervenes from the point of view of the citizen. I believe that this would be revelatory and could be stimulated by public participation being run directly by the Planning Service itself, rather than using intermediaries as is generally the case now, or by evaluating its outcomes in relation to health, environmental quality or (heaven forbid!) citizen approval, rather than just the time taken to process planning applications.

Conclusion

For autism in children progressive intervention can begin to overcome the two-way communication difficulties that frustrate the condition. Similarly, if there is one thing that the planning system in Belfast can do to overcome its failures, it is to listen to the frustrations and aspirations of its citizens. As a city, Belfast has some extraordinary attributes on which to develop a rich, sustainable and humane urban experience that could match most cities. It does, after all, have much to offer - a stunning location between water and mountain, the remnants of a grand civic architecture and even some good modern buildings. But as Shakespeare asked "What is the city but the people?" (Coriolanus). Belfast's planning system has been unable to comprehend this through its own morbid self-absorption and the community has suffered as a consequence.

References

Benvenisti, M. (1983) *Jerusalem: study of a polarised community,* Jerusalem, West Bank Data Project.

Boal, F.W. (1996) Integration and division: sharing and segregation in Belfast, *Planning Practice and Research*, 11(2), pp.151–158.

Bollens, S. A. (1999*) Urban peace-building in divided societies: Belfast and Johannesburg*, Boulder, Westview Press.

Bleuler, E. (1911) *Dementia praecox oder gruppe der schizophrenien* (J. Zinkin translation 1950), New York, International University Press

Cooper, J., Granzow, E., Ryley, T. and Smyth, A. (2001) Contemporary lifestyles and the implications for sustainable development policy - lessons from the UK's most car dependent city, Belfast, *Cities*, 18(2), pp.103-113.

Cumine, V., Leach, J. and Stevenson, G (1998) *Asperger's Syndrome: a practical guide for teachers*, David Fulton Publishers, London.

Department of the Environment/Department of Regional Development (1991-1998) *Vehicle Kilometres of Travel Survey of Northern Ireland: Annual Reports 1991-1998*, Belfast, HMSO.

Ellis, G. (2000) Addressing inequality: planning in Northern Ireland, *International Planning Studies*, 5(3), pp.345-364

Ellis. G. (2001) The difference context makes: planning and ethnic minorities in Northern Ireland, *European Planning Studies*, 9(3), pp.339 – 357.

Fawcett, L. (2000) *Transforming transport in Northern Ireland*, London, Transport 2000.

Imrie, R. and Thomas, H. (eds.) (1993) *British urban policy and the Urban Development Corporations*, London, Paul Chapman Publishing.

McEldowney, M. (2000) Planning and transportation: the need for integration, *Northern Ireland Environment Fact Sheet*, 1(2), pp.6-7.

Montgomery, J. and Thornley, A. (eds.) (1990) *Radical planning initiatives*, London, Longman.

Robinson C.A. (2004) *Planning decision-making: the impact of institutional culture*, Unpublished Working Paper, School of Environmental Planning, Queen's University, Belfast.

Romme, G. and Dillen, R. (1997) Mapping the landscape of organisational learning, *European Management Journal,* 15(1), pp.68 – 78.

Tantam, D. (1987) *A mind of one's own*, London, National Autistic Society.

Wing. L. and Gould J. (1979) Severe impairments of social interaction and associated abnormalities in children epidemiology and classification, *Journal of Autism and Childhood Schizophrenia*, 9, pp.11-29.

Wing. L. (1981) Language, social and cognitive impairments in autism and severe mental retardation, *Journal of Autism and Developmental Disorders*, 11, pp.115-129.

Wing. L. (1996) *The autistic spectrum*, London, Constable.

Section Five:

PERSPECTIVES ON PLANNING GOVERNANCE

Chapter 17

Towards a Theory of State-Community Partnerships: Interpreting the Irish Muintir na Tíre Movement's Experience

Tony Varley and Diarmuid Ó Cearbhaill

Introduction

Over the past decade or so the notion of 'partnership' as a means of restructuring the nature of democratic governance, and stimulating local development, has become hugely fashionable in Irish public policy discourse. Much of the impetus for the rise of the partnership approach, at least in its main guises, can be attributed to the influence of the European Union, particularly in its sponsorship of a whole series of area-based partnership programmes (Sabel, 1996; Walsh *et al.,* 1998; Geddes, 2000).[1] While much of what has transpired within the area-based programmes is of relevance to our discussion, our focus here will fall on the now frequently encountered suggestion that relations between the state and organised community interests should also be structured along partnership lines. The nature of state-community movement partnership-type relations will be explored with specific reference to the experience over recent years of the long-established Irish community development movement, Muintir na Tíre (People of the Land).

We begin our discussion in this chapter with the possibility that state-community interest partnerships can be understood in two very different ways. The idea of starting out with what we will term the optimistic and the pessimistic models of how the partnership approach to state-community interest relations is structured reflects our belief that these help summarise competing accounts of reality. Generally speaking, these two models correspond broadly and respectively to the 'consensus' and 'conflict' perspectives that stand out as fundamental benchmarks in contemporary social science (Alexander, 1987, pp.8-9).

Our optimistic model is inspired by that tradition of social theorising that highlights the phenomenon of consensus in social life. At the level of aspiration and ideology, many community interests (and Muintir na Tíre is no exception here) show a preference for seeing the world in consensus terms. They are encouraged to do this by an all-inclusive ideology that desires to represent everyone in the local community and to ensure that the benefits of community development are spread as widely as possible. They also believe that if community development is to succeed in advancing the 'common good' it must proceed by formalising arrangements that allow community interests to work in tandem with the state to their mutual advantage. For their part, state sector decision makers, as is borne out by the official rhetoric surrounding the area-based partnerships in Ireland, may be equally disposed to view the world in consensus terms, at least in their public pronouncements. At the level of general ideological orientations, our optimistic model thus helps illuminate some of the broad preferences of the community and state actors we will be considering in Ireland.

Much light is shed by the pessimistic model in considering the context of the actual practice of partnership in which the realities and consequences of power differences may loom large for community partners. What the consensus way of thinking overlooks above all, according to the conflict theory assumptions of our pessimistic model, are the power imbalances that gulf wide between state and community partners. Recognition of such imbalances leads to the further suggestion that power differences allow state actors to manipulate community interests for their own purposes. Initial inequalities between state and community interest partners, therefore, threaten to undermine the possibility of any real equality and, in the worst case, result in state actors manipulating community interests for their own purposes to the point of co-optation and disempowerment.

Our approach to building a theory of state-community interest partnerships does not stop with isolating and elaborating the different elements of these pessimistic and optimistic interpretative frameworks, and drawing on them to interpret an Irish community movement's experience of partnership. We seek to go beyond all this to theorise how community interests might devise strategies to exploit the new opportunities the partnerships bring (highlighted by the optimistic model), and to resist the co-optation and disempowerment which the pessimistic model sees as a likely consequence for community interests under the partnership approach.

It is the possibility that community interests can learn from their experiences that opens the door to the activist model. The prospect the activist model conjures up is that community activists can learn to exploit the opportunities the partnerships bring and to resist the co-optation that leaves them at risk of becoming accomplices in their own subordination. The importance in all this of the *strategies* community interests devise to shape partnership relations more to their own advantage encourages us to call our third perspective the 'activist' model.

Modelling Partnerships

The use of models or ideal types can serve a number of different purposes for the student of society (Burger, 1987, pp.154-79). Strictly speaking, the optimistic and pessimistic models now to be elaborated cannot be said either to *describe* or to *explain* specific empirical realities. All that can be expected of them is that they can represent or stand for reality, but in a way that is capable of facilitating the interpretation of empirically possible patterns and sequences of events, such as those to be encountered in Ireland presently. The interpretations of Muintir na Tíre's experience of partnership the optimistic and pessimistic models permit will clear the ground for introducing a third (activist) model, which we hope will advance our theoretical understanding of partnerships.

The building of these three models of state-community interest partnership relations is aimed at providing us with a *general* approach to the interpretation of how *specific* partnerships are put together and develop over time. We can, at the very least, look to our three models to suggest a number of possibilities and questions that can be used to help us locate specific instances of state/community interest partnerships in a useful interpretative framework.

Once our optimistic and pessimistic models have been outlined (Table 17.1), we will turn to the Irish case with two aims in mind. We wish, firstly, to consider where the ideal and practice of 'partnership' have featured within the experience of Muintir na Tíre (hereafter Muintir) over recent years. This descriptive account will be preliminary to an attempt at interpreting how well the Muintir experience of partnership has lived up to the assumptions and characterisations of our optimistic and pessimistic models. The examination of Muintir's experience of partnership will involve exploring its activists' ideological proclivity to think in partnership terms. It will also consider the constraints and the opportunities the movement now faces in seeking to survive within a context in which the ideal of 'partnership' has become firmly implanted in Irish public policy discourse. What we have to say about Muintir at the national and local levels is based on a series of interviews with Muintir activists, as well as on documentary research undertaken at Muintir's head office and in a number of Irish archives (Ó Cearbhaill and Varley, 1988, 1996).

The Optimistic Model of Partnership

Lying at the core of our optimistic model (Table 17.1) is an ethical commitment to the centrality of community life and to the empowerment of local communities. It is possible to characterise this communitarian commitment as populist. 'Many populist writers', Midgley (1995, p.90) points out 'place emphasis on the community as a locus for people's activities. They believe that communities form the basis of society and that the enhancement of community life offers the best opportunity for promoting people's happiness, a sense of belonging and identity.'

The most basic of our optimistic assumptions is that ruling politicians and state functionaries, as well as community activists, are disposed to see the world through eyes that are sympathetic to communitarian populism. Consequently, these ruling politicians and functionaries can be expected to refrain from treating community interests as simply a means to the achievement of their own ends. More positively, ruling politicians and functionaries can be assumed to be genuinely committed to achieving development and change in order to promote community empowerment as one strand of a vigorous and dynamic civil society. The optimistic view, therefore, is that, once there is an official willingness to contemplate power sharing in 'partnership'-type development schemes, the control that state elites can exert will be more enabling or facilitative than *dirigiste* or directive. When this happens the state's approach comes to be based on treating community movement/groups as something akin to equals who are to be trusted, respected and encouraged to push ahead with projects that can at once be jointly agreed and be mutually beneficial. A serious commitment to equality on the state's part implies the devolution of power to community interests.

For local community interests to be at the centre at all stages of state/community interest partnerships, their representatives would obviously need to stand formally equal with those of other partners on partnership boards as well as be in a position to perceive themselves to be equal in practice. Representatives of community interests would need, in addition, to be able to use the resources the partnerships make available to advance their own projects, and so extend the community (however understood) dimension of local development more generally. This optimistic scenario obviously implies not only *equality* between partners, but also the *active* participation of the representatives of local community interests at all decision-making levels within the partnership process.

When optimistic assumptions hold good, the state's commitment to taking the side of community interests amounts to what Midgley (1986, p.44) calls a 'participatory mode' that is characterised by a willingness to countenance 'a real devolution of power'. The optimistic expectation is that entering into partnership-type relations with community movements/groups may become an important means whereby the state devolves power to community interests. The opportunities the partnerships bring stand to empower community interests by adding to their resources, experience and organisational capacities, thus allowing them to advance existing aims and to take

274

on new ones.

Community development, based on our optimistic assumptions, may imply a radical break with the past, but just how radical this break proves to be will obviously depend on circumstances. In Ireland, for instance, crucial elements of the wider context, a historically heavily centralised and bureaucratised state and a deeply clientelist political culture (Higgins, 1982; Coakley, 1996), can be read as generally unsympathetic to the ideal of communitarian populism we have described above.

The Pessimistic Model of Partnership

The pessimistic model's understanding of state-community interest partnership-type relations begins from the gap that is assumed to exist between the official rhetoric of community empowerment *via* partnership and the reality of large power differences between state and community interests as prospective or actual partners (Table 17.1). Partnership-type relations between the state and community interests, notwithstanding any official rhetoric to the contrary, are assumed to be likely to carry the stamp of the state's power to control what goes on for its own ends. The basic pessimistic fear is that community interests will inevitably be disadvantaged as long as the relevant parameters of partnership activity - what is considered worth funding, funding levels, reporting and supervisory procedures and the duration of programmes – are controlled by the state or by supra-state political entities such as the European Union (EU).[2]

In thinking further about pessimistic scenarios we can again turn to Midgley, this time to his treatment of the so-called 'manipulative' mode of state-community group relations. Behind this manipulative mode lurks the notion that the state's willingness to support 'community participation' springs from 'ulterior motives', such as 'a desire to use community participation for purposes of political and social control' or as a means of reducing 'the costs of social development programmes and facilitat[ing] implementation' (Midgley, 1986, p.40).

The ever-present danger with the manipulative mode for community interests is 'co-optation'. This Midgley (1986, p.41) defines as 'a process by which the state seeks to gain control over grass-roots movements and to manipulate them for its own ends'. But manipulation and co-optation are by no means the whole story. Community interests can be imagined as having two broad options when faced with state interests intent on manipulation and co-optation. They can either succumb to manipulation and co-optation, or they can attempt to fashion strategies so as to resist and escape manipulative state control. It is this possibility of resistance that supplies one crucial facet of our activist model of partnership, to be introduced later on.

Table 17.1: Two models of state/community partnerships

Optimistic	Pessimistic
Vision based on principled, long-term commitment	Vision based on rhetoric and short-term crisis management
Participatory mode	Manipulative mode
Community as end in itself	Community as means to an end
Equal standing of partners	Unequal standing of partners
Power-sharing	Co-optation
Community empowerment	Community disempowerment

Dimensions of Partnership in Muintir

It is with these optimistic and pessimistic models of state/community interest partnership-type relations in hand that we now turn to look at the experience of one set of community interests with the partnership phenomenon in Ireland. Muintir, whose long career began as far back as the 1930s (Devereux, 1993), enjoys the distinction of being the oldest, still extant locality-based community movement in the Republic of Ireland. The movement, organised at both the national and local levels, currently describes itself as 'a national voluntary organisation for promoting, through the process of community development, the social, economic and cultural welfare of the people of Ireland' (Armstrong, 2001, p.392; see also http://www.muintir.ie/). Muintir's national organisation consists of a representative and executive body as well as a head office run by a handful of paid staff. Its 140 currently affiliated local units – known as community councils (CCs) – are spread unevenly across the country.

Although the contemporary notion of 'partnership' may be of recent origin, thinking more broadly in terms of partnership has for long been a feature of Muintir. The movement was conceived in the 1930s as an attempt to bring together elements in local communities that had been bitterly divided by civil war (1922-3) and by a flare-up of rural class conflict in the course of the nationalist revolution (1916-21) (O'Connor, 1988). The all-together ideal of uniting diverging and potentially conflicting interests, around a platform of developing local communities and pursuing the common good, remains at the core of Muintir's present-day CC-based approach to community development.

As well as being representative in the sense of being elected on a universal adult franchise, Muintir's local CCs are expected to be capable of assembling and giving voice to a local consensus behind a programme of collective self-help activity. This consensus-building process can again be construed in terms of producing and reproducing a partnership-type coalition between different social elements in local society. The notion of partnership arises in yet another guise in Muintir's suggestion, one enjoying great currency since the 1960s and conforming to the underlying thrust of the optimistic model, that effective community development requires the creation of partnership-type relationships between Muintir (at national and local levels) and the state.

Interestingly, acceptance of this state-centred version of partnership was not always a feature of national Muintir. The society into which Muintir emerged in the 1930s was heavily rural and Catholic. No longer was this so overwhelmingly the case by the 1960s and 1970s, decades that proved to be ones of great transition, not alone for Ireland but for Muintir's thinking on 'community development'. By then the principles that had been central to the movement's early ideology and local organisation – subsidiarity and vocationalism – were either abandoned or heavily modified.[3] In 1970, a decision was taken to replace the old vocationalist parish guild/councils (in existence since 1937) with new representative community councils.[4] Muintir had by 1970 become a firm convert to the United Nations' view that effective 'community development' required the building of partnership-type relations between voluntary groups (such as Muintir's parish-based local councils) and the state. This new preference for partnership with the state stood in sharp contrast with the subsidiarity-inspired desire of Muintir's founder, Fr. John Hayes, to keep a studied distance between his movement and the state.

The Quest for Partnership with the State

It is against the backdrop of these ideological and organisational changes that Muintir's first attempt at building a specific partnership-type relationship with the state (or, more precisely, with the EU) was initiated. Muintir's new direction was already clearly signalled in 1971 when a specially constituted review committee proposed to the Irish state that it bestow on Muintir national responsibility for promoting and establishing CCs and for meeting their training and information needs. A professionally staffed development unit was contemplated that, with adequate state funding, would service the needs of a steadily expanding number of Muintir-affiliated CCs (Muintir na Tíre, 1971, pp.36-37).

By the mid-1970s Muintir's national organisation was breaking new ground, having succeeded in attracting EU funding for a pilot project aimed at advancing the Muintir approach to community development. A team of *animateurs* or organisers set to work in bringing new CCs to life. At this point hopes were high within national Muintir that a bright future lay ahead. The new partnership mode it had opted to operate within, and indeed was helping to create and shape, appeared to be paying dividends. However, the official funding that underpinned Muintir optimism did not survive the pilot phase of the EC scheme that concluded in 1979. In consequence, much of the organising work then on hand had to be scaled back or even abandoned.

In spite of this reverse, national Muintir remains committed to the partnership ideal as the means of extending and strengthening its CC-based approach to community development. Ideological acceptance of partnership as a normative ideal is one major reason for this continuing commitment. Another reason, reflecting the absence of a 'captive market' for the services it provides to CCs and a desire to become a genuinely country-wide movement, flows from the national movement's almost total dependence on the state/EU for funding to maintain even its current activities. Although Muintir has been in receipt of a small state-provided annual grant-in-aid for many years,[5] the pattern of intermittent funding, established by the EU-funded pilot project of the 1970s, has continued to the present day. Most recently it is evident within the EU's LEADER (*Liaisons entre actions de développement de l'économie rurale*) II programme (1994-9),[6] by means of which Muintir was able to hire three animateurs to organise new CCs in three of the Republic's 26 counties.

Muintir draws on certain strengths in seeking to convince the state (or some elements of it) of the need to fund an extension of its CC-based approach to community development. An obvious advantage is that it has survived for such a long time and has numerous successes to its credit. Among these successes, the movement currently lists the provision of 'community centres, small-scale industrial development, sport and recreational facilities, care of the aged, housing, children's playgrounds, community crime prevention, youth projects, community information centres (now citizen information centres), adult education, tourism, arts facilities and training, group water schemes, local community radio, tidy towns, environmental activities, land and river drainage, research and publications'.[7] Compared to the early 1970s, however, Muintir's case that the state should grant it national responsibility for organising CCs has become a lot harder to make. Some of the difficulties it faces here relate to Muintir itself, others (to be considered in the next section of this chapter) relate to the Irish state and to the nature of the EU's area-based partnerships.

Most basically, perhaps, the movement's case has not been helped by the fact that it does not look as if it has the ability, certainly in the near term, to cover the country with a dense network of affiliated CCs. While some progress was made under the recent LEADER 2 funded organisational drive, the number of Muintir affiliated CCs remains disappointingly low. Arguably, the obstacles encountered in expanding the number of CCs reflect not alone the absence of a well-funded and sustained organising campaign, but some fundamental difficulties with the entire Muintir approach, at least as currently practised. A basic problem is that CCs can be established along Muintir lines without affiliating with the movement. In addition, there is the tendency for once-affiliated CCs to disaffiliate. A further difficulty stems from the drift away from Muintir guidelines on the part of some CCs that remain affiliated (see Ó Cearbhaill and Varley, 1996).

Negotiating Crisis Conditions *via* the Partnership Approach
In the troubled circumstances national Muintir has found itself in since the late 1980s, the possibility of creating new partnership-type relationships with the state/EU has appeared to the national leadership to be crucial to any effort to restore the fortunes of their movement. By far the most important new partnership-type initiative Muintir has become involved in is the Community Alert Programme whose origins can be traced to the formation of local vigilance groups in the mid-1980s to protect the rural elderly from the depredations of roving gangs of violent robbers. The form of community policing, into which Community Alert has evolved, is organised by local community groups in association with the Gardaí (police).

Community Alert, which continues to attract funding from the Departments of Health and Justice, has enabled Muintir to employ five full-time organisers in establishing and maintaining Community Alert (CA) groups. Over 80 per cent of the 1,130 of these CA groups (as of July 2001) can be directly attributed to the exertions of Muintir's organisers. Significantly, however, these CA groups are not typically organised as multi-purpose CCs. Nor do CA organisers necessarily see it as a major part of their role to encourage CA groups to become fully fledged CCs.[8] Instead, CA groups are offered the opportunity to become 'associates' of Muintir which allows them to qualify for 'charitable status' for tax purposes. These associates pay a nominal annual fee of £10, as compared to the £50 payable by affiliated CCs. So far about 30 per cent of CA groups have opted to become associates of Muintir.

Behind Muintir's success in making rapid strides with the organisation of CA groups lies the state's willingness to grant Muintir a monopoly of sorts in organising new CA groups and to provide what has so far proved to be stable funding. The state, as we have seen, is not similarly disposed to support Muintir's efforts to increase its pool of CCs. Community Alert has undoubtedly contributed to restoring Muintir's national profile and to demonstrating its practical relevance, though many people identify Community Alert with the Gardaí primarily. National Muintir is confident, as the only voluntary body in receipt of a direct grant for organising CA groups, that it will retain its quasi-monopolistic 'ownership' of the CA scheme and that it can extend the programme's scope beyond the crime prevention needs of the elderly. Involvement in the programme, however, has also had more ambiguous benefits for national Muintir, particularly in so far as it represents a departure from its long-established core activity – organising new CCs and servicing their ongoing needs.

Interpreting Muintir's Experience

How well does Muintir's experience of partnership with the state conform to the expectations of our optimistic and pessimistic models? Muintir's future as a national movement has long been seen internally as depending critically on the willingness of the state/EU to fund an ongoing campaign to organise and maintain CCs. Muintir activists still hold to this view, and continue to work to restore the sort of partnership-type arrangement negotiated with Europe in the 1970s. The difficulties in achieving this, as we have seen, can be partly attributed to Muintir's own troubles with its CC-based approach to community development. National Muintir activists, of course, also suggest that had the Irish State in the 1970s conferred on Muintir what would amount to a quasi-monopoly in the organising of new CCs and the servicing of existing ones, the movement would be in a far more robust condition today.

Can we say from this suggestion that the Irish State is not well disposed to the optimistic model's communitarian populism? To go by the official rhetoric of community empowerment surrounding the area-based partnerships, an optimistic reading of state-community interest partnerships would appear to carry conviction. A feature of the area-based partnerships over the past decade or so is that 'local communities' have been constituted, at least in much of the official rhetoric, as holding one solution to some of Ireland's economic and social problems. Local communities have been presented as possessing a capacity to engage in economic activity and create employment, deliver a range of social services and even be the means of revitalising local government and regional planning. The very first of the recent series of national plans, the National Development Plan 1989-1993 (Government of Ireland, 1989, p.65), in addressing 'integrated rural development', thus confidently announced that 'the priorities will be set by the communities themselves, who will be responsible for ensuring that local potential will be realised'.

However much national-level Muintir activists view the creation and funding of partnership as indispensable to their movement's ability to survive, they realise the risks associated with depending so heavily on partnership arrangements with the state. Muintir activists may subscribe to partnership with the state as an ideal, but experience has taught them that the official rhetoric of community empowerment is often no more than a chimera. For one thing, state interests are perceived as using this rhetoric very selectively. It may be applied to community participation in the area-based partnerships, and even to Community Alert, but not to the project of advancing Muintir's CC-based approach to community development. In part this selectivity is seen as reflecting the fragmentation of the state that results from the division of labour between, sometimes, competing state departments and agencies. Not only does the state fail to qualify as a unitary entity, in the view of Muintir activists, but none of its arms has emerged to assume an overall co-ordinating role where community development is concerned.

Selective use of the rhetoric of community empowerment is also seen as reflecting the state's typical crisis-management mode of operation where community development is concerned. The area-based partnerships, we should remember, were all born out of economic and social crisis conditions. Community Alert itself was conceived initially in response to a crisis of law and order. Above all, perhaps, the state's crisis-management mode of operation is viewed as having encouraged its various branches to regard community interests (Muintir included) as a means of contributing to the achievement of certain crisis management ends rather than as an end in themselves, worth supporting as an indispensable element of the civic culture of democratic societies. Consistent with pessimistic model assumptions, Muintir's national-level activists are well aware from experience of the centrality of this feature of state policy towards organised community interests; as one of them perceptively puts it, the Irish State (and the EU for that matter) is 'more interested in projects than in organisations'.

To avoid incurring an ongoing commitment to funding organised community interests, the Irish State historically has insisted on preserving the principle of voluntarism (Varley and Curtin, 1999, pp.64-5). In the present period of increasing liberalisation (one strongly driven by the EU), the idea of giving any one community movement a quasi-monopoly in organising community groups (along the lines Muintir has been seeking since the early 1970s) is foreign to the way of thinking of the general run of politicians and state functionaries. In fact, the last decade has seen the emergence of a number of new alliances (the Irish Rural Link and the Community Workers' Co-operative in particular) that also claim to represent and service rural community interests.[9] That Muintir now finds itself competing with new alliances of Irish community groups in speaking on behalf of CCs is entirely in harmony with the state's current emphasis on achieving efficiency *via* enhanced competitiveness.

In spite of retaining respect for the ideal of partnership, national Muintir activists, in view of concrete experiences going back to the 1970s European Community funded pilot project, would dismiss any suggestion of equality between state and non-state partners as a distortion of the reality of very large and very real power differences. This is not to say, however, that our Muintir activists would view themselves as *inevitably* manipulated to the point of co-optation, in the way Midgley describes. They would choose to see Community Alert more optimistically as a major opportunity to revive their movement to the point where a convincing case for the CC-based approach to community development can be made. Such a view can be read as consistent with the optimistic model's suggestion that the partnerships present community interests (such as Muintir) with significant new opportunities.

It would nonetheless be hard to conclude, on the basis of its experience to date, that empowerment of the sort conjured up by our optimistic model has been the order of the day for Muintir at either the national or local levels. To state the matter in somewhat different terms, the building of social capital can be said to require the formation of trust and co-operation (see Putnam, 2000; OECD, 2001). Whether the conditions that apply to the Irish partnerships are conducive to the building of state-community interest relationships of trust and co-operation in the longer term (see Government of Ireland 2000, chapter 5) is highly questionable. Why this is so reflects the tendency (flagged by our pessimistic model) of a fragmented state to treat community interests as a means rather than an end, the start-stop development that follows from short-term funding and the official setting of the other key parameters regardless of the wishes of community interests.

In significant respects, in fact, the case of Muintir (at the national level especially) highlights the heavy costs community movements and groups must sometimes pay as the price of participation in partnerships (see Frazer 1996). These costs stem from the power of the state-like external actors to set the relevant parameters of partnership activity, what is considered acceptable work, funding levels, reporting procedures and the duration of programmes. Muintir, as we have seen, has admittedly made some headway within the LEADER 2 area-based programme. But a defining feature of all the area-based partnerships is that they cannot, as fixed term programmes, be relied on to provide the sort of ongoing funding that Muintir is keen to attract so as to place its CC-based approach to community development on a more solid footing. The conditions, in other words, do not permit anything close to that 'real devolution of power' that forms a crucial plank of our optimistic model.

The Muintir case reflects the assumptions of our pessimistic model in important respects. It illustrates how the power to lay down the broad parameters around which partnerships operate can make for dominance that restricts community movements' strategic and tactical options, perhaps to the point of being able to constitute them in the image desired by state actors. Muintir, by virtue of its heavy involvement in Community Alert, is arguably being diverted from its core activity of organising new CCs and servicing existing ones. The mildest pessimistic interpretation of this state of affairs would be that Muintir has at least been left at risk of co-optation, as Fr. Hayes, the founder of Muintir, feared many years ago would happen if his movement were to become excessively dependent on the state.

Does this characterisation of national Muintir's experience of the

282

partnership phenomenon apply to the local level of the movement as well? The same enthusiasm for building partnership-type relations with the state/EU is not universally found at the movement's local level (see Ó Cearbhaill and Varley, 1996). Indeed, one significant area where drift is evident from the nationally set guidelines is in the local CCs' very partial acceptance of the national movement's emphasis on the desirability of steering clear of adversarial or confrontation tactics in their dealings with the state (Muintir na Tíre N.D., pp. 4-5).

Local government has historically comprised the one branch of the state in which there was something of a formal basis for the creation of partnership-type relations between statutory bodies and CCs. Under the 1941 Local Government Act community groups were permitted to apply for 'approved' status that could result in some small-scale material assistance and possibly even the delegation of some statutory functions. However this provision, reflecting lack of official interest as much as an absence of pressure from below, is now largely defunct. CC activists may even see 'approval', in the cases where it applies, as restricting their room to manoeuvre. One group of western CC activists, for instance, involved in a protest campaign to prevent the downgrading and possible closure of a local hospital, felt so constrained by the implications of this form of partnership that they decided to throw off their CC's 'approved' status.

What some CC activists claim to know from experience is that the state is anything but a unitary entity and that scale and capacity differences rule out anything other than symbolic 'partnership'. Actual experience of dealing with the local government authorities and other branches of the state has resulted historically in considerable cynicism about the state's commitment to any form of genuine partnership (O'Donohue, 1982). Several instances might be given to illustrate how critical some CCs have become of their local authorities over such matters as poor quality roads and refuse disposal facilities (see Ó Cearbhaill and Varley, 1996).

Enter an Activist Model of Partnership

The likelihood that community interests will strive to exploit the opportunities flagged by the optimistic model, and resist the disempowerment signalled by the pessimistic model, allows us now to contemplate a third model of state/community interest partnerships. This activist model focuses on the manner community interests see the world and on their capacities for collective agency. Its emphasis on activism in the form of strategies designed to exploit the opportunities and negotiate the constraints associated with partnerships permits us to go some distance towards resolving the differences between the optimistic and pessimistic models. Above all, the activist model directs its gaze at the optimistic possibility that community interests may succeed in using the partnership approach instrumentally to advance their own prospects. Whether partnerships eventually evolve into something akin to genuine power-sharing arrangements will ultimately depend on experience and imagination in waging power struggles, and on the ability of community interests to strategically and skilfully pursue their own instrumental objectives.

The challenge for the observer is to specify the circumstances in which community interests can create sufficient room to manoeuvre to allow them grasp the opportunities that partnerships with the state bring with them. We can in broad terms construe the ability of community interests to build up a capacity for agency that allows them exploit the opportunities the partnerships bring as a learning process that involves the acquisition over time of knowledge and skill (see Korten, 1980).

How is the ability of community interests to resist the co-optation and disempowerment the partnerships threaten to bring to be construed? We have seen how the pessimistic model, drawing on another conflict theory insight, holds out the prospect of community interests resisting state manipulation and co-optation. Of course, the form such resistance may take can vary widely, from outright withdrawal to a plethora of struggles aimed at improving the relative standing of community partners.

The question then becomes: how well has Muintir actually succeeded in exploiting the opportunities and negotiating the constraints the partnership regime has bestowed upon it? Our analysis suggests that it would be a mistake to characterise Muintir (no less than the state) as a fully uniform entity. The differences evident between national and local Muintir activists' views on partnership, and in the strategies forged to deal with them, reflect varying degrees of dependence on the state. Some local activists, it is clear, have seen their position more in terms of negotiating constraints than seizing opportunities.

Muintir's national activists, as we have seen, remain upbeat about Community Alert not alone as a partnership opportunity in itself, but as one important means of reviving the state's interest in funding the CC-based approach to community development on a partnership basis. A dilemma national Muintir now faces is that while it may not have benefited greatly under the partnership regime (at least as far as its work with the CCs is concerned), it sees itself with no real option but to make the best of whatever partnership opportunities come along. It needs to do this not only to survive in the short term but also to keep alive its ambition to become a more dynamic and self-assured national community development movement in the longer term. There are, therefore, real material reasons as to why national Muintir activists' ideological commitment to partnership should persist, despite an experience that departs significantly from the promise of empowerment.

How successful has local Muintir been in using the partnership approach instrumentally to advance its own projects? In comparison to the national organisation, small local Muintir CCs are significantly less dependent for their survival on state funding. Some local Muintir activists have even come to see the state (in part at least) as a dominating force and remain to be convinced of the merits of building partnership-type relations with certain branches of the state. At the local level, opting out of partnership emerges as one distinguishable strategy of dealing with the fear of co-optation.

Conclusion

This chapter has presented and applied to an Irish case what we would suggest is a useful general theoretical framework to approach the interpretation of specific instances of partnership-type relations between community interests and the state. We have shown, drawing on what we have termed optimistic, pessimistic and activist models, how a range of elements are relevant to an interpretation and understanding of the different realities surrounding partnership-type relations between the state and community interests in Ireland. In seeking to build a theory of community interest/state partnerships, we have pushed beyond our initial pessimistic and optimistic models to propose an activist model of partnership. Lying at its heart is the ability of community interests to learn from experience and to assert their own capacity for collective agency by devising strategies to exploit the opportunities and negotiate the constraints associated with partnerships more to their own advantage.

Four broad steps, posed as questions, can now be identified as following from the three-model approach we have adopted to building a theoretical framework to interpret the involvement of community interests in partnerships with the state. The first of these steps involves inquiring how community interests see their prospects within particular partnerships. Do they see their prospects more in terms of empowerment or disempowerment, along the lines envisaged by our optimistic and pessimistic models? Answers to this question are likely to vary over time and to be influenced by the play of various contingencies.

Linked to the issue of how community interests see their prospects is the question of whether community activists see their position more in terms of seizing opportunities than negotiating constraints. Once this question in turn is answered, we can press on to ask about the actual strategies community activists resort to in availing themselves of opportunities and in negotiating constraints. How community activists fare with the strategies they opt to pursue constitutes our fourth question. Here again, as the Muintir case illustrates, a range of conditions may impinge on the success community activists actually experience in pushing forward with their favoured strategies.

Acknowledgement

This chapter was originally publised in *Journal of the Community Development Society,* 2002, Vol.33, No.1.

Endnotes

1 These area-based partnership programmes bear some resemblance to the US federal government's empowerment zone/enterprise-community initiative of the 1990s (see Wetherill, 1995; Gaventa *et al.*, 1995).

2 The designation (European Union came to replace that of European Economic Community once the Treaty of Maastricht was ratified by the individual member states on 1 November 1993).

3 Society, according to the Catholic version of subsidiarity, was to be conceived as a series of interlocking but largely autonomous spheres, in relation to which the liberal democratic state would have no more than 'an overall co-ordinating role' to play (O'Leary, 2000, p.12). The closely allied ideal of 'vocationalism' called for a reorganisation of society around substantially self-regulating 'vocational groups' (O'Leary, 2000, pp.18-19).

4 Under the system of vocational organisation, representation on the Muintir parish councils was typically offered to farmers, labourers, professionals and business people, with women and adolescents being sometimes admitted as distinct sections in their own right (Newman, 1963, pp.20, 24).

5 A fiscally hard-pressed Irish state felt obliged to cut this grant from £30,000 to £15,000 in 1987, thereby precipitating an immense financial crisis for the national organisation (see Ó Cearbhaill and Varley, 1996).

6 For further information on the LEADER 11 programme in Ireland, see http://www.pobail.ie/en/Rural Development/LEADER).

7 See http://www.muintir.ie/head_off/business/mission.htm).

8 Some west of Ireland CC activists have complained that CA development officers have not consulted them adequately or have even bypassed them in favour of other local groups.

9 Information relating to the Community Workers' Co-operative is available at the website address: http://www.cwc.ie/

References

Alexander, J.C. (1987) *Sociological theory since 1945*, London, Hutchinson.

Armstrong, J. (ed.) (2001) *Administration yearbook and diary 2002*, Dublin, Institute of Public Administration.

Burger, T. (1987) *Max Weber's theory of concept formation: history, laws and ideal types*, Durham, Duke University Press.

Coakley, J. (1996) Society and political culture, in J. Coakley and M. Gallagher (eds.) *Politics in the Republic of Ireland.* Limerick, PSAI Press.

Devereux, E. (1993) The lonely furrow: Muintir na Tíre and Irish community development, 1931 - 1991, *Community Development Journal,* 28(1), pp 45-54.

Frazer, H. (1996) The role of community development in local development, in P. Conroy *et al.*(eds.) *Partnership in action: the role of community development and partnership in Ireland*, Galway, The Community Workers' Co-operative.

Gaventa, J., Morrissey, J. and Edwards, W.R.. (1995) Empowering people: goals and realities, *Forum for Applied Research and Public Policy,* 10(Winter), pp.116-121.

Geddes, M. (2000) Tackling social exclusion in the European Union? The limits to the new orthodoxy of local partnership, *International Journal of Urban and Regional Research,* 24(4), pp.782-800.

Government of Ireland (1989) *National Development Plan, 1989-1993*, Dublin, Stationery Office.

Government of Ireland (2000) *White Paper on a framework for supporting voluntary activity and for developing the relationship between the state and the community and voluntary sector*, Dublin, Stationery Office.

Higgins, M.D. (1982) The limits of clientelism: towards an assessment of Irish politics, in C. Clapham (ed.) *Private patronage and public power: political clientelism in the modern state*, London, Frances Pinter.

Korten, D.C. (1980) Community organisation and rural development: a learning process approach, *Public Administration Review,* 40, pp.480-511.

Midgley, J. (1986) *Community participation, social development, and the state*, London, Methuen.

Midgley, J. (1995) *Social development: the developmental perspective in social welfare.* London, Sage.

Muintir na Tíre (1971) *Review Committee report on Muintir na Tíre*, Tipperary, Muintir na Tíre Publications.

Muintir na Tíre (N.D.) *Community development and the representative Community Council*, Tipperary, Muintir na Tíre.

Newman, J. (1963) The 'specific situation' of Ireland in relation to community development, in J. Newman (ed.) *Organising the community*, Tipperary, Muintir na Tíre.

Ó Cearbhaill, D. and Varley, T. (1988) Community group/state relationships: the case of West of Ireland Community Councils, in R. Byron (ed.) *Public policy and the periphery: problems and prospects in marginal regions*, Belfast, International Society for the Study of Marginal Regions.

Ó Cearbhaill, D. and Varley, T. (1996) An Irish community development movement's experience of crisis conditions: Muintir na Tíre's struggle for survival, *Journal of the Community Development Society,* 27(1), pp.1-16.

O'Connor, E. (1988) *Syndicalism in Ireland*, Cork, Cork University Press.

O'Donohue, K. (1982) How do people help themselves? in P. Berwick and M. Burns, (eds.) *Conference on poverty*, Dublin, Council for Social Welfare.

OECD (2001) *The well-being of nations: the role of human and social capital*, Paris, OECD Centre for Research & Innovation.

O'Leary, D. (2000) *Vocationalism and social Catholicism in twentieth-century Ireland: the search for a Christian social order*, Dublin, Irish Academic Press.

Putnam, R.D. (2000) *Bowling alone: the collapse and revival of American community,* New York, Simon and Schuster.

Sabel, C. (1996) *Ireland: local partnerships and social innovation*, Paris, OECD.

Varley, T. and Curtin, C. (1999) Defending rural interests against Nationalists in 20th century Ireland: a tale of three movements, in J. Davis (ed.) *Rural change in Ireland*, Belfast, The Institute of Irish Studies, Queen's University, Belfast.

Walsh, J., Craig, S. and McCafferty, D. (1998) *Local partnership for social inclusion?* Dublin, Oak Tree Press in association with the Combat Poverty Agency.

Wetherill, G.R. (1995) Empowerment holds key to rural revitalization, *Forum for Applied Research and Public Policy,* 10(Winter), pp.117-120.

Chapter 18

Community Planning in Northern Ireland: Participative Democracy in Practice?

Colin Knox

Introduction

Community planning has now entered the lexicon of public administration reformers in Northern Ireland and marks a significant shift in the role envisaged for local government and community based initiatives such as local strategy partnerships in future governance arrangements. More fundamentally, this new emphasis on community planning delineates a distinction between participative and representative democracy and brings into focus tensions which arise as Northern Ireland oscillates between an active political forum in the form of a functioning devolved Assembly (now suspended for the fourth time since October 2002), Direct Rule from Westminster, and an omnipresent civil society.

Community planning, however, is part of a wider agenda rooted in the Labour Government's modernisation agenda which asserts that 'government matters' – its role should be to improve the quality of our lives through the provision of policies, programmes and services. 'People want effective government, both where it responds directly to their needs (health, education, social services)…and where it acts for society as a whole (environment, crime)' (Cabinet Office, 1999, p.10). The community planning process provides a practical mechanism for demonstrating effective community leadership, for developing a sense of vision or direction, and for 'joining-up' the work of the various agencies at the local level. It needs to be seen as a vehicle for making connections, to promote long term sustainable development. Although community planning in Northern Ireland has been given prominence through the current Review of Public Administration, it poses more fundamental questions about the capacity which proposed new councils would have to deliver this role and their relationships with Local Strategy Partnerships.

This chapter, therefore, attempts to do three things. First, it considers proposals emerging for community planning within the context of the 'well-being' debate now mainstream, in other parts of the United Kingdom. Second, it looks at the (default) role played to date of PEACE II Local Strategy Partnerships in developing community planning in the form of local integrated strategies. Third, in light of the mixed experience and nugatory impact of partnerships in this area, it considers the future of community planning in the uncertain environment where PEACE II funding ends and the functions and form of local government remain undecided. In sum, this chapter offers a retrospective and prospective narrative on whether community planning is or can be effectively embedded in the evolving mechanisms of governance in Northern Ireland.

Community Planning and Local Government
Community planning and community leadership are inextricably linked within the Labour Government's modernisation agenda. In 1999 the initiative *Modernising Government* aimed to: ensure that policy making is more joined up and strategic; public service users, not providers, are the focus, by matching services more closely to people's lives; and to deliver public services that are high quality and efficient (Cabinet Office, 1999). Alongside this, the Government set out proposals to modernise local government through *Modern Local Government: In Touch with the People* (DETR, 1998).

At the local government level the modernisation programme stressed three themes:
- community leadership or the role of local authorities working with their partners and with local people in meeting economic, social and environmental needs;
- democratic renewal, building a new and active relationship between local authorities and their citizens;
- improving performance in meeting needs and in providing services.

Community leadership was given expression through powers of well-being and the duty to undertake community planning. To strengthen local authorities' position and role in providing leadership, the Government enshrined in law the role of councils as the elected leader of their local community with a responsibility for the well-being and sustainable development of their areas. Hence the Local Government Act 2000 gives local authorities in England and Wales powers to promote or improve the economic, social and environmental well-being of their area – commonly referred to as the powers of well-being. The same Act also laid a duty on local authorities to prepare a strategy to achieve these goals and contribute to sustainable development in the United Kingdom. Similar provisions have been introduced by the Local Government in Scotland Act 2003. The Local Government Act 2000 does not apply to Northern Ireland.

There is no prescription on what community strategies should contain but guidance was issued on general principles. Hence community planning should:

- engage and involve local communities;
- involve active participation of councillors;
- be prepared and implemented by a broad 'local strategic partnership' through which local authorities can work with other local bodies; and
- be based on a proper assessment of needs and the availability of resources (DETR: 2000, p.7).

Similarly, there is no definition of what actions constitute the promotion of well-being, although guidance to local authorities highlights the need for an integrated approach to tackling social exclusion, reducing health inequalities, promoting neighbourhood renewal and improving local environmental quality. Given the absence of key functional responsibilities for councils in Northern Ireland, the power of well-being has even greater significance if local authorities are to have oversight of the many central government and quango service providers in their areas.

Community planning has featured on the policy agenda in Northern Ireland through the ongoing Review of Public Administration, initiated in June 2002. Its task is to review the existing arrangements for the accountability, administration and delivery of public services in Northern Ireland, and to bring forward options for reforms which are consistent with the arrangements and principles of the Belfast Agreement, within an appropriate framework of political and financial accountability (Terms of Reference: Review of Public Administration, 2002).

The devolved system of public administration in Northern Ireland is a mosaic of departments, agencies, non-departmental public bodies and local government. The restructuring of the pre-existing government departments from six to eleven following devolution compounded an already complex system of public administration. This made no administrative logic but was the outcome of political negotiations to secure a power-sharing executive within a devolved Assembly. Add to this an assortment of around 100 public bodies, some of which have responsibility for major public services though appointees (housing, health and education), emasculated local government, and we have the Byzantine system that is the Northern Ireland public sector.

The fragmentation in our administrative structures has inevitably led to disjointed public services typified by the different boundaries within which health, education, housing and local government (to name but a few) are delivered. This problem has been identified in the Review of Public

Administration consultation document as an issue that needs to be tackled to improve our public services.

> Many people are concerned about the lack of 'joined-up' government both at central and local level… In Great Britain and in the Republic of Ireland this problem has been addressed through a formal process of community planning. All the agencies in an area come together under the leadership of the council to develop a community plan and play a continuing role in contributing to and monitoring the way these plans are put into practice. Given the different structures here, collaborative processes are less well developed in Northern Ireland. (Review of Public Administration Consultation Document, 2004, p.16)

The Review Team envisages 'joined-up' government happening through: a formal system of community planning; the establishment of common boundaries; and greater collaboration.

Under a 'community planning model' local councils will become the locus of several public bodies (e.g. health, policing, economic development, civil service departments, and housing) providing services in their areas through an integrated local strategy or community plan. The Review of Public Administration Team proposes a community planning model as a way of illustrating the pivotal role of local government therein (see Figure 18.1).

Figure 18.1: Proposed Community Planning Model[1]

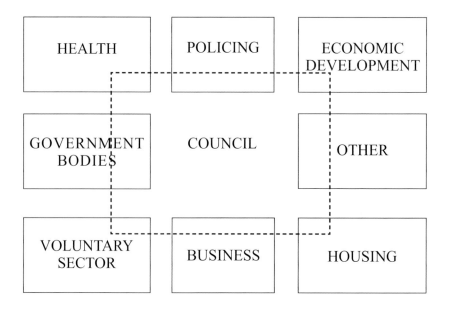

Evidence emerging from the Review sets out how Minister Ian Pearson sees the respective roles of central and local government and the importance of community planning for future governance arrangements:

> I envisage the Assembly with departments sitting at regional level with responsibility for policy, strategic planning, setting standards and monitoring performance. At a local level, larger more powerful councils could have responsibilities for an increased range of functions such as regeneration, environmental services, some planning functions and possibly local roads. I see councils having an important role in ensuring co-ordinated service delivery in their area and this co-ordination could be further enhanced by giving councils a major role in community planning for their local population. (Pearson, 2004)

All of this heralds a significant new role for local government at the centre of the community planning process. In the British model the advice to local authorities was that the most effective way of ensuring the commitment of other organisations to community planning was for councils to work with statutory, non-statutory and voluntary organisations through a local strategic partnership. Importantly, however, a local strategic partnership is a voluntary framework based on local co-operation. While it is local authorities in Great Britain that are legally required to prepare community strategies, they must recognise the operational autonomy of their partners. Hence, it is at the discretion of participating partners to sign up to the long-term vision contained in the plan and to commit the necessary resources for its implementation.

Key to all of this, through guidance given to local authorities from the Office of the Deputy Prime Minister, is that 'the organisation that leads a local strategic partnership needs to command the confidence of the other partners' (Office of Deputy Prime Minister, 2003, p.26). Given the relatively insignificant role envisaged for local government in Northern Ireland *vis-à-vis* key sectoral players in, for example, health, policing and economic development, it is highly unlikely that the proposed councils (under the Review of Public Administration) could assume such a lead role. In short, claims by the Review Team that local government in Northern Ireland will play a pivotal role in community planning (as set out in Figure 18.1) may well turn out to be vacuous when dwarfed by much larger public sector bodies.

Community Planning and Local Strategy Partnerships
Thus far, in the Northern Ireland context, unlike the rest of the United Kingdom, which vests statutory responsibility with local authorities to prepare community strategies, this role has been assumed by Local Strategy Partnerships in Northern Ireland on a non-statutory basis. Northern Ireland, like other parts of Europe, has embraced partnership arrangements mainly in areas of economic development, health, urban regeneration and peace and

reconciliation. Initiatives such as 'Making Belfast Work', the 'Derry/Londonderry Initiative' were launched in the late 1980s in response to problems of multiple deprivation – physical dereliction, social deprivation, high long-term unemployment, and difficulties attracting private sector investment into the cities. Partnership working through voluntary/community organisations, the private sector and Government became the norm as integrated strategies evolved to tackle these deep-rooted problems.

European funds, however, institutionalised the model of partnership working in Northern Ireland. EU Community Initiatives such as URBAN have assisted local partnerships in deprived urban areas to support schemes for economic development, social revitalisation and environmental protection. The INTERREG cross-border programme has funded projects aimed at strengthening economic and social cohesion by promoting cross-border transnational and interregional co-operation and balanced development – local authority cross-border (between Northern Ireland and the Republic of Ireland) partnerships have been central to this Community Initiative.

The European Union Special Support Programme for Peace and Reconciliation launched in 1995 (PEACE I: 1995-99), however, promoted partnership working to a new level. The aim of the programme was to support social inclusion of those at the margins of economic and social life, and exploit opportunities arising from the peace process in order to stimulate social and economic regeneration. One of the most innovative aspects of the programme was the development of 26 District Partnerships coterminous with local authorities with responsibility for some 15 per cent of the total funding package (£375m). Partnership boards were established from 3 sectors – one-third councillors, one-third voluntary and community sector representatives, and one-third made up from other partners – business, trade unions and statutory organisations (in equal numbers).

The partnership approach was considered important beyond the confines of the individual funded projects. The process of partnership working cut across traditional political cleavages and fostered cross-sectoral working relations. Commenting on their effectiveness in this regard, Hughes *et al* note:

> The European Peace and Reconciliation Initiative has opened up participation and partnership in a way that has recast democracy towards a model that brings together participatory and representative models. Their lead role confirms the value of local partnerships as a permanent feature of civic culture in the region, not least because of their enormous potential to make a lasting contribution to peace and reconciliation in a divided society. (Hughes et al, 1998, p.232)

PEACE II (2000 – 2004) takes forward the overall aim of its predecessor but with a new economic focus. District Partnerships were replaced by Local Strategy Partnerships which are responsible for locally based regeneration and development strategies, addressing grassroots needs with local delivery mechanisms. The partnerships (again based on the 26 council areas) have been reconfigured and comprise two equal strands: local government and the main statutory bodies; and the four pillars of the social partners – private sector, trade unions, voluntary and community sector, and agricultural and rural development. They have been allocated 20 per cent of a €595m funding package to deliver local economic initiatives for developing the social economy, and human resource training and development strategies (Priority 3 – PEACE II).

Beyond their role in delivering PEACE II, however, Local Strategy Partnerships are expected to engage in integrated planning within district council areas (Table 18.1). In other words, they must ensure that services provided to the public are better integrated across administrative boundaries and more responsive to the needs of local communities. Guidelines for the partnerships suggest 'this is a process for agencies, stakeholders, communities, local councillors and individuals to engage in collaborative decision making about tackling key issues – jobs, education, health, crime and so on – for local people' (SEUPB, 2001, p.6).

To do this, the partnerships were tasked to develop an integrated local strategy and action plan that will become the framework for sustainable regeneration and development in each district council area beyond the lifetime of PEACE II. This integrated local strategy 'will seek to improve the economic, social and environmental conditions in a local area and contribute to sustainable development' (SEUPB, 2001, p.8). The Peace II Operational Programme provides guidance as to what an effective integrated local strategy should encompass but at the same time suggests that may differ from area to area.

Table 18.1: Common Elements of an Effective Integrated Local Strategy[2]

- the identification of what different public, private, voluntary and community bodies are doing in the area. Integrate representatives in the partnership structure and use their input in a transparent consultation process;

- the development of a long-term vision for the area focusing on outcomes;

- the identification of European, national and regional policy priorities and the availability of resources attached to them;

- on this basis, an analysis highlighting gaps in provision and defining opportunities to realign activities in the area, and in particular in the pursuit of the objectives of peace and reconciliation;

- the identification of the groups/communities, areas and sectors most affected by the conflict;

- the development of an agreed action plan identifying short-term priorities and activities what will contribute to the achievement of long-term outcomes;

- the establishment of a shared commitment to implementing the local area strategy and action plan by those best placed to deliver them;

- agreement of arrangements for monitoring the implementation of the local area strategy and its action plan by the Local Strategy Partnership structure and through the reporting system of the Programme.

A recent evaluation of the 26 Local Strategy Partnerships reveals a very mixed picture on the development and implementation of integrated local strategies (Deloitte, 2004). All 26 had drawn up strategies but these are at very different stages of development. The evaluation reports that there was an initial flurry of activity when integrated local strategies were being promoted as 'the most significant development in local government for decades', but this dissipated when devolution was suspended in October 2002 – the political focus 'fell through the floor'. Without this strategic political will to drive the integrated local strategy process what became important to its success was: how influential the Local Strategy Partnership manager was with other relevant organisations; the attitude of the Chief Executive of the local council to the partnership; and the seniority and commitment of statutory sector representatives (Deloitte, 2004 p.100). The Northern Ireland Regional Partnership Board in a research paper identified four main barriers faced by

Local Strategy Partnerships in the development of integrated local strategies:
- poor understanding of the integrated local strategy concept and rationale;
- lack of consensus regarding the strategic direction of the integrated local strategy;
- limited resources on the part of all co-operating organisations, but particularly the Local Strategy Partnerships;
- authority to 'force' co-operation. (NI Regional Partnership Board, 2004)

The evaluation of the partnerships revealed that more than a third of them received limited co-operation from statutory agencies in the development of their integrated local strategy. Statutory representatives, on the other hand, queried the capacity of relatively small and inexperienced organisations such as Local Strategy Partnerships to effectively co-ordinate major and specialised service delivery mechanisms in local areas. In addition, the evaluation noted that consultees in both the European Commission and the Special EU Programmes Body did not anticipate monitoring the implementation and impact of the integrated local strategies as they did not view them as high priorities within the overall programme. The evaluation concluded that the integrated local strategy process 'is considerably more difficult than envisaged by the Special EU Programmes Body in drafting the Peace II Operational Plan' (Deloitte, 2004, p.ix).

Conclusions

Has the foray of Local Strategy Partnerships into the field of community planning on a non-statutory basis, 'persuading' rather than 'requiring' full co-operation from council and other statutory agencies ended in failure? If so, what does this mean for the future of community planning? The evidence on Local Strategy Partnerships appears less than convincing in terms of their capacity to deliver community planning within current operational parameters. This is not to reject the notion of partnership governance. Indeed there is enthusiasm from some influential figures to embed partnerships in the long-term governance of Northern Ireland. The former Deputy First Minister (Mark Durkan) suggested in an Assembly debate:

> Partnerships will have a vision and purpose which will last well beyond the horizons of the PEACE II programme... In the context of the new institutions, I see an opportunity for the partnership process to be widened and deepened at both regional and local level. We do not want the partnership approach to be confined to European funding, nor do we want it to wither away when that source of income has ceased. The whole purpose of our approach is to increase the scope and significance of decision-making at the local level. (Durkan, 2001, p.16)

Interestingly, Taylor (1997, p.20) in her earlier work on partnerships in Great Britain argued that they were 'not a quick fix but had potential to be the basis for new forms of local governance that will last into the next century'. To do this, she argued that partnerships 'cannot be tacked onto the edges of existing systems'. The former Deputy First Minister seems intent on mainstreaming partnership governance in Northern Ireland.

So where should community planning reside given the state of political flux? A devolved government in Northern Ireland (despite its suspension for the fourth time since October 2002) offers a welcome return to representative democracy but it cannot, of itself, deliver stability on the ground and requires active engagement with civil society as key stakeholders in the community. There is also a balance to be achieved in ensuring that accountable forms of representative government sit alongside participative mechanisms for civic engagement. In a society still deeply divided along traditional ethno-national cleavages, cross-cutting sectoral contributions from social partners through Local Strategy Partnerships can act as an effective counterbalance. Achieving the optimal balance between participative and representative democracy is the task which faces the Northern Ireland Executive as it reviews the future role of local government and relationship with its 'partners' in the form of the voluntary and community sectors.

If a stronger local government emerges from the Review of Public Administration it could, with confidence, broker relationships with other stakeholders in rebuilding civil society which did not threaten, but complement, the role ascribed to the devolved legislative Assembly. The natural centripetal tendencies of the Assembly could be moderated and a stronger local government established, with the potential for strengthening participative democracy, through collaboration with Local Strategy Partnerships.

What is missing in all of this is a mechanism to improve co-ordination between the Northern Ireland Assembly/Executive, the new emerging councils and their partners, working through Local Strategy Partnerships. There is a danger that with 11 government departments, disjointed messages are sent out from central government though separate silos to local government and social partners. The Audit Commission in Great Britain referred to this as the 'humpty dumpty effect' where local agencies must put fractured policies back together again (Audit Commission, 2004, p.15). What is needed is a model to give new councils, within the context of Local Strategy Partnerships, more leverage over how to join up activity in support of local priorities – a new system of participative governance. This could be styled diagrammatically as in Figure 18.2.

Hence a smaller number of large multi-purpose or unitary local authorities could assume a statutory role for the power of well-being. The existing 26

Local Strategy Partnerships would retain the task of developing community plans reflective of local needs which must, in turn, manifest Programme for Government priorities. The final product is a local area strategy (covering the new local authority boundaries) to which all community planning partners sign up. Could this fulfil a modernising agenda for Northern Ireland which exhibits the pre-requisites: community leadership; democratic renewal by building an active relationship between councils and their citizens; and, a community plan which defines needs and provides joined-up services to meet those needs?

Figure 8.2: Joined-Up Government

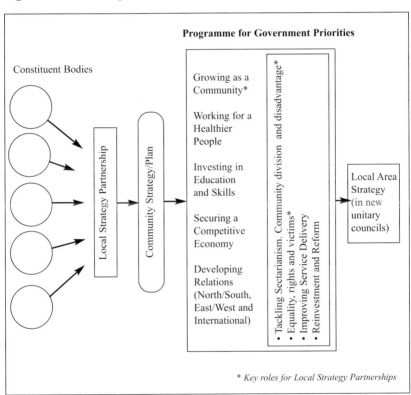

Endnotes

1   Review of Public Administration: Presentation given by Greg McConnell – 7th September 2004.
2   Peace II Operational Programme.

References

Audit Commission (2004) *People, places and prosperity: transforming national priorities into local well-being*, London, Audit Commission.

Cabinet Office (1999) *Modernising government*, Cm 4310, London, HMSO.

Deloitte (2004) *Mid-term evaluation of Local Strategy Partnerships – Stage 1 Report*, Belfast, Deloitte.

Department of the Environment, Transport and the Regions (DETR) (1998) *Modern local government: in touch with the people*, London, DETR.

Department of the Environment, Transport and the Regions (DETR) (2000) *Preparing community strategies*, London, DETR.

Durkan, M. (2001) *Local Strategy Partnerships,* Hansard, Northern Ireland Assembly, 27th March.

Hughes, J., Knox, C., Murray, M. and Greer, J. (1998) *Partnership governance in Northern Ireland: the path to peace*, Dublin, Oak Tree Press.

Northern Ireland Regional Partnership Board (2004) *Review of integrated local strategies*, Belfast, NIRPB.

Office of the Deputy Prime Minister (2003) *Preparing community strategies: Government guidance to local authorities*, London, ODPM.

Pearson, I. (2004) *Improvements to quality of service key to public administration reform*, Office of the First and Deputy First Minister, News Release, 19th July.

Special EU Programmes Body (2001) *Local Strategy Partnerships – guidelines*, Belfast, SEUPB.

Taylor, M. (1997) *The best of both worlds: the voluntary sector and local government*, York, Joseph Rowntree Foundation.

Chapter 19

Cross-border Tourism Co-operation on the Island of Ireland: Learning Lessons for Future Partnership Development

Jonathan Greer

Introduction

Over the last two decades partnerships have been increasingly embraced as a service delivery mechanism and have emerged as a central theme in public administration (Prior, 1996; Darwin, 1999). Within this relatively short period of time, partnerships have also become well established in tourism development as economic and technological changes have created an increasingly complex and multifaceted industry. On this basis, national tourism administrations have sought to facilitate co-ordination among ministries and work in partnership with a range of actors including non-governmental organisations, the private sector, professional, and voluntary / community groups to implement strategic tourism initiatives (Goymen, 2000). To date, partnerships in tourism have largely been located at the local and regional levels with much research being focused on the extent of community participation *vis-à-vis* administrative authorities (Joppe, 1996; Godfrey, 1998; Bramwell and Sharman, 1999; Tosun 2000). Indeed, this experience has been reflected within Northern Ireland and the Republic of Ireland as both administrations have sought to co-operate with local communities and develop tourism initiatives (Murray and Greer, 1993; Walsh 1997/98). The tourist authority in Northern Ireland, the Northern Ireland Tourist Board (NITB), has also established a series of public / private partnerships at the sub-regional level which have the responsibility to work alongside the NITB and formulate an integrated marketing plan (NITB, 2004).

Considering the backdrop of increasing European cross-border co-operation (Loughlin, 2000), what is interesting in the case of Ireland, however, is that the partnership approach has also been adopted at the trans-jurisdictional level between the respective tourist authorities, the Northern Ireland Tourist Board (NITB), and Fáilte Ireland (previously Bord Fáilte) in the Republic of Ireland. A trans-jurisdictional partnership was first initiated in the 1960s, but over the last two decades in particular, the level of co-operation has substantially increased with the implementation of cross-border programmes and the introduction of a joint marketing initiative to promote the island of Ireland as a single tourist destination. Moreover, in recent years, the partnership has developed a new dynamic and is one of the six 'matters for co-operation' for the North-South Ministerial Council (NSMC) set up under the 1998 'Good Friday' Agreement. As part of this process a publicly owned limited company, Tourism Ireland, has been established by both tourist authorities with the responsibility for planning and delivering international tourism marketing programmes. Given the emergence of this partnership relationship and the continuing peace process, a number of commentators such as Gray (1995), Tansey (1995) and Leslie (1996) have outlined the potential opportunities of cross-border co-operation for boosting tourism throughout the island of Ireland. Despite this, very little is known about the operation of trans-jurisdictional tourism partnerships in general and the co-operation between the NITB and Fáilte Ireland in particular. This chapter aims to fill the gap in this research by examining the evolving relationship between the two tourism authorities and outlining lessons for future partnership development on the island of Ireland.

First, as a means of providing a framework to examine the relationship between the tourist boards, this chapter begins by outlining the factors which influence the development of partnership. Secondly, tourism on the island of Ireland will be reviewed by setting out the roles and responsibilities of the tourist boards, discussing the history of cross-border co-operation, and identifying the new structures established under the 'Good Friday' Agreement. Following that, the chapter critically assesses the development of the partnership between the two tourism authorities over the last two decades. Reflecting on the future of cross-border co-operation in tourism on the island of Ireland, the chapter concludes by presenting a number of important lessons for the future development of tourism partnership at national, regional and local levels.

Conditions Influencing the Development of Partnerships
Given the variety and diversity of partnership arrangements (Bryson and Crosby, 1992; Prior, 1996), there are a wide range of conditions cited in the literature which influence partnership development. Therefore, for the purposes of this discussion, each of the conditions is subdivided into four categories: contextual, stakeholder, decision making, and operational.

Contextual conditions

Contextual issues focus on the background or environment in which partnerships operate and can be highlighted as important factors which influence partnership arrangements. First of all, it is argued that partnerships are more likely to succeed if each participant believes that working together will achieve greater benefit than acting individually (Huxham, 1991; Selin and Chavez, 1995). If stakeholders agree that co-operation will improve service delivery or achieve greater economic and operational efficiency, this will motivate each partner and create a favourable partnership environment.

Moreover, Bramwell and Sharman (1999) argue that partnerships need to operate within a contextual environment of understanding and respect. If the partner organisations respect the traditions and values of each other, this works to break down barriers and facilitate interaction between stakeholders. On the other hand, it is maintained that if a partnership is operating against a background of historical and political confrontation this could have a profound impact on the success of the relationship. Historical and political conflict can combine to raise tensions between the stakeholders and entrench different groups in the partnership into traditional camps with each seeing the other as the enemy (Gray, 1989).

Stakeholder conditions

When reviewing the role of stakeholders, Bramwell and Sharman (1999) maintain that an unequal balance of power between organisations can lead to the failure of partnerships. In partnerships that vary in power, participant organisations will have a different level of ability, meaning some organisations will see others as irrelevant. This causes disagreement within partnerships leading to conflict and eventual failure.

In addition, a partnership is likely to face difficulties if the stakeholder organisations view each other as a threat or perceive that working together will lead to fragmentation of their organisation or a loss of authority (Mattessich and Monsey, 1992; Gray, 1989). Fear or loss of autonomy is particularly true when partners view the other to be lower in status and legitimacy, or if one stakeholder believes that a lack of resources will generate an inferior exchange position. Maintaining determination, commitment and stamina among participants is also an important condition for facilitating partnership. Huxham and Vangen (1996) comment that collaborations often fail to make progress as the participants are unwilling to pledge their full commitment. Conflict arises if commitment is not equally spread, with some organisations placing more importance on the collaboration than others.

Decision making conditions

The decision making process focuses on the relationships and interactions between organisations and individuals within collaborative arrangements. To develop an effective decision making process, Mattessich and Monsey (1992) argue that it is important to facilitate the participation of all individual organisations and ensure consensual agreement. Consensus decision making and participation encourages a common approach, guards against isolating individuals, and increases the perceptions of equality of status internally and fair representation externally.

Following on from this, Mattessich and Monsey (1992) and Forester (1993) comment that in collaborative relationships it is essential that the partnership decision making process is open and informal. This decision making environment seeks to encourage participation from all individuals and organisations and helps to build relationships among the partners. Furthermore, within an open forum partners are permitted to voice their concerns and discuss problematic and contentious issues. Establishing effective communication channels between the participant organisations is another condition for facilitating partnership (Huxham and Vangen, 1996). Differences between the organisations' working practices, culture and language can lead to conflict if each organisation adopts different interpretations over problems. In this case achieving a common position will be difficult. Therefore, it is essential to establish good communication in which participants can seek to understand each others meaning and language, and accept the need for tolerance. In addition, Hutchinson (1994) argues that time is important for a partnership decision making process, particularly when developing links with the other organisations and learning to understand different agendas.

Partnership operation

A final consideration when discussing the conditions which influence partnership development relates to the operation or activities of partnerships. Wide agreement exists among commentators that partnerships must first develop clear strategies (Boyle, 1989; Mattessich and Monsey, 1992; Wilson and Charlton, 1997). Formulating a strategy is essential as it shapes the development of the initiative in the early stages, defines the scope of activity and provides a constant reminder to stakeholders of the aims and objectives of the partnership. Developing a strategy at the outset is also important, not only in arriving at a common definition of a problem, but in designing the partnership processes and procedures, and understanding how important each of the problem issues are. Furthermore, when formulating a strategy, Gray (1989), Mattessich and Monsey (1992), Wilson and Charlton (1997), support the view that partnerships must involve all partners or the wider community in the decision making process. It is believed that greater involvement and participation will create equality within the partnership, ownership of policy formulation and implementation, and a more effective decision making process. Finally, it is maintained that the allocation or accessibility of sufficient funds is an important condition for development as resources are required to support partnership programmes and operations (Mattessich and Monsey, 1992).

Having outlined the conditions which influence partnership development, the chapter now goes on to provide the necessary background to the examination of the relationship between the NITB and Fáilte Ireland by reviewing the emergence and development of cross-border co-operation in tourism on the island of Ireland.

The Development of Cross-border Co-operation in Tourism

The role and responsibilities of government in tourism
From its establishment in 1948, the NITB has been central to the development and promotion of tourism in Northern Ireland, working in conjunction with the Department of Enterprise, Trade and Investment (DETI) (formally Department of Economic Development, DED) and local authorities. The role of the government department in tourism has traditionally been focused around administration and funding, providing the annual grant and directives on policy matters to the NITB. The NITB on the other hand, is responsible to the DETI, and undertakes the functions of promotion, administration, registration, research and marketing. In addition, local authorities have certain responsibilities for leisure and tourism, which include the attraction of tourists to their areas, the provision of tourism advisory and information services, and the upkeep of amenities and services for visitors (Deegan and Dineen, 1997).

In the Republic of Ireland, Fáilte Ireland is the main agency responsible for the promotion and development of tourism. Fáilte Ireland was formed in May 2003 with the merger of the former national tourism authority, Bord Fáilte (established under the Tourist Traffic Act 1939), and the Tourism Training Organisation (CERT). Reporting to the Department of Arts, Sport and Tourism, Fáilte Ireland has responsibility for implementing national tourism policy, direct enterprise support, and product and infrastructural development. In this role Fáilte Ireland also works in conjunction with the Regional Tourism Authorities (RTAs) which have a general operational function seeking to encourage greater local and regional effort from local authorities and the private sector in tourism development (Pearce, 1990; PriceWaterhouseCoopers, 2005). Therefore, while the RTAs aim to promote a regional tourism product, Fáilte Ireland promotes national tourism on their behalf. There are currently seven regional tourism areas, six of which are the responsibility of the RTAs. Shannon Development manages the seventh.

Cross-border co-operation in tourism
The origins of cross-border co-operation in tourism can be traced back to the meetings in 1965/66 between the then Taoiseach of the Republic of Ireland, Seán Lemass, and the Prime Minister of Northern Ireland, Terence O'Neill, which provided a whole new impetus to partnership and opened up relationships between the two Boards (Clarke and O'Cinneide, 1981). Towards the end of the 1960s, co-operative tourism initiatives began to emerge with the NITB, the British Travel Association (British Tourist Association (BTA) from 1969) and Bord Fáilte (the then national tourism authority in the Republic of Ireland) working together on marketing tours abroad to promote holiday tours and packages to Great Britain, Northern Ireland and Ireland.

However, just as this tripartite relationship began to take shape, the civil disturbances in Northern Ireland escalated and were followed by a sustained campaign of terrorist violence. The period between 1969-1971 is generally regarded as a watershed for tourism with tourism numbers falling in Northern Ireland and the Republic of Ireland (Hannigan, 1995; Bord Fáilte, 1972). In response to the conflict, the marketing and promotion of Northern Ireland was significantly curtailed (NITB, 1972), and the opportunities for co-operation became limited as a result.

It was not until the 1980s, when tourism numbers gradually began to recover (Buckley and Klemn, 1993; Hannigan, 1995), that both governments started to take a stronger interest in tourism and its potential for economic growth. Greater strategic focus to improve the sector was provided with the publication of a series of policy documents, notably, the 1989 DED policy statement *A View to the Future*, in Northern Ireland, and the 1989-1993 National Development Plan in the Republic. However, what is also important is that these initiatives were published at a time when additional funding was made available for tourism from the International Fund for Ireland (IFI)[1] and the European Union (EU). These monies provided for an extensive programme of tourism infrastructure development (Wilson, 1993; Deegan and Dineen, 1997), and acted to facilitate greater North - South co-operation. The IFI's tourism programme, for example, has been administered jointly by the NITB and BF and has injected resources to develop accommodation amenities, other tourism amenities, and marketing programmes (IFI, 1996). Similarly, the EU INTERREG Programmes (1991-1993, 1994 – 1999 and 2000-2006) and the EU programmes for peace and reconciliation[2] have awarded funding to the Boards, local authorities and RTAs to implement cross-border tourism projects (Fitzpatrick and McEniff, 1992; Coopers and Lybrand, 1997; PriceWaterhouseCoopers, 2003a; PricewaterhouseCoopers, 2003b).

Marketing the island of Ireland
During the 1990s, greater cross-border linkages within the tourist industry were established with the introduction of two major marketing programmes to promote the island of Ireland, the Overseas Tourism Marketing Initiative (OTMI) and Tourism Brand Ireland (TBI). The OTMI was set up in 1993 by the tourism industry to launch a marketing campaign in the USA, Britain, France and Germany (OTMI, 1997) while the TBI marketing initiative was developed by the two Boards in November 1996 to promote the island of Ireland as a single tourism destination.

Tourism Ireland
In December 2000, co-operation was given further expression with the launch of Tourism Ireland. Tourism Ireland is a publicly-owned limited company which was established by Bord Fáilte and NITB in December 2000, in response to the requirement contained in the 'Good Friday' Agreement (1998) that co-operation be pursued in the field of tourism. The company operates under the policy direction of the North South Ministerial Council and service level agreements to both Fáilte Ireland and the NITB. Tourism Ireland has the primary remit of planning and delivering international 'above the line' tourism marketing programmes in partnership with tourism industry representatives in the Republic of Ireland and Northern Ireland. More specifically, the tourism company provides the following services:

- planning and delivering an international tourism marketing programme, including programmes in partnership with the industry North and South. In this role the new company would subsume the existing OTMI and TBI programmes;
- market research, provision of information and other appropriate assistance to help this industry develop international marketing expertise; and
- co-operation with, consulting, and assisting other bodies or associations in carrying out such activities (Trimble / Mallon, 1998).

Having considered the role of government in tourism and the emergence of cross-border co-operation, attention now focuses on analysing the evolving relationship between the NITB and Bord Fáilte / Fáilte Ireland.

Partnership between the Northern Ireland Tourist Board and Bord Fáilte / Fáilte Ireland

A contentious political environment
In the partnership between the two tourism authorities, the terrorist violence in

Northern Ireland and the political sensitivities surrounding cross-border co-operation have had a damaging influence on the relationship. During the 1980s when the NITB and Bord Fáilte engaged to develop cross-border programmes and initiatives, both Boards held feelings of distrust and suspicion. Within the NITB political sensitivities emerged in partnering a government agency from the Republic of Ireland, at a time of heightened political tension in Northern Ireland and following a prolonged period of isolationist or 'back to back' development. In these initial stages the NITB was suspicious of cross-border co-operation and wary of the possible political ramifications that may follow.

By contrast, the underlying concerns of Bord Fáilte did not rest with the political sensitivities surrounding cross-border co-operation. At first, Bord Fáilte was reluctant to enter into co-operation because by partnering with Northern Ireland, the tourist product in the South could become tainted by association with terrorist violence. In the 1970s, as the increasing civil disturbances in Northern Ireland made a significant contribution to the decline in tourism numbers within the Republic of Ireland, Bord Fáilte gradually began to distance itself from the events in the North. It then became difficult for Bord Fáilte in the 1980s and early 1990s to engage in co-operation with the NITB when terrorist violence was still ongoing. Therefore, as both Boards mainly focused on their own priorities cross-border co-operation received minimal attention, even neglect. Steps towards co-operation were initiated but in reality considerable distance remained between the Boards, particularly in relation to marketing and promotion.

However, from a position of mutual distrust the two tourist boards have maintained and developed a partnership. Co-operation has been extended to include the Tourism Brand Ireland (TBI) marketing programme involving joint stands to promote the island of Ireland. One of the most important events which has changed the nature of the relationship between the tourist boards has undoubtedly been the paramilitary cease-fires and the development of the peace process. The peace process has helped transform the partnership by creating a more stable political environment which is supportive of cross-border co-operation. Secondly, with sustained peace a greater opportunity now exists to develop and promote tourism in Northern Ireland without the hindrance of civil disturbances comparable to the 1970s and 1980s. Therefore, with the advent of the cease-fires and the peace process, a major obstacle to partnership development has been removed allowing co-operation to be more open and transparent.

A dominant partner

Although the peace process has created a more supportive environment, imbalance between the two Boards has also heightened the sensitivities of the

NITB over cross-border co-operation. During the last twenty years the Republic of Ireland has been attracting a larger number of tourists and receiving a greater amount of overseas tourism expenditure than Northern Ireland. In 2004 tourism visits to the Republic of Ireland reached 6.4 million with tourist expenditure worth €3.4 billion[3]. By contrast, despite significant growth in recent years, tourism in Northern Ireland is a more minor part of the economy with tourism visitors numbering 2 million in 2004 and spend totalling £406 million (NITB, 2005).

Therefore as Fáilte Ireland in the Republic of Ireland promotes a much larger industry than the NITB in Northern Ireland, Fáilte Ireland in theory can be regarded as a stronger partner. This imbalance has impacted on the relationship between the Tourist Boards as some members of the NITB at times feel that they are being overshadowed by Fáilte Ireland, the larger, more dominant partner. However, as one means of dealing with this sensitivity, the NITB has been afforded favourable exposure in joint marketing programmes when compared to funding contributions. By receiving a disproportionate level of publicity in programmes such as TBI and OTMI, this has helped to allay fears of the NITB that the identity of Northern Ireland tourism may be compromised and diluted in an all-Ireland marketing campaign.

Co-operative competition – a contradiction in terms?
Although the Tourist Boards aim to work together in partnership, the NITB and Fáilte Ireland have found it difficult to co-operate while they still see each other as competitors. In certain areas of co-operation such as marketing, competitive tensions have accentuated the feelings of suspicion and distrust and inhibited the development of partnership. Operating through Tourism Ireland, the Tourist Boards have worked well together when promoting Ireland in the global markets in America, Australia or mainland Europe. As such, both boards have been able to market the tourism products and attractions throughout the island of Ireland, maximise tourism potential and reduce duplication. However, in the home market, tensions have come to the fore between individuals who wish to promote either Northern Ireland or the Republic of Ireland and who essentially see the Tourist Boards to be in competition. This has caused friction and placed strains on the partnership, making it difficult for the Boards to present a united front.

The role of government
Given the sensitivities and tensions in cross-border co-operation, both Boards have needed government to take a strong and proactive role in directing the partnership. However, before the 'Good Friday' Agreement, this role from government was generally not forthcoming. Broad policy was formulated in both jurisdictions covering aspects of co-operation but no firm or clear

direction to work in partnership was delegated to the Boards. Therefore, in the initial stages of co-operation, both Boards enjoyed a great deal of flexibility. In practice this meant the NITB and Bord Fáilte prioritised their own interests giving minimal attention to cross-border arrangements. Under loose direction from government the Boards tended to view each other with suspicion and distrust, particularly in relation to marketing. At this stage, the relationship was almost maintained on an artificial basis as the partnership was centred on implementing cross-border programmes which provided external funding for co-operation.

With the advent of the peace process and creation of the 'Good Friday' Agreement, both governments have now taken a more proactive role in facilitating greater co-operation and providing focus and direction for the tourism authorities. Cross-border co-operation is now seen as part of a wider government strategy in Britain and Ireland to support the peace process and a political settlement. Political will, clear government policy and the establishment of Tourism Ireland have helped to facilitate greater co-operation and give strong unambiguous direction to the boards. Under this situation any overriding concerns about co-operation have been set aside as partnership is now a priority government policy. There is clear government commitment to co-operation and this has filtered down to the Tourist Boards and individuals within the organisations. Indeed, despite the stalled political process and the suspension of the Northern Ireland Assembly, Tourism Ireland is one of the key organisations established under the 'Good Friday' Agreement which has continued to function and develop.

The partnership process

In the initial stages of the relationship, both the NITB and Bord Fáilte found it difficult to develop an open and effective partnership process from operating against a backdrop of tension and distrust. Decision making was conducted in committees composed of members of the Board and senior executives from both organisations who met only three or four times a year. This established an artificial process as suspicions between the Boards permeated down to individuals. At the committee level decision making between members of Bord Fáilte and the NITB was conducted on a formal and structured basis, with meetings being very focused and both Boards strictly adhering to a clear agenda. In this approach decision making became static, leaving little opportunity to exchange information and share experience.

Furthermore, in the decision making structures much consideration was given to establishing parity between the Boards. This ensured that an equal number of representatives from the North engaged with those from the South, particularly at the local project level which involved members from district councils, RTA's, local tourism interests, and representatives of Bord Fáilte and the NITB who administer the EU and IFI programmes. Although this has contributed to alleviating tensions within Northern Ireland about being overshadowed by a dominant partner, equal representation has been strictly applied in too many circumstances. In these instances parity hindered the partnership decision making process as it emphasised rigidity and formality, did not allow partners to engage on a personal, informal and open basis, and placed too much attention on establishing parallel relationships.

Within the last number of years, however, the decision making process has been re-invigorated and there is now an opportunity for members from each of the Boards to meaningfully engage. With the creation of Tourism Ireland and all-island marketing programmes, more urgency has been applied to the partnership and this has transferred to the decision making process. The structured, formal process has been sidelined for a more open, informal negotiation which is conducted at all levels between the tourism authorities, not just at committee level. Now the issue in decision making is to find a solution, not to protect priorities, which has given both partners greater opportunity to develop synergy.

In a similar vein, the partnership process at the local project level has been undergoing transition. Decision making is now less structured and ordered and is conducted within a more informal process allowing the partners to open up and talk about problematic issues. Working on a greater number of projects over a period of time with limited staff, has helped to build working relationships and lay the necessary foundations to set up an open and fluid decision making process. Building good relations has been difficult and has taken a long time; however, this provided a necessary incubation period to allow individuals to get to know one another, build relationships, develop dialogue and gain acceptance of different attitudes and experiences.

Strategic development

Before the implementation of the 'Good Friday' Agreement, the partnership between the NITB and Bord Fáilte had been based on an informal, co-operative arrangement meaning no overall strategy existed. This often created confusion over the roles and organisational responsibilities of both boards and led to a loose *ad hoc* approach to marketing and tourism development. As a result, the Boards experienced difficulties developing tourism in the Irish border region. Both the NITB and Bord Fáilte excluded cross-border programmes from their principal strategies and they have generally been regarded as an 'add on'. Projects have been developed in relation to the different funding programmes but not based on the needs of tourism development. Projects have been implemented which are vulnerable and unsustainable, leading to the criticism that the Boards are simply co-operating as a means to attract external funding from the EU and IFI. This problem is exacerbated by the point that the success of projects is often determined by the nature of the relationships between representatives from Northern Ireland and the Republic of Ireland rather than through specific commercial criteria. In the absence of a strategic approach, concerns have also been voiced by tourism interests in the Republic of Ireland who feel that the joint marketing programme encourages tourists to travel into Northern Ireland. Tourist interests largely based in the extreme south are anxious about co-operating in all-Ireland marketing initiatives as they feel this may upset the traditional pattern of tourists who travel between Dublin and Galway and visit the south west and east. In addition, concerns have been raised over the issue of sustainability, as co-operating together to attract more tourists to Ireland may lead to the problems of mass tourism which could have a detrimental effect on the tourist product.

With the creation of Tourism Ireland and a common marketing strategy, however, more direction has now been provided to the partnership as the NITB and Fáilte Ireland have a clear understanding of their roles and functions in the relationship and of the specific areas for co-operation and future development. In addition, the management of Tourism Ireland and the formulation of a common marketing strategy have provided a focus, helping the tourist authorities to interact and contributing to the overall gelling process.

However, while Tourism Ireland has helped to clarify roles between the NITB and Fáilte Ireland, organisational implications of the partnership still remain to be resolved at the regional level. Although Tourism Ireland is responsible for product marketing, the RTAs in the Republic of Ireland are involved in a range of consumer, trade and product marketing activities aimed at the domestic and international markets. This has created a proliferation of marketing activities, fragmentation of effort and lack of integration of national and regional efforts (PriceWaterhouseCoopers, 2005).

Developing Cross-border Tourism Partnerships
With a view to examining the future of cross-border co-operation in tourism on the island of Ireland, a number of lessons can be identified for developing trans-jurisdictional tourism partnerships. Moreover, by reflecting on the experience of NITB and Bord Fáilte / Fáilte Ireland, important insights are also provided into key preconditions and concepts central to building partnership across different local and regional administrative boundaries.

An integrated and sustainable development strategy
First, it is important that a common marketing plan is coupled with an integrated tourism development strategy. In the relationship between NITB and Bord Fáilte in previous years, too much consideration was often devoted

to building the concept of partnership and developing relationships between stakeholders. Political as opposed to economic criteria determined the success of partnership, creating unsustainable projects and hindering product output. However, now that the partnership process has developed interpersonal relations, development needs to be co-ordinated with other mainstream economic, social and environmental objectives within an overarching integrated strategy to ensure that projects and programmes are implemented on the basis of tourism needs and sustainability. While marketing the island of Ireland and seeking to maximise tourism potential through Tourism Ireland, it is important that the NITB and Fáilte Ireland also work together and give consideration to environmental monitoring and management. Both authorities need to examine the carrying capacities of tourist areas in a process that embraces the physical capacity of a destination, but also the levels of use at which the ecology is protected, the visitor experience is undiminished and the resident community is not overwhelmed. Overall, this approach would highlight areas where infrastructure or environmental issues would pose an obstacle to development of tourism and proactively address any infrastructure gaps which exist or may emerge. To this end, the function of co-operation must be extended beyond purely marketing to provide overarching strategic direction and linkage with broader product and local or regional development.

A participative planning process

Secondly, in seeking to formulate a common sustainable strategy, it is important to initiate a participative planning process to establish commitment among all tourism stakeholders. To date, the role of the private sector in cross-border co-operation in Ireland has been limited and concerns have been expressed by tourism interests in the very south of the Republic of Ireland who feel an all-island marketing strategy may direct tourists towards Northern Ireland. If members of the tourist industry feel that their interests are not being promoted they may frustrate the development of the new strategy as they are not committed towards its implementation.

In learning from this experience, there is a need for government departments and Tourist Boards to facilitate an inclusive planning process to broaden participation and create widespread ownership of strategic development across the public, private and voluntary / community sectors. This will also raise awareness of local tourism issues, and provide a forum for building consensus and transferring knowledge between different sectoral interests and ensure that tourism promotion will be driven by the needs of the industry.

Furthermore, a participative approach will establish vertical partnership arrangements and allow local and regional tourism interests greater input into wider strategic development. This will ensure greater integration of tourism development, particularly in relation to marketing activities at the regional level, and more balanced regional tourism growth across the island of Ireland. In addition, linkage between the national, regional and local levels can develop greater innovation capability and enable the tourism sector to react swiftly to changing consumer trends. In regard to identifying the carrying capacities of tourist areas, a participative approach will also provide the opportunity to establish local planning processes. This would allow local communities, the tourism industry, local authorities and other tourism interests to come together to agree peak season carrying capacities and then put in place local development strategies which are in harmony with these targets.

Understanding political sensitivities
Thirdly, tourism stakeholders need to be constantly aware of the historical and political environment in which the partnership operates. The experience of the relationship between NITB and Fáilte Ireland / BF has demonstrated that stakeholders need to recognise and deal with diversity and difference among partnership actors. Certainly, granting the NITB disproportional influence in joint marketing programmes has facilitated an inclusive approach, but stakeholders must also be sensitive to the political environment to avoid raising tensions. For example, despite the peace process the emotive political environment in Northern Ireland still has the potential to hinder partnership development. In the relationship with Fáilte Ireland, the NITB have been placed in a difficult position as the organisation aims to equally reconcile the interests of the Nationalist and Unionist communities and not upset political sensitivities. In particular, the NITB is mindful that a significant section of the Unionist population are cautious about the development of deeper links with the Republic of Ireland. In a similar vein, it is important that Fáilte Ireland and the Irish Government understand the political tensions surrounding cross-border co-operation and adopt a sensitive approach to partnership with the NITB.

Partnership balance and learning processes
Finally, where there is an unequal distribution of power between the stakeholders, it is important to achieve a degree of balance in partnership arrangements. In the relationship between the NITB and Fáilte Ireland, favourable marketing exposure in the all-island campaign helped to allay the fears of the NITB that the identity of Northern Ireland may be compromised. This demonstrates that during the difficult initial stages in particular, disproportional influence can weaken the fears and sensitivities of the smaller partner, build trust and facilitate joint learning between the partners.

However, in the developing relationship between the stakeholders, the concept of partnership balance may need to be reviewed. Over time, as the partners establish synergistic relationships and develop a partnership process, equal weight must be given to funding contributions and influence as the smaller partner becomes more stable and assertive within the arrangement. In future years this will be important in cross-border tourism development as the NITB maximises the Tourism Ireland resource and commitment and develops the potential in Northern Ireland to achieve "catch-up". Learning transfer in the partnership, however, will not be confined to a one way process. Indeed, as concerns have been raised over the increasing uncompetitive nature of the tourism product in the Republic of Ireland, benchmarking with the tourism industry in Northern Ireland will become an important feature of future partnership.

Conclusion

The relationship between the NITB and Fáilte Ireland / BF has demonstrated that developing trans-jurisdictional tourism partnerships is a complex and difficult task. However, from this experience a number of important lessons can be identified which can further partnership development across national, regional or local administrative boundaries. It has been highlighted that co-operation can be maintained by formulating an inclusive and integrated tourism strategy, developing a participative partnership approach, understanding political sensitivities and establishing partnership balance and learning processes.

Endnotes

1   The International Fund for Ireland (IFI) was established by the British and Irish Governments and backed by donations from the EU, the governments of the USA, Canada, Australia and New Zealand. Since its inception in 1986 the IFI has funded projects across a wide spectrum of social and economic activity including community led economic regeneration in deprived urban and rural areas, and the encouragement of all-Ireland business initiatives and local enterprise parks.

2   The EU Special Support Programme for Peace and Reconciliation Programme 1995-1999 (Peace I) and the EU Programme for Peace and Reconciliation in Northern Ireland and the Border Region of Ireland 2000-2006 (Peace II).

3   CSO, Central Statistics Office.

References

Bord Fáilte (1972) *Bord Fáilte Eireann - Irish Tourist Board: Report and Accounts for year ended March 31st 1972.*

Bord Fáilte (1999) *Tourism Facts.*

Bord Fáilte (2000) *Tourism Development Strategy, 2000-2006.*

Boyle, R. (1989) Partnership in practice, *Local Government Studies*, 15(2), pp.17-27.

Bramwell, B. and Sharman, A. (1999) Collaboration in local tourism policy making, *Annals of Tourism Research,* 26(2), pp.392-415.

Bryson, J.M. and Crosby, B. (1992) *Leadership for the common good*, San Francisco, Jossey-Bass.

Buckely, P.J. and Klemm, M. (1993) The decline of tourism in Northern Ireland: the causes, *Tourism Management*, 14(3), pp.184-195.

Campbell, H. (2000) Success story knows no bounds, *Belfast Telegraph Business*, 26th September.

Clarke, W. and O'Cinneide, B. (1981) *Understanding and co-operation in Ireland: tourism in the Republic of Ireland and Northern Ireland*, Paper 5, Co-operation North, Belfast and Dublin.

Coopers and Lybrand (1997) *Special Support Programme for Peace and Reconciliation and the Border Counties of Ireland 1995-1999, Mid Term Evaluation Final Report.*

Darwin, J. (1999) Partnership and power, in L. Montanheiro, B. Haigh, D. Morris, and M. Linehan (eds.) *Public and private sector partnerships: furthering development*, Sheffield, Sheffield Hallam University Press.

Deegan, J. and Dineen, D.A. (1997) *Tourism policy and performance – the Irish experience*, London, International Thompson Business Press.

Fitzpatrick, J. and McEniff, J. (1992) Tourism, in *Ireland in Europe: a shared challenge – economic co-operation on the island of Ireland in an integrated Europe*, Dublin, Stationery Office.

Forester, J. (1993) *Critical theory, public policy and planning practice*, Albany, State University of New York Press.

Godfrey, K. B. (1998) Attitudes towards 'sustainable tourism' in the UK: a view from local government, *Tourism Management*, 19(3), pp.213-224.

Goymen, K. (2000) Tourism and governance in Turkey, *Annals of Tourism Research*, 27(4), pp.1025-1048.

Gray, A. (1995) The economic consequences of peace in Ireland, *Accountancy Ireland*, 27(5), pp.23-34.

Gray, B. (1989) *Collaborating. Finding common ground for multiparty problems*, San Francisco, Jossey-Bass.

Greer, J. (2001) *Partnership governance in Northern Ireland: improving performance*, Aldershot, Ashgate Press.

Hannigan, K. (1995) Tourism policy and regional development in Ireland: an evaluation, Paper presented to *Regional Studies Association Conference*, Maynooth, Co. Kildare. 14th September, 1995.

Healey, P. (1996) Consensus-building across difficult divisions: new approaches to collaborative strategy making, *Planning Practice and Research*, 11(2), pp.207-216.

Hutchinson, J. (1994) The practice of partnership in local economic development, *Local Government Studies*, 20(3), pp.335-334.

Huxham, C. (1991) Facilitating collaboration: issues in multi-organisational group decision support in voluntary, informal collaborative settings, *Journal of Operational Research Society*, 42(12), pp.1037-1045.

Huxham, C. and Vangen, S. (1996) Working together: key themes in the management of relationships between public and non-profit organisations, *The International Journal of Public Sector Management*, 9(7), pp.5-18.

International Fund for Ireland (1996) *Annual Report 1996*, Belfast and Dublin, International Fund for Ireland.

Joppe, M. (1996) Sustainable community tourism development revisited, *Tourism Management*, 17(7), pp.475-479.

Leslie, D. (1995) Northern Ireland, tourism and peace, *Tourism Management*, 17(19), pp.51-69.

Loughlin, J. (2000) The cross-border challenges and opportunities posed by the transformation of European governance, paper presented to the International Conference, *European Cross-Border Co-operation: Lessons for and From Ireland*, Queen's University Belfast. 29th September – 1st October, 2000.

Mattessich, P and Monsey, B. (1992) *Collaboration: what makes it work*, Amherest, H. Wilder H. Foundation, St. Paul, Minnesota.

Murray, M. and Greer, J. (1993) Rural development in Northern Ireland, in M. Murray and J. Greer (eds.) *Rural development in Ireland*, Aldershot, Avebury Press.

NITB (1972) *25th Annual Report 1972*, Belfast, Northern Ireland Tourist Board.

NITB (1998a) *Corporate Plan 1998-2001,* Belfast, Northern Ireland Tourist Board.

NITB (1998b) Special edition tourism strategy, *Tourist*, 4(1), Northern Ireland Tourist Board.

NITB (2004) *A strategy framework for action 2004-2007*, Belfast, Northern Ireland Tourist Board.

NITB (2005) *Draft corporate plan, 2005-2008, consultation document*, Belfast, Northern Ireland Tourist Board..

Overseas Tourism Marketing Initiative (1997) *OTMI review of the year 1997.*

Pearce, D.G. (1990) Tourism in Ireland - questions of scale and organisations, *Tourism Management*, 11(2), pp.133-153.

PriceWaterhouseCoopers, (2003a) *Ex-post Evaluation of Peace 1 and Mid-term Evaluation of Peace II,* Final Report, November 2003, Special European Union Programmes Body.

PriceWaterhouseCoopers (2003b) *Mid-term Evaluation of the Ireland INTRREG Programme, Ireland North / South*, Final Report, August 2003, Special European Union Programmes Body.

PriceWaterhouseCoopers (2005) *Review of Regional Tourism Structures in Ireland,* April 2005.

Prior, D. (1996) Working the network: local authority strategies in the reticulated local state, *Local Government Studies*, 22(2), 92-103.

Selin, S. and Chavez, D. (1995) Developing an evolutionary tourism model, *Annals of Tourism Research*, 22(4), pp.844-856.

Tansey, P. (1995) Tourism a product with a big potential, in M. D'Arcy and T. Dickson (eds.) *Border crossings developing Ireland's island economy*, Dublin, Gill and Macmillian.

Tosun, C. (2000) Limits to community participation in the tourism development process in developing countries, *Tourism Management*, 21(6), pp.613-633.

Trimble / Mallon Statement (1998) 'Trimble - Mallon statement on what was agreed', *Irish Times*, 19th December.

Walsh, J. A. (1997/98) Best practice in local development - the Ballyhoura model, *Pleanáil*, 14, pp.129-153.

Wilson, A. and Charlton, K. (1997) *Making partnerships work: a practical guide for the public, private, voluntary and community sectors,* York, The Joseph Rowntree Foundation, York Publishing Services Limited.

Wilson, D. (1993) Tourism, public policy and the image of the Northern Ireland since the troubles, in B. O'Connor and M. Cronin (eds.) *Tourism in Ireland: a critical analysis*, Cork, Cork University Press.

Chapter 20

The Rural-Urban Interface: Outskirts of European Cities

Malachy McEldowney

Introduction – Rural Idyll and Urban Hegemony

> While Northern Ireland is synonymous with particular societal divisions, its experience of a long-standing rural-urban dialectic is shared in common with other parts of Europe and North America. (Greer and Murray, 2003, p.3)

Greer and Murray, above, highlight the rural–urban dialectic as a significant issue in Northern Ireland. They also refer to its longevity and its ubiquity, at least within the European and North American contexts. This chapter is a contribution to that debate within the Western Europe context in general and the United Kingdom (UK) policy context in particular. It reports on the findings of a European working group on *Urban Outskirts* (Dubois-Taine, 2004) that investigated aspects of the interface between town and country in a number of European city-regions. This European experience is interesting in that it provides an antidote to the more familiar UK – and English, in particular – sentiment in relation to town and country. The early British planning system was pre-occupied with controlling urban growth because, amongst other more practical reasons, "the countryside was regarded as a bucolic backdrop to life in urban areas" (Newby, 1980). This is a nostalgic and idealised conception of the rural from an urban perspective, poetically captured by McEwan (1999):

> for city dwellers the countryside is a repository of longing and illusion; it is a place of nourishment, innocence and ancient wisdom; it is the garden from which we have been expelled'. (in, Barnett and Scruton,1999, p.vii)

A version of this attitude has transferred to official policy in Northern Ireland, where, in similar fashion, it underpinned early planning perspectives. Greer and Murray point to the 'hegemony of the urban' in this dialectic and the fact that the countryside is seen as 'residual' or, in the infamous words of official policy designation, 'the rural remainder'.

The 'urban hegemony' charge can also be applied to the broader research project that informs this chapter. Most of the contributors to the working party investigations are urban planners, architects and engineers and their perspectives are essentially urban, as the title 'urban outskirts' implies. Nevertheless, the range of case studies undertaken, from highly urbanised examples like the Paris region to the more dominant rural contexts of the Basque Country and the outskirts of Nicosia, provide comprehensive coverage of most spatial contexts, albeit from a generally urban orientation. They also provide a set of European perspectives, influenced by Scandinavian, Napoleonic and Germanic legislative codes and social attitudes (Newman and Thornley 1998), which contrast interestingly with the UK and Irish contexts.

The 'Outskirts' Concept

In the UK system there is no specific definition of 'urban outskirts' although the term 'urban fringe' is commonly used to describe the area beyond the built-up city that is subject to constant pressure for development, mainly housing. It is a version of the 'rurban fringe', a term first adopted by Coleman (1977) as a derogatory description of the ill-defined, mixed-use, low-density development at the urban edge which was a symptom of urban decentralisation and, in her eyes, the failure of the land-use planning system to protect agricultural land from creeping urbanisation. Subsequent geographical analyses (Best, 1981) showed these fears to be exaggerated, as urban sprawl declined with rapidly-falling population levels in the 1970s. More particularly, Best demonstrated the effectiveness of green belts in protecting agricultural land with the loss of farmland in the 1970s and 1980s declining to 30 per cent of its pre-war level as emerging structure plans strengthened and formalised green belt policy. The relationship between urban outskirts and green belt policy is, therefore, totally intertwined in the British experience, as it is to a slightly lesser degree in Northern Ireland.

Broader European conceptions of outskirts are uncomplicated by green belt policy intrusion for the most part, although various versions of the green wedge approach are evident, especially in Scandinavia. Ruegg (2004) traces the evolution of the rural-urban dichotomy into a rural-urban continuum as urban sprawl crossed administrative boundaries. For planning purposes, new descriptions of evolving city regions have become necessary: the 'stadtregion' in Austria, the 'verdichtungsraum' in Germany, the 'agglomeration' in France and Switzerland. Specifically in relation to the urban fringe, Sieverts (1997) has coined the term 'zwischenstadt' (in-between-towns) and Baccini and Oswald (1998) the term 'netzstadt' (network or patchwork town). Priebs (2001) has accepted the North American concept of 'post suburbia', while the

Swiss authors Eisinger and Schneider (2003) have introduced the term 'stadtland' (urbanscape) and Borsdorf (2004) the 'urban archipelago'. In France the terms 'ville emergeant' (emerging town) and 'campagne urbaine' (urban countryside) are both applied.

Language is important, and subtle differences of meaning and emphasis are incorporated within these terms. For that reason the slightly vague but all-encompassing term 'outskirts' was used to initiate the transnational investigations. A working definition of the concept was simply the twentieth-century accretions to the urban built-up area, incorporating pre- and inter-war suburbs as well as mid-century outlier settlements and late-century commercial/industrial edge cities. A common theme in all these areas is a pressurised version of the 'rural –urban dialectic' identified at the beginning of this chapter. In order to attempt to understand what is happening in these places, the research project focused on the 'structures' (social, economic, political, physical) that underpin them, on the 'dynamics' (demographic, accessibility-based, lifestyle-focused) that currently characterise them, and on the 'governance' issues (static administrative units versus dynamic network-based activities) that confront them.

This chapter reports three case studies from that project: the Basque Country outskirts of Bayonne/Biarritz in France, the prosperous Limmatal Valley east of Zurich in Switzerland, and the southern fringes of Nicosia in Cyprus. These have an urban scale and rural significance that is somewhat similar to the Belfast region and, thus, are mutually comparable. Moreover, they offer useful contrasts with Northern Ireland, not only in relation to planning, but also in their divergent and interesting cultural and political contexts.

Bayonne/Anglet/Biarritz (BAB) and the Basque Country

The outskirts issues in this area relate to three interlocking sets of spatial relationships: those between the three towns of Bayonne, Anglet and Biarritz, those between the declining rural hinterland and the burgeoning coastal strip, and those between the French and Spanish components of the Basque linear metropolis which extends from Bayonne to San Sebastian, with a total population of approximately 600,000 (Figure 20.1). The parallels with the Northern Ireland situation (McEldowney, 2004) are interesting. The Belfast Metropolitan Area with its competing local municipalities, the urban-rural dialectic within the Regional Development Strategy context, and the cross-border Dublin-Belfast linear city concept represent comparable spatial planning challenges, albeit at different scales and within different contexts.

Figure 20.1: BAB context map

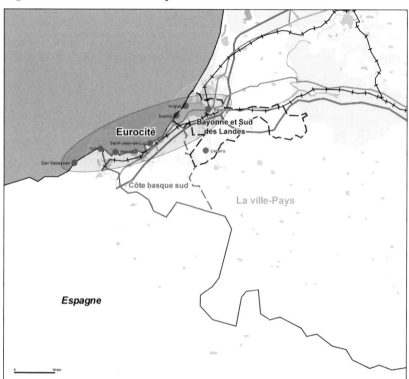

With regard to the three towns, the issue is one of the 'outskirts becoming the centre' in a laissez-faire planning policy context. Bayonne and Biarritz are both distinctive and well-established urban centres. Bayonne is a historic 'secteur sauvegarde' with a strong retail, administrative and tourist economy. Biarritz is a prosperous Napoleonic watering-hole for the rich and famous, whose tourist economy has diversified and recovered from recent relative decline. Anglet, however, is a relatively nondescript suburb for both of these towns which has drawn strength from the success of its American-style commercial 'strip' and the complementary development of out-of town office, light industrial and recreational facilities to the extent that it now claims to be the new 'centre' for the BAB urban area. This is acknowledged in political terms by the voluntary establishment of a 'super commune' incorporating the three existing official communes and the location of some central administrative functions in Anglet. This may be a source of wounded pride for the two established towns, but it represents less of an economic diversion than would be the case in, say, the Belfast-Sprucefield example, due to the strengths of their tourist economies.

In relation to the urban-rural debate, the problem is one of inland rural depopulation in the face of the growing popularity of the coastal areas, which in turn leads to local congestion and environmental pollution along the narrow coastal corridor which carries the intensively-used road and rail infrastructure linking France and Spain. There is a cultural/political dimension to this dynamic also, in that it represents a loss to the Basque language-speaking heartland and its cultural traditions, particularly of younger members of its population. Ironically, and in contrast to the suburbanisation of the Northern Ireland countryside, this helps protect the character of traditional Basque settlements, which also display a nucleated spatial pattern and a strong aesthetic code (white-rendered walls and red-tiled roofs) that is generally respected in new development.

As for the cross-border linear city, the unifying factors are relative proximity (San Sebastian is less than 50 kms from Bayonne), the shared Basque culture (San Sebastian recently hosted Biarritz's European Cup rugby quarter-final in its larger stadium), and the existence of a functional multi-modal transportation corridor that links major European cities such as Paris and Madrid. However, there are distinct differences in political, economic and physical terms. Expressions of Basque cultural nationalism are less dominant on the French side, and its economic base is service-oriented accounting for 70 per cent of total employment. The San Sebastian area is part of industrialised northern Spain. Physically the French side has a low-density, dispersed settlement pattern, while the Spanish side retains much high-rise, densely populated apartment development alongside its traditional industrial complexes.

Nevertheless, along the Basque coastal corridor strategic spatial planning is more advanced than it is currently for the Dublin-Belfast corridor, with liaison between municipalities and regional authorities having already produced a series of strategic spatial planning options. These contain measures for the promotion of second-tier 'key settlements' to address rural decline on both sides of the border, physical prescriptions to lessen the severance problems caused by the transport infrastructure and a range of spatial development options for the economically buoyant settlements along the coast.

Zurich and the Limmat Valley (Limmatal)

The 'outskirts' issues in this prosperous part of Switzerland are noteworthy in that they are perceived positively rather than negatively. Here the rural-urban dialectic has possibly reached some level of synthesis or resolution. A combination of topographical determination, bottom-up governance and a benign and diversified economic climate provides for a situation in which the admixture of rural and urban elements can be presented as 'interesting' and 'surprising' rather than problematic (Schumacher *et al*, 2004). This provides an obvious contrast to prevailing official attitudes in Northern Ireland and, perhaps, offers some support to advocates of a 'living and working countryside' as opposed to those of rural protectionism.

The Zurich metropolitan area is the economic fulcrum of Switzerland. Its y-shaped physical form (similar to that of Belfast) is dictated eastwards by development along both sides of the Zurich lake and westwards along the Limmat river valley in a 25-kilometre corridor to the smaller city of Baden. It can be regarded as a dynamic and diverse multi-functional corridor, providing intensive public and private transport infrastructure, numerous service and shopping centres, large and small-scale industrial complexes, and a wide range of residential choices including high-rise apartments, single-family homes and rural village cottages (Photograph 20.1 and Photograph 20.2). It has also been described, by its local inhabitants, as 'a gastro-intestinal tract for the greedy city of Zurich', a reflection of functional value, perhaps, but also of some perceived exploitation.

Photograph 20.1: Good quality high rise residential development in the Limmatal Valley

Photograph 20.2: Shopping centre development in the Limmatal Valley

The expansion of development up the Limmatal is largely a twentieth-century phenomenon, although the opening of the railway in 1847 provided the initial impetus, with the Baden hydroelectric power plant in 1909 and the Wettingen electricity works in 1930 establishing key infrastructural foundations. From the 1950s the small settlements south of the river began to merge into an industrial/service residential strip, while on the northern slopes (the sunny side of the valley) high quality residential development for the middle-classes began to augment traditional village settlements. Here the positive qualities of Limmatal's diverse character are most obvious: organic earth-houses cheek by jowl with traditional farm dwellings and medium-rise luxury apartments, all located alongside agricultural smallholdings, pocket vineyards and public recreational facilities (art and industrial heritage trails), beneath the protected woodland (the 'holy forest') at the top of the valley slope.

The reason for this diversity lies in the governance of the river valley. Its administrative structure is a patchwork of small municipalities, within two of Switzerland's twenty-six cantons – Canton Aargau to the west and Canton Zurich to the east. Bottom-up governance is highly valued in Switzerland and the municipalities have relatively powerful legal land-zoning responsibilities within the canton's coordinating master-plan. Both levels have considerable autonomy from federal authority, so inter-municipal and inter-cantonal competition is a feature of Swiss life. Differential local tax regimes are used to attract certain types of commercial activity, or wealthy resident, to particular areas. In the Limmatal, for example, Canton Aargau has laxer laws than Canton Zurich in relation to 'concubinage' (unmarried couples living together) that has caused an influx of younger residents to burgeoning border settlements like Spreitenbach. It also has a more favourable tax regime for large-scale commercial developments which encouraged the development of Shoppi, Switzerland's first out-of-town shopping mall, close enough to Zurich to benefit from its catchment population, but outside its cantonal control and higher property-taxes.

While there is interest and vitality in the situation outlined above, there are also, inevitably, problems relating to inequitable taxation on the one hand and unsustainable development patterns on the other. There is, generally, a poor match between static governmental designations and dynamic economic activities. The Swiss federal government has recognised this by permitting the concept of 'agglomeration' between municipalities on a voluntary basis (Rueegg, 2004). This creates, in effect, larger governmental units to provide more strategic regulation. It has also, interestingly, introduced the concept of 'siedlungstrennguertels' (settlement separation belts) to control urban sprawl. These are analogous to the recently introduced 'urban landscape wedges' in the Belfast Metropolitan Area Plan in that they promote higher densities within defined urban boundaries and protect the individual character of established settlements.

Municipal zoning and construction regulations are under local democratic control and promote a higher architectural design ethic than is evident in Northern Ireland. Seventy per cent of Swiss people live in urbanised areas but most still consider themselves part of rural village communities, a reflection of the strength of rural tradition and the accountability of local governance. In general, the Swiss are more at ease with the unrestricted interplay of urban and rural environments than the British. The mountain and valley topography (in which natural landscape is generally visible, if not proximate) provides a rural patina to a suburban lifestyle and the tourism-based service economy relies on a positive alliance of urban and rural attractions.

Nicosia and Central Cyprus

The Nicosia situation is in many ways the most obvious comparison with Belfast and its outskirts. The 'divided city' at the heart of a clearly-defined rural region, with a 1970s British model of governance under a contemporary challenge from changing cultural attitudes and a top-down centralised planning system necessitated by years of political instability is a description that could apply to both city regions. There are obvious differences in the strength and dominance of the Cypriot tourist economy, and the intractable nature of its political division. But in terms of scale, stage of development, aspects of governance and location on the periphery of the European Union, both territories share common problems, particularly in relation to planning at the urban fringe.

Nicosia is a relatively small city in European terms (approximately 230,000 people in an island population of 800,000) whose natural expansion has been distorted by the annexation of its northern section by the Turkish invasion of 1974. Inevitably, most post-war expansion has been southward comprising mainly private, low-density suburbs along private-transport corridors (public transport in Cyprus is seriously under-developed), with publicly-funded refugee housing complexes on the periphery for some 40,000 refugees from the Turkish-occupied north of the island. An extensive buffer-zone (the Green Line) separates the Greek and Turkish areas north of the city centre (Photograph 20.3). This comprises some 18,000 vacant properties and a wide swathe of cleared and sterilised landscape. Nicosia presents an unusual type of 'outskirt', one that symbolises current divisions, but may present environmental opportunities in the future.

Photograph 20.3: Derelict streetscape in the buffer-zone, Nicosia

An aspiration of a better future is the basis of the Nicosia Master Plan which is a unique bi-communal development plan, drafted under the auspices of the United Nations Development Programme, for the combined Turkish and Greek controlled urban area. This has no legal status, and is somewhat selective in focus. Its initial phase (1981-84) had a strategic perspective on the city as a whole, its second phase (1984-86) addressed urban sprawl and its effect on the viability of the city centre, while its current phase concentrates on the protection and promotion of the historic walled city. The changed emphasis reflects more modest ambitions and the reality of division, but the initiative is valuable in planning terms for its highly unusual cross-community perspective and endeavour, involving professionals from both the Turkish and Greek Cypriot administrations.

Conventional planning by the Greek-speaking government for its part of Cyprus follows British planning codes laid down initially in the 1960s, but not formally ratified until the early 1990s because of the invasion and its aftermath. The codes give powers to central government (the Ministry of the Interior) for the production of Local Plans and Action Area Plans for the country's four major urban areas, and of a Policy for the Countryside to cover the rest of the island. Development control is exercised on the basis of these policy documents. The comparison with the powers of the Department of the Environment for Northern Ireland is striking, although the local plans' emphasis on physical aspects such as zoning and density, and the absence of a regional strategic plan (like the Regional Development Strategy in Northern Ireland) suggests comparisons also with the pre-1970s development plan system in Britain. Public participation, even at the formal public inquiry stage, is very limited, and the private development industry exerts strong political and economic power, supported by a strong constitutional commitment to the ownership of private property (cf. the Republic of Ireland).

In consequence, the southern outskirts of Nicosia exhibit a low-density scatter of large residential units on relatively small plots (Photograph 20.4), with only basic infrastructural services and little or no public provision in terms of transport, recreation or even, at times, footpaths. The refugee housing is of good architectural quality, but of impermanent character, while even the private houses have a dynamic quality with reinforcing rods protruding upwards from concrete structures for future enlargement as the family expands. This dynamism extends to many aspects of the Cypriot way of life. The tourist-based service economy is booming, with full employment and growing work-based immigration, so the quality of residential life is high, if possibly unsustainable. Traditional rural attachment to land and family, in many ways similar to the situation in rural Ireland, means strong resistance to even modest planning restrictions, particularly as the rural landscape, unlike that in the Belfast city region, is often barren and desolate. The development of housing for the suburbanising urban population or the incoming residential tourists is frequently the most valuable use of rural land, as it now is in many parts of rural Ireland.

Photograph 20.4: Urban sprawl in Nicosia

While public attitudes are favourable to this interplay of rural and urban, the striking difference with the Swiss case discussed above, is the profligacy of land utilisation in Cyprus and the absence of public local control and provision. The planning system, in keeping with its British ethos, tries to preserve urban/rural distinctions by local plan zoning of fringe areas as 'non-urbanised land' (non-agricultural development is prohibitted except under very strict physical criteria). This is a diluted form of green belt policy, but it is increasingly undermined by compensation claims under the pro-landowner Constitution, and by the active opposition of local politicians (Demitriou, 2004). A stricter policy, involving the imposition of an 'urban growth boundary' (cf. Portland, Oregon, USA) and the refusal of water and sewerage services to development beyond it, is now under consideration, but is highly unlikely to command political support. The clash between British and Mediterranean attitudes to town and country, and to development freedom and regulation, continues.

Conclusions

This chapter has considered issues of urban expansion and rural protection that are of particular importance in relation to planning policy for the urban/rural fringe around Belfast. The case studies also reveal a diverse set of attitudes, experiences and policy responses that reflect very different physical, cultural, economic and governance contexts.

In **physical** terms, there are obvious differences between the inland plains of south west France, the barren landscapes of central Cyprus and the picturesque sub-alpine surroundings of the Limmatal in Switzerland. In the France and Cyprus case studies the outskirts land has less scenic value (and in the Cyprus case less agricultural value) than either the Swiss or Northern Ireland situations, and in practice a more laissez-faire attitude to urban sprawl pertains. However, in both Switzerland and Cyprus the architectural quality of outskirts development is higher than in the Belfast city region. In Switzerland the landscape amenity is always visible, if not proximate, and strict protection is given only to the 'holy forest' on the upper slopes of the valley. An interesting admixture of rural and urban pockets characterise the valley floor, and the architectural detail of most development, particularly the innovative residential schemes, is of high quality. Here development control has to be fine grained and sensitive, and some reconciliation between urban and rural character results from a light-touch approach to regulation. Koch (2004) describes it thus: "the settlement pattern is not a concept, it is a provocation".

It is interesting that in two of the case study areas, what might be termed macro **cultural** divisions relating to issues of language, nationality and religion are part of the policy-making context. In Cyprus there is the well-publicised divide between the Greek-speaking and the Turkish-speaking sections of the population; in the Basque Country there are the Basque and French-speaking communities, not to mention the cross-border French/Spanish complication of the issue. These case studies highlight the need for policy sensitivity and, indeed, policy acceptance and, in overall terms, they resonate with our Northern Ireland experience. Moreover, the case studies point to the importance of common micro cultural issues dealing with urban and rural attitudes to land. In rural Cyprus and the Basque country (as in rural Ireland) there is a strong cultural attachment to land ownership as an expression of family status and autonomy, and this has a massive influence on settlement patterns in the urban fringe. The fact that Cyprus (along with Ireland) may have a post-colonial attitude to an established British planning ethos accentuates the cultural dimension, something which is less apparent in the more integrated French and Swiss examples.

In **economic** terms the rural-urban dichotomy may be crudely characterised as a conflict between laissez-faire and regulated approaches to economic development and planning policy. In Ireland, for example, the recent relative success of the Dublin, as opposed to the Belfast, city region economy has been attributed, *inter alia*, to the less regulated planning regime in its urban fringe. Zurich, and to a lesser extent, Biarritz/Bayonne also exemplify healthy local economies in less restricted planning regimes, although many other economic factors are obviously at play. A consistent presence on the urban fringe in all countries, and particularly evident in Cyprus, is the property development industry, with its substantial outskirts land holdings and an influential voice in local politics. While this is also true in Northern Ireland, it may be that the regulated UK system is now out of step in its attitudes to the emerging network society and its spatial manifestation in edge cities. These are no longer a solely American phenomenon, being well established in France and other parts of Europe. Even in Britain, their advance is recognised, albeit their environmental impact is unloved. As Barker (1999) comments: "Edge cities now flourish like *leylandii* cypress whilst city centres show every sign of affliction by an urban version of Dutch Elm disease." (p.210)

In terms of **governance** the contrast is between British-influenced and French/Swiss (Napoleonic, to use Newton and Thornley's (1996) legal/administrative classification) systems, the former in Cyprus (and Northern Ireland), the latter in BAB and the Limmatal. The essential difference between these lies in the power and autonomy of the commune (local municipality) in the Napoleonic system, as compared with the top-down approach in the British tradition, where the local authority is simply the service provider for a higher tier of government. Hence, the application of urban growth boundaries in Cyprus (and green belt policies in Northern Ireland) reflects a regulatory policy tradition which, interestingly, is somewhat at odds with local cultural traditions and preferences. Such local preferences are better catered for in the French and Swiss systems (Reugg, 2004), where the commune provides a fine-grained, zone-based local control, allied to stronger local democratic accountability, but eschews large-scale regulation and, to some extent, strategic coherence.

References

Bacchini, P. and Oswald, F. (eds.) (1998) *Netzstadt: Transdisziplinare methoden zum umbau urbaner systeme,* Zurich.

Barker, P. (1999) Edge city, in Barnett, A. and Scruton, R. (eds.) *Town and country,* London, Penguin.

Best, R.H. (1981) *Land use and living space*, London, Methuen.

Borsdorf, A. (2004) On the way to post-suburbia, in Borsdorf, A. and Zembri, P. (eds.) *European cities - insights on outskirts - structures,* Paris, METL/PUCA.

Coleman, A. (1977) Land-use planning – success or failure ? *Architects Journal*, (Jan), pp.94-124.

Demetriou, C. (2004) Nicosia Urban Area, in Dubois-Taine, G. (ed.) *European cities - insights on outskirts*, Paris, METL/PUCA.

Dubois-Taine, G. (ed.) (2004) *European cities – insights on outskirts*, Paris, METL/PUCA.

Eisinger, A. and Schneider, M. (eds.) (2003) *Stadtland Schweis,* Basel.

Greer, J. and Murray, M. (2003) Unravelling the rural in Northern Ireland, in Greer, J. and Murray,M (eds.) *Rural planning and development in Northern Ireland,* Dublin, Institute of Public Administration.

Koch, M. (2003) *Mapping the unmapped, seeing the unseen,* COST Action C10 Seminar, Zurich.

McEldowney, M. (2004) The Belfast Metropolitan case study, in Dubois-Taine, G. (ed.) *European cities – insights on outskirts ,* Paris, METL/PUCA.

McEwan, I. (1999) Preface, in Barnett, A. and Scruton, R. (eds.) *Town and country,* London, Vintage.

Newman, P. and Thornley, A. (1996) *Urban planning in Europe,* London, Routledge.

Newby, H. (1980) *Green and pleasant land,* London, Penguin.

Priebs, A. (2001) Postsuburbia, *Beitrage zur Regionalen Entwicklung 90,* Hannover.

Ruegg, J. (2004) *Urban/rural interface in European urban regions,* Technical Annex, COST C25 Application (unpublished), Fribourg.

Ruegg, J. (2004) Governance of urban outskirts, in McEldowney, M. (ed.) *European cities - insights on outskirts - governance,* Paris, METL/PUCA.

Sieverts, T. (1997) *Zwischenstadt,* Bauwelt Fundamente 113, Braunschweig, Wiesbaden.

Schumacher, M., Koch, M. and Ruegg, J. (2004) The Zurich Limmatal, in Dubois-Taine, G. (ed.) *European cities - insights on outskirts,* Paris, METL/PUCA.

Chapter 21

Campus and Community: Changing Times for the Urban University

Frank Gaffikin

Introduction

UK universities face many new opportunities. Not only is student intake rising, as third level education moves from being an elite to a more mass experience, but academy is also becoming economically prominent in the context of a shift to a knowledge society. Yet, alongside such positive trends, the sector faces many challenges. Public funding has not been commensurate with student demand for at least 15 years, with the consequent drop in resources per student impacting negatively on both staff morale and student learning experience in many institutions. Even allowing for the recent real 6 per cent increase in public spending for higher education over a three-year period, the estimated investment 'gap' in teaching and research facilities stands at £8bn. (White Paper, January 2003). Such a significant shortfall threatens the global competitiveness of the sector, and is prompting many colleges to radically reappraise their strategic direction. This chapter explores some key implications of these shifts for the role of the university in the city-region, particularly its relationship with the most distressed communities.

Policy Context

One outcome of the funding gap is the increased commercialisation in academia, and with it, a renewed question about academic freedom and educational mission. Perhaps, to date, this has been most evident in 'Oxbridge'. For instance, Cambridge has seen corporations like BP, Shell, ICI, Glaxo, Price Waterhouse, and Marks & Spencer all sponsor chairs, while others like Rolls Royce, Microsoft and AT&T have installed research centres. Such corporate largesse can be massive – £25 million from BP in the case of Cambridge, £20 million from Wafic Said in the case of Oxford, where also Rupert Murdoch endows a chair in English and a visiting professorship in Broadcast Media (Monbiot, 2000). Though it can be argued that the imperatives of world-class research demand the lucrative financing associated with large corporate sponsors, such beneficence poses serious issues about the skewing of research agendas. For instance, five times as much research money is devoted to the oil and gas industry as compared to renewable energy, hardly coincidental given the prominence of companies like BP amongst the donors (Muttitt and Grimshaw, 2000). The extent to which such influence compromises the intellectual integrity of Higher Education emerged in the controversy over Nottingham University's acceptance of a substantial sum from the premier tobacco company British American Tobacco (BAT) to research and advance business ethics. In more general terms, such sponsorship may tend to privilege utilitarian considerations such as commercial advantage over traditional university commitment to research that is intellectually exacting and socially beneficial. Nevertheless, such patterns comply with the overall attempt to create a new mixed economy of welfare, whereby government funding and responsibility are complemented by wider benefactor partnerships.

Within this more marketised context, public policy prioritises three goals for the university sector that do not always sit comfortably together: to raise academic standards; to improve equality of access across the social classes; and to extend the global reach and reputation of research. This search for both excellence and equity can lead to some contentious resource decisions. For instance, 27 'elite' universities like Oxford and Cambridge are to be offered extra financial inducements – £18 m over three years – to attract a higher share of state school pupils. It could be argued that this is an inequitable case of the better-endowed institutions being rewarded for their 'under-performance' in this regard to date. In a wider sphere, the increased emphasis attached to the sector's role in advancing the UK's competitiveness in the new globalised economy could demote other potential agendas for the academy, such as working with under-developed communities to promote greater social equity and inclusion.

Universities increasingly attempt to be global in their purpose and profile because they recognise the imperative to be internationally competitive. In essence, they are competing with each other for staff; resources to attain state-of-the-art facility and technology; research grants; market-based and patented spin-offs; and, finally, international students, particularly post-graduates, who are the most lucrative catch in terms of fees. But, this keenness to be global in focus has tended to imply that the local is no longer an appropriate arena for world-class research, particularly if that 'laboratory' is judged to be a 'place apart' like Northern Ireland.

This shift in agenda has to be contextualised in the university's typical three main tasks: teaching, research and service to the community. Often the latter has been residualised relative to the core status of the other two, and the three have tended to function separately rather than supportively (Stukel, 1994; Bender, 1988). Certainly, in recent times, there has been a re-awakening about the pertinence and potential of academy for society, and of the reciprocal benefits involved in links between the two (DeMulder and Eby, 1999). Taken alongside the literature about the distinctiveness of place and the significance of locality in development trajectories (Harloe *et al*, 1990; Sayer, 1991), the role of the university in improving the soft infrastructures of research capacity for economic development (Best, 2000; Checkoway, 1997) has been much highlighted. Together with an understanding of the university's wider civic duty (Kennedy, 1997) and its great potential for participation in the building of communities (Rubin, 1998), an ambitious agenda for the role of academy as a key urban institution has been advanced. Interestingly, the literature around this discourse has been particularly prominent in the United States (US) (Bok, 1982).

University-Community Partnerships in the US
In 1994, the US Department of Housing and Urban Development (HUD) established the Office of University Partnerships to support the development of partnerships between universities and communities in order to redress urban problems. Designed to link the significant assets of a powerful urban institution – physical, economic, political, technical and intellectual – to the capacities of the poorest neighbourhoods, the initiative emphasised the gains to both (US HUD, October 1996; COPC, 2001).

Of course, universities in the US had been involved in service and community outreach work for many decades. But, the argument was that the scale and pace of urban change and the challenge to the university as a democratic civic institution demanded that the contemporary relationship extend beyond the narrowness of the typical 'outreach' model (Feld, 1998). To take a simple example, in UK universities, there are individual faculty members linking their teaching and research to the challenges of regeneration and social inclusion. But, in many instances, these tend to be operating as 'lone rangers' without a 'posse' of collegial and institutional support. Certain subjects such as planning and social policy lend themselves most readily to direct association with the community (Zeldin, 1995), and unsurprisingly these are the subject areas that appear most relevant to the regeneration needs of deprived areas. The assistance they can offer lies in areas of: contextual research, technical assistance, data analysis, evaluation, planning, and human and organisational resource development. But, increasingly, it has been recognized that urban challenges are multi-dimensional in character and resolution. Thus, in terms of the academy's intervention, this needs a more extensive transdisciplinary reach across the curriculum to involve most, if not all, faculty in direct community engagement.

In turn, this demands a new mindset among the university's leadership and a new scholarship among the academic staff (Boyer, 1996; Schon, 1995). One

335

aspect of this is to acknowledge the complementarity of the formal knowledge of the academy and the experiential and 'tacit' knowledge of the community. Another is to locate all such activity within a comprehensive vision of the democratic cosmopolitan civic university (Benson and Harkavy, 2000), and the third is for the two partners to openly recognize their own current strengths and weaknesses.

Campus and Community: Traits and Trials

In the case of the latter, it is instructive to identify these features more precisely to help identify the potential for paradox and tension in the university-community relationship (Silka, 1999). Universities are high profile resource-rich urban institutions, enjoying social status, and benefiting from the institutional continuity that facilitates forward strategic planning. Unlike many other forms of economic investment, they are more 'rooted' to place. To their local urban-regions, they can provide civic leadership, together with significant economic multipliers in terms of their consumption and employment. Moreover, their role in the local property market can be significant. For instance, in Belfast, in terms of real estate value and share of listed buildings, Queen's University ranks high among the top property holders in the city.

Use of their applied research can help to clarify and to redress social problems, while their role in knowledge, skills and technology transfer can support capacity-building and self-help within the community. In the shift to the integrated development of spatial planning, their cross-disciplinary perspectives can penetrate the linked dimensions of sustainable local development. Comparative policy analysis can illustrate on an internationally comparative basis the good practice that has been most transformative. Moreover, academy can support also the urban networking that underpins effective social capital, and, particularly in the case of contested societies, it can provide a safe dialogic space for difficult discourses between protagonists, with university facilitation where appropriate. The scholarship that links teaching to community needs enriches the student learning experience, in the same way that student community service also provides participants with a 'real life' learning arena that connects theory to practice.

At the same time, universities can suffer from the cumbersome bureaucracy and tradition associated with large durable organizations. Their reward system is disinclined to value community engagement highly. As property developers, they can gentrify rather than cooperatively re-make their own hinterland. Cross-faculty collaboration can be difficult because of the disciplinary panel system that assesses research, while the tradition of staff autonomy means that staff have to be persuaded individually rather than recruited en bloc to any collective project. Indeed, the kind of participative action-research demanded by good processes of community engagement is time-consuming, and thereby involves opportunity costs for researchers in terms of the time they could otherwise spend on the current gold standard of research appraisal, namely refereed journal articles. As explained earlier, the current fiscal stress induces universities to focus on commercially-oriented knowledge transfer rather than on knowledge exchange with poor communities. At the same time, such communities can view the university through a stereotypical lens that depicts it as an elite detached body, given to the abstract and theoretical rather than to practical dividend.

For its own part, at its best, the community can contribute many assets to the partnership, including: local knowledge, credibility and legitimacy; regeneration experience and expertise; the enterprise and inventiveness that can attend adversity; a focused agenda that emphasizes concrete change within clear time schedules; often distinctive and enriching cultural traits; and the voluntary effort and civic leadership that support social capital and accord local projects vital community ownership and endorsement. Yet, it contains also a set of limitations that curb its capacity. It operates mostly at relatively small neighbourhood level, minimizing the scale and scope of its interventions, and sometimes its perspectives. Naturally engaged with the very immediate manifestations of decline and decay, it can either adopt a tactical rather than strategic approach, or concentrate on time-consuming efforts to enhance community infrastructure, a process-driven agenda that may end up valuing outputs over outcomes. Its attempts to cope with the multi-dimensional features of decline can diffuse its efforts to deal coherently with any single aspect of disadvantage. Often, the long haul that is demanded in the redress of deeply rooted problems means that it is difficult for community organizations to hold on to a core membership over time. People come and go with great frequency and this transient character is a debilitating mismatch with the persistent problems that the community sector addresses.

Within the community sector, the imperative to collaborate across localities for mutual support and strength can be compromised by the competitive rivalry to win shares of the limited funds targeted at deprived areas. With respect to funding, the sector's obligation to demonstrate to benefactors relatively quick tangible return on their investment can distract from its strategic approach to long-term regeneration. Moreover, behind the apparent unifying and bonding traits of 'community' lies the reality of internal dissensions and diversity of interest, and the arbitration of such factionalism is problematic. Finally, there is a contemporary debate about the 'eclipse' of community in a globalising age, whereby old solidarities around shared social space are splintered, partly by the new segmentations in the labour market, and partly by the many new networks within which people operate beyond neighbourhood.

Moving from Stereotype to Partnership

Such strengths and weaknesses within both the campus and community can prompt each side to stereotype the other, leading to a dialogue of the deaf between 'the remote ivory tower' and 'the ever demanding, ever complaining community'. US experience suggests that beyond such misunderstandings, partnerships can be built between the two interests. In a review and evaluation of university-community partnerships, certain conditions for effective collaboration are identified (Cityscape, 2000):

- mutual understanding of the respective 'worlds' of community development and academia requires continuous investment and sensitivity;
- differences in interest, culture, class and power need to be openly acknowledged;
- productive division of responsibility between partners that may, for instance, separate roles in academic research and community advocacy, can be helpful. But, this should not deny the integrity of participatory action-research, which involves a total integration of both partners in the process;
- institutional support and 'imprimaturs' from the leadership of both partners are required for a long-term strategic alliance;
- progress in the relationship demands patient processes of capacity-building within both partners; and
- overall, a written protocol between the two sides is useful, laying out in clear detail the mutual obligations and supports, so that ambiguities and confusion do not confound the relationship.

Engaged Urban Universities

As indicated earlier, in the 21st century, there are many pressures on universities to rethink their mission. In considering what this new role might be, it is instructive to re-visit the three models of academy that have predominated to date (Gaffikin, 2001; Perry, 2005).

1. *The 'ivory tower' model* of detachment from the wider society is no longer tenable. This 'Platonic' concept of elitist and contemplative learning sites the university as 'a place apart'. From this perspective, the university best protects its integrity and currency by removing itself from the demands and problems of its immediate environment. A version of this argument was used during the height of the 'Troubles' by a Vice-Chancellor in Queen's University to suggest that if the university was drawn too deeply into the local conflict, it risked being cast as partisan, thereby jeopardizing its autonomy and institutional neutrality:

Direct university involvement in society negates professional independence and academic style... Universities who play politics can have politics played on them. (Froggatt, 1977, p.6)

2. *The 'service' model* sees a modest role for the university in encouraging staff to respond voluntarily to requests from deprived communities for assistance and expertise. In this approach, the power, status and discretion rest exclusively with the institution. Moreover, there is a tendency for this model of knowledge production to generate a class system within the university: the 'higher class' staff devote themselves to recognized and rewarded research, while the 'lower class' staff undertake the time-intensive service work with community, an investment that receives little incentive from the institution.

3. *The 'outreach' model* has the academy as more proactive in extending itself into city and community. Indeed, often it will set up 'offices of extension' to coordinate the delivery of such expertise. But, the 'outreach' perspective risks being paternalistic and restrictive, assuming that the dynamic is between a brimful 'jug' of knowledge and grateful empty 'mugs' of relative ignorance.

The radical alternative to these standard models is that of *the 'engaged' university*, one that seeks an equitable and mutually supportive relationship between academy and wider community. In essence, this model seeks to transform the relationship between the two in the production and application of knowledge. Traditional and simplistic dichotomies between the 'experiential' knowledge of community and 'formal' knowledge of the academy are dissolved, as both parties explore a new synthesis of how collaboratively they can compose, exchange and use knowledge. This is 'knowledge without boundaries' (Walshok, 1995). Indeed, in the complex environments that constitute contemporary city-regions, this process acknowledges the synergy between traditional and non-traditional sites of knowledge. Institutional outreach to the community and city is complemented by civic in-reach to the academy. A protocol between the two enshrines commitment to a long-term strategic partnership, involving not only the minority of staff already attached to such work, but rather *the very core* of the university.

Importantly, this does not transform academics into consultants or community workers. They continue to do what they can contribute best, namely research. But, it is *engaged research*, based on three distinctive metrics that assume, but go beyond, the professional robust research methodologies and ethics (Perry, 2005):

1. it involves **partnership** between academy and civic agency;
2. it is **inter-disciplinary**, reflecting the reality that problems are multi-dimensional;
3. it has **high impact**, both in terms of its public policy and development transferability for cities everywhere, and of its extension of both knowledge boundaries and the linked aspects, such as good quality university teaching.

Beginning the Process

A starting point involves the systematic examination of the research and teaching resources of universities to determine how these can best be operated in an on-going partnership with deprived communities and city-region development agencies. For example, how can:

- student placements and specialist projects be systematically linked with the regeneration agendas of local partnerships in deprived communities?
- this work, in turn, inform the structure of courses taught at the institutions?
- tailored courses, including on-line courses, be developed to enhance the knowledge and qualification of local development workers in these areas?
- an international network of educational exchange be developed around the regeneration and planning agenda?
- isolated social researchers in the universities be brought together in flexible inter-disciplinary research teams to achieve an economy of scale and scope that can only occur with a critical mass research community?
- the research agenda of the local universities be made systematically more relevant to the development needs of these areas?

But, behind these kinds of explorations and arrangements, evidence from practice elsewhere, such as the US experience outlined earlier, suggests that the following platform is needed:

- the *'imprimatur' from the university authorities* to endorse and support this mission (Gates and Robinson, 1998);
- corresponding systems of *recognition and reward* that give staff incentive to participate;
- the *appropriate structures* to facilitate inter-disciplinary collaboration – perhaps, a distinctive Institute charged with clustering staff for periods of secondment for such research projects, and resolving any dilemmas around attributions for the Research Assessment Exercise;
- long-term partnerships/memoranda of understanding between the *institution as a whole* and leading community and civic agencies.

Encountering the Reservations

Given the financial and globalising imperatives faced by universities at present, these ideas will probably encounter scepticism and resistance. In two recent focus groups, involving academics and civic interests, and facilitated by the author to address this issue, the following discourse emerged.

It may appear that universities face hard choices. For instance, they can take comfort in their traditions or embrace the risks of change. But, given that change is all around – the shift to new economy; the re-invention of governance; the re-alignment of welfare towards mixed funding and provision; and the transformation of community – it would be foolhardy of academy to seek insulation from this general dynamic. So, there is no respite in 'enclave'. Indeed, the apparent choice as to whether to operate behind academic walls, or whether to be open for engagement is, in fact, an illusory choice. Related to this, given the myriad new sites of research, information, and learning, there is no real choice about whether to be involved in exclusive or inclusive forms of knowledge creation and distribution. Only the latter will produce a credible epistemology in the contemporary period. Similarly, other apparent choices on offer – for instance, between the local and global research agendas – are not, in fact, so dichotomous. Good local research, rooted in a problem-solving methodology, with appropriate international comparative, has global worth and transferability. In short, an institution like Queen's University, Belfast, for example, does not enhance its global ambitions by abandoning the Belfast component, as if it was some kind of virtual campus. Rather, seen from this perspective, Belfast is its major asset, its international recognition and 'calling card'.

Nevertheless, there remain many difficulties in translating this agenda into a form that accords with the mission of contemporary universities. The rhetoric of partnership comes easy, but often disguises the reality of continued dominance by powerful interests (Barnekov *et al,* 1989; Squires, 1989). In this respect, it would be naïve to under-estimate the impulse for universities to prioritise knowledge transfer that yields the most commercial return. At the same time, even genuine partnerships do not erase these inequitable dynamics simply by offering a table at which the relatively disadvantaged can speak truth to power.

Often, the urban campus, in its design and setting, has conveyed a deliberate Arcadian pastoral impression of being anti-urban, almost a refuge from the city. The remaking of 'campus' outlined here liberates the university from these boundaries, and in so doing, enfranchises academy to be a good neighbour to its city-region.

References

Barnekov, T., Boyle, R., and Rich, D. (1989) *Privatism and urban policy in Britain and the United States*, New York, Oxford University Press.

Bender, T. (ed.) (1988) *The university and the city: from medieval origins to the present*, New York, NY, Oxford University Press.

Benson, L. and Harkavy, I. (2000) Integrating the American system of higher, secondary and primary education to develop civic responsibility, in Ehrlich, T. (ed.) *Civic responsibility and higher education*, Washington, DC, American Council on Education and Oryx Press.

Best, M. (2000) *The capabilities and innovation perspective: the way ahead in Northern Ireland*, Research Monograph 8, Belfast, Northern Ireland Economic Council.

Bok, D. (1982) *Beyond the Ivory Tower: social responsibilities of the modern university*, Cambridge, MA, Harvard University Press.

Boyer, E. (1996) The scholarship of engagement, *Journal of Public Service and Outreach*, 1, pp.11 - 20.

Checkoway, B. (1997) Reinventing the research university for public service, *Journal of Planning Literature*, 2(3), pp.307-319.

Cityscape: A Journal of Policy Development and Research (2000) Community Outreach Partnerships Centers: connecting communities and institutions of higher education, 5(1), special edition..

Community Outreach Partnerships Centers (COPC) (2001) *COPC annual report 2000*, Washington, DC, US Department of Housing and Urban Development (HUD).

DeMulder, E. and Eby, K. (1999) Bridging troubled waters: learning communities for the 21st Century, *American Behavioral Scientist*, (42)5, pp.892-901.

Feld, M. (1998) Community Outreach Partnership Centers: forging new relationships between university and community, *Journal of Planning Education and Research* 17(4), pp.285-290.

Froggatt, P. (1977) *The university as an instrument of social change: a dangerous or desirable concept?* Paper presented to Conference of Universities and Schools, Belfast, Queen's University, Belfast.

Gaffikin, F. (2001) *Universities in contested space*, Unpublished Seminar Paper, Belfast, University Of Ulster.

Gates, R. and Robinson, G. (1998) Institutionalizing university-community partnerships, *Journal of Planning Education and Research*, 17(4), pp.312-322.

Harloe, M., Pickvance, C. and Urry, J. (eds.) (1990) *Place, policy and politics: do localities matter?* London, Unwin Hyman.

Kennedy, D. (1997) *Academic duty*, Cambridge, MA, Harvard University Press.

Monbiot, G. (2000) *The captive state, the corporate takeover of Britain*, London, Macmillan.

Muttitt G. and Grimshaw, C. (2000) *Degrees of involvement: an examination of the relationship between the upstream oil and gas industry and UK higher education institutions*, London, CorporateWatch.

Perry, D. (2005) Discussions with Dr Perry, Director of the Great Cities Institute, University of Illinois, Chicago. David offered many insights into 'the engaged university' and these have informed this chapter.

Rubin, V. (1998) The role of universities in community-building initiatives, *Journal of Planning Education and Research*, (17)4, pp.302-311.

Sayer, A. (1991) Behind the locality debate: deconstructing Geography's dualisms, *Environment and Planning A*, 23, pp.283-308.

Schon, D. (1995) The new scholarship requires a new epistemology, *Change*, 27, pp.26 - 35.

Silka, L. (1999) Paradoxes of partnerships: reflections on university-community collaborations, *Research in Politics and Society*, 7, pp.335-359.

Squires, G. (ed.) (1989) *Unequal partnerships: the political economy of urban redevelopment in postwar America*, New Brunswick and London, Rutgers University Press.

Stukel, J. (1994) Urban and metropolitan universities: leaders of the 21st century, *Metropolitan Universities*, 5(2), pp.87-92.

US Department of Housing and Urban Development (1996) *University-community partnership: current practices*, Volume 2, Washington, HUD.

Walshok, M. (1995) *Knowledge without boundaries: what America's universities can do for the economy, the workplace, and the community*, San Francisco, Jossey- Bass.

White Paper (2003) *The future of Higher Education*, London, Department for Education and Skills (DFES).

Zeldin, S. (1995) Community-university collaborations for youth development: from theory to practice, *Journal of Adolescent Research*, 10, pp.449 - 469

Publications of
John V Greer

GREER, J V (1966) *The changing village*. Essay submitted as part of the Final Examination (Part One) of the Town Planning Institute.

Craigavon New City: Second Report on the Plan (1967) with Craigavon Development Commission and Department of Housing, Local Government and Planning, Craigavon.

Londonderry Area Plan – Costing and Implementation (1968) with James Munce Partnership, Belfast.

Londonderry Area Plan – Ballycarnett / Shantallow District (1969) with James Munce Partnership, Belfast.

GREER, J V (1972) Environmental planning in Northern Ireland, in *Urban and Industrial Policy*, Ministry of Development, Belfast.

Report on landscape treatment of open space in Brooke Park Estate (1972) with J C Moughtin, Belfast.

Ballinasloe: Development Plan Review (1973) with Brady Shipman Martin, Dublin.

GREER, J V (1976) Planning education: the crisis of relevance, *Northern Architect*, December.

Arklow Development Plan (1978) with Brady Shipman Martin, Dublin.

Roscommon Small Towns Study (1978) with Department of Town and Country Planning, The Queen's University of Belfast.

Killybegs Development Plan (1979) with Brady Shipman Martin, Dublin.

Erne Catchment Study (1980) with Brady Shipman Martin, Dublin and PA International, Belfast.

West Region Study: Development Strategy to 2004 (1983) with Brady Shipman Martin, Dublin.

Caldwell, J H and GREER, J V (1984) *Physical planning in rural areas of Northern Ireland*. Occasional Papers in Planning, No 5, Department of Town and Country Planning, The Queen's University of Belfast.

The demand for retail space: Development Plan manual- number 3 (1984) with An Foras Forbartha, Dublin.

GREER, J V (1984) Integrated rural development: reflections on a magic phrase, *Pleanail, The Journal of the Irish Planning Institute*, Vol 1, No 4, pp.10-15.

Jess, P M, GREER, J V, Buchanan, R H and Armstrong, W J (eds.) (1984) *Planning and development in rural areas*, The Report of a Conference held at Magee College, Londonderry in September 1983.

Caldwell, J H and GREER, J V (1984) Physical planning for rural areas in Northern Ireland, in Jess, P M, GREER, J V, Buchanan, R H and Armstrong, W J (eds.) (1984) *Planning and development in rural areas*, The Report of a Conference held at Magee College, Londonderry in September 1983, pp.63-86.

GREER, J V and Jess, P (1987) Town and country planning, in Buchanan, R H and Walker, B M (eds.) *Province, city, people: Belfast and its region*, Greystone Books, Antrim in association with the Northern Ireland Committee of the British Association for the Advancement of Science, pp.101-124.

GREER, J V and Murray, M (1988) *A recreation strategy for Mourne Area of Outstanding Natural Beauty*, The Sports Council for Northern Ireland, Belfast.

Murray, M and GREER, J V (1989) Rural development, recreation provision and amenity landscape conservation – a new challenge, *Business Outlook and Economic Review*, Vol 4, No 1, pp.24-28.

GREER, J V (1990) Planning and development in rural communities: the Ardboe experience, *Proceedings of an International Symposium on Rural Housing Policy*, The Northern Ireland Housing Executive, Belfast, pp.53-54.

Murray, M and GREER, J V (1990) Prized landscapes and recreation policy in Northern Ireland: the Mournes exemplar, *Irish Geography*, Vol 23, No 1, p.p43-49.

Murray, M and GREER, J V (1990) Rural development – a challenge of the 1990s: a Northern Ireland response, Business Outlook and Economic Review, Vol 5, No 2, pp.16-18.

GREER, J V and Murray, M (1991) *Development strategy for Ardboe, Ballinderry and Moortown*, Ronan Press, Lurgan.

GREER, J V (1991) Review of Prestwich, R and Taylor, P, Introduction to Regional and Urban Policy in the United Kingdom, in *Regional Politics and Policy*, Vol 1, No 3, pp.308-310.

Murray, M and GREER, J V (1991) Integrated rural development in Northern Ireland – reflections on policy progress, *Business Outlook and Economic Review*, Vol 6, No 3, pp.17-22.

Murray, M and GREER, J V (1991) Landscape resources and tourism, in McDowell, D and Leslie, D (eds.) *Tourism resources: issues, planning and development*, University of Ulster and Leeds Polytechnic, pp.20-30.

GREER, J V and Neill, W (1991) The plan as symbol – a case study of Belfast, *Pleanail – The Journal of the Irish Planning Institute*, No 19, pp.90-112.

GREER, J V (1992) The rural environment: asset or constraint? in O'Cinneide, M and Cuddy, M (eds) *Perspectives on rural development in advanced economies*, University College Galway, Galway.

GREER, J V and Murray, M (1992) *Causeway Coast Area of Outstanding Natural Beauty Access Strategy*, Countryside and Wildlife Branch, Department of the Environment for Northern Ireland, Belfast.

GREER, J V and Murray, M (1992) *Rural planning strategy review in Northern Ireland*, Community Technical Aid, Belfast.

Murray, M and GREER, J V (1992) Rural development in Northern Ireland: policy formulation in a peripheral region of the European Community, *Journal of Rural Studies*, Vol 8, No 2, pp.173-184.

Murray, M and GREER, J V (eds.) (1993) *Rural development in Ireland – a challenge for the 1990s*, Avebury Press, Aldershot.

GREER, J V and Murray, M (1993) Rural Ireland – personality and policy context, in Murray, M and GREER, J V (eds.) *Rural development in Ireland – a challenge for the 1990s*, Avebury Press, Aldershot, pp.3-20.

Murray, M and GREER, J V (1993) Rural development in Northern Ireland, in Murray, M and GREER, J V (eds.) *Rural development in Ireland – a challenge for the 1990s*, Avebury Press, Aldershot, pp.55-67.

Murray, M and GREER, J V (1993) Rural development and paradigm change, in Murray, M and GREER, J V (eds.) *Rural development in Ireland – a challenge for the 1990s*, Avebury Press, Aldershot, pp.255-268.

GREER, J V and Murray, M (1993) *Tydavnet development strategy*, R and S Printers, Monaghan.

Murray, M and GREER, J V (1994) State-community relationships in rural development, *Community Development Journal*, Vol 29, No 1, pp.29-37.

GREER, J V and Murray, M (1994) Fields of vision, *Perspective: The Journal of the Royal Society of Ulster Architects*, Vol 2, No 5, pp.29-30.

Murray, M and GREER, J V (1994) *Who re-draws the boundaries?* Rural Community Network for Northern Ireland, Coookstown.

GREER, J V and Murray, M (1995) *BRACE 2000: a development strategy for the Blackwater Rural Agency for Community Enhancement*, R and S Printers, Monaghan.

Murray, M and GREER, J V (1995) Strategic planning for access to the countryside in Northern Ireland, *World Leisure and Recreation*, Vol 37, No 2, pp.21-26.

Murray, M and GREER, J V (1995) Engaging with rural communities for local development in Northern Ireland, *Business Outlook and Economic Review*, Vol 10, No 3, pp.35-41.

Murray, M, GREER, J V and Walsh, J A (1995) Economic restructuring within the European periphery: the experience of Ireland, in Hardy, S, Albrechts, L and Katos, A (eds.) *An enlarged Europe: regions in competition?* Jessica Kingsley Publishers, London, pp.295-309.

Murray, M and GREER, J V (1997) Planning and community-led rural development in Northern Ireland, *Planning Practice and Research*, Vol 12, No 4, pp.393-400.

Murray, M and GREER, J V (1997) Interactive strategic planning and community development: the Northern Ireland experience, *Journal of Community Practice*, Vol 4, No 4, pp.27-48.

Voices of the people (1997) with The Queen's University of Belfast, The Urban Institute and Community Technical Aid, The Stationery Office, Belfast.

Murray, M and GREER, J V (1998) Strategic planning for multi-community rural development: insights from Northern Ireland, *European Planning Studies*, Vol 6, No 3, pp.255-269.

Murray, M and GREER, J V (1998) Reshaping rural development in Northern Ireland: partnership governance and regional competitiveness, *Economic Outlook and Business Review*, Vol 13, No 4, pp.47-53.

Murray, M and Greer, J V (1998) Evaluation insights from village and small town regeneration in Northern Ireland: a community perspective, *Pleanail – The Journal of the Irish Planning Institute*, No 14, pp.154-170.

The West Rural Region – a strategy for people, partnership and prosperity (1998) with Cookstown District Council, Dungannon and South Tyrone Borough Council, Fermanagh District Council, Omagh District Council and Strabane District Council.

Murray, M and GREER, J V (1999) The changing governance of rural development: state-community interaction in Northern Ireland, *Policy Studies*, Vol 20, No 1, pp.37-50.

Murray, M and GREER, J V (1999) *State – community interaction in the changing arena of rural development policy in Northern Ireland*, Association for Voluntary Action Research in Ireland, Coleraine.

GREER, J V and Murray, M (1999) Changing patterns of rural planning and development in Northern Ireland, in Davis, J (ed.) *Rural change in Ireland*, The Institute of Irish Studies, Belfast, pp.167-187.

Murray, M and GREER, J V (2000) The Republic of Ireland National Development Plan 2000 – 2006: some strategic planning implications for Northern Ireland, *Economic Outlook and Business Review*, Vol 15, No 1, pp.37-42.

Murray, M and GREER, J V (2000) *Rural settlement patterns and physical planning policy in Northern Ireland*, Policy Discussion Paper, Rural Community Network, Cookstown.

Murray, M and GREER, J V (2000) The Northern Ireland Regional Strategic Framework: a progress review, *Economic Outlook and Business Review*, Vol 15, No 2, pp.50-54.

Murray, M and GREER, J V (2000) *The Northern Ireland Regional Strategic Framework and its public examination process: towards a new model of participatory planning?* Research Monograph, Rural Innovation Research Partnership, Belfast.

Murray, M and GREER, J V (2001) *Participatory village planning: practice guidelines workbook*, Rural Innovation Research Partnership, Belfast.

Murray, M and GREER, J V (2001) The Regional Development Strategy for Northern Ireland: the end of the beginning or the beginning of the end? *Economic Outlook and Business Review*, Vol 16, No 4, pp.58-63.

Murray, M and GREER, J V (2001) Rural planning in Northern Ireland, *Northern Ireland Environment Link – Environment Fact Sheet*, Vol 1, No 3, pp.10-12.

GREER, J V, Houston, D, Murray, M and Murtagh, B (2002) Baselining rural services in Northern Ireland (research note 1), *Economic Outlook and Business Review*, Vol 17, No 2, pp.30-32.

GREER, J V, Houston, D, Murray, M and Murtagh, B (2002) Baselining rural services in Northern Ireland (research note 2), *Economic Outlook and Business Review*, Vol 17, No 3, pp.44-45.

GREER, J V, Houston, D, Murray, M and Murtagh, B (2002) Baselining rural services in Northern Ireland (research note 3), *Economic Outlook and Business Review*, Vol 17, No 4, pp.

Murray, M and GREER, J V (2002) Participatory planning as dialogue: the Northern Ireland Regional Strategic Framework and its public examination process, *Policy Studies*, Vol 23, No 4, pp.283-294.

GREER, J V, Houston, D, Murray, M and Murtagh, B (2003) *Services in rural Northern Ireland*, The Rural Development Council for Northern Ireland, Cookstown.

GREER, J V and Murray, M (eds.) (2003) *Rural planning and development in Northern Ireland*, Institute of Public Administration, Dublin.

GREER, J V and Murray, M (2003) Unravelling the rural in Northern Ireland: a planning and development perspective, in GREER, J V and Murray, M (eds.) (2003) *Rural planning and development in Northern Ireland*, Institute of Public Administration, Dublin, pp.3-35.

GREER, J V and Murray, M (2003) Rethinking rural planning and development in Northern Ireland, in GREER, J V and Murray, M (eds.) (2003) *Rural planning and development in Northern Ireland*, Institute of Public Administration, Dublin, pp.283-308.

Murray, M, GREER, J V and Scott, M (2003) The National Spatial Strategy (2002-2020) for the Republic of Ireland, *Economic Outlook and Business Review*, Vol 18, No 1, pp.63-66.

Murray, M and GREER, J V (2004) Participatory regional planning in Northern Ireland, in Lovan, W R, Murray, M and Shaffer, R (eds.) *Participatory governance: planning, conflict mediation and public decision-making in civil society*, Ashgate, Aldershot, pp.145-161.

Murray, M, GREER, J V, and Sterrett, K (2005) The public value of public involvement: insights from participatory village planning in Ireland, *Administration*, Vol 53, No 1, pp.3-15.

INDEX

Italicised page numbers refer to chapters
Emboldened page numbers refer to tables and illustrations
NI = Northern Ireland
RI = Republic of Ireland

Aalen, F. 189
Abercrombie, Sir P. 225-6, 227
accordion theory of retailing 254
activist model of partnership 283-5
Adorno, T. 79
Agenda 2000 107
Agerard, E. 249, 255
Agriculture, Food and Rural
    Development (RI), Department of 115
Agriculture and Rural Development
    (NI), Department of xiv, 174
Albrechts, L. 187
Alexander, J.C. 271
Alexander, N. 254, 256
Allpass, J. 249, 255
Anderson, T. 51
Angel of History 68, 74
Antrim Arms Hotel 161
Ardagh, J. 66
Armstrong, J. xvii, 276
Arthur, P. 21
Arts, Sport and Tourism, Department
    of 305
Ascherson, N. 21
Ashworth, G.J. 21
Assembly, NI 177, 289, 293, 298, 310
Atlas of Ireland 132-3
Audit Commission 298
autism of planning 265-7

BAB (Bayonne/Anglet/Biarritz)
    321-**2**,323, 330-1
Bacchini, P. 320
Baek, J. 256
Baer, W.C. 239
Bagguley, P. 24
Bain, G. xviii

Baker, A.R.H. 18
Balfour, A. 66
Ballybeg study 50-1
Bannon, M.J. 103, 104
    on Border, Midland and Western
        (BMW) Region *107-24*
Bardach, E. 241, 242
Barker, P. 330
Barnekov, T. 341
Barritt, D.P. 46
Bartetzko, D. 66, 67
Basque Country 321-**2**, 323
Bass, S.J. 255
Bassett, J. on rural housing *139-56*
Bates, A.D. 255
Batty, M. 228
Bayonne/Anglet/Biarritz (BAB)
    321-**2**,323, 330-1
Belfast Agreement 57, 291, *see also*
    Good Friday Agreement
Belfast Metropolitan Area 60, 321, 326
Belfast Metropolitan Residents
    Group 180
Belfast planning problems *261-8*
    roads 262-4
Belfast Telegraph 28, 252
Belfast Travel to Work Area 181
Bender, T. 334
Benjamin, W. 68-9, 70, 73
Benson, J. 250
Benson, L. 336
Benvenisti, M. 265
Berlin Babylon 63-88
Berlin planning and German
    identity 66-8
    Jewish Memorial 75-82
    nationalism 64-6

Planwerk Innenstadt 70-4
to forget the past 68-70
to remember the past 74-5
Berlin Wall 63, 70-1, **72**, 74
Berry, J. 243, 244
Best, M. 335
Best, R.H. 320
Blackman, T. 27
Bliss or Blitz conference 151, 158
Bloch, M. 5
BMW *see* Border, Midland and Western
 Region
Boal, F.W. 23, 37, 50, 265
Bodemann, M. 77
Bok, D. 335
Bollens, S.A. 265
Booher, D. 184
Bord Bia 119
Bord Fáilte 306, *see also* Fáilte Ireland
Border, NI 126, 130, 131
Border, Midland and Western (BMW)
 Region
 administration 99, 100, 102, 107-24
 demographic dimensions 110
 and Dublin-Belfast corridor 126
 economic dimensions 112-13
 European aid to 114-**15**, 116-**17**, 118
 and FAS 117
 fishing industry 116-17
 future of 120-3
 higher education 123
 physical dimensions 109
 state aid to 118-20
Borsdorf, A. 321
Bourdieu, P. 149, 153, 154
Boyer, E. 335
Boyes, R. 78, 83
Boylan, T.A. on regional policy *91-106*
Boyle, D. 158
Boyle, G. 104
Boyle, R. 304, 341
Bradley, J. 104
Braithwaite, J. 242
Bramwell, B. 301, 303
Braniff, P.L. on methodology *225-34*
Braudel, F. 5
Breheny, M. 253
Brennan, A. 233
Brett, C.E.B. 159, 161, 163

Briassoulis, H. 187
Brittain, P. 254
Brown, S. 257
Brown, T. 19
Brownlow **30**-3
Bryson, J.M. 302
Bubis, I. 77, 78, 80, 82
Buchanan, C. and Partners 94, 101,
 103, 122
Buchanan, R.H. 18, 20, 21
Buckley, P.J. 306
Building Preservation Trust 166
Burby, R. 243, 244
Burg, A. 66, 67
Burger, T. 273
Burrows, P. 241, 242, 244
Buruma, I. 64

Cabinet Office 289, 290
Caldwell, J. xvii, 171
Calvert, D. 46
CAP *see* Common Agricultural Policy
Carnwath, R. 235, 237
Carolan, B. 27
Carson, W.G. 241
Carter, C.F. 46
Carter, R. 172-3
Caygill, H. 68
Celtic Tiger 99, 100, 121
Central Statistics Office (CSO) 112,
 132, 315
Chambers, G. 45
Chambliss, E. 241
Charlton, K. 304
Chavez, D. 303
Checkoway, B. 335
Cheshire CC v Woodward 236
Chorianopoulos, I. 232
CIDO (Craigavon Industrial
 Development Organisation) 35
CIO (Committee on Industrial
 Organisation) 93, 103
clachans 13, 144-**5**
Clarke, W. 306
Claval, P. 18
Clinch, P. 120, 190
CNIC (Craigavon New Industries
 Council) 35
Co-operative Society 256

Coakley, J. 275
Cockcroft Committee 172-4, 182-3
  Report xvii, 151
Coe, B. 250
Cohesion Fund for Ireland **115**-16, 121
Coleman, A. 320
Common Agricultural Policy (CAP)
  and BMW 114, 120, 121
  and rural economy 205, 207-8, 214,
  216, 218-19
Common Fishery Policy 214
Community Alert Programme 279-82,
  284
Community Outreach Partnerships
  Centers 335
community planning in NI *289-300*
  and local government 290-3
  Local Strategy Partnerships 293-5,
  296, 297
  model **292**
Community Technical Aid 175-7
Community Workers' Co-operative 281,
  286
conflict theories of retailing 256-7
Connolly, K. 74
Conradi, P. 81
conservation, architectural 159-67
consultation and housing *169-86*
  Cockcroft Committee 172-4
continuity 8-10, 12, 13, 15
Continuous Household Survey 45
Convery, F. 190
Cooke, P. 24
Cooper, J. 262
Coopers and Lybrand 306
Cormack, R.I. 45
Cornforth, J. 164
Countryside Policy Areas 151, 176
Cowan, R. 66
Cox, R. 254
Craig, G.A. 64
Craig, P. 21
Craig, S. 271
Craigavon
  Borough Council 34, 45
  Development Commission xv, 27, **28**,
  29, 34
  Industrial Development Organisation
  (CIDO) 35

Master Plan 28
  New Industries Council (CNIC) 35
Craigavon project
  background 25-32
  business and industry 33-5
  ethno-sectarian identity 36-41
  local attitudes 32-3
  trades union culture 35-6
  unemployment rates 39-**40**
Cranston, R. 241
Cronin, M. 19
Crosby, B. 302
Crown Solicitor's Office 237
Crozier, M. 21
CSO (Central Statistics Office) 112,
  132, 315
Cuddy, M.P. 104
  on rural economy *205-21*
Cumine, V. 266
Curry's Cottage 163-**4**
Curtin, C. 44, 281
cyclical theories of retailing 253-5
Cyprus 326-**7**, 328-**9**

Darwin, J. 301
Davidson, W.R. 255
Davies, N. 64
Davies, R.L. 249, 252, 253, 257
Daviestown study 51
Davoudi, S. 196
Dawe, G. 21
Dawson, J.A. 256
Day, G. 24, 43-4
de Valera, E. 14
Dean, J.A.K. 163
Deegan, J. 305, 306
Deloitte 296, 297
Demetriou, C. 329
DeMulder, E. 335
depopulation, rural 197-8
Deputy Prime Minister, Office of 235,
  293
Derry/Londonderry Initiative 294
Development, Ministry of 27
development plans, local 199-201
development, rural sustainable *see*
  sustainable development
Devereux, E. 276
Devlin, H. 165

Dhalla, N.K. 255
Diepgen, E. 81
Dillen, R. 266
Dilley, R. 23
DiMento, J.F. 241
Dineen, D.A. 305, 306
District Councils 172-9, 182
District Partnerships 294-5
District Towns Strategy 172
Dobry, G. 235, 237
Donegal development 193-201
Donnan, H. 24, 44, 51
Douglas, J.N.H. 23, 37
Drumbeg lockhouse **162**
Dublin-Belfast corridor 121
    NSS and RDS 125-35
    and outskirts 321, 323, *see also* GDA
Dubois-Taine, G. 319
Duffy, P. 190
Durcan, P. 17, 21
Durkan, M. 297-8

Easthope, A. 64
Eby, K. 335
Economic Cooperation and
    Development, Organisation for
    (OECD) 104, 169, 282
Economic Development (1958) 93, 103
Economic Development, Department
    of 46, 177-8, 306
Economic and Social Committee of the
European Parliament 229
Economic and Social Council, National
    (NESC) 97-8, 100, 103, 126
Economic and Social Research Institute
    (ESRI) 126
Edelman, L.E. 241
Edwards, W.R. 286
Eipper, C. 23
Eisenman, P. 75, 80-2
Eisinger, A. 321
El Ansary, A.I. 256
Ellis, G. 58
    on Belfast planning problems *261-8*
Endlich, S. 76, 81
enforcement in NI *235-47*
    criticisms 237-8
    facilitation 243
    regulations 238-42
    system 235-7

engagement, models of 338-40
Enterprise Ireland 118, 119
Enterprise, Trade and Investment,
    Department of 305
Enterprise Trust 35
Environment Committee, House of
    Commons 147, 174
Environment, Heritage and Local
    Government, Department of 100, 107,
    131-2, 166, 192
Environment and Heritage Service 158
Environment and Local Government,
    Department of 253
Environment, NI Department of
    compared to Cyprus 328
    and consultation 172, 174
    and Craigavon project 46
    and enforcement 238
    Planning Policy Statement 6 166
    Planning Policy Statement 14 181
    Planning Service 175-6
    and preservation 168
    and territorial identity 60
    and vernacular housing 148, 149, 151,
    152
Environment, Transport and the
Regions,
    Department of 290, 291
environmental protection
    BMW 118
    and consultation 176
    and methodology 226-7
    and rural economy 206, 214, 216
    and sustainable development 187
Equality Impact Assessments 58
Erne Catchment Area Study (1980) xvi
ESRI (Economic and Social Research
    Institute) 126
Estyn Evans, Emer xv
    as a contemporary resource 14-17
    critique of 12-14
    geographical context 4-6
    geographical themes 6-12
    on vernacular housing 141-5
EU agricultural payments 114-**15**
European Agricultural Fund for Rural
    Development 208
European Commission
    and BMW 107
    and community planning 297

and Dublin-Belfast corridor 126
and rational comprehensive model
228-32
and regional policy 99, 101
and rural economy 208, 219
European Regional Development Fund
116
European Social Fund 116, **117**
European Spatial Development
Perspective 104, 125-6, 128
Eversley, D. 45
Eyben, K. 51-2

Fáilte Ireland 302, 307-15
Faludi, A. 128
Family Expenditure Survey 45
Famine, Great 144
FAS (Foras Aiseanna Saothair) 117, 119
Faulkner, B. 46
Fawcett, L. 262
Featherstone, M. 153
Febvre, L. 5, 18n
Federation of Housing Associations, NI
160
Feld, M. 335
Ferriter, D. 123
Fessenden, H. 65
Field, B. 227
Finance, Department of 115
Finance and Personnel, NI Department
of 178
Finch, J. 254
Fink, S.L. 256
Finkelstein, N.G. 77
Finn, A. 51
First and Deputy First Minister,
Office of 58, 170
Fisher, D. 64
fishing industry 116-17
Fitzduff, N. on J.V. Greer xiii-xviii
Fitzgerald, J. 104
Fitzpatrick Associates 109
Fitzpatrick, J. 306
Fleure, H.J. 3, 4-5, 8, 10, 16, 20
Forde, C. 104
Forester, J. 304
Forfas Enterprise Strategy Group 119,
122
Foster, J.W. 19, 21
Fratesi, U. 219

Frazer, H. 282
Friedmann, J. 170
Froggatt, P. 339
Fukuyama, F. 216

Gaebler, T. 170
Gaeltacht 11
Gaffikin, F. on universities *333-44*
Gailey, A. 139-41, 143-6, 154
Gallent, N. 189
Gates, R. 340
gateways 101, 122, 127-30, 217-18
Gaventa, J. 286
Gayler, H.J. 250
GDA *see* Greater Dublin Area
Geddes, M. 271
Geddes, P. 227
geography
Irish 3-21
sectarian 23, 24, 26, 36-41
Gerz, J. 81
Giblin, T. 103
Gibson Institute xviii
Gillock, G. 69, 70
Gist, R.R. 256
Glasscock, R.E. 18
Glassie, H. 146, 147
Glenanne, Loughgilly and Mountmorris
Community Association 56-7
Glenanne study 52-**3**, 54-**5**
Glenarm Conservation Area 162
Godfrey, K.B. 301
Good Friday Agreement 127, 261, 302,
307, 309-311;, *see also* Belfast
Agreement
Goodyear 28, 29, 30, 43, 46
Gould, J. 266
Goymen, K. 301
Grabosky, P. 242
Graham, B. on Estyn Evans *3-21*
Graham, S. 75
Gramberger, M. 169
Granzow, E. 262
Grass, G. 73
Gray, A. 302
Gray,B. 303, 304
Greater Dublin Area (GDA) 110, 111,
112, 121, 122, *see also* Dublin-Belfast
corridor
green belts 151, 176

and outskirts 320, 329, 331
Greer, J. on tourism *301-18*
Greer, J.V.
  on Cockcroft Committee 173
  on consultation 171, 174
  contributions of xv-xviii
  on Dublin-Belfast corridor 127
  on Estyn Evans 3
  Fitzduff, N. on xiii-xiv
  on methodology 230
  on outskirts 319
  on preservation 158-9
  on rural economy 202
  on territorial identity 49, 57, 60-1
  on tourism 301
Gregory, D. 18
Grimshaw, C. 334
Gross Value Added 112-**13**
Gruffudd, R.P. 18
Guerra, M.W. 67
Gunningham, N. 240
Guy, C. 250, 252

Habermas, J. 65, 75, 76, 78, 79
Hain, S. 70
Hajer, M. 189
Halbwachs, M. 64
Hamilton, A. 51
Hamilton, D. 129, 130
Hanf, K. 240, 242
Hannigan, K. 306
Harkavy, I. 336
Harloe, M. 335
Harris, R. 50-1
Hartung, K. 72
Hasty, R. 250
Hattstein, M. 75
Hausner, V. 24
Hawkins, K. 241, 242, 244
Hayes, M. xiii
Healey, P.
  on methodology 228
  on sustainable development 187, 193,
  196, 200, 202
Health and Social Services, NI
  Ministry 46, 177
Heaney, S. 15
Hearth Housing Association 158-66
Heffernan, M. 18
Heimrod, U. 75, 76

Hellman, L. 167
Heritage Lottery Fund 166
Herries Davies, G.L. 18
Heslinga, M.W. 19
Hewitt, J. 3, 4, 12, 14, 15, 21
Higgins, M.D. 275
Hill, G. 19n
Hirschman, A. 103
Historic Buildings Council 148
Hitler, A. 64-6
Hohendahl, P.U. 79
Hollander, S.C. 254
Holocaust 65, 74, 75, 77-8
  Memorial (Berlin) 78-82, *see also*
  Memorial to the Murdered Jews of
  Europe; *see also* Mahnmal
Housing Executive, NI 149, 151-2, 159,
  163
Housing (NI) Order 158, 160
housing, rural vernacular *139-56*
  contemporary design 147-9
  contemporary dilemmas 149-54
  location and siting 144-7
  orgins and development 139-43
  and tourism 152-3
  and VAT policy 152
Howard, S.E. 241
Howe, L. 23, 42
Hower, R.M. 254
Howlett, M. 170
hubs 101, 122, 127, 129, 218
HUD (Housing and Urban
  Development, US Department of) 335
Hughes, J. 294
Hull, A. 196
Human Rights Commission, NI 57-8
Humanities and Social Science, Irish
  Research Council for 193, 203
Hunt, D. 103
Hutchinson, J. 304
Hutter, B.M. 240, 241, 242
Huxham, C. 303, 304
Huyssen, A. 79

IDA (Industrial Development Authority)
  94-7, 118
identity, territorial *49-62*
IFA (Irish Farmers' Association) 193
IFI (International Fund for Ireland) 306,
  310-11, 315

Ignatieff, M. 64-5
Imrie, R. 261
industrial development 91-4
Industrial and Economic Council,
  National 93, 103
Industrial Organisation, Committee on
  (CIO) 93, 103
industrial planning 94-9
industrial policy, White Paper 103
Ingram, H. 239, 243
Innes, J.E. 184
INTERREG 116, 117-18, 294
  and tourism 306
InterTradeIreland 252
Irish Landmark Trust 162, 165
Irish Planning Institute, Council of xviii
Irish Studies, Institute of 3
Irishness 10-16

Jacob-Marks, C. 80
Jeffreys, J.B. 251-2
Jencks, C. 67
Jenkins, R. 23
Jewish Museum (Berlin) 65, 68, 74
Jewish Museum (New York) 79
Jews in Germany, Central Council of 77
Johnson, J.J. 103
Johnson, N.C. 19
Johnston, T. 157
Jones, E. 20, 23
Joppe, M. 301

Kagan, R. 241, 242, 243
Kearney, R. 21
Kennedy, D. 335
Kennedy, K.A. 103
Kirby, D.A. 249
Kirk, T. 51
Klemm, M. 306
Knee, D. 251-2, 254
Knox, C. on community planning
  289-300
Koch, M. 324, 330
Kohl, H. 7, 66, 75, 76, 80, 81, 83
Korn, S. 77, 79
Korten, D.C. 284
Kramer, J. 66, 83
Kunzmann, R. 187

Labour Force Survey 45
Labour Party, NI 26
Ladd, B. 63, 66, 69
Landscape Architects, Institute of 149
landscape protection 195-6
Latimer, K. on preservation *157-68*
Leach, J. 266
LEADER 117, 193
  and partnership 278, 282
pobail.ie/en/RuralDevelopment/LEADER
  286
  and rural economy 208, 216, 218-19
Lefebvre, H. 72
Lehrer, U. 69
Lemass, S. 306
Lepick, A. 73
Leslie, D. 302
Leyton, E. 51
Libeskind, D. 64-5, 74, 80
Lindsey, G. 187
Lipsky, M. 240
Lipton, M. 103
Livingstone, D.N. 18
Livingstone, I. 103
local government
  1941 legislation 283
  and community planning 290-3
Local Strategy Partnerships 289, 293-5,
  296, 297-**8**
Location, Siting and Design standards
  147
Longley, E. 21
Loughlin, J. 301
Lovan, W.R. 170
Lowe, M. 253
Lowndes, V. 170
Lurgan *23-48*
Lynch, C. 190
Lynch, K. 74
Lyotard, J-F. 79

Maastricht, Treaty of 286
McCafferty, D. 271
McCarthy, T. 104
McCartney, C. 51
McCluskey, C. 45
McCourt, D. 20
McDonagh, J. 188
MacDonagh, O. 20

McDonald, F. 158
McDougall, G. 228
McEldowney, M. 58, 262
  on outskirts *319-32*
McEniff, J. 306
McEwan, I. 319
McFarlane, G. 24, 51
McGoldrick, P. 252
McGrath, B. 189
McGreal, S. 243, 244
MacGregor, B. 227
McHugh, D. 103
McKay, S. on enforcement *235-47*
Mackey, D. 33, 40
McNair, M.P. 254
McNeill, T.E. 21
MacSharry, R. 103
Maguire, C. 152, 159
Maguire, M. 45
Mahnmal 75-83
Making Belfast Work 57, 294
Malecki, E.J. 129
Mallon, S. 307
Mallory, J.P. 21
Manning, P.K. 241
Marchand, R. 255
Marcuse, P. 77
Mark-Lawson, J. 24
market sustainability 210-**13**, 214-16
Marvin, S. 75
Mason, J.B. 255, 256
Mattesich, P. 303-5
Matthew, R. 171-2
Matthew Report/Plan (1963) 26, 27,
  147, 301
Matthews, A. 104
May, P. 243, 244
Mayer, M.L. 255, 256
Mayo development 193-201
Mazmanian, D.A. 239
Mecke, B. 75
Memorial to the Murdered Jews of
  Europe 63, 68, 74, 75-**82**, 83
Meredith, D. 220
methodology *225-34*
  historic context 226-7
  rational comprehensive model 227-32
Midgley, J. 274, 275, 281
Millichap, D. 237
Mintel International Group Ltd. 251

Mitchell, F. 144
Monbiot, G. 333
Monsey, B. 303-5
Montgomery, J. 261
Morrissey, J. 286
Morrow, D. 51-2
Moughton, C. xiii
Mourne Homesteads Scheme 165-6
Muintir na Tíre *271-88*
Murdoch, J. 24, 43-4
Murray, M.
  on community planning 294
  on consultation and housing *169-86*
  on Dublin-Belfast corridor 127
  on outskirts 319
  on regional policy 104
  on rural economy 202
  on territorial identity 49, 50
  on tourism 301
Murtagh, B. 50, 52, 57
  on territorial identity *49-62*
Muttitt, G. 334
Myrdal, G. 103

Nash, C. 19
National Development Plan (NDP)
  and BMW 107, 116, 117, 119-**20**, 122
  and Dublin-Belfast corridor 126
  and partnership 280
  and regional policy 100, 102, 104
  and tourism 306
National Spatial Strategy (NSS)
  and BMW 107, 109, 122
  and Dublin-Belfast corridor *125-35*
  and regional policy 91, 100, 101,
  102, 104
  and rural sustainable development
  189-92, 200
National Trust, NI Committee of 159
  nationalism
    German 64-6
    Irish 4, 7, 9, 11, 31, 45
    Ulster 15
Naumann, M. 77
NDP *see* National Development Plan
Neafcy, E. 252
Neill, W.J.V. on Berlin planning *63-88*
NESC *see* Economic and Social
  Council, National
new cities 23-48

New Towns Act (NI) 27
Newby, H. 319
Newman, J. 286
Newman, P. 320, 331
Nicosia and central Cyprus 326-**7**, 328-**9**
NIHE (NI Housing Executive) 149, 151-2, 159, 163
North South Ministerial Council 132, 302, 307
Northern Ireland Act (1998) 57
Northern Ireland Affairs Committee, House of Commons xviii, 176, 237
Northern Ireland Executive *see* Assembly
Northern Ireland Office 237
Novick, P. 64
NSS *see* National Spatial Strategy
Null Stunde (Zero Hour) 65, 67, 75
Nurkse, R. 103
NUTS (Nomenclature of Territorial Units for Statistics) regions 107-8, **109**-10, **113**, **117**, 119-**20**, 121

O Tuathaigh, G. 21
Objective 1 status 99, 107-8, 110, 121
O'Cearbhaill, D. on partnership *271-88*
O'Cinneide, B. 306
O'Connor, B. 19
O'Connor, E. 276
O'Donohue, K. 283
O'Dowd, L. on Craigavon project *23-48*
O'Drisceoil, P. 18
OECD (Organisation for Economic Cooperation and Development) 104, 169, 282
Ogus, A.I. 241, 242, 244
Oinas, P. 129
O'Leary, D. 286
O'Leary, E. 104, 122
Oliver, J. 26
Olsen, P.A. 249, 255
O'Neill, T. 306
optimistic model of partnership 273-5, **276**
Oram, R. 159, 167
Orange Order 37
Ordnance Survey 13, 131, 132, 146
O'Ríordáin, S. 9
Ormsby, F. 21

Osborne, D. 170
Osborne, R.D. 45
Oswald, F. 320
outskirts *319-32*
  BAB and Basque Country 321-**2**, 323
  concept of 320-1
  Nicosia and central Cyprus 326-**7**, 328-**9**
  Zurich and Limmat Valley 323-**4**, **325**-6
Overseas Tourism Marketing Initiative 307
Owen, R. 227
Owen, S. 189, 199

paecon.net 265
PAFT (Policy Appraisal for Fair Treatment) 57
Palast der Republik 72-**3**
Parkes v Secretary of State (1978) 236
partition 130
partnership
  activist model 283-5
  approach to crisis 279-80
  campus/community *333-44*
  conditions of 302-5
  Local Strategy Partnerships 293-7
  optimistic and pessimistic 273-**6**
  state-community *271-88*
  and tourism *301-18*
Paterson, R. 243
Patton, M. 159, 165
Paulick, J. 68, 70, 71
pays 5-8, 11, 13-14, 16
peace process 310, 314
Peace and Reconciliation, EU Special Support Programme 49, 294, 315
  and community planning 290
PEACE II 116, 118, **120**, 295, 297, 299
Pearce, D.G. 305
Pearson, I. 293
Perrin study 51
Perroux, F. 93, 103
Perry, D. 338, 339
PESCA Community Initiative 1994-1999 116
pessimistic model of partnership 275-**6**
Petterson, S. 241
Pfeiffer, W. 142
Pickvance, C. 335

Planning and Development Act 95, 192
Planning (General Development) Order
  (NI) 1993 237
Planning (NI) Order 158, 236, 237, 238
Planning Policy Statement 9 238
Planning Policy Statement 14 181-4
Planning Service, NI Department of
  Environment 175-6, 265, 267
Plantations, Ulster 13, 14
Planwerk Innenstadt 63, 70-1, 72-4
PNIC (Portadown New Industries
  Council) 34, 46
pobail.ie/en/RuralDevelopment/
  LEADER 286
Pol, P. 232
Policy Appraisal for Fair Treatment
  (PAFT) 57
policy, regional *91-106*
Pollak, A. 21
Poole, M. 37
population, census of 133
Portadown
  and Craigavon Project **23-48**
  New Industries Council (PNIC) 34, 46
Potsdamer Platz 63, 68-70
pre-Celtic culture 9, 11, 13
preservation 157-68
PriceWaterhouseCoopers 305, 306, 312
Priebs, A. 320
Prior, A. 238, 242
Prior, D. 301, 302
Programme for Government 299
Promoting Social Inclusion 58
Proudfoot, L.J. 19, 20, 21
Public Administration, Review of 289-
  92, 293, 298-9
Public Examination 177, 179-80, 183-4
Public Record Office, NI 173
Putnam, R.D. 282

Queen's University 151, 177, 178, 336
Quinn, A.M. on retailing *249-60*

Range, P.R. 65
rational comprehensive model 227-32
Rauterberg, H. 73
Read, A. 64
Reardon, J. 250
Redecke, S. 66, 67

Regional Assemblies 108
Regional Authorities 99
Regional Development, Department for
  58, 150, 167
  NI consultation 177, 180, 181-2, 184
  and retailing 252
Regional Development Fund,
  European (ERDF) 116
Regional Development Strategy for NI
  xiv
  and consultation 183
  and Craigavon Project 30
  and Dublin-Belfast corridor *125-35*
  and outskirts 321, 328
  and territorial identity 58-**9**, 60
Regional Development Theory 128-31
Regional Industrial Plans 95-6
Regional Partnership Board, NI 296-7
Regional Physical Development
  Strategy 1975-1995 172, 177
Regional Planning Guidance 179
regional policy
  EU Structural Funds, effect of 99-102
  and industrial development 91-4
Regional Strategic Framework (RSF),
  NI
  178-9, 180
regionalism 14, 15
  and environment 6-7
  Reichhardt, H.J. 66
Reichstag 67, 78, 79
Reid, J. 29
Reiss, A. 242
replacement policy, Department of
  Environment 152, 159
REPS (Rural Environmental Protection
  Scheme) 114, 122
resettlement grant scheme 28
retailing *249-60*
  accordian theory 254
  conflict theories 256-7
  cyclical theories 253-5
  factors driving change 249-53
  life cycle 255
  spiral movement theory 255
  wheel of 254-5
Rhodes, J. 233
Rhodes, R. 170
Rich, D. 341

Richardson, G.M. 241, 242, 244
Richie, A. 66
roads, Belfast 262-4
Roberts, P. 232
Robinson, C.A. 266
Robinson, G. 340
Rodriguez-Pose, A. 219
Rogers, D.S. 250, 251, 253
Romme, G. 266
Rosenbloom, B. 255
Rosh, L. 76, 77, 78, 80, 81
Ross, J. 78, 82
Ross, M. 103
Rothery, S. 158
Rowthorn, B. 24, 45
Rubin, V. 335
Ruegg, J. 320, 324, 326, 331
rundales 13, 14, 144
Rural Action Project xiii
Rural Community Network x, xvii, 50,
    174-5, 177
Rural Community Programme xiv
Rural Cottage Holidays Ltd. 153, 165
rural development
    Council xiv, xvii, xviii, 174-5
    equality agenda 57-60
    Interdepartmental Committee on xvi
    NI case studies 52-7
    Programme for NI xiii-xiv, 117
religion and segregation 50-2
role of villages 192
    White Paper on 126
rural economy *205-21*
    defining rurality 206-7
    government intervention 217-19
    market sustainability 210-16, **213**
Rural Environmental Protection Scheme
    (REPS) 114, 122
Rural Innovation and Research
    Partnership xviii
rural planning policy
    housing 171-86
Review Committee xvi
rural-generated housing 191
rural-urban interface *see* outskirts
rurality 8-10, 49, 91
    economic context 206-7
    and sustainability 188-9
rurban fringe 320

Ryan, C. 45
Ryan, M. 144
Ryley, T. 262

S&E (South & East) Region
Sabatier, P.A. 239
Sabel, C. 271
Salamon, L.M. 239
Sauer, C. 5
SAVE Britain's Heritage 166
Savitt, R. 257
Sayer, A. 335
Schaeche, W. 66
Schlusser, G. 75, 76
Schneider, A. 239, 243
Schneider, M. 321
Schoeps, J. 78
Scholz, J.T. 241, 243
Schon, D. 335
Schröder, G. 82-3
Schumacher, M. 324
Scott, M. on sustainable development
    187-204
Scott, P. 249
Seaforde 160-**1**
Secretary of State for NI 237
Seferens, H. 75, 76
segregation 37, 49, 57, 60
    rural 50-2
Selbourne, D. 65
Selin, S. 303
Serra, R. 80-1
Shaffer, R. 170
Shaffrey, M. 142
Shaffrey, P. 157-8
Shannon Development 119, 305
Shapiro, D. 24
Sharman, A. 301, 303
Shaw, G. 249, 250
Shaw, T. 187
Shucksmith, M. 189
Siegert, H. 63, 68, 70, 74
Sieverts, T. 320
Silka, L. 336
Simmel, G. 74
Single Act/Market 99
Sinn Féinism 14
Skelcher, C. 170
Smith, D.J. 45

Smyth, A. 262
Smyth, W.J. 20
social capital 216
Sontag, S. 74
Sorenson, P. 240
South & East (S&E) Region
  and BMW 108, 110-11, 113, **120**, 121
  and Dublin-Belfast corridor 126
  and regional policy 99, 100, 102
Spatial Data Archive 132
Special EU Programmes Body 295, 297
Speer, A. 66, 67, 75, 83
Spiegel, Der 66, 67, 80
spiral movement in retailing 255
Squires, G. 341
Statistical and Research Agency, NI 132
Staunton, D. 78, 81
Stelfox, D. 159, 167
Stern, L.W. 256
Stern, R. 63
Sterrett, K. 58
  on vernacular housing *139-56*
Stevenson, G. 266
Stimman, H. 70
Stone, D. 240
Stormont 25, 26, 27, 31, 34
Strategic Planning Guidance
SPG3 58-**9**, 60
SPG9 179
Structural and Cohesion funds, EU
  and BMW 107-8
  and methodology 226
  and NI consultation 178
  and rational comprehensive model
  228-32
  and regional policy 99-102, 104
  and rural economy 208, 218
Stukel, J. 334
Sussmuth, R. 81
sustainable development, rural *187-204*
  criteria for 187
  in Mayo and Donegal 193-201
Planning Policy Statement 14 181-4
  and Regional Strategic Framework
  180
Sustainable Development Strategy 126
Swoboda, H. 72
synergy 225, 228-32, 244

Taddeo, K. 256
Tansey, P. 302
Tantam, D. 266
Targeting Social Need 57, 58
Taylor, M. 298
Tesco 251, 254
Tewdwr-Jones, M. 189
Theakston, K. 170
Thomas, H. 261
Thomas, M.J. 228
Thornley, A. 261, 320, 331
Tosun, C. 301
tourism
  agency partnerships 305-12
  cross-border *301-18*
  future of 312-15
  RI dominance of 308-9
  and rural housing 152-3, 174, 196-7
Tourism Brand Ireland 307, 308
Tourism Ireland 302, 307, 309-12
Tourist Board, NI 153, 165, 301-2
  cross-border co-operation 305-15
Town and Country Planning Service, NI
  Department of Environment 238
Town Planners, European Council of
  xviii
Town Planning Institute, Royal xviii
trade, north/south 130
transport policy 178
transport and telecommunications 215,
  217
Trimble, D. 307
Troubles
  and Belfast planning problems 265
  and Craigavon project 23, 24, 29,
  38, 45
  effect on tourism 306-8
  and territorial identity 56
Tuan, Y.-F. 4, 21
Tunbridge, J.E. 21
Turnly's Tower **164**-5
Tyler, P. 233

Udaras Na Gaeltachta 108, 118, 119
Ulster Architects, Royal Society of 149
Ulster Architectural Heritage Society
  151, 154, 158, 159

Ulster Countryside Committee 158
Ulster Folk and Transport Museum 7,
   149
   Ulster Society for the Preservation of
   the Countryside 148, 173
Ulsterness 10-12
Undeveloped Areas Act (1952) 91-2
unionism and Unionists 4, 26, 31, 45
United Nations Development
   Programme 327
universities, urban *333-44*
   models of engagement 338-40
University of Ulster 177-8
URBAN II Community Initiative
   Programme 2000-2006 232, 294
urban-generated housing 191
Urry, J. 335

value added creation 209-**10**
Van den Berg, L. 232
Van der Meer, J. 232
Vangen, S. 303, 304
Varley, T. on partnership *271-88*
VAT policy 152, 158
Vidal de la Blache, P. 4-5
villages, role in rural development 192

Walby, S. 24
Walker, J. 242
Walser, M. 82
Walsh, B. 190
Walsh, J.A. 104, 271, 301
   on Dublin-Belfast corridor *125-35*
Walshok, M. 339
Walters, D. 254
Warde, A. 24
Wayne, N. 24, 45
Weinmiller, G. 80
Wenders, W. 69-70
West Rural Region 177, 178, 179, 180
Wetherill, G.R. 286
Whelan, K. 5, 8, 13, 18, 20, 21
White, P. 103
Whitecross study 52-**3**, **54**-7
Wilhelm, K. 66
Wilson, A. 304
Wilson, D. 51-2, 306
Wilson Report (1965) 26, 27, 30

Wilson, T.M. 44
Wilsonian perspective 239
Wing, L. 265, 266
Wise, M.Z. 66
Wolf, M. 253
Wrigley, N. 250, 253

Yeager, P.C. 240
Young, J.E. 79, 80, 81 82
Youth Council, NI 177
Yuseph, S. 255

Zeldin, S. 335
Zero Hour (Null Stunde) 65, 67, 75
Zurich and Limmat Valley 323-**4**, **325**-6